S0-AWP-542

UNIVERSITY *of*

DAYTON

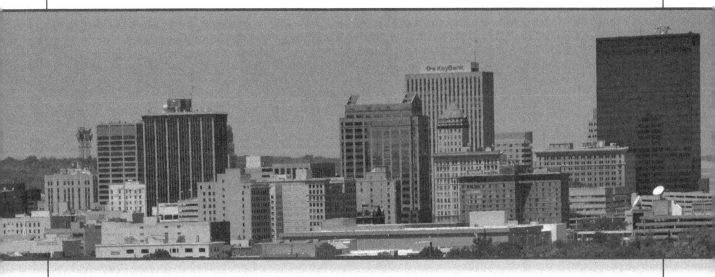

PRINCIPLES
OF
ORAL COMMUNICATION

2018 – 2019 Edition

FOUNTAINHEAD
PRESS

Fountainhead Press's green initiatives include:

Electronic Products and Samples. Products are delivered in non-paper form whenever possible via Xample, an electronic sampling system. Instructor samples are sent via a personalized web page that links to PDF downloads.

FSC-Certified Printers and Recycled Paper. All of our printers are certified by the Forest Service Council, which promotes environmentally and socially responsible management of the world's forests. This program allows consumer groups, individual consumers, and businesses to work together hand in hand to promote responsible use of the world's forests as a renewable and sustainable resource. Most of our products are printed on a minimum of 30 percent post-consumer waste recycled paper.

Designer: Susan Moore

For more information, please visit our website at www.fountainheadpress.com.

ISBN: 978-1-68036-761-4

Printed in the United States of America

The Department of Communication would like to thank the Basic Course Advisory Board for their help in developing this edition of the textbook:

Shawn Swavey, Department of Chemistry

Heather McLachlan, Department of Music

Peter Titlebaum, School of Education and Allied Professions

Thomas Whitney, Department of Civil and Environmental Engineering

Jamie Longazel, Department of Sociology, Anthropology, & Social Work

Nancy Mohan, School of Business Administration

Danielle Poe, Department of Philosophy

Katy Kelly, Roesch Library

Ryan Allen, Learning and Teaching Center

Gov. Robert Taft, School of Education and Allied Professions

PREP QUESTIONS

1. Describe the Common Academic Program (CAP) and explain how CMM 100 contributes to the learning objectives for UD undergraduates.

2. Explain three skills that CMM 100 is designed to help you develop. Provide two examples of how these skills could potentially be useful to you in your field of study/future career.

3. What is civil dialogue? Compare and contrast dialogue with the type of communication that is commonly practiced on news programs and talk shows.

4. What are some of the benefits of receiving training in civil dialogue? How could this type of training enhance your undergraduate experience in the UD community? How could it enhance your professional life?

5. What are the primary goals of CMM 100 and how do they compare and contrast with those of a course designed to teach public speaking?

6. What four courses make up the Humanities Commons and what are the six Student Learning Objectives in those courses? How do they connect with CMM 100?

LETTER FROM THE PROVOST

Dear CMM 100 students:

This textbook is designed and written specifically for the University of Dayton's new Communication course, CMM 100. This course delivers a required component in our new Common Academic Program (CAP) and promotes important learning objectives for all UD undergraduates. Because CAP seeks to embody fundamental goals for an undergraduate education at a Catholic and Marianist university, this textbook also reflects UD's broader educational mission, to link learning and scholarship with leadership and service.

"That is all well and good," you may think; "it's just the sort of thing that an academic administrator would say. But why do I have to take this course, when there are so many other things that I want to study before I graduate?" This is a fair question. I would note, first, that oral communication skills are highly prized in any professional field or area of academic study you may pursue. These are foundational skills, essential for a high quality liberal education and pursuit of your personal aspirations, whatever they may be.

CMM 100's focus on skills of civil dialogue and persuasive argumentation is especially relevant to the world you will inhabit as a UD graduate. In our time, the inevitable disagreements and conflicts that arise among human beings are more often addressed through emotionally combative, disrespectful, and poorly reasoned verbal attacks than through serious dialogue and even-handed, reflective exchanges of persuasive evidence. Persons educated to resist incivility and demagoguery through careful understanding of others' standpoints and thoughtful exchanges of reasons for their own judgments and actions will be sought after and admired as wise colleagues, influential leaders, responsible community members, and trusted friends.

The skills that you will gain and refine in CMM 100 are also particularly important for UD's mission to educate leaders who serve and build community among diverse people, advancing the ends of social justice and the common good. As our *Commitment to Community* (C2C) document emphasizes, striving to live in community on campus and to experience community living as a central ingredient of your education requires that you embrace certain ethical principles and develop certain habits. As you will see, the ethical principles and habits necessary for community living also are important to the subject matter of CMM 100.

This course is vitally important to your UD education—as important as any you will take—and it should be fun besides. Any UD student should enjoy thinking through controversial, contemporary issues, crafting clear, well-reasoned explanations of complex ideas, and attempting to persuade fellow UD students. Regardless of other courses you want to take during your UD career, CMM 100 should be personally engaging and practically useful.

I hope that the course is at once stimulating and challenging for you, and that this book is a valuable resource for your future studies at UD. I look forward to hearing your reactions to our new Communication course.

Paul H. Benson
Provost, University of Dayton
June, 2013

LETTER FROM THE CHAIR

Dear CMM100 Student,

Welcome to CMM100 Principles of Oral Communication! I want to take a moment and share with you how unique this class is. You may hear your friends at other schools refer to their communication course as "public speaking," but at UD that is not what the class is—in fact there is no course like this one around the country!

When we designed this class we met with departments across the university, from Business, to Engineering to Education, and identified key oral communication skills that your faculty felt were essential for your success. What we have done is create a class that shows how the skills of effective oral communication are about so much more than just traditional public speaking. In CMM 100 you will learn how to deliver a speech, but more importantly you will begin to develop the ability to explain complicated information to non-experts. You will also develop effective problem solving and communication skills within small group contexts. Perhaps the most unique part of this class is the emphasis on civility and how to disagree with others without being seen as disagreeable or offensive. These are all things your faculty and prospective employers believed needed to be emphasized in this class.

CMM100 has been designed specifically for UD students. You will notice that in each chapter specific events and concepts central to UD are highlighted as examples. You will also be asked from time to time to think through challenging issues pertinent to the UD community that relate to course content. In fact several chapters of the book were written by your UD faculty so that they were more relevant to you—and this just heightens the special nature of the course which you are about to take.

From the interteaching sessions, to the content of the book, to the performative assignments and in-class activities your instructor will facilitate, all of the distinctive elements of CMM100 are the product of adapting the course each year based on student and instructor feedback. Much like communication itself, this course is not static. In fact, thanks to your fellow students and your instructors, the course has changed for the better each semester we have offered it. While the syllabus, all of the graded assignments, and course policies are the same for every section of CMM100, the lectures and discussions will be specific to the learning community in your classroom. You will even have the opportunity to help your instructor tailor review sessions by giving feedback regarding concepts on which you need more information. Besides the valuable critical thinking skills you will learn, one of the best parts of CMM100 is that you get to pick your own speaking topics within the semester theme so you get to play a role in how you experience the course!

One final aspect of the class that bears noting is its connection to the rest of your education here at UD. You will note that in the first chapter we discuss some foundational figures in communication, people like Plato and Aristotle and Cicero. What is interesting is that you will also encounter many of these great thinkers in other classes, such as History or Philosophy, but from a different perspective. These connections will help you see how your classes support and complement each other, because we have made a conscious effort to build a cohesive UD education that integrates different disciplines and ways of understanding the world.

I hope that you enjoy your semester in CMM100 and that you find new ways to think about the world around you. Throughout the semester, you will notice that you are constantly engaging with new people and new ideas. The more you open your mind to these new opportunities, the more you will find this course useful and enjoyable. I invite you to let CMM 100 be the beginning of a long conversation, one that continues in every class you take at UD from here on out!

Joseph M. Valenzano, III
Chair, Department of Communication

LETTER FROM THE UNDERGRADUATE DIRECTOR

Dear CMM 100 Student,

Congratulations on your decision to enroll in CMM 100 this semester! Not only will this course fulfill a University requirement, but it will allow you to gain essential knowledge and practical skills in explanation and advocacy as practiced in civil dialogue. Those people trained and experienced in civil dialogue tend to be much better listeners, better analysts, better at building the relationships that are critical in organizations, and they are perceived to be more informed and more competent professionals. As we continue to move toward becoming a culture of specialists, the ability to explain complex and specialized knowledge to non-specialists is a necessary ability.

Along with training in oral communication, the Department of Communication offers courses and concentrations in Journalism, Public Relations, Communication Management, and Electronic Media. Please let me take a moment of your time to describe some of the opportunities available if you choose to major in Communication, concentrating in one of those four areas.

The field of *Journalism* is becoming more complex as the news industry continues its transition. The industry is heading toward *media integration* which will create a multiple-platform industry with newspapers, web news, broadcast television and radio, and cable outlets rolled together into a new "shape." Even so, the skills of this 21st century organization will continue to require strong writing skills and a solid foundation in the legal, ethical, and social issues essential to the professional journalist. Students in the journalism concentration are exposed to writing, editing, design, research, and production experiences with special attention to detail and accuracy. Our journalism students graduate prepared to enter careers with newspapers, television and radio outlets, wire services, magazines, web publishers, book publishers, corporations, and nonprofit organizations.

Public Relations students learn how corporations, nonprofit groups, organizations, and individuals manage their public image, control internal and external communication, and establish themselves as good and productive citizens in a community. PR training in the Department of Communication includes both theory and professional skills based on a solid foundation of strong and precise writing, strategic planning, message design, ethics, and research. Our students have established careers as media planners, media strategists, event planners, crisis communication specialists, public information officers, public opinion researchers, community affairs liaisons, and many others.

If the thought of telling stories and sharing information across a variety of media platforms sounds exciting to you, then you should investigate our *Electronic Media Concentration*. The focus is on television and radio broadcasting, audio and video production, and multimedia production. You can gain an understanding of principles and get practical experiences through production, script writing, and carefully designed class activities. The program encourages cross training on multiple media platforms to increase adaptability and to make our graduates more attractive in the professional marketplace. Careers include traditional broadcast and cable television and radio, corporate production for training and promotions, independent production and post production, public television, nonprofit organizations, education, advertising, script and screen writing, multimedia design and production, and many others.

Our concentration in *Communication Management* can prepare you for a challenging career: managing people in organizations. Trying to get people to cooperate and accomplish an organization's goals can seem nearly impossible! To complicate matters, you will likely be working with at least some people that you will never meet; people who are in different zip codes, time zones, or even on different continents. Managing people in organization requires keen attention to interpersonal relationships, group decision making, persuasion, cultural differences, clear explanations, and especially conflict management. The Communication Management concentration will help you learn to be an influential and positive presence in your organization through coursework, research experiences, and practical application gained from innovative class projects and internships. Careers include organizational management, sales, staff development, human resources, customer relations, consulting, and a variety of others.

Even if you don't consider a career in Communication, please take full advantage of the CMM 100 class that you are enrolled in right now. The class offers a unique perspective on skills considered absolutely essential by employers for positions in virtually every professional arena. If you find yourself interested in other Communication classes, or even a minor in Communication, please don't be shy! Feel free to contact me at swallace1@udayton.edu so you can meet with a faculty member who can answer your questions.!

I hope you have a great semester in CMM 100!

Sam Wallace
Director of Undergraduate Studies
Department of Communication
swallace1@udayton.edu

THE HUMANITIES COMMONS AND CMM 100:
PRINCIPLES OF ORAL COMMUNICATION

As a student in CMM 100, you may also be enrolled in one or more of the four courses which comprise the Humanities Commons:

English 100 or ENG 200H: Writing Seminars
History 103: The West and the World
PHL 103: Introduction to Philosophy
REL 103: Introduction to Religious and Theological Studies

These are the foundational courses of the Common Academic Program (CAP) which begin the process of integrating all aspects of a student's university experience via the seven mission related Student Learning Outcomes (SLO's). Each Humanities Commons course will emphasize six common learning objectives that have been identified and agreed upon by faculty from each of the four departments. In these courses students will:

1. read a variety of primary texts closely and critically (including self-critically).

2. analyze, in writing, a variety of texts contributing to larger historical conversations, debates, and traditions and as resources for understanding and appreciating the complexities of human identity, dignity, and experience.

3. develop an understanding of their place in community, country, and world in relationship to multiple others, with particular attention to differences–such as class, gender, and race–upon which social inequalities are constructed and maintained.

4. engage central concepts of Catholic intellectual tradition as they contribute to humanistic inquiry and reflection in the relevant academic discipline (English, History, Philosophy, or Religious Studies).

5. examine the question of what it means to be human from a disciplinary perspective, and in the process make connections among disciplines and develop an appreciation for the ways in which learning is a process of integrating knowledge.

6. understand and practice academic honesty as foundational to the making and sharing of knowledge as a community of learners that is both local and global.

Your CMM 100: Principles of Oral Communication course will enable you to participate more fully via oral communication in these courses and beyond, explaining, persuading and dialoguing with classmates, instructors and others, while the humanities commons courses will provide the experiences, subject matter and perspectives about which you will communicate. You may (and should!) see the similarities and differences in oral versus written communication, and the variety of communication models across disciplines and diverse speakers.

SCENARIOS

Scenario 1

You are the Vice President of a marketing consulting firm and you are interviewing three candidates for a managerial position. This person will report to one of the senior partners, and will be responsible for training incoming associates, planning and leading weekly staff meetings, overseeing project management, and daily communication with clients, among other duties. With your group members, devise three interview questions to ask the candidates that would help you assess their communication knowledge and skills. Work to develop questions that would help you to get a sense of the candidate's ability to do each of the following (one question for each would be ideal):

1.   Explain complex ideas to non-experts

2.   Persuade others by making a compelling case

3.   Engage in dialogue with people whose ideas are different from their own

Scenario 2

Who is the best communicator you know? Who is the worst? Why? Work with your group members to generate a list of 5 things that good communicators do well, and 5 things that you wish people would do better when they communicate. Based on these lists, identify what you think are the 3-4 most important communication skills for today's college graduates and be able to provide reasoning for your answer (work to achieve group consensus on this).

Scenario 3

Detail the benefits to an education when classes cover similar material in different ways. What topics might you see covered in both the Humanities Commons and CMM 100?

Scenario 4

According to the *Civility in America* report, 86% of Americans say that it is uncivil when someone you are eating with is on the phone. Almost as many agree that it is uncivil behavior when someone talks loudly on a cell phone in public. A third of Americans believe these problems stand to get worse over time. Identify two examples of incivility that you have recently experienced, and then work with your group members to determine practical ways of responding to and managing these situations.

Scenario 5

In what ways are the skills in explanation, advocacy (the ability to present a persuasive case), and civil dialogue important in your field of study/desired career? Give an example of a complex idea in your area of study here at UD that you may one day have to explain to a non-expert. Give an example of a controversial issue (an idea or subject about which people disagree) within your field of study that you may one day have to discuss with others. Talk with your group to generate and share ideas.

Table of Contents

SPEAKING OF CIVIC ENGAGEMENT BOXES

SPOTLIGHTING THEORISTS BOXES

The Practice of Public Communication

CHAPTER OVERVIEW

1

- Explores long tradition of approaching communication as civic engagement
- Identifies three ways of contributing to the discourses of one's community through communication
- Discusses the principles and practice of ethical communication

Practically SPEAKING

Imagine being tutored by one of the greatest minds ever to live. Imagine personal attention from the man responsible for some of the most important writings in history. Of course, such an opportunity is not really available today, but it was in the classical world, and one person managed to receive such an education: Alexander the Great of Macedon. From his early teenage years Alexander was personally tutored by Aristotle, the man who wrote books that are still considered foundational texts for communication studies, philosophy, political science and even the natural sciences. You might think that such an opportunity came about largely because of the wealth and power of Alexander's family, and in that you would be only partially correct.

In 343 BCE Philip of Macedon, Alexander's father, approached Aristotle with an offer to tutor his son, then thirteen years old. At the time, Aristotle had not written many of his works and had only recently finished twenty years of studies at Plato's Academy. In fact, he was little more than a roaming refugee in exile since Philip himself had ordered the complete annihilation of Aristotle's home city, Stagira.[1] So, the fact that Philip chose him is interesting. There was also a personal connection between Philip and Aristotle in that they knew each other from childhood when Aristotle's father, Nicomachus, was the personal physician to Phillip's father. Perhaps the combination of the childhood connection, Aristotle's education under Plato and Philip's possible desire to extend an olive branch to the remaining people of Stagira led to the choice of Aristotle as personal tutor to Alexander.[2]

It did not take long for Aristotle to accept the offer and begin schooling Philip's son and a few other sons of nobles at Mieza, a spot of land west of the Macedonian capital of Pella.[3] While there, Alexander learned about medicine, ethics, literature, Greek culture and other subjects while sitting outdoors on stone benches. One can easily see the impact these lessons had on the young prince. When he became king and began his conquest of the known world, Alexander would collect samples of flowers and animals and send them back to his former tutor for study.[4] He also carried a volume of Homer's *Iliad* with him that Aristotle had personally edited. An even more practical impact was the fact Alexander used his knowledge of medicine garnered from his time with Aristotle to personally treat wounded soldiers on the battlefield![5]

The education of Alexander by Aristotle provides us with an early example of what we may now call a classroom, and the broad outline of what we call a liberal arts education. Alexander was schooled in a wide array of subjects from ethics, philosophy, and rhetoric to politics, medicine, and physics. Today, universities take a similar approach in designing a general education for students. The lasting impact of the way schools were structured and students taught in classical Greece and classical Rome can still be seen today.

In this chapter we will explore some of the great thinkers of classical Greece and Rome and look at how their schools were structured. It is important to note, some did have schools, like Plato and Aristotle, but others were more like wandering tutors. All of these individuals and groups, however, understood the importance of education and the place of speech in it. To cover this much history in such a short space we will highlight aspects of classical education relevant to our focus on communication and introduce you to figures such as Aristotle and Cicero, whom we will revisit later in the book. We will also discuss some more contemporary contributions to our understanding of message construction and reception. We will conclude the chapter with a brief discussion of different contexts today where the lessons of these ancient Greeks and Romans remain relevant.

Prep Questions

Part 1: Key Concepts

1. Define civic engagement. Explain how communication can be a way of participating in the discourses of one's community with a spirit of civic engagement.

2. List and define the three components parts of persuasion as defined by Aristotle.

3. List the four functions of rhetoric according to Aristotle. Explain how these four functions are reflected in the three major performance assignments in this course.

4. List and define Cicero's five canons of rhetoric. Explain how Cicero's framework can provide a structure for preparing a message for public communication.

5. List nine principles of ethical communication from the National Communication Association's Credo for Ethical Communication.

Part 2: Application

1. A company that advocates for the adoption of orphaned children comes to you for help in creating a commercial to motivate people to adopt a child. Describe a commercial that you could create for this purpose. Explain how your commercial would incorporate each of Aristotle's three components of persuasion.

2. Many social issues have received attention in the news media. Explain how one specific individual, group, or organization is using communication as a form of civic engagement to address one of these issues. Would you consider their communication to be ethical? Justify your answer using the National Communication Association's Credo for Ethical Communication.

COMMUNICATION AS A FORCE IN OUR LIVES

Right now, all across the country students are sitting down and learning how to communicate better. They are taking a similar class to the one you are enrolled in; some courses are titled Oral Communication, others maybe Introduction to Public Speaking, and others still perhaps refer to the class as Speech Communication. The point is, you are not alone, and what you are doing is nothing new. In fact, instruction in communication is rooted in a long tradition that we can trace back to classical Greece (approximately 490–322 BCE).

One of the fundamental tenets of an education in the Greek city-states or Roman Empire was *rhetoric*, which for them essentially meant the ability to speak well and persuade audiences. There were some who decried rhetoric in favor of philosophy, but there was no denying the importance placed on teaching people to speak well in the classical period. Today's education system, however, has moved away from this emphasis. Students are often only introduced to formal training in speech at the college level—and even there for only one semester with a focus on public speaking, instead of communication in a variety of contexts. Education today does not emphasize the importance of speaking well, and one of our aims with this book is to show you how speaking well should be as important today as it was in the days of the Greeks and Romans.

rhetoric
the ability to speak well and persuade audiences

Despite their different views about how best to teach communication and the definition and utility of rhetoric, the thinkers and practitioners of classical times agreed on the important role it serves in public life. They all knew public speaking could move people to action, change their beliefs, and educate the masses, and history has proven their understanding accurate. At key moments in our history, speech has helped moved us to war, shaped public attitudes and policies, and enabled us to express a definition of our identity with each other. There also have been important technological advances that have affected our ability to use communication to accomplish those tasks. In this section of the chapter we will briefly discuss the power of communication as a means of civic engagement. Communication is a primary way of participating in the life of one's community and, through one's words and actions, shaping the thoughts, attitudes, and actions of others.

Public Communication as Civic Engagement

The ability to use symbols to communicate with each other is what makes us human. Neuroscientists recognize that speech is the one cognitive ability that separates humans from other animals. In addition, communication is the way we negotiate and construct society's rules, values, and beliefs. To a considerable extent, the social world operates on the basis of assumptions that people share regarding what is good, right, or true. Consider the class that you are taking. Your behavior in this class from one day to the next is based on assumptions that you, your classmates, and your teacher share about your respective roles, the purpose of your being in the class, and the manner in which the class should operate. If you were to share different assumptions, then your class might operate very differently from how it does. Social reality, in a sense, is co-constructed by those who participate in it.[6]

civic engagement
·······················
acting upon a sharp awareness of one's own sense of responsibility to his or her community

The constructed quality of social reality highlights the degree to which human beings have choice and responsibility for the social world. If people want social reality to be different than what currently exists, then they must take responsibility for making it into what they desire it to be. *Civic engagement* occurs when people act upon a sharp awareness of their own sense of responsibility to their community. Unfortunately, our collective commitment to each other has seen a marked decline in recent years, despite enhancements in technology that make it easier than ever for us to communicate with each other.

For instance, Robert Putnam argued that our sense of community involvement and civic engagement has drastically decreased since the end of World War II, as evidenced by low voter turnout, decreased membership in civic organizations like the Rotary Club and Knights of Columbus, and reduced subscription rates to newspapers. These developments would shock the Greeks and Romans we discussed earlier, who saw civic engagement as one of the most fundamental duties of a citizen.

Even though we may not experience it in the intense way the Greeks and Romans did, communication remains central to civic engagement. Have you ever wondered how to "have your voice heard" on a subject? Perhaps your state is thinking of raising tuition. How do you respond? Communication! Maybe your town wants to raise property taxes. How do you fight such an action? Communication! Or how do you let a congressional representative know that you don't like his behavior? Communication! Communication is central to understanding and participating in public life.

The crowd at the G-20 protest in London in April 2009

At a meeting of the G-20 in London, England in March 2009, several thousand people rallied against the foreign leaders who gathered to talk about the world's economic troubles. How did they make their voices heard? They chanted, held posters and gave speeches throughout the day. This is an example of civic engagement at its finest. Without communication, all that would have happened would be a bunch of people standing together in the middle of the street. Communication provided meaning for them, their purpose, and their protest. It allowed them to take an active role in the well-being of their community.

Many classical scholars recognized the relationship between communication and civic engagement. They understood that rhetoric was central to a thriving democracy and that people needed to be taught how to effectively and ethically communicate their ideas to others. Good people who spoke well could create a healthy and thriving community. That belief still holds true today, and many contemporary communication scholars continue to explore ways to speak well and encourage civic engagement.

Aristotle and the Practice of Communication

One contributor to the long tradition regarding communication as a form of civic engagement—perhaps the greatest contributor—was Aristotle. Aristotle lived in ancient Greece during the Fourth Century BCE Aristotle defined rhetoric as the means of identifying probabilities inherent in an issue or interpretation. When the truth of a matter could not be settled through philosophical means because the premises on which people might reach a decision were not known with absolute certainty, Aristotle believed that people could ascertain the good and true through rhetoric. He focused on rhetoric as a persuasive process. Despite his more favorable view of rhetoric, Aristotle understood the dangers inherent in a purely technical understanding of speech, so he conducted an exhaustive analysis of how persuasion works. In this analysis, he identified three component parts of persuasion, recognized two forms of proof for arguments, and urged communicators to reflect three stylistic virtues in their efforts to influence others.

ethos
the credibility of the speaker

Aristotle taught his students about the interconnection of three component parts of persuasion. The first part he called *ethos*, or the credibility of the speaker. He felt that the more believable, honest, and learned on the subject a speaker was, then the more persuasive the message. In addition to ethos, Aristotle proposed that *logos*, or the logical dimension of the appeal, contributed to a message's persuasive effect. Aristotle believed that persuasive messages must follow a logical order that makes the case in a clear and cogent fashion to the recipients of the message; without this orderly argument, persuasion is much less likely to occur. The evidence that a communicator provides in support of her or his claims and the quality of the communicator's reasoning in connecting this evidence to her or his conclusions are also key elements of logos. The third source of persuasion Aristotle called *pathos*, which referred to the audience's disposition toward the topic. He said that language can be used by a speaker to emotionally connect audience members with a topic and thus move them to an ethical and correct action.

logos
the logical dimension of the appeal

pathos
the emotional dimensions of the appeal that can influence an audience's disposition toward the topic, speaker, or occasion

Aristotle referred to ethos, pathos, and logos as *artistic proof*. Artistic proof consists of those elements of persuasion that the speaker has created through his or her interaction with the audience. The speaker's credibility depends on how

artistic proof
constructed by the speaker for the occasion; concerns ethos, pathos, and logos

the audience perceives the speaker relative to the occasion and the topic. What the speaker says or does over the course of the communication can impact those perceptions in consequential ways. The emotions of the audience also relate to the topic and the occasion, and what a speaker says or does as she or he delivers the message can have a profound effect on what the audience feels. Similarly, a speaker develops the logic of the argument in a way that relates to what the audience understands and knows. In this way, ethos, pathos, and logos all are forms of artistic proof. The other form of proof identified by Aristotle, *inartistic proof*, concerns all the evidence, data, documents, and other elements that the speaker did not craft through his or her own efforts, yet nevertheless help to persuade the audience. For instance, if a event occurs shortly before a speaker delivers his or her message that motivates people to think about an issue in a way that favors what the speaker wants, then the event functions as inartistic proof for the argument that the speaker is making. The speaker did not create the event; the event occurred through forces outside his or her control. Nonetheless, the event adds to the persuasiveness of the speaker's argument. However, if the speaker incorporates the event into his or her argument, perhaps by telling a story about what happened and offering it as one of many cases supporting a particular claim that he or she is making, then the speaker's use of the event as evidence functions as artistic proof. The speaker has appropriated something outside her or his control and made creative use of it in delivering her or his message.

Aristotle also understood that the approach that a communicator takes plays a part in the success or failure of persuasive appeals, so he laid out three virtues of style that *rhetors*, or speakers, should reflect in the messages they create. These virtues of style stand as ideals that speakers should strive to attain in their efforts to communicate. The first stylistic virtue is *clarity*, or the ability of speakers to clearly articulate what they wish to say. Clarity manifests itself with simple, direct sentences, and we will discuss more about how to construct such messages in the chapter on language. For the moment, however, take note that the ability to develop clear messages is essential when speaking to one or one hundred people. Aristotle's second stylistic virtue, *correctness*, relates to the accuracy of information presented and the honest representation of the speaker. Quite obviously, this virtue is intimately tied to being an ethical speaker, which will be discussed further later in the book. Finally, Aristotle emphasized the virtue of *propriety*, or good behavior and faithfulness to what one considers moral and just. Propriety relates to the idea that a speaker should be both ethical and clear in content, but also in delivery. It is an overarching virtue that essentially encompasses both clarity and correctness, and is an important part of developing healthy relationships with other people.

Aristotle viewed rhetoric as an important component of civil society. Specifically, he noted that rhetoric, as a means rather than an end, fulfilled four functions in an open society. First, rhetoric allows for true and just ideas to prevail through open discussion, because he noted all things in debate are not equal and capable speakers need to advocate for them to win out. Second, in addition to the preservation of truth and justice, Aristotle also believed rhetoric offered the ability to instruct people on how to connect their ideas with the experiences of their audiences; in short, it allows us to teach others. Third, Aristotle saw rhetoric

inartistic proof
all the evidence, data, and documents that exist outside of the speaker and the audience, but nevertheless can aid in persuasion

rhetors
speakers

clarity
the ability of speakers to clearly articulate what they wish to say

correctness
the accuracy of information presented and the honest representation of the speaker

propriety
good behavior and faithfulness to what one considers moral and just

as the means of analyzing both sides of a question. Finally, Aristotle understood rhetoric as a means to defend oneself, noting that speech and rational thought are abilities unique to human beings.[7] He understood communication as one of the most important tools a person can possess for engaging in civic life. Table 1.1 notes how these four can pragmatically be used today:

Table 1.1

Aristotle's Four Functions of Rhetoric	
Function	Example
Upholding truth and justice	Defending an innocent client in a courtroom
	Advocating for a law that will benefit residents of a community
	Urging fellow students to support a particular social justice cause in a classroom
Teaching an audience	Explaining a concept from one's field to a fellow student not in that field
	Providing information to one's colleagues in a meeting at work
	Telling others in one's neighborhood about a program that could be initiated
Analyzing both sides of a question	Listening to the views of the prosecution and the defense while on a jury
	Having a dialogue with people of different races about their differing experiences
	Considering pros and cons relating to a particular decision
Defending oneself	Giving testimony about one's innocence relative to a certain charge
	Refuting a criticism that someone has made about you or your performance
	Arguing for how responsibility should be understood in light of a given problem

Aristotle felt that through the use of ethical and proper communication, people could search for truth. Societies would become more open and therefore a sense of justice and fairness would be encouraged. He trained his students to examine arguments, defend themselves, and ultimately be able to teach the next generation these important skills. It is safe to say that Aristotle saw good communication skills as the foundation of a lasting productive civil society.

Aristotle's functions of rhetoric still have relevance today. The communication that one undertakes in one's professional life or in one's interactions in the community at any given moment likely reflects one or more of these functions. In this course, the four functions are reflected in the major performance assignments that you will carry out. Each assignment has an overarching goal, what we might call its general purpose. The ***general purpose*** of any given communication is the primary aim that the speaker tries to achieve, apart from her or his specific topic. General purposes of communication relating to this course include to explain, to persuade, to explore, and to understand. Others include to entertain and to commemorate, though this course does not focus on these. In one assignment, you will explain a complex idea or concept to someone who is not an expert regarding that topic. The general purpose of this assignment, to explain, reflects especially Aristotle's function of teaching an audience. In another assignment, you will advocate for a particular position using logic and credible evidence. Depending on the argument that you make, the general purpose of this assignment, to persuade, would reflect especially Aristotle's function of upholding truth and justice and possibly defending oneself—or, in some cases, others. In the third performance assignment, you will engage in civil dialogue with a small group of your classmates about controversial issues. The general purposes of this assignment, to explore particular topics with others and to understand their differing views, relate especially to Aristotle's function of analyzing both sides of a question, though for any one of these topics, there might be many sides to explore, not just two. The ***specific purpose*** of any communication is the general purpose combined with the particular topic that the speaker wishes to address. For instance, in a conversation with a client, a civil engineer might have the specific purpose, "to explain to the client how concrete sets." This specific purpose is a combination of the general purpose, "to explain," and the particular topic that the speaker wishes to address.

general purpose
the primary aim that the speaker tries to achieve in that communication, apart from her or his specific topic

specific purpose
the general purpose combined with the particular topic that the speaker wishes to address

Cicero: An Example of Civic Engagement

Another scholar who exemplified civic engagement was Marcus Tullius Cicero. Cicero was one of the most influential figures in the history of rhetoric. Born in

Cicero

106 BCE near Rome, he received a strong education in Roman schools and began a career in the courts, later moving into the Senate. Eventually he rose to the highest position in the Roman Republic, that of consul, and developed a reputation as a well-spoken champion of the people. Like many people in today's world, Cicero lived during tumultuous times, watching the rise and fall of Julius Caesar and the subsequent establishment of the Roman Empire under Octavian. Throughout his career, Cicero fought against the threat of military dictators, and it ultimately resulted in his death.

Cicero contributed much to our understanding of communication. He himself was a gifted orator, but eventually his speaking ability got him into trouble. During the Roman Civil War between Octavian and Marc Antony which followed the death of Julius Caesar, Cicero vocally fought against a dictatorship and found himself at odds with Marc Antony. Eventually, Antony had him killed and nailed his tongue

SPOTLIGHTING THEORISTS: ARISTOTLE

Aristotle (384–322 BCE)

Born in the village of Stagiros, near what was then considered Macedonia, in northern Greece, this Greek philosopher and teacher was responsible for many contributions to rhetoric and public speaking. During his life he accomplished a great many things, including mentoring Alexander the Great of Macedonia.

Due to Aristotle's close connection to the kingdom of Macedon, many Greeks, especially those in Athens, probably viewed him with a great bit of suspicion. In 367 BCE Aristotle moved to Athens to study under Plato at the Academy. Despite his fondness for Plato, Aristotle was much more realistic and practical in his approach to philosophy than his teacher. Aristotle used his education and exposure to great thinkers of his time while at the Academy to guide his academic pursuits. He was the first to outline what we refer to as formal logic, and he crafted an ethical code grounded in living a happy life rather than adhering to religious codes. Further, he developed a political philosophy vastly different from Plato's that found as its inspiration the democratic and constitutional governments of his time— approaches Plato clearly held in disdain.

In the 350s BCE Aristotle taught rhetoric at the Academy, largely as an attempt to compete against the school opened by Isocrates. Aristotle's rhetoric courses focused on logic, in direct contrast to what Isocrates and his Sophistic plan of study offered. In 347 BCE, just around the time Plato died, Aristotle left Athens and went abroad where he studied other subjects, like biology. Around 343 BCE, however, he moved back to his roots at the request of King Philip of Macedon in order to educate the prince, Alexander.

Within eight years, but well after his tutelage under Aristotle ended, Alexander conquered Athens and Aristotle returned to the home of his mentor. In 335 BCE Aristotle opened the Lyceum—his version of the Academy—and taught students there until the death of Alexander the Great in 323 BCE. When Alexander passed, Aristotle gave his school over to his most prominent student, Theophrastus, and died a year later on the island of Euboea.[11]

Aristotle wrote extensively on a variety of subjects and remains one of the most influential philosophers on oratory, philosophy, logic, and politics in all of history. He serves as an excellent example of the importance of education. Even today he is one of the most recognized of all classical Greek thinkers and figures.

and hands to the door of the Senate as a sign for all those that might have aligned themselves with Cicero against him. The hands and tongue were symbols of Cicero's ability to persuade others, and the nails a warning to those who followed in his footsteps. Such was the death of Cicero, and the beginning of the Roman Empire.

Despite Cicero's unfortunate and untimely end, his story is an example of civic engagement. Cicero used his words to persuade others to adopt what he believed was good and right for his society, even in the face of strong opposition. In doing so, he was acting upon a sharp awareness of his own responsibility for his community. We as practitioners of communication can follow Cicero's example and even use some of the methods and approaches that he advocated.

In his works, notably *De Oratore* and *De Inventione*, Cicero explored what he called the five "canons" of rhetoric. A canon is a principle, rule, or criterion by which something can be judged or assessed. Cicero's five canons provide a structure for developing a strong speech or any other complex message that you might wish to deliver to an audience or listener. The first is ***invention***, which is when you identify the best arguments for your case in a given situation. This is the creative dimension of message construction where you find the best possible way to convince someone to agree with you. If you wanted to argue that Mickey Mantle was the best baseball player of all time, you would invent, or choose, the way to support your case by deciding what to present about Mickey Mantle that supports your position and what not to present. You might need to do some research about Mickey Mantle to know what you could present in the first place, especially if initially you do not know much about him.

invention
the first canon of rhetoric in which you choose the best possible arguments for your case

The second of the five canons concerns organizing your arguments in the most effective manner. ***Arrangement***, or finding the most effective way to organize your case for the topic and the audience, can be done in a variety of different ways. To arrange points in the best possible way requires that you understand your topic and your audience, because the most effective arguments on a given topic may not be the same for different audiences hearing a speech on the same topic. For example, political candidates make different arguments to different audiences when trying to get each group to vote for them. In some cases, you might choose to organize your message in a predetermined manner and might even create an outline of your main points. In other cases, you might decide to create a less rigid structure consisting of a number of talking points, which you could discuss in the moment, if your interaction with the audience seems to warrant addressing those points in a given order. We will look at various arrangement options available to you when we look at how to craft the different types of messages later.

arrangement
the second canon of rhetoric in which you determine the most effective way to organize your case for the topic and the audience

Cicero's third canon refers to how you design the specifics of your speech. ***Style*** involves your word choices, phrasing, and the level of formality in the language you use to present your case to the recipient. All speakers have their own language style, and discovering yours will make this creative stage much easier and more enjoyable. Of course, style must also fit the situation and the audience. We cover the nuances of style in greater detail when we discuss language in a later chapter.

style
the third canon of rhetoric; involves word choice, phrasing, and the level of formality in the language you use to present your case to the audience

Delivery, the fourth of Cicero's canons, refers to the manner in which you physically and vocally present your message. Although today many people erroneously assume that a strong delivery implies effective communication, for Cicero, delivery was part of the process of communication, not the sole determining element of its effectiveness. In this way, he recognized the power of good delivery, but also by connecting it to the content itself cautioned against the dangers of overemphasizing physical and vocal delivery.

delivery
the fourth canon of rhetoric; the manner in which you physically and vocally present the speech

The final canon of rhetoric proposed by Cicero is less important today than it was during his time, but still remains a part of the communicative process. *Memory*, according to Cicero, refers to one's ability both to use memory to recall names and important information in the middle of an interaction as well as to deliver a cogent message without notes. The ability to speak without notes is less of a concern today thanks to things like PowerPoint and teleprompters, but in Classical Rome performing speeches without notes was a sign of eloquence and intelligence. That said, the ability to recall information relevant to a conversation or meeting and incorporate it into a response is still a valued skill today, and communicators must make decisions about how they will help themselves to remember the message once they begin interacting with the audience.

memory
the fifth canon of rhetoric; refers to one's ability to recall names and important information in the middle of a speech as well as to deliver a cogent speech without notes

Cicero's five canons provide communicators with a general structure that they can follow as they craft a message for an audience. Each canon can be understood as a set of interrelated tasks that a communicator must carry out as she or he prepares to engage an audience. One need not go through these tasks in a strictly linear manner. One can move back and forth among tasks as one makes decisions about the message that one is crafting and the manner in which she or he is planning to deliver it. Nonetheless, these tasks are likely to follow more-or-less the order in which Cicero lists the five canons, with invention coming first, arrangement and style following it, and delivery and memory being addressed last.

PARTICIPATING IN THE DISCOURSES OF ONE'S COMMUNITY

Today, scholars and students explore communication in a wide range of contexts. Cicero, Aristotle, and other early rhetoricians were interested especially in speeches that members of a given community would give in public forums. Although many scholars and students today still examine political figures and their comments, others analyze the messages that everyday folks create in the context of their professional work and their involvements in the community. Conversations such as these are not simply empty talk. Through these interactions, people negotiate what is real and what is not, what is good and what is bad, what is right and what is wrong, and what ought to be done and what ought not to be done in given situations. Earlier in the chapter, we described the constructed character of social reality. The communication that we have with others might seem to be mundane and unimportant, yet each interaction is a site where people determine many aspects of the world in which they do live, as well as what sort of world in which they want to live. Conversations and other forms of communication are important contexts within which people figure out what it means to be members of a given community.

Community as a Field of Discourse

When many people talk about social reality in a similar or even shared way from one conversation to the next, a *discourse* exists. Metaphorically, a discourse can be understood as a stream of talk that flows throughout society, through which that society's members negotiate their social reality. Such talk consists not only of statements that people make about a given topic, but also practices in which people

discourse
communication of thought by words; conversation; a stream of talk flowing through society, through which members negotiate social reality

engage that have significance for themselves and others. On a college campus, such practices might include how people dress, with whom they sit when they visit the cafeteria, how they interact nonverbally with people whom they pass on their way to class, how they decorate their dorm rooms and houses, and even the classes that they take—any of which might communicate something to themselves and others about the social order. In any given community, there are many discourses, including discourses relating to race, ethnicity, gender, socioeconomic class, religion, politics, and age. A community such as the University of Dayton campus can be understood as a ***discursive field*** where many different discourses converge, intersect, flow together, and even move against each other. Within any of these discourses, there might be different, even competing views of what is true and what is not, what is good and what is not, and what should be done and what should not be done. There also might be certain voices within a given discourse that carry a lot of influence, even authority, while other voices speak from a more marginalized place. As these streams of conversation flow within this field, people come to understand in particular ways the social world that they share and make decisions about how to live and act.[8]

For instance, at the University of Dayton, there are many discourses of religion. One dominant discourse on campus is a discourse of Catholicism. This discourse is often reflected in the messages that University administrators craft and transmit to the campus as a whole and the conversations that occur in official events and activities on campus. Administrators use words such as "Marianist," "faith," "social justice," and "service." There are also other discourses of religion on campus, ones that reflect the concepts, ideas, values, and experiences associated with other faith traditions, such as Judaism, Islam, Hinduism, Parsee, and Bahá'í. Moreover, there are secular discourses that form the basis of people's sense of morality and purpose but are not associated with any religious tradition. These discourses, though they might be viewed with respect, have a more peripheral status in the field of discourses at the University, taken as a whole. The holy days associated with some of these traditions, for instance, are not officially observed on the campus calendar. Many of the concepts and ideas that have significance to the followers of these traditions are typically not expressed in official documents or statements at the University as prominently as those that have meaning within the dominant Catholic discourse. Within each of these discourses, whether dominant or peripheral, people strive to understand their everyday lives and to decide how they should conduct themselves from one situation to the next, and not all adherents of a particular discursive tradition speak and act in the same ways. For instance, not all Catholics share the same beliefs or attitudes regarding their faith, nor do they practice their faith in the same ways. Sometimes people speak and act from a place that straddles two different discourses—for instance, if they identify with or have experience with two different religious traditions, perhaps because of diverse experiences within their family. When people participate in multiple discourses, they often can ask questions and contemplate possibilities that might not be visible to people speaking and acting from within any one of the discourses alone.

discursive field
....
a space where many different discourses converge, intersect, flow together, and even move against each other

Key Contexts of Communication

A good communicator in today's world, just like those in the days of Aristotle and Cicero, needs to be knowledgeable about the discourses within his or her community, so that she or he can create and deliver messages that will have the greatest potential for shaping the social world in ways that are both effective and ethical. There are many ways in which one might participate in the discourses of the community—or even the society—in which one lives and potentially have some influence on how others understand and act with regard to their shared social reality. Each of these ways of communicating with others makes up a particular context, or situation, within which communication occurs. Each context evokes particular expectations among communicators and accordingly brings particular opportunities and challenges. In this course, you will learn about three of them.

One way in which people participate in the discourses of their society is through *public speaking*. In public speaking, communication moves typically from one speaker to an audience of many. Certainly, you will give many presentations during the course of your professional life, regardless of the field that you enter. You also might be called upon by friends and neighbors, community organizations, or local governing bodies to present to audiences in the local community as well. Your purpose in giving a presentation can be informative or persuasive in nature; there are also other purposes as well. In this course, you will create and give a speech with the general purpose of persuading your audience. In doing so, you will have an opportunity to contribute to the discourse here at the University and potentially influence people's beliefs, attitudes, and actions regarding some topic or issue.

public speaking
speaking where communication moves typically from one speaker to an audience of many

A second way whereby people can participate in the discourses of their society is by engaging in *dyadic communication*, or one-to-one conversation. A one-to-one conversation is similar to a speech in that the speaker might have prepared in advance what she or he wants to say and might be expected to take a leading role in the conversation that ensues. However, it differs from a speech in that conversations have a give-and-take quality, for participants share responsibility and ownership for the interaction in a manner that is more equal than in a speech. Accordingly, no one has full control over what happens. The listener might have questions or ideas or opinions to offer, which can change the trajectory of the interaction. Understanding needs to be created through the ongoing exchange between speaker and listener, even if the speaker and listener still expect to participate in the interaction to differing degrees. Similar to a speech, a one-to-one talk can have a variety of purposes, and one of the participants might play a more directive or leading role in the interaction. In this course, you will learn how to plan for and lead a talk to explain to your listener some concept, idea, person, place, process, or thing. An explanation involves giving information to a listener and helping him or her to understand that information. In this regard, it differs from persuasion in that your goal is not to change someone's attitude or to prompt them to take action in some way, but rather to help them to understand. What they do with that understanding is theirs to decide.

dyadic communication
a one-to-one conversation in which participants share responsibility and ownership for the interaction in a manner that is more equal than that in a speech

Speech to the NAACP Comparing Improving Childhood Obesity to the Civil Rights Movement
by Michelle Obama

Delivered July 13, 2010, Kansas City, Missouri

First Ladies in the United States generally have a national agenda. Michelle Obama's cause is childhood obesity and she established a program entitled "Let's Move" to promote efforts to reduce childhood obesity.[20] She announced the program in early 2009 and it has remained a focus of her time as First Lady. She has delivered many speeches on the topic and in doing so she has kept a focus on the health of America's children. One of the reasons for her success is that she has what Aristotle would have termed strong ethos.

When Mrs. Obama spoke to the NAACP in Kansas City, Missouri, she had ethos, or credibility, not only due to the fact that she was the First Lady, but also because she was a working mother who had faced the task of feeding her children. She used this ethos effectively to reinforce her message.

Mrs. Obama noted some troubling statistics and spoke of the necessity to act immediately. She noted actions the government was taking but called on communities to get involved and individuals to exercise personal responsibility. Perhaps most importantly she told her audience that the battle could be won. In the conclusion of the speech, Mrs. Obama called for action from the NAACP by linking the childhood obesity problem to the struggle for equal rights. Here is an excerpt from her address that shows how she did just that: "Surely the men and women of the NAACP haven't spent a century organizing and advocating and working day and night only to raise the first generation in history that might be on track to live shorter lives than their parents. And that's why I've made improving the quality of our children's health one of my top priorities."[21] Her speech in Kansas City is an example of ethos, but more importantly of how speech is central to civic engagement and can be a source of positive change in society.

dialogue
....
an interaction in which people with different perspectives seek to understand each others views; speaking so that others want to listen and listening so that others want to speak

A third way whereby people can participate in the discourses of their society is to engage in small group communication. Small group communication involves a few or several participants. While one or a couple of these participants might act as a facilitator for the group, typically the group members more or less share responsibility for their interaction. The general purpose of their communication can vary and is often shaped by the intentions of the facilitator. However, small group communication can be an important context for dialogue. In *dialogue*, the primary goal is not to persuade or to explain, but to achieve mutual understanding. A dialogue is not a debate, so the aim is not to "win" or otherwise overcome the arguments that others put forth. Rather, the goal is to explore some topic on which there are different views, in a manner that allows the participants to understand each other's perspectives regarding the topic or issue at hand. Dialogues can be powerful spaces for ensuring that different perspectives within a community can be heard alongside each other without those who hold those perspectives falling into opposition. A dialogue also can be a space in which discourses that are more marginalized or peripheral have a greater opportunity to be explored than they otherwise might be. In this course, you will participate in at least one instance of small group dialogue, perhaps more. These dialogues will have the general purpose of exploring certain controversial issues and fostering understanding of the views that different participants express.

Throughout this book, you will encounter examples of communicative events accompanied by a brief discussion of the issue the speaker addressed and how she or he approached it. Several of these examples are featured in the "Speaking of Civic Engagement" inserts. What they all have in common is a genuine appreciation of the power of communication to affect their communities and the lives of their fellow citizens, and they all demonstrate an effective reading of the discourses already occurring within the communities that they addressed. For instance, take a look at the box in this chapter that discusses a speech by former First Lady Michelle Obama in which she sought to motivate the NAACP to get behind her fight against childhood obesity. After reading about Mrs. Obama's efforts, consider what the context of her communication was, which discourses in the national community she addressed, and how she took up her communication in that context as a way of shaping those discourses and accordingly as a form of civic engagement.

SOME ETHICAL CONSIDERATIONS IN COMMUNICATION

As we engage others in communication and attempt to shape the discourses of our community, the effectiveness of our communication must not be our only concern. Preparing and delivering our message so that we can accomplish our goals is a key consideration; however, we must also think about the ethicality of our communication. Ethicality and effectiveness are both integral to the practice of communication.

Scholars and practitioners in ancient Greece noted the importance of ethics in communication, although they focused their attention on providing speakers with guidance for ethical message construction. They understood the immense power speech had over the actions of the public, and so in their schools they often took care to teach not just the skills of message construction and delivery, but how to wield them for the public good. For them, and for us today, why you say something is just as important as what you say and how you say it.

Isocrates and Plato: Two Early Advocates

Like Cicero and Aristotle, Isocrates was early advocate of communication as a form of civic engagement. He lived in ancient Greece during the Fourth Century BCE. He opened a school where rhetoric and speech were core components of the education his students received. The School of Isocrates was expensive and highly selective. Isocrates was one of the first scholars to offer a view of communication as a form of ethical participation in the life of the community.

The Struggle for Human Rights
by Eleanor Roosevelt

Delivered September 28, 1948, Paris, France

Former First Lady of the United States, Eleanor Roosevelt, lived a privileged existence. Despite her well-off origins, however, she witnessed much hardship and human suffering during her life: the Great Depression and World War II. To her, human rights were a fundamental issue worth fighting for. After her time in the White House alongside her husband, Franklin Delano Roosevelt, she confronted her growing concern over the expansion of the Soviet Union and how its policies infringed on human rights.

Mrs. Roosevelt became an advocate for human rights and delivered many speeches on the subject. One of the more notable of these speeches was given at the Sorbonne in France, where she noted: "It was here the Declaration of the Rights of Man was proclaimed, and the great slogans of the French Revolution—liberty, equality, fraternity—fired the imagination of man."[5] Speaking at virtually the front door of the Soviet Union and its allies on these issues would have been a risky proposition for any speaker, but Mrs. Roosevelt found it important and necessary to do so.

Mrs. Roosevelt noted that the charter of the recently formed United Nations concerned human rights and that the Human Rights Commission was working on language concerning those rights. She also commented on the objections of the USSR and a few other countries and outlined differences between the United States and the Soviet country.

Mrs. Roosevelt recognized that achieving universal human rights would be difficult, but she concluded her speech with a prayerful message of hope: "I pray Almighty God that we may win another victory here for the rights and freedoms of all men." [6]

Isocrates taught his students that a person's capacity to know things was limited, and therefore to expect to know the right course of action in every situation and on every issue was impossible. For Isocrates, only a well-educated person could determine the best course of action through a well-informed, yet incomplete, opinion. He believed that "it is much better to form probable opinions about useful things than to have exact knowledge of useless things."[11] Essentially, Isocrates felt that in order to speak well in any context people needed to be well learned on a variety of subjects.

Isocrates also believed that good speakers were morally sound individuals who could discern right from wrong. He felt that education on many subjects was the best way to ensure ethical goals for a speaker. He also believed that ornate language and lofty sentence construction within a message about a worthy topic—which could only be identified by well-informed individuals—indicated an ethical and moral person. This emphasis on style and content represents a sort of fusion of the approaches taken by Gorgias and Protagoras, two well-known teachers of rhetoric. It also illustrates an emphasis on teaching people to think before they speak, and not to profess to know things which they do not know.

Isocrates believed you could not teach people the appropriate thing to say in any given moment with a handbook, only through extensive repetition and exposure to civic life. This exemplifies Isocrates' approach to education commitment to the strength of community. He recognized that communicating effectively and ethically with one's own neighbors and fellow citizens was the bedrock upon which a thriving and vibrant community was built. That said, Isocrates influenced many great orators in his time and in the years that followed, especially those in the Roman rhetorical tradition.

A contemporary of Isocrates, Plato held a less than favorable view of the practitioners and writers in his time who advocated what has become known as the Sophistic approach to communication. The *Sophists* were itinerant teachers who traveled from city-state to city-state in classical Greece, training people in public speaking. While there was little unity to their various approaches, the Sophists focused principally on technique. Plato was skeptical of this approach. First, he believed that a focus only on technique was dangerous and not conducive to living what he termed "a good life," where understanding, justice, and living a just life were the ultimate goal for an individual. Plato referred to rhetoric as "a knack," or trick and felt that the Sophists trained people in how to achieve personal goals through the use of persuasion that used language to manipulate public opinion. He believed, instead, that education should focus on philosophy, or the search for truth, rather than persuasion. Additionally, Plato felt not everyone was capable of conducting the arduous task of seeking and knowing the truth. He believed that the only people capable of doing so, and thus the only people who could tell the difference between good and bad, were philosophers, and therefore they should lead the people. In his famous book *The Republic*, Plato argued that leaders of this kind might still need to employ the knack of rhetoric to deceive the public for its own good. Rhetoric in a just society, for Plato, was a tool for the philosopher to convince the population to embrace those ideals that the philosopher as a ruler had identified as what was true and good.

Sophists
•••••••••
itinerant teachers who traveled from city-state to city-state in classical Greece, training people in public speaking

Plato was skeptical, at best, regarding the use of rhetoric. He understood the way it was employed during his day as an evil, but when used properly in his vision of a just society, it became a utopian tool for philosophers. Regardless of the debate over which was better or more important—rhetoric or philosophy—Plato foreshadowed discussions about the power and purpose of speech that last to this day. He understood its power and, more importantly, its relationship to shaping the world around us.[12]

Some Principles of Ethical Communication

The ethical principles and duties laid out by classical thinkers, such as Isocrates and Plato, still apply today. Just as it was then, when we speak to the public today— be it to our fellow students, our church congregation or at a rally—we are asking them for their time, attention, and trust. Whenever we speak, we ask them to place value in our message by committing time and energy to listening to us. That value depends on their believing that we are interesting with them with goals that are greater than our own self-interest and that we are using ethical means of communicating with them. Consequently, when we communicate with others, we must give attention to both the goals that we are bringing to the interaction and the means whereby we intend to accomplish those goals.

Ethical communication requires, first, that the speaker is seeking a goal that has the audience's best interests in mind. One instance when a speaker addressed a group of people with the global community's best interests in mind came after the second World War, when former First Lady Eleanor Roosevelt spoke about human rights to a group in France, which is described in another "Speaking of Civic Engagement" insert. The issue of basic human rights is something that affects all of us, and speaking on behalf of protecting those rights represents a good and ethical goal. If we have good goals, we should also share our intentions with the audience honestly, and acknowledge any personal interests or biases we may have related to the topic.

As a more current example, let us take a look at charity work here on campus. Every December as the semester ends, UD delivers "Christmas on Campus." This celebration symbolizes the Catholic and Marianist tradition of the University of Dayton by inviting local families to campus to celebrate Christmas early. UD students "adopt" a child from the Dayton community and bring them to a decorated campus for an evening of fun and celebration. Every year students seek support for Christmas on Campus in the form of donations of time, treasure, and talents from members of the UD community. Talking to your friends to encourage support for Christmas on Campus would fit this description of ethical speaking because you would be seeking a good goal, and good speakers must have good goals. They must have more than their own self-interest in mind.

But ethical speaking is not just about achieving good goals or ends; it is also about the means we use to achieve those ends. Let's suppose you are seeking donations from your classmates for breast cancer research. As a piece of evidence, you state that there is a 75% chance that the other person's mother will develop breast cancer—except this data is not accurate and you do not even provide a source for the information. In fabricating the statistic, you would violate the principles of ethical speaking because you would not be defending the truth. Despite the fact this story may help your case and move someone to donate for a noble cause, the ends were achieved through deception and manipulation—two things not characteristic of ethical action. Additionally, it will damage your ethos, if the audience were to discover that you were using such means to convince them.

Determining which goals and which means for seeking those goals in communication sometimes can be a challenge. Among the various ends that we might seek in a given situation through our interaction with others, we might have difficulty as we weigh particular alternatives against each other. The same might be true for the means that are available to us. Having a set of principles that generally define ethical communication might help us to assess the options before us in any given situation or to evaluate the communication in which others have engaged in which we ourselves might have a stake.

Fortunately, there is a broad consensus among communication scholars and practitioners about what constitutes ethical communication, which scholars have articulated in formal statements that people can use as a reference in making these challenging decisions. One large, highly reputable community of scholars and practitioners, the National Communication Association, has offered its own credo regarding ethical communication. At the start of its credo, the National Communication Association explains the importance of ethical communication:

> Questions of right and wrong arise whenever people communicate. Ethical communication is fundamental to responsible thinking, decision making, and the development of relationships and communities within and across contexts, cultures, channels, and media. Moreover, ethical communication enhances human worth and dignity by fostering truthfulness, fairness, responsibility, personal integrity, and respect for self and others. We believe that unethical communication threatens the quality of all communication and consequently the well-being of individuals and the society in which we live.

It then identifies several principles for ethical communication, which people can use to assess the ethicality of the communication in which they participate or that they observe among others in their lives, should they face a need to make such evaluations:

> We advocate truthfulness, accuracy, honesty, and reason as essential to the integrity of communication.

> We endorse freedom of expression, diversity of perspective, and tolerance of dissent to achieve the informed and responsible decision making fundamental to a civil society.

> We strive to understand and respect other communicators before evaluating and responding to their messages.

> We promote access to communication resources and opportunities as necessary to fulfill human potential and contribute to the well-being of individuals, families, communities, and society.

> We promote communication climates of caring and mutual understanding that respect the unique needs and characteristics of individual communicators.

> We condemn communication that degrades individuals and humanity through distortion, intimidation, coercion, and violence, and through the expression of intolerance and hatred.

> We are committed to the courageous expression of personal convictions in pursuit of fairness and justice.

> We advocate sharing information, opinions, and feelings when facing significant choices while also respecting privacy and confidentiality.

> We accept responsibility for the short- and long-term consequences for our own communication and expect the same of others.[15]

integrity
. . . .
a quality of discerning and acting on one's ethical principles

Acting in accordance with principle is fundamental to conducting oneself with *integrity*. Law professor Stephen Carter describes integrity as having three elements: "(1) *discerning* what is right and what is wrong, (2) *acting* on what you have discerned, even at personal cost, and (3) *saying* openly that you are acting on your understanding of right from wrong."[16] These principles require that you give thoughtful attention to the question of what makes something high or low in ethical quality, and that you then act in an ethical manner. The latter can be difficult to do, because others may disagree with your ethical judgment or may want you to act differently, even if they know it is not right. For example, if a professor asks you directly if your friend cheated on an exam, your guilty friend will likely be unhappy with you if you tell the truth, even if that friend recognizes truthfulness as the moral response. So, Carter acknowledges that doing the right thing won't always work out so well for you. But, if you are to maintain integrity, you have to accept those consequences. Living with integrity means sometimes suffering for doing what is right.

Communicating in a principled way demands that one develop certain qualities of character. One of the greatest lessons you can learn about communication is that your communication is shaped by your character. Various religious and secular perspectives throughout the ages have invoked the concept of character in their efforts to describe what constitutes ethical conduct. In his book *Nicomachean Ethics*, Aristotle defined character as a form of moral excellence. One's character can be described in terms of specific *virtues*, or personal qualities that manifest moral excellence and make one capable of performing noble deeds.[17] Aristotle explained that virtues are expressed when one finds the mean between extremes as one takes action. He identified several, including generosity, courage, temperance, gentleness, friendliness, truthfulness, fairness, and magnanimity. For instance, the virtue of courage is the mean between cowardice and foolhardiness. If one leans too far to one extreme as one responds to a situation, then one has failed to be courageous by acting out of fear. One, however, can lean too far towards the other extreme and act in a manner that is rash or reckless. This too is not courage. To be courageous, Aristotle argued, one must find the middle way between the two extremes. Only then could one's actions within the given situation be understood as virtuous.

virtues
. . . .
personal qualities that manifest moral excellence and make one capable of performing noble deeds

Accordingly, you'll have to think carefully about what values you hold and how you live those values if you want to develop the type of integrity necessary to be effective at communication in a manner that goes beyond technical proficiency. Fortunately, UD offers many opportunities for you to do this through many CAP courses, co-curricular programming (such as through the Fitz Center or Campus Ministry), and elsewhere. Take advantage of this time to consider your values and develop your integrity, and it will serve you well in the workplace as well as in your personal life.

Some Unethical Means of Communication

When people do not approach their communication with others on the basis of principle, they are likely to resort to various means of unethical communication. One of these means is demagoguery. Unfortunately, many speakers today rely primarily on demagoguery when crafting appeals, even if they do not communicate outright mistruths. *Demagoguery* refers to speech that attempts to win over an audience through appealing to their prejudices and emotions, particularly those of fear, anger, and frustration. Unfortunately, the practice of demagoguery has become even more common with the advent of mediated communication and 24-hour news channels.

demagoguery
speech that attempts to win over an audience through appealing to their prejudices and emotions, particularly those of fear, anger, and frustration

Demagogues originally referred to leaders of the common people in classical Greece, but like today, the term carried a negative connotation that implied deceit, selfishness, and a desire to create mischief in thepopulation. Demagogues typically seek to gain power for themselves by activating and exacerbating the darker side of human emotions. For example, Huey Long, governor of Louisiana in 1928, won election by demonizing the wealthy and corporate interests while promising a utopian community where "every man is a king, but no one wears a crown." He referred to the wealthy as "parasites" and used them as a target for the anger of the Louisiana public that had begun to feel the effects of an economic downturn.

Perhaps the most famous demagogue in American history was Senator Joe McCarthy who, in the 1950s, accused high-ranking officials, Hollywood celebrities, and even newsman Edward R. Murrow of being either communists or communist sympathizers bent on destroying the fabric of American society. This period, now referred to as the Red Scare, saw many people lose jobs and suffer damaged reputations that could not be repaired, even after McCarthy's accusations were discovered to be baseless and unfounded. His accusations created a public frenzy by playing solely on the public's fears of communism. —> History repeats itself

Emotions are an important part of effective message construction, but when communicators use emotions to further their own ends at the expense of reasoning and evidence or play on the stereotypes that their audiences hold, appealing to emotion becomes unethical. There are plenty of emotional appeals that are both ethically constructed and designed to achieve ethical ends, but as a speaker we must be cognizant of both the means we use to move people to action and the action toward which we move them. Demagogues violate both of these principles by capitalizing on an audience's emotions to achieve personal, rather than communal, goals.

Those who resort to demagoguery often use language in derogatory or abusive ways to shape people's perceptions. Language is a creative—and also potentially destructive—part of our lives, but it is central to all things that make us human. It can create strong relationships, and also, if used without care, can destroy associations with others. It can influence and evoke emotions and move us to action. It can teach us things about ourselves, others, and the world around us. It is the cornerstone of community. Language is a powerful tool that helps you accomplish the goals of any presentation or interaction. As the adage goes, though, with great power comes great responsibility, so you must be careful not to abuse language when interacting with other people.

Two ways in which communicators can use language that can cross the line from edifying to abusive are profanity and hate speech. *Profanity* consists of coarse and irreverent language. To profane something is to treat something that is held to be sacred or worthy of reverence without respect. One can find profanity

profanity
coarse and irreverent language

everywhere: on the street, in movies, within songs, and in various other spaces. Often, people use this language without much thought because they feel intense emotions that stretch the limits of their self-control. However, in many cases, people use this language because they find it to be normal or customary in their relationships with specific others or perhaps even in general.

While one might argue that there is nothing inherently unethical about particular words or phrases, use of profanity without consideration for one's audience can violate their sense of what is decent and proper. This can lead to unnecessary tension, alienation, or even conflict with others. One might feel that others are overreacting and do not have any right to make such judgments; however, such a view ignores that, in using such words without consideration for these others, one is also making judgments about what is morally acceptable and what is not. In a diverse society, there are no guarantees about how any person will view what is right and good, and to assume that others should simply conform to one's own moral vision assumes a certain attitude of moral superiority that others might resist. Regardless of how people might speak in private circles, many people view using profanity in public settings, especially in formal organizational contexts such as a workplace, to be unprofessional. Using profanity in these contexts might risk losing credibility. Moreover, it should be remembered that certain profane words and phrases also might imply derogatory judgments about particular demographic groups that others find especially to be objectionable, even hurtful. Whatever one's personal views about the acceptability of using profanity might be, avoiding its use in favor of language that people view generally as more edifying towards others can be a way of approaching one's public interactions with others as having a certain measure of "sacredness" that warrants courtesy, politeness, and respect. These qualities are essential components of civility, a concept that we will explore later as we learn about dialogue.

hate speech
rude and crude speech that attacks or demeans a particular social or ethnic group many times with the intent of inciting action against that group

The second way in which language can be used unethically is **hate speech**. Hate speech attacks or demeans a particular social or ethnic group, many times with the intent of inciting action against that group. Hate speech uses offensive and emotional language to incite anger in the audience, and neither the language nor the goal it is used to achieve is ethical. In the 1930s and 1940s Adolf Hitler used such language to move his country to war. He blamed the ills Germans faced on the Jewish community and began a program of systematic elimination of that group that we now refer to as the Holocaust. Kenneth Burke, a rhetorician who lived in the twentieth century, published an essay in 1939 that pointed out the power rooted in Hitler's unethical language.[18]

dehumanization
making people seem less than human in order to more easily motivate action against them

Burke's analysis of Hitler's rhetoric provided the foundation for quite a bit of scholarship on similar language. Burke noted that Hitler's hate speech followed a particular structure whereby a social ill is found, a cause is identified, a defense of the good qualities of society is presented, and then action must be taken to rid society, or purify it, of the ill. One especially damaging quality of hate speech is the **dehumanization** of a particular social group. Dehumanization means making people seem less than human in order to more easily motivate action against them. For Hitler, Jews were portrayed as less than human, thereby making it easier to purge them from society. In other cases people compare enemies to rats, insects,

SPOTLIGHTING THEORISTS: RICHARD M. WEAVER

Richard M. Weaver (1910–1963)

Richard Weaver was born in North Carolina. Five years later his father died and his mother moved the family to Lexington, Kentucky. Weaver worked his way through school at the University of Kentucky and graduated with a degree in English in 1932. Upon graduating, Weaver was unable to find work given the poor economic climate created by the Great Depression. The young graduate was bitter and joined the Socialist Party, but after a few years its ideas fell out of favor with him and he left the party.

He eventually received a scholarship to Vanderbilt University and studied under John Crowe Ransom, where he was introduced to southern agrarianism, an anti-progress movement. In 1942 Weaver achieved a Ph.D. at Louisiana State University and began a career teaching and writing about rhetorical theory and composition.[6]

Weaver was very interested in the nature of human beings and how language was used in expression. Weaver became known for describing such ways of knowing as argument by definition. He was enthralled with orator Edmund Burke and the Lincoln-Douglas debates of 1858. Weaver was also interested in understanding how orators could use loaded words to make a point. He labeled these "god terms" and "devil terms." Weaver noted that god words, such as science, progress, freedom, and democracy, had positive cultural connotations, whereas devil words, such as communist and fascist, had negative connotations.[7] Weaver later declared that no words are value-free, because each contains a worldview.[8]

Weaver also wrote about culture and rhetoric's place in it. He felt that society in general was declining. Weaver noted that scientific progress was not all that should be considered when analyzing culture. He pointed to things such as scientism and cultural relativism as warning signs in the structure of societies.

Weaver died at age 53 in 1963.

or even diseases to make the audience appear better than the hated group and more willing to take action. Scholar Robert L. Ivie later took Burke's work and expanded it to illustrate that dehumanizing enemies in a battle makes it easier to motivate people to fight wars. Hate speech dehumanizes a particular group of people to make it easier for an audience to agree to action against them. For this reason it is often much more dangerous than profanity.

Rhetorician Richard Weaver also built upon the work of Burke by noting an additional way in which dehumanizing language manifests itself. He labeled certain loaded words *god terms* and *devil terms* and argued that society imbued such terms with positive and negative connotations that can affect the meaning of a message. He argued "god terms" like "science," "progress" and "democracy"

god/devil terms
loaded words imbued generally in society with positive and negative connotations that can affect the meaning of a message

always conveyed something positive to people, whereas words like "communist" and "tyranny" always connoted something negative. When someone or something was described using these words it circumvented arguments and immediately promoted a positive or negative view of an object or person. In hate speech, devil terms are prominent and help to bypass reason to capitalize on a person or group's emotions. Such efforts are both uncivil and unethical.

In general, we believe that practicing communication with civility is fundamental to conducting oneself in an ethical manner. We will explore civility in much greater depth in Chapter 11; however, it is valuable to take a moment to reflect on civil discourse as it relates to listening and speaking. Based on what you have already read in this chapter, it is easy to see that using language in ways that do not offend, alienate, or dehumanize others goes hand-in-hand with civility. We have all probably witnessed behaviors we would not call civil such as name calling, lying, gossiping, or even judging others based on gender, race, socioeconomic status, and/or age, just to name a few. We may have even engaged in some of this behavior ourselves. If we, as individuals, lived according the "Golden Rule" (do unto others as you would have done to you) perhaps we would all speak ethically and thereby help to create discourses that are edifying rather than debilitating in the communities of which we are part.

SUMMARY

In this chapter, we discussed how fundamental communication, understood as rhetoric, was to education in the classical period. We considered how communication can serve as a primary way of participating in the life of one's community and explored how two classical scholars, Cicero and Aristotle, contributed to a long tradition of understanding communication as civic engagement. We identified three ways in which people can participate in the discourses within their community through which people negotiate and co-construct their social world. Communicators must strive to communicate with audiences on the basis of certain ethical principles, while avoiding certain unethical communication practices. These practices include demagoguery and two unethical uses of language: profanity and hate speech.

KEY TERMS

arrangement 16

artistic proof 7

civic engagement 6

clarity 8

correctness 8

dehumanization 24

delivery 12

demagoguery 5

devil terms 25

dialogue 16

discourse 13

discursive field 14

dyadic communication 15

ethos 7

general purpose 10

god terms 25

hate speech 24

inartistic proof 8

integrity 22

invention 12

logos 7
pathos 7
profanity 23
propriety 8
public speaking 15
rhetoric 5

rhetors 8
Sophists 19
specific purpose 10
style 12
virtues 22

REVIEW QUESTIONS

1. What is civic engagement?
2. What are three elements of persuasion identified by Aristotle?
3. What are the five parts of a message as proposed by Cicero?
4. What are the two major ways in which a greater emphasis on rhetoric in today's curriculum would improve our abilities?
5. What are some key principles for ethical communication?
6. What does it mean for a speaker to act as a demagogue?
7. What are two unethical uses of language?

ENDNOTES

1. Peter Green, *Alexander of Macedon: A Historical Biography* (Berkeley, CA: University of California Press, 1991), 54–56.
2. Ibid.
3. Ibid., 54.
4. Paul Cartledge, *Alexander the Great: The Hunt for a New Past* (Woodstock, NY: Overlook Press, 2004), 84.
5. Philip Freeman, *Alexander the Great* (New York, NY: Simon & Schuster, 2011), 24.
6. Peter L. Berger and Thomas Luckmann, *The Social Construction of Reality: A Treatise on the Sociology of Knowledge* (New York, NY: Anchor, 1967).
7. James A. Herrick, *The History and Theory of Rhetoric,* 4th ed. (Boston, MA: Pearson, 2009), 39.
8. Stanley Deetz, *Democracy in an Age of Corporate Colonization: Developments in Communication and the Politics of Everyday Life* (Albany, NY: SUNY, 1992).
9. http://blogs.abcnews.com/politicalpunch/2010/07/michelle-obama-to-the-naacp-now-is-not-the-time-to-rest-on-our-laurels.html (accessed April 30, 2017).
10. Ibid.
11. Quoted in Thomas M. Conley, *Rhetoric in the European Tradition* (Chicago, IL: University of Chicago Press, 1990), 18.
12. Herrick, 72.
13. http://www.americanrhetoric.com/speeches/eleanorroosevelt.htm (accessed May 9, 2011).
14. National Communication Association, Credo for Ethical Communication, https://www.natcom.org/advocacy-public-engagement/public-policy/public-statements, 2017.
15. Ibid.
16. Stephen L. Carter, *Integrity* (New York: Harper Perennial, 1996), 7.
17. Aristotle, *Nicomachean Ethics* (Indianapolis: The Bobbs-Merrill Company, Inc., 1962).
18. Kenneth Burke, "The Rhetoric of Hitler's Battle," *The Philosophy of Literary Form,* 3rd ed. (1941; Berkeley, CA: University of California Press, 1973), 191-220.

Interteaching Session

Dialogue

In 2010, on his show, MSNBC news commentator Keith Olbermann delivered a strongly-worded criticism of Scott Brown, then a candidate for the open Senate seat in Massachusetts. Olbermann called Brown an "irresponsible, homophobic, racist, reactionary, ex-nude model, Tea Bagging supporter of violence against women, and against politicians with whom he disagrees." Initially refusing to apologize, Olbermann added "sexist" to the list of complaints in his following broadcast. After being criticized for the comments by other media outlets, including by comedian Jon Stewart, Olbermann apologized for the remarks.

1. Is Olbermann's remark an example of demagoguery? If so, explain why?

2. What are three specific examples of demagoguery you have heard in the media in the past year? Explain how each appeals to the prejudices of their intended audience and what negative emotions it attempts to evoke for that audience.

3. While Olbermann was eventually let go by MSNBC, he soon found a job on another news network. Why do you think these kinds of messages find their way into the public media?

Performance

Suppose that you have been asked to give a speech to a group of high school students in a government class, explaining the contributions of one of the following classical thinkers to understanding communication as civic engagement: Aristotle, Cicero, Isocrates, or Plato. Your speech must include an explanation of key concepts that each of these thinkers addressed and provide examples that illustrate these concepts. Using the five canons of rhetoric as a framework for your work, prepare the speech. What decisions do you need to make as you translate into action each of the five canons? Your speech should last approximately five minutes. Be prepared to give your speech to your CMM 100 class.

Communication as a Transactional Process

Many people suffer from phobias of one sort or another. For example, those who suffer from arachnophobia fear spiders of all shapes and sizes. Then there are those who fear animals, who suffer from zoophobia. Perhaps you know someone with aerophobia, the fear of flying. Maybe one of your friends has nyctaphobia, the fear of the dark. There are other more unique fears, like triskaidekaphobia—the fear of the number thirteen—or the fear of old people (gerontophobia). One of the most debilitating fears happens to be agoraphobia, or the fear of public spaces that comes from a feeling of inescapability. People who suffer from this fear cannot even go outside their own homes without risk of severe anxiety.

Fear is as human an emotion as love or happiness, and so it is not a bad thing to be afraid of something. In fact, it can make you function better. Take the example of Oscar-winning actor Sir Laurence Olivier. Olivier, named to the American Film Institute's list of Greatest Male Stars of All Time,[1] suffered from debilitating anxiety attacks before performances.

From as early an age as five or six, Olivier demonstrated a penchant for drama and acting, creating a makeshift stage in his parents' house from window curtains and a wooden chest to perform for his sister, visiting neighbors, or extended family members. Olivier's formative years took place during World War I, a time when England's image of itself as Europe's dominant force came under fire. Despite his commitment to the lines of each of the plays and roles he would perform, Olivier still suffered stage fright, or performance anxiety.

One of the more poignant insights he offers to this fear was, "It comes in all sorts of forms; I suppose it's always there, but most of the time it hovers unseen."[2] Olivier also suffered from fear right before going on stage, describing it as "nothing like first-night nerves . . . the breathing becomes affected: the breath becomes shorter when you want it to become longer and deeper . . . you try to calm down but the sweat breaks out again. The voice in the head starts to ramble."[3] Do any of these feelings and emotions sound familiar when you prepare to deliver a speech? Well, fear not, because Olivier mastered his fear, made it work for him, and went on to become a world-renowned performer.

In this chapter, we explore communication as a transactional process through which senders and receivers exchange messages and create meaning. While many people experience fear or nervousness as they participate in this process, called communication apprehension, there are strategies that people can adopt that can help them to cope with those feelings. The success of communication depends upon the ability of participants to overcome distractions, such as communication apprehension, and arrive at an understanding of each other's messages. With such an understanding, communicators are more able to make critical decisions. They also can find greater enjoyment in the process, as they appreciate more fully what others are saying to them.

Prep Questions

Part 1: Key Concepts

1. List and define the key elements of communication represented in the Transactional Model of Communication. Explain briefly how these elements work together as parts of a process.

2. List the four types of listening. Explain what one does when engaging in each type of listening.

3. Describe the three types of distractions that can interfere with listening. Give one strategy for coping with each, identified in the chapter.

4. List and define the four types of non-listening. Give a concrete example of each type.

5. Define communication apprehension. Give six strategies for coping with it, identified in the chapter.

Part 2: Application

1. Consider your first major performance assignment in this class: an explanatory talk that you will give to one of your classmates on a topic of your choice. The talk will take place in front of the class, even though you as a speaker will not be addressing the class. Using the Transactional Model that you have drawn, explain what will take place during this conversation. Make sure that you include all of the elements identified in the model: sender, receiver, noise, feedback, encoding, message, channel, decoding.

2. Give an example of a situation in which each of the three types of listening would be most appropriate. For each type of listening, list specific behaviors that a person in that situation should perform in order to listen with effectiveness.

CONTEMPORARY VIEWS OF COMMUNICATION

The classical scholars whose views we explored in the previous chapter represent a small sampling of those who contributed to the long tradition of understanding communication as civic engagement. They tended to focus on formal presentations because that is the type of communicative event that dominated the time in which they lived, but their contributions provided much of the foundation for the study and practice of communication today. Throughout this book we will introduce you to various other noteworthy figures and their contributions, some from the classical period and others from more contemporary times. The important thing to understand is that the practice of good communication between people and our understanding of rhetoric, speech, and persuasion have evolved over time. That evolution began with the works of these important individuals from classical times, yet today it has come to include the concepts and insights that innumerable contemporary scholars have offered through their own original research. In fact, contemporary scholars have developed different models that help explain the communication process that the Greeks first studied. Let's take a look at these more modern models and explore the components of the communication process as we understand it today.

The Linear Model of Communication

One of the first models that scholars and practitioners advanced was the linear model of communication. The linear model essentially describes communication as a process much like injecting someone with a drug. There are seven components to this model of communication. First, there is a *sender*, or the person who desires to deliver a message to another person or group of people. That person uses a symbol system, normally language, to encode the subject matter they wish to send. *Encoding* is the process of attaching symbols to your ideas and feelings so that others may understand them. The subject matter that is encoded is the *message*, or the actual content you send to an audience, and it can be both intentional and unintentional. That message is then sent through a *channel*, or the modes through which it is conveyed to another party. The traditional modes for transmitting messages is the voice or the written word; however, in today's society we also send messages through electronic channels like the radio, television, or the social media.

sender
the person who desires to deliver a message to another person or group of people

encoding
the process of attaching symbols to ideas and feelings so that others may understand them

message
the actual content you send to an audience, both intentional and unintentional

channel
the mode through which the message is conveyed to another party

noise

anything that interferes with the encoding, transmission, and reception of a message

As the message travels through its channel it competes with other forces that sometimes disrupt its transmission. These disruptive forces are broadly referred to as *noise*. This term constitutes anything that interferes with the encoding, transmission, and reception of a message, and it can take many forms. When you think about noise, don't simply assume it is auditory, or the result of some loud "bang" or "boom." Noise certainly can include sounds, but it also includes environmental distractions such as scenery and temperature, personal biases and predispositions, anxiety, and confusing word choice by the speaker. It is an umbrella term for elements outside the message that can hamper its transmission from one party to another.

receiver

the person or persons who receive the encoded message sent by the sender

The sixth and seventh components of the linear model of communication involve the party opposite the sender of the message. The *receiver* is the person or persons who receive the encoded message sent by the sender. Receivers are not always those for whom the message is intended. Think about when you have conversations with friends in Kennedy Union, or at a coffee shop. Yes, they will hear you and they are to whom you are speaking, but the workers and others in the room will also hear parts of, or even the whole conversation you have with your friends. They will not care much about it, but they still receive the message. There are always unintended recipients to messages we send, which only underscores our duty to pay close attention to what we say and where we say it. After all, how many times have you overheard something from a nearby conversation and then told someone else what you heard? Or, perhaps someone told you about a conversation they overheard.

decoding

the process of taking a message that has been sent and using one's own experiences and knowledge to give it meaning

Unintended receivers are only one of the potential issues that we need to be aware of when it comes to this part of the communication process. We also must understand that receivers decode messages using their own knowledge and experiences, and so they may not decode the same message you encoded for them. *Decoding* is the process of taking a message that has been sent and using one's own experiences and knowledge to give it meaning. Think about times when you have listened to a lecture in class and thought you heard the teacher say one thing, when they actually said something else. Sometimes this is due to words sounding alike, other times it is due to not paying close enough attention, and yet other times it happens when a speaker misspeaks or mispronounces something. Ultimately, we cannot control how an audience will decode the messages we send, but we can maximize the potential for their doing so accurately.

linear model of communication

depiction of communication process that features a sender who encodes a message and sends it through a channel where it competes with noise on its way to a receiver who decodes the message

In summary, there are seven components to the basic *linear model of communication*: a *sender* who *encodes* a *message*, sends it through a *channel* where it competes with distracting forces called *noise* while on its way to a *receiver* who then *decodes* the message.[4] (see Figure 2.1). This model of communication is very speaker centered, as it puts the focus of communication on the sender and places the receiver at the end of the process.

It is important to remember that the linear model is not a type of communication; rather, it is a particular way of depicting the communication process. Because it assumes that communication moves in only one direction, it best explains communication in situations in which a sender has a high degree of control over the

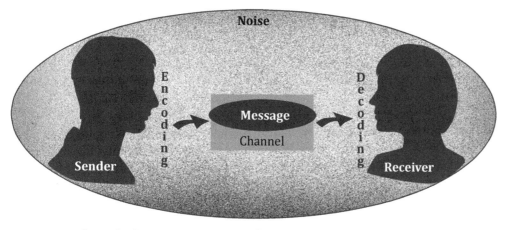

Figure 2.1
Linear Model of Communication

message and sends the message to an audience that has little ability to engage her or him in response. Consider, for instance, someone who creates a website but does not provide any features for making comments or sharing thoughts or reactions about the site. While those who see the website might find some way of engaging the person who posted the page, there likely will be a considerable delay before such a response reaches her or him, and by that time, the site's creator might have moved onto other projects. The one-way orientation of the linear model makes it suited for explaining what is happening in this communication, for the reactions of the audience other than interpreting what they have seen in the message have little bearing on what happens in the communication.

The Transactional Model of Communication

The linear model of communication, despite its strengths, does not adequately explain how all communication occurs. Because of its one-way orientation, it has difficulty in explaining how communication in which the receiver can respond quickly, even immediately after decoding the message. In fact, much of the communication that occurs in one's everyday life does not occur in a one-way manner, but rather involves a constant exchange between the sender and the receiver.[5] A more accurate model for explaining communication in these cases is the *transactional model of communication*, which expands the linear model by recognizing that communicators serve as senders and receivers simultaneously

transactional model of communication
••••••••••••••••••••
recognizes that we simultaneously send and receive messages; a cyclical model of the communication process

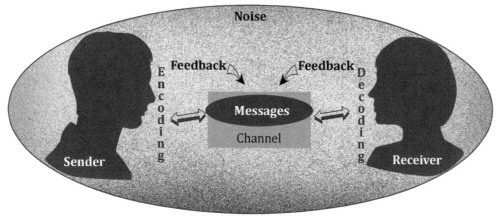

Figure 2.2
Transactional Model of Communication

and adds an eighth component to its depiction of the communication process: feedback.

feedback
....
the responses and reactions to the messages transmitted by the sender; is itself a new message sent back to the original sender

Feedback consists of the responses and reactions to the messages transmitted by the sender and is itself a new message delivered to the original sender. The notion of feedback allows the both parties in the message process to simultaneously serve as sender and receiver of messages (see Figure 2.2). Feedback can be verbal, nonverbal, or both and it plays an important role in any interaction, thus making the transactional model of communication a more appropriate explanation for communication.

The feedback we provide in a communication situation can alter an unfolding interaction and can let senders know about our impressions of the speaker and their message. Confused looks from a message recipient can tell a speaker to slow down and more thoroughly explain a concept, while head nods alert a speaker that the recipient agrees with what the speaker is saying. We will further explain audience feedback, what it means to you when delivering a speech, and how to adapt to it as a speaker when we cover audience analysis.

There is one very important aspect to take away from the transactional communication model of communication. We must always keep in mind that communication is an ongoing process, meaning that even as you deliver a message to an audience, the audience members communicate with you as well. Paying attention to the dynamics of the communication process when interacting with others will help enable you to better adapt to the moment and increase your effectiveness at getting your messages across to an audience.

Both the linear and transactional models of communication provide us with a logical way of understanding the communication process, but they cannot be understood as the "be all, end all" of the study of communication. In fact, several scholars have warned against emphasizing the development of models to the detriment of the more creative aspects of communication like language. Most notable among these contemporary thinkers is Marie Hochmuth Nichols, a former president of the Speech Association of America, which eventually became the National Communication Association, whose ethical credo we studied in the first chapter. As recounted in the "Spotlighting Theorists" insert, she called upon her colleagues to understand the power of the spoken word.

LISTENING AND COMMUNICATION

hearing
....
the physiological process of processing sounds, conducted by one's ears and brain

listening
....
the psychological process of making sense out of sounds

Understanding communication as a transaction between sender and receiver emphasizes the central importance of listening in communication. People often confuse listening with hearing when in fact they are quite different. *Hearing* is a physiological process of capturing sound, conducted by ears and brains. *Listening* is the psychological process of making sense out of sounds, and involves paying attention to the external world. Listening is an important skill for both speakers and audiences. To listen effectively, one must negotiate the many elements of the communication process in a way that allows one to make sense of the message that the other person has sent as she or he intended it to be understood.

SPOTLIGHTING THEORISTS: MARIE HOCHMUTH NICHOLS

Marie Hochmuth Nichols (1908–1977)

Marie Hochmuth Nichols's influential career covered more than three decades. She was one of the more preeminent rhetorical scholars, teachers, and leaders in the communication discipline during the twentieth century. She was the first female president elected by the entire membership of the Speech Communication Association in 1969 and shepherded the discipline through a tumultuous period of transition.[15] Nichols also served as editor of the most prestigious periodical of rhetoric and public address, *The Quarterly Journal of Speech*. In 1976 she was awarded the Speech Communication Association's Distinguished Award.[16]

Nichols was a scholar of both theory and criticism in the neo-Aristotelian tradition. She also was heavily influenced by the work of Kenneth Burke and I. A. Richards.[17] Nichols published many essays; two of the most prominent were "Lincoln's First Inaugural Address" in 1954 and "The Criticism of Rhetoric" in 1955. In these and other essays she argued in defense of the discipline of communication and called on people to focus less on developing models and paradigms, and more on the ends and purposes of speech. Specifically, she contended that the communication discipline is, and always will be, about understanding the uses and power of verbal symbols.

So highly regarded was Dr. Nichols that the National Communication Association (formerly the Speech Communication Association) named one of its most prestigious awards, the Marie Hochmuth Nichols Award, in her honor. It is awarded for published works in public address. In 1983 Kathleen Hall Jamieson issued the highest of praises for Nichols: "Some of us command an encyclical; some of us command a single rhetorical theorist; some of us command a rhetorical period. Marie Hochmuth Nichols commanded the tradition."[18]

Sometimes, to do this, one must overcome considerable apprehension. For some communicators, knowing that many people with be paying attention to them when they speak causes a high level of anxiety and is a contributing factor to their fear of communication. For others, the intense focus of communication on one or a few people in an interaction can cause discomfort. However, once we understand how listening works and can acquire some familiarity with ways of improving it, our level of discomfort in either situation is likely to decrease. This part of the chapter will help you understand the complex nature of the different types of listening audiences employ, as well as discuss the importance of listening for all parties in a communicative interaction.

Listening should be thought of as more than simply making sense of sounds, as it encompasses paying attention to nonverbal messages and processing them as well. Speakers listen both to the audience's verbal responses to statements—which can be as simple as making grunts of agreement or disagreement, or shouts of praise, or as complicated as logical expressions of agreement or disagreement—

and their nonverbal actions which can include leaving the presentation, staring off at something else, or even nodding off during a conversation. All of these actions indicate to a speaker who listens that changes need to be made in order to return the audience's attention to the message.

Speakers engage in listening to gauge how their audience has received their message and how to adapt if they determine that the audience members have interpreted their message in a way that differs from what they have intended. Listening skills are especially helpful during a question-and-answer session or dialogue following a presentation. In fact, the questions that audience members ask can tell a speaker a lot about how they have understood the message. If they do not wish to be direct in the way whereby they respond to audience members, speakers can use questions to guide the audience to a particular understanding of the issue. In ancient Greece, Socrates developed such a method. As described in the "Spotlighting Theorists" insert, he would ask questions to another communicator in response to her or his answers to previous questions, and these successive questions would lead the other person to the truth of the matter. Known as *Socratic questioning*, this method now bears his name. When a lawyer cross-examines a witness in a courtroom, they employ a similar method. Communicators can use Socratic questioning in other contexts as well, especially if they want people to come to certain conclusions through their own reasoning, rather than through being told what they ought to understand regarding the matter at hand.

Socratic questioning
the process of asking questions of a speaker focused on the responses to previous questions; its ultimate goal is to uncover the truth

Audience members face a harder time listening than speakers do because there are so many distractions that can keep them from focusing on the message. After all, the average human attention span is not very long and ranges anywhere from a few seconds to about 10 minutes, depending on the subject to which they are paying attention. When audience members do not pay attention to a speaker and the speaker notices, it may heighten the speaker's level of anxiety as they may believe the speech is boring and lose confidence in their speaking ability. It also may aggravate the speaker. Consider a phone call with a friend or family member when you suddenly feel like the person on the other end is not paying attention. Or, think about a moment when you told someone a story and the listener started to check their phone or look around the room. These are evidence of not only poor listening, but incivility and a lack of respect toward the speaker. It is, therefore, an audience's ethical obligation to maintain attention to the speaker and the message as much as possible.

Three Purposes in Listening

Often when people speak to an audience, they feel apprehension. One of the main reasons why having an audience who is listening to them makes speakers feel nervous is because they are afraid that the audience will catch them making a mistake or saying something inaccurate. Although you might find yourself someday in a situation in which your audience is trying to find fault with what you are saying, this is not a common situation. Often, when people listen to someone, they are simply trying to understand the message. Sometimes, they are weighing the content of the message but only so that they can decide what their own view is. In some cases, they are listening because they are enjoying what the speaker

SPOTLIGHTING THEORISTS: SOCRATES

Socrates (469–399 BC)

Virtually all we know of Socrates comes to us by way of his student, Plato, and his contemporaries Xenophon and Aristophanes, because he himself did not write any philosophical texts. Socrates perfected the art of listening to criticize through what we now call the Socratic method and Socratic questioning. In Ancient Greece, Socrates would wander through the marketplace questioning the political and moral positions of people in Athens. He did so by carefully listening to them and then asking questions about their statements. His questions almost invariably illustrated significant problems with the philosophies of his contemporaries. This would not have been possible had Socrates not carefully listened to, and critically analyzed, the positions they took. He can rightly be considered the father of modern logical intellectual inquiry, but even more to the point, he demonstrated the power and purpose of listening carefully to the messages of others.

Socrates was an Athenian who devoted his life to teaching philosophy, although according to Plato he did not accept payment for his educational services. He went through life financially poor, but was highly regarded by his students. In addition to his teaching efforts he also served in the military during three Athenian campaigns.

Socrates lived in Athens during a time of turmoil, when neighboring Sparta and its allies defeated Athens. After this defeat, Athenians seemed to have doubts about democracy, and from Plato we can see how Socrates may very well have shared those doubts. One of his greatest roles during this time was as moral and social critic of the city he loved, leading to eventual problems with those in power at the time. Greeks at the time held a "might makes right" philosophy toward justice and governance and Socrates vehemently disagreed with this position.

Plato called Socrates the "gadfly of the state" because he spurred Athens into action through his various encounters with leaders, philosophers, and politicians. The story goes that one of Socrates' friends asked the Oracle at Delphi who was wiser than Socrates, and the Oracle responded that no such person existed. Upon hearing what he believed to be an erroneous statement, Socrates set out to show that there were wiser people throughout Greece by entering into dialogues with politicians and philosophers.

He used a dialectic method of discussion in these conversations whereby he would solve what he saw as problems by breaking problems down into a series of questions that eventually produced the answers sought by those around them. These discussions almost always centered on moral and social dilemmas and the concepts of justice and goodness.

Socrates' questioning agitated the leaders of Athens because he often made them look foolish. They eventually had him arrested. When convicted he was sentenced to death, and despite the opportunity to flee and escape prison, he decided to stay and face judgment. Socrates was forced to drink a cup of hemlock, a poison, and died in his cell. His philosophy, however, has survived 2,400 years and greatly influenced Western thought.

is saying. Knowing about these three purposes of listening might help you to feel more relaxed when communicating with others and to adapt what you are saying to them.

listening for appreciation
listening for enjoyment; not high in cognitive commitment

The first listening purpose is for appreciation. *Listening for appreciation* encompasses activities where you listen for enjoyment. Starting your favorite playlist on your way to work or listening to the radio is an example of listening for appreciation. It also occurs in the company of friends and family when you are joking around and relaxing. People often listen for appreciation when others tell stories that resonate with and move them. In these moments, audiences are not waiting in the wings to pounce on an incorrect statement or to disagree with a speaker; they are listening to relax. Audiences often do not employ high levels of cognitive commitment when they are listening for appreciation, though they might be highly engaged emotionally or in other ways—for instance, if they too are participating in the telling of a story or are contributing to the enactment of a particular episode, rendering, or performance.

listening to comprehend
listening to understand a concept or message

A second purpose of listening is *listening to comprehend*. When we try to understand a message or learn about something we do not know we listen to comprehend. This listening purpose involves a higher level of cognitive commitment than listening for appreciation because we pay attention to the message in order to gather and store information about a topic. Think of classroom lectures, business meetings, discussions about household matters with a spouse or partner, or watching news broadcasts as examples of listening to comprehend. We do not look for things to argue about in an instructor's lecture; rather, we take notes so we can learn about something with which we are unfamiliar. It is about understanding the messages presented by others, and obtaining clarification if there is confusion after the speaker is finished.

paraphrasing
relaying back to the speaker what she or he has communicated to you

Three skills that are integral to effective listening for comprehension are paraphrasing what the other person has said, perception checking to ensure that you are reading accurately the feelings and intentions behind the message, and asking questions. *Paraphrasing* means feeding back to the speaker what she or he has communicated to you. One can paraphrase the content of the message. To do so, one summarizes as accurately and objectively as possible what the speaker said. When the precise wording of the message is key, the listener can include it in this summary. In general, when paraphrasing, one should refrain from including your interpretations of the message and rather focus on the actual content of the message in as descriptive of a manner as possible. Being able to accurately paraphrase what the speaker has told you signals to the speaker that you are listening to him or her with your full attention. Accordingly, it can motivate the speaker to share more of his or her information and insight.

perception checking
feeding back to the speaker the emotions or intentions that you as the listener are perceiving behind the speakers words

One also can engage in perception checking. *Perception checking* involves feeding back to the speaker the emotions or intentions that you as the listener are perceiving behind the speaker's words. To check your perceptions, you must communicate your reading of the speaker's emotions or intentions in as nonjudgmental of manner as possible. You are not trying to evaluate these emotions or intentions; you are trying to make sure that you are understanding them accurately. You might use phrases such as "it seems to me that you are feeling frustrated when you say that" or "you seem to be wanting support right now." Adding a tag question such as "is that right?" or something similar invites the speaker to verify whether or not the perception that you have shared is accurate. Perception checking highlights how understanding another communicator's emotions is a component of achieving an accurate understanding of her or his message, for the content of a message is not purely informational, but also emotional in nature.

Asking questions is a primary means through which one can develop an understanding of others in communication. There are many types of questions that one can ask. *Clarifying questions* seek to understand the meaning of particular words or phrases that the speaker used in the message. For instance, if a speaker says, "I'm not sure that adopting that proposal would be the prudent thing to do," then you might ask, "What do you mean when you say that you don't think that the proposal would be 'prudent'?" in order to gain a clearer understanding of the speaker's intended meaning for that word. *Probing questions* are used to follow-up with what a speaker says and gain additional information. Questions such as who, what, where, when, why, and how can be useful in extending your understanding of a speaker's intended meaning. Asking "why" can be helpful if it focuses on causes or motivations, but one must take care that it does not come across to the other person as criticizing her or his reasons for doing something. If a speaker tells a story about a particular experience that she or he had while studying abroad, for instance, you as a listener could seek additional information by asking any of the aforementioned questions: "Where did you go?" "How did you get there?" "Who else was with you?" "When did you arrive?" "Why did the group select that location?" "What happened when you arrived?" If one's goal is to understand the speaker's meaning, then one must be careful that one's questions are not thinly veiled vehicles for expressing one's own views. These are called leading questions. *Leading questions* are stated in the form of a question but actually express a judgment or opinion. "Don't you think that this position would result in higher costs?" is only outwardly a question; it actually has the function of expressing the questioner's viewpoint. Later in the book, we will learn more about asking questions especially in the context of a dialogue. In the meantime, practicing these three communication skills—paraphrasing, perception checking, and asking questions—will strengthen your ability to listen for comprehension, regardless of the context.

The final purpose of listening is *listening to evaluate*. It involves paying attention to the information and the argument that the speaker has presented, so that one can make a judgment about the message. Listening to a political candidate's speech to determine whether or not you agree with the message and listening to the position that a friend has taken in a debate on a particular subject to decide what you think about her or his position are common examples of listening to evaluate. Listening to evaluate is sometimes called listening to criticize. The word "criticize" often carries a negative connotation, such that people sometimes associate criticism with being personally attacked. Negative feedback can be helpful, if someone wishes to improve their performance or to correct their behavior; however, how it is delivered can have an impact on how someone receives it. Critical listening is an important part of any thriving democracy and is not something to fear, if it is

clarifying questions
questions that seek to understand the meaning of particular words or phrases that the speaker used in the message

probing questions
questions that are used to follow-up with what a speaker says and gain additional information

leading questions
questions that are stated in the form of a question but actually express a judgment or opinion

listening to evaluate
listening to make a judgment about a message; involves a high level of cognitive commitment on the part of the audience

given in a civil manner. Ideally, when we listen with a critical orientation, we are not looking to attack the speaker or to make negative judgments about them as people; we are trying to evaluate their message on the basis of its merits.

To employ effective critical listening, one first must make sure that one first understands the ideas presented by the speaker, before issuing any assessment of those ideas. Accordingly, one might begin listening to a speaker by adopting an orientation focused more on comprehension than evaluation and only after one believes with some confidence that one has understood the message as the speaker intends it to be understood, one can begin listening to the message with a critical ear. Some questions that one might ask include:

- What specifically is the speaker claiming?
- What evidence does the speaker give for that claim?
- What is the source for that evidence?
- How credible is that source?
- What bias is reflected in that source?
- How can the accuracy of the information that the speaker is giving be verified?
- What is the speaker assuming in making this argument?
- Are these assumptions accurate? How can these assumptions be verified?
- Does the speaker's conclusion follow logically from the evidence?
- How could we test this logic?
- What standpoint does the speaker's argument reflect? Has the speaker identified him or herself with particular social identities, in terms of race, ethnicity, gender, religion, socioeconomic class, occupation, or political affiliation?
- Are there other ways of interpreting the evidence that the speaker is presenting?
- What is not known about this topic?
- What is still in dispute among those who have some expertise about this topic?
- Who else is in a position to have some relevant knowledge or experience about this topic? Whose voice have we not heard in this conversation so far?
- What are the advantages of accepting the position that the speaker is advocating? What are the disadvantages?
- What practical implications follow from the speaker's position?
- What are some ethical dilemmas that follow from taking this position?
- What actions does the speaker's position warrant?
- How ethical are these courses of action?

A communicator could consider these questions while listening to the speaker's argument, yet there are many advantages to engaging the speaker in a dialogue through which she or he can be invited to answer these questions directly. We will explore how to create a dialogue with others later in this book.

Being an Active Listener

In general, people should strive to engage in what is called *active listening*. Active listening occurs when audiences have high cognitive involvement with the speaker's message, and seek to understand the message. In other words, they are processing, storing and potentially evaluating it as it is being delivered. In this regard, active listening is most likely to occur when someone is listening to comprehend or listening to criticize. Moreover, active listening also involves some form of reaction by the listeners to demonstrate that they are gathering the data being presented.

active listening
listening to understand a message by processing, storing, and potentially evaluating a message; also involves reactions by the listener in some form

In contrast, *passive listening* is listening without reacting, although the listener may well receive the information presented. Passive listeners do not raise hands or inquire during a presentation, and typically show no reaction in a conversation either. This is the "sponge" approach to listening and can be risky if you do not understand something being said. Listeners are more likely to take a passive approach if they are listening to comprehend or listening for appreciation. When it takes place during the latter then the sounds are often referred to as background noise. While in some cases, it might be safe to put less energy and attention into the listening process, if it is important to understand the message accurately, to make a critical decision about what is being said, or to have a deep appreciation for the message, then one must resist the temptation to be passive, given the many obstacles that one is likely to face when listening to others.

passive listening
listening without reacting

One reason why active listening is important is because there is a difference between how you speak and how your brain functions. You speak at a rate of approximately 120 to 150 words per minute, but your brain processes words at over 600 words per minute, resulting in lots of time for your mind to wander. This time is referred to as *spare brain time*, or the time available for your mind to wander due to your ability to process messages faster than it takes to construct them. Spare brain time makes it easy for your mind to focus on things other than the speaker's message. Being an effective listener requires concentration, which can be difficult if you are engaging in passive listening. To stay focused, you can make the spare brain time work for you, by using the space between sentences to review what the speaker has said. If you have the ability to take notes, you can write down key points that the speaker has made. You also can stay focused by asking questions, paraphrasing, or checking your perceptions when you have a turn in the conversation. While such behaviors do not eliminate the spare brain time, they can help to keep you in the mode of active listening, which means that the extra time that your brain has is likely to be focused on the other communicator's message.

spare brain time
the time available for your mind to wander due to your ability to process messages faster than it takes to construct them

Some noise, like background noise, does not affect a person's ability to concentrate or listen attentively; however, other noise can interfere with a person's ability to receive a speaker's message. These noises are distractions. In the next section, we will explore several types of distractions that can negatively impact someone's ability to listen and thereby can create a more challenging atmosphere for effective communication to take place.

Overcoming Distractions

Distractions can create an uncomfortable atmosphere for senders and receivers. Some of these distractions occur because of a person's reactions to fear, while others are external to the people involved in the interaction. Nevertheless, all of these can inhibit a person's ability to listen.

Biological reactions to the environment in both speakers and audience members can distract them from listening. Think about a situation where you are in a room that is too cold, or perhaps too hot. How hard is it to pay attention to the lecture in that room? It is likely difficult. Or perhaps you are ill, have a headache, or are hungry—all biological responses that diminish your capacity to pay attention to a message. Such experiences also can interfere with people's efforts to speak. When some people get hungry, their mood becomes irritable, and if this is a spouse or partner it creates a delicate communication situation. So, how do we overcome these distractions?

Table 2.5

Dealing with Distractions	
Type of Distraction	**Coping with Distractions**
Biological	Be sure to get enough rest and food and water, and if ill let the audience know
Environmental	Clear focus and acknowledge them to the audience
Hecklers	Ignore them Directly address them The audience may support the speaker

Unfortunately, there are few remedies other than concentration and focus. You could try and eat or drink before a speech if you are hungry, and in fact if you are the speaker you should go into the presentation with a satisfied stomach. If you are ill, you could take medication, but even then the best course would be to acknowledge the illness to the people you are interacting with at the outset so they are aware of it and do not spend time distracted by your reactions to the affliction.

In addition to biological distractions, there may be environmental occurrences that draw attention away from the presentation. Airplanes flying overhead, cars driving by, people coughing or sneezing, and even the howling of the wind can all cause both speakers and listeners to turn their attention somewhere other than the message. Again, the best answer to these distractions is to focus on the interaction and not the environment. After all, the brain is physically incapable of multitasking, so choose which is more important to pay attention to: the conversation or the airplane flying overhead.

The final type of distraction we will cover is the rarest of them, and predominantly concerns the context of public speaking: hecklers. Hecklers are those individuals who seek to interrupt a presentation to inject their own viewpoint, either through insult, unsolicited questions, or unwarranted commentary. Heckling could quite possibly be the most unethical behavior an audience member can display. Hecklers have appeared at political speeches, guest lectures by faculty, and even during comedy shows.

There are two ways speakers can deal with hecklers, and two ways audience members can help deal with hecklers as well. Speakers can choose to ignore hecklers in the hopes that they will eventually quiet down because they are not receiving attention. Rhetors also can acknowledge the hecklers and ask them to be quiet or face removal from the area. Audiences can also help control hecklers by ignoring them, especially if this follows the lead of the speaker. They also can confront the heckler and express their displeasure with that person's behavior. Either way, hecklers can make both speakers and audiences uncomfortable for as long as they are making their unwanted intrusions loud enough that people can hear them. Choosing to be an attentive listener who allows speakers the opportunity to say their piece prevents this type of behavior from occurring and contributes to creating a more comfortable atmosphere for a presentation.

Types of Nonlistening

Oftentimes we think we listen, when in fact we do not. What we are doing is called *nonlistening*, or providing the appearance of listening without actually paying complete attention to the message. Nonlistening comes in a variety of forms, and in each instance we believe, or pretend, that we are listening, but in fact are not.

nonlistening
providing the appearance of listening without actually paying complete attention to the message

The first, and perhaps most common, form of nonlistening is called *pseudolistening*. This occurs when listeners attempt to hide their inattention to the message by appearing as though they are listening attentively to the speaker. Think about phone conversations you may have had where you take the phone away from your ear only to come back in time to say something like "uh-huh" to make it sound as though you were listening to the person on the other end. Or perhaps, when you went to lunch with someone you had to ask "are you listening to me?" because he or she seemed not to understand what you said. Finally, you engage in pseudolistening while sitting in class, looking at the professor, perhaps occasionally nodding your head, and just pretending to pay attention. These are all examples of appearing to listen, but not actually paying attention to the message.

pseudolistening
when people attempt to hide their inattention to the speaker's message

A second form of nonlistening is *glazing over*. At some point in all our lives we started to look out the window or stare at a wall during a lecture in school, only to realize later that we missed important information. This daydreaming is a form of nonlistening common to situations where the audience is not enthralled with the topic. Although it may appear somewhat benign, speakers may internalize this as

glazing over
daydreaming instead of hearing the message

their poor speaking skills creating boredom in their audience. Your lack of focus thus can negatively impact the other person in ways you may not intend.

ambushing
selective listening in which the audience ignores the strengths of a message and hears only the weaknesses

Ambushing is a third form of nonlistening in which audiences may engage. This involves selecting only the weaknesses of a message and ignoring the strengths of the speaker's argument. It is a negative form of nonlistening that can encourage a hostile atmosphere that increases a speaker's anxiety toward participating in an interaction. It is important to listen to someone with an open mind and judge the message on all its merits, not only on selected points that are made. This is the listening version of the straw man fallacy in crafting a logical argument, which we will discuss later.

prejudging
entering into a presentation with a judgment already formed about the message being delivered

Prejudging is the last form of nonlistening we will explore. It is dangerous and a potentially negative form that stems from an audience member's inability to enter the presentation with an open mind. Audience members have an ethical obligation to enter into any interaction with an open mind and allow a person to make their case. If you have already formed an opinion prior to the event and are unwilling to change it, then the interaction is pointless. For example: Suppose your university has been raising student fees quite often. An SGA representative is coming to your organization and you know they support yet another increase in mandatory student fees. Your passion and attitude about the topic would make it easy for you to already have a decision made before they even begin their speech.

Most times a speaker can easily determine whether people have prejudged the speech and the speaker before a word is spoken, which is not fair to the audience or the speaker. Listen for the evidence and the argument and then make your judgment.

Listening is an important skill for communicators and it should be treated as such. When both sides are attuned to the message, they create a more comfortable speaking situation and help to reduce speech anxiety for everyone involved.

Managing Communication Apprehension

For many people, communicating with others can evoke feelings of considerable apprehension. These feelings can affect how one participates in the communication process with respect to any of its elements: how they encode messages, how they decode, how they perceive the context of the interaction, the channels they select for transmitting a message, and how they send and receive feedback from others. Speaking in front of others is one of the most frightening experiences for some people, especially when it occurs in the context of public speaking. Sometimes called "performance anxiety" or "stage fright," such fears are a specific manifestation of *sociophobia*, the fear of people or social situations. It usually come from some combination of fears, including the fear of speaking, of rejection, of criticism, of judgment, or of failure.

sociophobia
the fear of social situations or people

communication apprehension
the fear or anxiety associated with real or anticipated communication with another or others

Academics call the fear of speech *communication apprehension* and define it as "the fear or anxiety associated with real or anticipated communication with another or others."[9] Communication scholars apply this definition to a variety of speaking situations, as it also helps to define shyness in interpersonal situations. Here you see why there are multiple ways of describing fear of public communication. People often use the terms fear and anxiety to mean the same thing, even though academics might use these terms to refer to different experiences.

What is important to realize is that everyone experiences both fear and anxiety in their lives. Perhaps things get really busy at work and you become easily agitated over things that normally do not bother you. Some individuals experience

abnormal levels of anxiety, or who become anxious for no reason at all. These people have what psychologists call an *anxiety disorder*. An example of someone with an anxiety disorder is the fictional character Sheldon Cooper from the CBS award winning show *The Big Bang Theory*. Sheldon suffers from multiple phobias as well as obsessive compulsive disorder, significantly hampering his ability to function in mainstream society. His anxiety prohibits him from functioning, whereas normal anxiety does not do that, although it does cause a level of discomfort.

anxiety disorder

abnormal mental outlook in which individuals experience high levels of apprehension that keep them from living life

Causes of Communication Apprehension

Communication apprehension is often the result of a variety of factors, ranging from specific fears about the situation, aspects of a person's personality, or the physiological makeup of an individual. Environmental factors concern those things in the physical situation in which you find yourself. Psychological factors that influence speech anxiety include your approach to everyday life and how you handle stress. Finally, different people have different physiological reactions, in which their bodies involuntarily respond to stimuli that are present in their surroundings.

Three environmental factors influence a person's level of anxiety when speaking, and each stems from fundamental differences in the nature of the communication situation. The first two involve the audience. An audience for a speech is typically much larger than that of any conversation, and so we often find groups intimidating. That intimidation can sometimes increase even more when we are not as familiar with the people to whom we are speaking. For example, you probably feel more nervous talking to a group of strangers than you would to a group of friends. The third environmental influence is *spotlight syndrome*, or the perception encouraged by the room setup that all eyes are focused on you as the speaker. This can affect students in a classroom by inhibiting them from asking questions or making comments.

spotlight syndrome

the belief encouraged by the room setup that all eyes are focused on you as the speaker

Environmental factors don't only manifest when we're delivering presentations or are in front of large, unfamiliar crowds. Consider a first date. The audience for the evening is just one person, but the desire to connect with and impress that person can cause a great degree of pressure. The same effect is what causes nervousness in job interviews and in meeting roommates for the first time. So, just as large audiences can intimidate people, smaller and more intimate environments can as well.

The public speaking environment is different from the atmosphere for most conversations in other ways as well. Public speaking uses more formal language, has a very structured format, and involves more than just a few people. Conversations are less structured, often employ slang, and typically involve only a few people. Differences aside, the two situations share certain characteristics, and understanding those common components can help reduce anxiety over speaking in public or interpersonally.

Conversations and public speaking share several elements that make them more similar than they are different. Both entail extensive nonverbal communication when delivering messages and receiving feedback. Both call on you to logically organize your thoughts. Public speaking and conversation also require you to adapt to audience feedback in order to tell a story in the most effective manner possible. Finally, in both situations you need to tailor your message to the audience. All told, conversations and public speaking have far more commonalities than differences! So, just think of public speaking as having multiple conversations at the same time and your anxiety will be dramatically reduced. Or, think of conversations as different formats for presentations and put as much preparation into what you say in those situations as you would preparing to deliver formal remarks.

Table 2.2

| Differences and Similarities in Conversation and Public Speaking ||
Differences	Similarities
• Public speaking has more formal language • Public format is more structured • Public speaking involves more than a few people	• Use of nonverbal communication • Logic is needed • Must adapt to feedback • Message is tailored to the audience

The environment is only one set of influences on people's anxiety; their mental approach also can contribute to heightened stress in advance of an interaction. Thus, some psychological factors may cause us apprehension, as well. Many people believe that effective communication is a talent and not a skill. The fact is communication is a skill, something that can be learned, and not a talent that they're either born with or not. They enter into a speaking situation under the false assumption that they lack the tools necessary to effectively deliver a message to another person. In other cases, they falsely believe they are naturally good at persuasion or explanation and so become too overconfident in their abilities. Through practice and experience you can become a very effective communicator.

self-fulfilling prophecy
believing that something will happen before it actually does, and then when it does come true it reinforces the original expectation

Psychological elements can also contribute to a person's reluctance to engage others in conversation. Many people, especially as their time to speak draws near, allow worrisome thoughts to creep into their mind, creating a *self-fulfilling prophecy*. If you convince yourself that you will not perform well, you will invariably not practice well, and then the performance will be poor, resulting in the original expectation coming to fruition. This and other forms of worrisome thoughts can cloud a speaker's mind to the point where it increases their anxiety and gets in the way of a successful performance or interaction.

Nerves are not merely psychological; they appear in physical ways as well. When we get nervous we experience involuntary physiological reactions like an increase in heart rate, blushing and perspiration. These are our bodies' ways of responding to stress, and often we jump to the conclusion that 1) everyone around us notices, and 2) everyone is attributing them to our nervousness. Neither of those beliefs, however, is necessarily always true. Often, people do not see perspiration, or notice our blushing, or even see our hands shake. The truth is that we can hide the physiological manifestations of nerves without even trying; other people see only a fraction of what we feel, and usually do not attribute it to anxiety.

Now that we are aware of the environmental, psychological, and physiological factors that affect speech fright we can address how to manage performance anxiety and eventually make it work for us. In the next section we discuss several strategies for handling and reducing the anxiety present before and during a speech.

Coping Strategies

Fear is one of the most potent human emotions, and when you are afraid of something fear grips you and controls your thoughts and actions. It can be paralyzing, but it does not need to be so. Many people feel the best way to overcome a fear is to confront it head on and immerse yourself in it until you realize that there is nothing to fear. For example, they would tell someone who
is afraid of heights to climb to the top of the tallest building around and stare out over the edge of the roof. Do that until you get used to it. Although this immersion technique sounds logical, albeit a bit cruel, there is some truth to it.

Experience with that which makes you fearful will ultimately help you manage your fear. Unfortunately, this technique fails to address how you handle the fear while it is still present. Thankfully, overcoming performance anxiety entails both immersion and incremental management techniques. On the one hand, the more experience you get interacting with others in a wide array of contexts, the less nervous you will become with doing so in the future. On the other hand, there are several strategies for helping you manage the fear if it manifests itself during a communicative event, because you will not manage or master your fear overnight.

One of the ways you can combat the worrisome thoughts and self-fulfilling prophecy we mentioned earlier in the chapter is through visualizing success. Thinking positively about the interaction and imagining yourself successfully handling the situation will increase your belief in your ability to do so. A positive approach and visualizing the event without any problems will also allow you to practice more comfortably.

Changing your mental approach also can minimize the influence of physiological factors on your anxiety levels. Understanding that people cannot see your nerves, and that there are a multitude of other reasons why you might sweat or blush, alleviates the worry that people might see that you are nervous. You might be perspiring because the room is hot, or blushing because of the same reason. Your shakes might be because you are sick, or the room is cold. Just because you know that you are anxious does not necessarily mean others know that too.

Table 2.3

Manifestations of and Reasons for Stress		
Physical Manifestations of Stress	Could Be Caused by . . .	But It Might Be Caused by . . .
Perspiring	Nervousness	Room temperature
Blushing	Anxiety or embarrassment	Illness or room temperature
Trembling	Apprehension	Room temperature or illness
Breathing heavily	Anxiety	Physical exertion

Breathing can also help you combat nervousness and get more comfortable in front of an audience. You do not need to start to speak immediately when the other person finishes, or even once you get behind the podium. If you are feeling tense then take a deep breath or two before you begin speaking. If you find your nervous state is still there, or that it returns during the delivery, do the same thing. Breathing increases your intake of oxygen, reduces blushing, and calms your nerves, so always remember that stopping and taking a breath is an option available to you when you get nervous before or during an interaction. During meetings you might be more willing to contribute if you take notes so that you can refer to them when it is your turn to speak. Having your reactions written in front of you reduces the risk of forgetting what you want to say, or saying the wrong thing, and makes it more likely that you would contribute to the discussion.

Table 2.4

Strategies for Dealing with Speech Anxiety
• Directly confront it by presenting speeches and interacting with others • Visualize success • Realize the audience only sees a portion of what you feel • Take deep breaths for calmness • Adequately prepare and practice • Take notes

Finally, and perhaps most importantly when it comes to public speaking contexts, proper preparation will undoubtedly make you more relaxed when you deliver a speech. The easiest thing you can do to gain more confidence in your ability to speak is to practice often, in advance of a speech. The more you practice, the more comfortable you get with the material, and the more comfortable you get with material the more you know it when you get in front of an audience. Practice and experience breed confidence, and confidence is the strongest tool you can develop to fight your fear. Realize that you do not have to present the message using the exact same words each time. Focus on the content. As an example, you may talk to one friend about a date you just had, then talk to a different friend about the same experience but not relay the content using exactly the same words, tone, or even content. You may not say the same thing as word choices may vary, but the content, or purpose, will be the same.

SUMMARY

In this chapter, we explored two models of communication that contemporary scholars use to understand communication as a process: the linear and the transactional models of communication. Many scholars today see the transactional model as being more able to account for the complex and dynamic quality of communication. Understanding communication as a transactional process highlights listening as a key process whereby people attend to and interpret the messages that others send to them. Avoiding nonlistening behaviors, overcoming distractions, and actively paying attention to the speaker's message will help the listener to make sense of the speaker's message. Many people, as they communicate with others, experience communication apprehension, which can interfere with their ability to understand the messages that others send. Thankfully, there are a variety of ways to counter and manage this feeling so that any interference that it might introduce into communication is minimized.

KEY TERMS

active listening 45

ambushing 48

anxiety disorder 49

channel 35

clarifying questions 43

communication apprehension 48

decoding 36

encoding 35

feedback 38

glazing over 47

hearing 38

leading questions 43

linear model of communication 36

listening 38

listening for appreciation 42

listening to comprehend 42

listening to evaluate 43

message 35

noise 36

nonlistening 47

paraphrasing 42

passive listening 45

perception checking 42

prejudging 48

probing questions 43

pseudolistening 47

receiver 36

self-fulfilling prophecy 50

sender 35

sociophobia 48

Socratic questioning 40

spare brain time 45

spotlight syndrome 49

transactional model of communication 37

REVIEW QUESTIONS

1. What are the components of the linear and transactional models of communication?

2. What are the three listening purposes and the two listening types?

3. What are the common forms of nonlistening?

4. What are three factors that can cause communication apprehension?

5. What are some strategies for combating communication apprehension?

ENDNOTES

1. American Film Institute, "AFI's 100 Years... 100 Stars," http://www.afi.com/tvevents/100years/stars.aspx (accessed June 25, 2008).

2. Laurence Olivier, *On Acting* (New York, NY: Simon and Schuster, 1986), 181.

3. Ibid., 183.

4. Claude E. Shannon and Warren Weaver, *The Mathematical Theory of Communication* (Urbana, IL: University of Illinois Press, 1949).

5. For example: Michael Dunne and Sik Hung Ng, "Simultaneous Speech in Small Group Conversation: All-Together-Now and One-at-a-Time?" *Journal of Language and Social Psychology* 13 (1994): 45-71.

6. Marie Hochmuth Nichols. http://natcom.org/Default.aspx?id=73&libID=94 (accessed June 11, 2011).

7. Marie Hochmuth Nichols. http://blog.umd.edu/ncapublicaddress/2011/03/09/call-for-nominations-2011-nichols-award/ (accessed June 11, 2011).

8. Ibid.

9. James C. McCroskey, "Oral Communication Apprehension: A Review of Recent Research," *Human Communication Research* 4 (1977): 78-96.

Interteaching Session

Dialogue

Take the Personal Report of Communication Apprehension (PRCA) at the following site: https://www.hawaii.edu/gened/oc/PRCA-24.pdf. Then score the instrument according to the instructions for doing so. After you have scored the instrument, share your scores with your groupmates and discuss them. As you do, consider the following questions:

1. For which of the four contexts of communication did you receive the highest score: group discussion, meetings, interpersonal conversations, and public speaking? Tell your groupmates how accurate you feel this result to be. If it is accurate, explain why you experience the highest apprehension regarding communicating in this context.

2. For which of the four contexts of communication did you receive the lowest score? Tell your groupmates how accurate you feel this result to be. If it is accurate, explain why you feel that you experience the least apprehension regarding communicating in this context.

3. Share with your groupmates about a time when you experienced communication apprehension but were able to cope with it successfully. What did you do that worked well?

4. If you have experienced a time when you experienced communication apprehension but did not cope well with it. What might you do differently in the future if you find yourself in a similar situation?

Performance

With your groupmates, find a short video clip—no longer than one minute or so—from a favorite movie, television show, or other media program that shows ineffective listening. Analyze what goes wrong in the communication using the Transactional Model of Communication and what you have learned in this chapter about problems that can arise while people are listening to others. Prepare a five minute presentation in which you show the video clip to the class and, using the Transactional Model and these other ideas from the chapter, explain what went wrong.

Audience in Context

3

- Discusses how audiences can be classified and analyzed
- Explains how audience analysis can be employed in developing points and using language
- Outlines how to effectively adapt during an interaction

Practically SPEAKING

The 2008 presidential primaries represented the first time in over a half century when neither a president nor vice president sought his party's nomination for president. The campaigns for both the Democratic and Republican contenders were bitterly divisive, and each candidate needed to find a way to appeal to groups that normally would not support them. For instance, Republican Senator John McCain needed to quell criticism over what some party members saw as his questionable conservative record.[1]

In 2007 the Conservative Political Action Committee (CPAC) invited all the major candidates to speak at the conference and McCain was the only one not to attend.[2] As a result, he was crushed in the straw poll by his competitors and many conservatives refused to support him.[3] As the year progressed, McCain took further criticism from the right for his immigration policies, refusal to vote for the Bush tax cuts a few years prior, and his maverick nature. The criticism became so severe for McCain in 2007 that his campaign almost went bankrupt.[4]

The Arizona senator's fortunes changed, however, in 2008 when voting began. By the time he reached the podium at CPAC he was the likely Republican nominee for president. He had won significant election victories the previous week, and just a few hours before his speech his chief rival, Mitt Romney, announced the suspension of his campaign. McCain could now attempt to unite the party behind him. Unfortunately for the senator, the audience still viewed him with skepticism at best, and hostility at worst.

McCain needed to tailor his speech to the scene he faced. He knew he faced conservatives, but what kind? What was their age? Where did they come from? What was their economic status? Would race play a part in their perceptions of him? Were they ready to believe in his candidacy? Which political principles did they espouse? The answers to these and other questions influenced the word choices within his speech and the evidence he chose to use to deflect their potential criticisms. But even with knowing these things in advance, McCain still needed to be attuned to his audience while delivering the speech. All of these assessments are part of audience analysis, an essential skill for any communicative situation.

This chapter will show you the various elements of audience analysis that can help you craft and deliver messages tailored to your listeners, whether they consist of one person or one hundred people. It begins by discussing the various dimensions of a communication context that influence your message, and then discusses how that information can be used to inform your decisions on phrasing and organizing your message. Finally, we will explain how audience analysis continues during the interaction, and is not restricted to advance preparation. The chapter provides tips and suggestions for how to gauge the affectivity of your message while delivering your positions to listeners.

Prep Questions

Part 1: Key Concepts

1. Define context. List the six components of the context.

2. Define stereotyping. Explain how one risks stereotyping in doing demographic analysis.

3. Define the rhetorical situation as Bitzer understood it. List and define the three elements that make up the rhetorical situation.

4. Explain why Vatz disagreed with Bitzer's understanding of the rhetorical situation. Describe the implications of Vatz's view for a communicator.

5. Describe three different strategies from the chapter whereby a speaker can use what she or he learns about an audience in developing the content of her or his message.

Part 2: Application

1. Read the following script for a commercial for a hypothetical service:

   Still trying to get that yard into shape? Enough is enough, I say! A real man isn't afraid of asking for a little help, is he? Well, I know when I called Landscape 911, they helped me out of a real bind. You see, my in-laws were coming from overseas and were expecting to see a garden paradise. With weeds everywhere, yellow grass, and a lump of who-knows-what in the corner, I needed help fast. Because it was an "emergency" as they called it, they arrived almost immediately with a crew that would have impressed a military general. Needless to say, calling Landscape 911 saved my yard, my skin, and probably my marriage. Check 'em out at their website. Landscape 911, 'cause you never know when you'll need them.

   Now answer the following questions:

   a. In demographic terms, who is the target audience for this advertisement? Give evidence from the advertisement that this audience is being targeted.

   b. What does this advertiser assume to be important to the people in these demographic groups: that is, their values?

c. What does this advertiser assume that the people in these demographic groups believe?

d. How well do you believe this message has been designed to appeal to its intended audience? Justify your answer.

2. Marshall McLuhan said that "the medium is the message." Come up with one situation in which each medium below would be appropriate for someone to use and one situation in which it would be inappropriate to use. Explain your answers.

a. A phone call

b. A text message

c. A social media status update

d. An email

e. A face-to-face conversation

UNDERSTANDING THE CONTEXT: SIX COMPONENTS FOR ANALYSIS

The first step to any effective communication with others is understanding the *context*. The context is the circumstances in which communication occurs as experienced by the communicators themselves. Understanding the context is important because it influences the meaning of the moment and the messages that communicators exchange through their interaction. The context has several components: it consists of the who, what, when where, why and how of the interaction between the communicators. Understanding the context increases the likelihood that you will achieve your goals for the interaction, in part because you are better able to adjust your message to your audience. In this chapter, we will explore each of these elements in detail and explain how each plays a role in influencing how and what we say to others.

context
the circumstances in which an event occurs that influences the meaning of the moment and the message

Who Is the Audience?

No matter what situation you find yourself in, knowing to whom you are speaking is essential for successfully developing and sending messages. The "who" refers to both the identity of the other person or people in an interaction, as well as an appreciation of them in relation to you. It is important to understand the term *audience* as meaning those who are listening to you in a given context. Therefore, you can have an audience of one other person, or an audience of many other people. Throughout this chapter think about audience in both ways so that you better appreciate how audience analysis is a tool to be used in any communication situation—not just public speaking. In today's society we often break down individuals and audiences into *demographic* categories, or groups determined by select population characteristics. Such an approach is both positive and negative.

demographic
groups determined by select population characteristics

Demographic categories measure a variety of different aspects of a population. They detail observable and identifiable characteristics through survey techniques. Every time you place a check mark next to your race or provide your age on a document you are contributing to demographic information databases. Think about your college applications: You checked these off and sent them back to the universities of your choice. The universities then used this information to examine the appeal of their colleges to certain populations they targeted. Demographic information is powerful, and for that reason the use of it for anything other than description is prohibited by law.

In the United States most demographic categories are protected by law from discrimination. Race, age, sexual orientation, and religious affiliation represent specific groups shielded from discrimination. So, on the aforementioned college application you could not be rejected from a school for checking the box next to, say, "African American" or "Hispanic" or "Caucasian." So, demographic information—understood as a piece of data—can be helpful to corporations, universities, and other groups when trying to tailor appeals to large segmented parts of the general public.

Market researchers make use of demographic data all the time. In one clear ethical violation of the use of such data, Camel cigarettes was fined for targeting young people with their cartoon based advertisements. More common and appropriate, however, is how universities collect demographic data from their applicants to devise recruiting strategies for future classes. Demographic data are immensely useful when tailoring messages to specific audiences.

stereotyping
....
assuming qualities in a specific individual because of membership in a larger group

Just as the Camel story from a moment ago illustrates, demographic data can be dangerous. When we use one piece of demographic data to assume qualities in an individual because the larger group exhibits a tendency or preponderance for that particular belief we run the risk of *stereotyping* a person. That is to say, we assume qualities in a person based on qualities of a larger group to which they belong. These types of generalized assumptions are risky, and often wrong. The fact of the matter is that people belong to numerous demographic categories at the same time, and each of these groups may exhibit opposite trends, so it is important to remember to be careful when making assumptions in the face of possible conflicting data. Moreover, unless we ask the audience members themselves about the social identities with which they identify, we might be assuming that they identify with certain social identities only because we perceive certain observable physical characteristics in them. Just because a person has physical traits or mannerisms that one might associate with a certain population, for instance a particular racial or ethnic group, these characteristics do not guarantee that the person identifies with that group. While we might need to make certain assumptions about our audience, especially as we prepare the message that we want to communicate to them and consider the manner in which we want to deliver that message, we must be very careful that the assumptions that we make are as reasonable as they can be.

One way of grounding any assumptions that we make about our audience in data beyond our own limited experience is to research what specific demographic groups believe and the attitudes that they hold regarding specific topics. Two prominent and reputable organizations that conduct demographic research are the Gallup organization and the Pew Research Center. For instance, if you are interested in learning about the attitudes that American Muslims have regarding immigration in the United States, or what African-Americans believe about healthcare in this country, you can search the data reports that these organizations provide at their websites. The website for the Gallup organization is www.gallup.com. The website for the Pew Research Center is www.pewresearch.org. Having such information never guarantees that the specific people in your audience feel this same way about the topic in question, for demographic research is typically based on a sample of a given population, not the entire population. However, because researchers use sampling methods that allow them to generalize with high levels of probability the patterns that they observe to the populations that these samples represent, a speaker can have greater confidence in the assumptions that they are making about the audience than if they made those assumptions solely on the basis of their limited personal experience.

In large companies, different divisions need to communicate effectively with each other for projects to be successful, so again a proper understanding of "who" the other party is becomes essential for success. Take the case of a large international engineering firm tasked with creating a proposal for a client's new building. Obviously, engineers develop the plans, but accountants are responsible for purchasing and pricing the materials needed for the job. Neither of these two professions likely understands the details of the other, but they need to communicate with each other to finish the building. Engineers thus need to appreciate where the accountants come from when talking about money and financing, while the accountants also must appreciate the expertise of the engineers in identifying proper materials. These types of meetings are only successful when both parties understand the "who" dimension of the context when they interact with each other.

Take the case of Mary Church Terrell, a nineteenth-century social activist who spoke out against gender and racial discrimination. Terrell often had to balance her speeches with examples that appealed to women and African Americans at a time when the experiences of both had some commonalities, but also some significant differences. Terrell needed to pay attention to the racial demographic of her audiences each time she gave a speech to make sure she used the best possible examples. You can read about how Mary Church Terrell achieved an understanding of these audiences that allowed her to communicate effectively with them in the "Speaking of Civic Engagement" insert in this chapter.

What Does the Audience Know?

Once you have determined who your audience is, you must strive to understand, to the best degree possible, what they know about you and your topic. This is not the same as determining in general the beliefs and attitudes of people in demographic groups with which your audience might identify. It is rather considering the knowledge of the specific audience members who will be the recipients of your message. Are they unfamiliar with the topic under discussion? Do they know a little about it, or do they know a lot? What do they know about you? Answering these questions before and during an interaction can often make the difference between success and failure in a meeting. If you assume they know nothing, when they actually have some knowledge of a topic, then you might come across as condescending and arrogant. If you assume they know more than they do, then they might not be able to keep up with or understand what you're trying to say. It is also important to understand that just because people are unfamiliar with you or your field it does not make them unintelligent. You most likely do not know much about their area of expertise.

Your instinct might tell you that you can assume knowledge based on the person or group's level of education, economic status, or even other demographic categories. However, if you're assuming qualities about a people based solely on the demographic groups they belong to, you are stereotyping.

As an example of audience analysis crossing over into stereotyping let's take the case of a possible classroom interaction at UD. You know that UD is an expensive school and that most people in the class probably have some disposable income.

What It Means to Be Colored in the Capital of the U.S.
by Mary Church Terrell

Delivered October 10, 1906, to the United Women's Club, Washington, D.C.

In 1906 the United Women's Club invited African American advocate and teacher Mary Church Terrell to speak, and she delivered a scathing commentary on racial equality in Washington, D.C.[5] Terrell noted in her opening that the nation's capital had been labeled the "colored man's paradise" but declared such a title must have been bestowed out of irony, because "it would be difficult to find a worse misnomer for Washington."[6] Terrell also argued that conditions for African Americans had worsened in the 15 years of her residence there, and that although many other minorities could find lodging, unless a black person had acquaintances they likely could not find a bed. She noted that if she resisted current standards then she would be "cast into jail and forced to pay a fine for violating the Virginia laws."[7] Such issues reflected the direct experiences of African Americans of her day, but her speech was not simply about race—after all it was delivered at the women's club!

Ms. Terrell vividly described the limitations on the possibility of education, specifically that black school children received a lower quality education than that of white children. Within her speech she also referenced many more examples of injustice and discrimination, all designed to connect the causes of women and African Americans, as the causes of these two groups were priorities in her life.

In the closing paragraph of her speech, Ms. Terrell made a statement of a stern tone: "It is impossible for any white person in the United States, no matter how sympathetic and broad, to realize what life would mean to him if his incentive to effort were suddenly snatched away."[8] Mary Church Terrell lived to see the successes of the women's suffrage movement and the significant victory of *Brown v. Board of Education*, dying shortly thereafter at the age of 90. In recognition of the power of her voice on civil rights issues, the United States Post Office honored her with a stamp in 2009.

Furthermore, you look and see that the majority of people wear clothing from well known brands. You take this information and then assume the entire audience shares these qualities, when in fact, that is not true. In saying something that implies everyone has name brand clothes, you might be offending or alienating classmates who do not. That said, sometimes knowing the position of the individual or individuals you are speaking to can help you determine what they know about a topic—especially if the topic relates specifically to their area of expertise. For example, speaking to pre-med students about privacy you might infer that they know something about the subject, specifically as it relates to doctor-patient confidentiality.

One of the best ways to determine audience knowledge of a topic is to check your perceptions before and during the interaction. This is particularly useful with smaller audiences, but can also work in larger situations. Simply asking people how familiar they are with something can help circumvent needless background information and allow you to get right to the point of the proceedings. If, however, they admit to not knowing something, then you are prepared to elaborate on it for them. The topic, though, is not the only thing with which they need to be familiar.

Another key component of the "what do they know" part of context is knowing what the audience is aware of about you. In some instances, like interviews, your conversational partner knows a bit about you thanks to your résumé. In other instances, such as sales calls to potential new clients, the other party may be completely unfamiliar with you and your company and so you need to spend time introducing yourself and your company. If there is any question about what the audience knows about you going into a discussion, it is a good idea to open by asking them. That way you can establish a baseline for what the audience knows about you.

Where Is the Meeting Taking Place?

A third factor in determining context involves the place in which the meeting or presentation takes place. Where the meeting occurs can be informative and can significantly alter the dynamic of an interaction. Certain topics and relationships lend themselves to specific locations. When delivering more formal presentations the scene of the interaction can provide insight into the other party's disposition and interests.

It is not a stretch to call your own space, be it a home or an office, your "home field" as you feel most comfortable there. Meetings in your office or home provide you with an advantage, especially when discussing business with other people. You can control the setup of the room to influence the flow of a conversation. Your professors at UD for instance, arrange their offices to either encourage or discourage interaction with people. Desks can serve as barriers for discussions with people. Some professors put their desks in corners of offices and create more open and inviting spaces for an interaction, thus making office hour visits and conversations much more comfortable. Even open and closed doors play some role in how we interpret a person's availability and interest in conversation.

Office and home setups can also provide a great deal of information about a person. Many people choose to decorate their office space in a way that reflects their personality and interests. Even those who occupy cubicles hang posters or put pictures up that show support for issues or even sports teams. Paying attention to such surroundings can help you find ways to identify with the other party in an interaction.

Not all meetings and interactions take place in an office or a home. In fact, off-site meetings in local coffeeshops or diners have become more and more common in our culture. These meeting places can provide an atmosphere more conducive to a relaxing interaction where neither party has the "home field advantage". Off-site meeting places are also helpful when the topic of a discussion is sensitive. Public places, in this way, provide an ironically more private setting because those around you do not know who you are or what you are talking about.

When Is the Meeting?

It may sound strange, but the time of day, month, or even year influences the context of an interaction in several ways. Research actually shows that different people function better at different times of day, and understanding this will help you in any interaction. The amount of time you have before a meeting, presentation, or conversation can also influence the different tools you can employ to gather information about your audience.

In his book *Brain Rules*, molecular biologist John Medina explains the three different types of people in terms of when they function best. The first group, called larks, consists of those of us who function best in the morning and are often early risers. This group represents about 10% of the population. For our purposes, these people would prefer to meet and discuss issues in the morning. The second group, called owls, often works best in the evening and late night hours, staying up often until early in the morning. Owls, obviously, do not function well in morning meetings and may, in fact, become irritated more easily if they are asked to do so. This group represents roughly 20% of the population. The final group, hummingbirds, leans more toward either larks or owls, but generally functions fine during "normal" daytime hours.[9] Knowing to which one of these groups you and your audience belong can be immensely helpful in determining when to schedule meetings with other people. Of course, this is not always possible.

open-ended questions
items on a survey that allow room for the person taking the survey to answer in his/her own words

fixed-response questions
items on a survey that allow only for prescribed answers

In addition to the influence of time of day on an individual's focus, knowing how much time you have before a meeting or presentation can also affect your preparation. With enough time you can conduct research into your audience to learn how they feel about you and your topic, or even collect demographic data about them that can influence your message construction. You can use surveys that contain *open-ended questions* or *fixed-response questions*. Open-ended questions can be useful tools for gaining depth of understanding about particular issues, while fixed-response questions help gather specific data. Surveys are quite useful if you have the time, but a lot goes into their creation, distribution, collection, and analysis.

Another technique for discovering information about your potential audience when you know you have time before the meeting to do so is through interviewing. If you have enough lead time and some knowledge of who is in the group with whom you will be speaking, you may try and arrange appointments with them to gather specific information you need to help you determine the best ways to approach the meeting. Interviews primarily consist of open-ended questions because demographic questions are simply not suited for conversation, and the answers to some of them (like race and gender) are readily identifiable without asking the person. An added advantage to the interviewing strategy is that throughout the course of the interview you will develop a relationship with one of the people who will attend your talk later, thus increasing your comfort level when you actually deliver the address. They are much more personal than a survey and if used correctly and creatively, interviews can provide extremely useful information.

Time is an important part of context both in understanding when you and your audience function best, but also in determining how much time you have to find out information about your conversational partners.

Why Are You Meeting?

There are many reasons why people get together and communicate, and these reasons play a role in determining the context of the interaction. In this section of the chapter we will identify two common reasons why people get together and talk, and illustrate how the reason for the conversation influences the meaning of what is said.

The first reason why people engage in a discussion is to develop personal relationships. That is to say, it is not related to business, but rather developing or maintaining a personal relationship. In these instances we tend to use less formal language, focus on topics of common interest and disclose personal feelings, emotions, or experiences to others often in the hope they reciprocate. Think about your personal lives and the language and topic choices you make. They surely differ from when you talk to people at work or in a business setting.

The second reason people engage in discussion is to advance business goals. In business settings we typically refrain from colloquial language and avoid the use of slang. We also focus on more task-oriented topics that relate to the business at hand. In many business meetings an agenda needs to be accomplished. This is not to say that "small talk" is out of line; in fact, most meetings begin with it to establish a rapport between the parties, but it rarely, if ever, goes deeper than superficial topics.

Now, things can be complicated when business partners develop friendships, and so in these moments it becomes essential to pay attention to why the meeting is taking place. If the motive is business, keep your language and discussion topics limited to business, but if the main reason for getting together is personal, then you can relax your expectations a bit. Just remember that if the person you are with is a supervisor or even someone whom you supervise, then you still need to pay careful attention to what you do and do not say. Remember that civility requires us to not speak ill of others, whether the meeting is for business or personal relationships. This rule becomes especially important when we are with colleagues who are also our friends.

How Are You Meeting?

This next component of the context relates to the channel whereby the communication occurs. For much of human history face-to-face interactions were the only way to communicate; however, recent technological achievements changed this quite a bit. We still meet in small intimate settings with another person, or even a group of people. We also still engage in presentations and public speeches to larger groups, but these are increasingly rare for the average person. Some of the more common ways we interact with people today are through the telephone, web, email, and streaming video. We can send quick text messages, write a somewhat longer email to one or more people, or even have live video conferencing with multiple groups at once. Social media, such as Instagram, Snapchat, and Facebook, have opened the doors for entirely new ways of sending messages between people, each of which affects communication in particular ways.

As described in the "Spotlighting Theorists" insert in this chapter, the late Canadian communication scholar Marshall McLuhan once wrote that "the medium is the message." With this statement, McLuhan implies that the channel through which you choose to deliver your message shapes the meaning of the message as much as the content of what you say. The late Canadian communication scholar Marshall McLuhan once wrote that "the medium is the message," meaning that the manner in which you choose to deliver your message tells the audience just as much as the content of what you say. By "medium" he referred to technological media, and primarily television; however, the principle still stands with other manners of interaction. The environment you choose to speak through—the "how" you plan on meeting with other people—can send as powerful a message as the content of what you say.

For example, suppose that a client for a company has a question about one of the company's products. An IT support staff member for a company may choose to send a technical expert to a client to demonstrate how a product works, or she might create an instructional video addressing the client's questions and electronically share it with the client. The same message can be delivered both ways, but each channel potentially sends a different message to the client. The visit from the technical expert, while perhaps costly, might make the relationship with the client seem more important, one worthy of the cost of sending an expert to the client's location. The instructional video is likely more cost-efficient to the company, but use of this channel might carry a different meaning than the visit. You must pay attention to the medium through which you communicate to another person and anticipate how your use of that medium will shape the meaning that your audience makes as they receive and decode the message. The same message can be delivered both ways, but the manner in which it is packaged sends another message to the audience as well. You must pay attention to the

SPOTLIGHTING THEORISTS: MARSHALL MCLUHAN

Marshall McLuhan (1911–1980)
Media analyst and theorist Marshall McLuhan was born in Edmonton, Alberta, Canada, on July 11, 1911. He earned a B.A. and an M.A. at both the University of Manitoba and Cambridge University. He taught at, among other places, the University of Wisconsin–Madison and St. Louis University.

In 1963 the President of the University of Toronto appointed McLuhan to develop a Center for Culture and Technology.[9] The center studied the relationship between technology, media, and human cognition. McLuhan had many other appointments in business and government throughout his storied career. In addition to these jobs, McLuhan wrote *Understanding Media: The Extension of Man*, which challenged the assumptions many had of media and its uses and powers in a technologically advancing society. He was also concerned with the consequences of media on society. McLuhan is perhaps best known and remembered for this statement that "the medium is the message." This phrase is used in various contexts in academe, including but not limited to media studies, rhetorical studies, film studies, and English.

medium through which you communicate with another person, and how you and your surroundings may be perceived through that medium.

There are some pitfalls and potentially hazardous dimensions to the seemingly wonderful ability to communicate with people across the globe so quickly through media. Text messages work best when the person you text knows who you are, and the messages are short. In fact, there is a specific language code for text messaging that allows for shorter written words—but this type of writing does not translate well to other written forms of communication, even email. Keep in mind that there are plenty of situations where delivering a message face-to-face is much more effective than through text or email.

For example, in business settings email may not always be the best mode of communication, especially when trying to build trust and relationships between yourself and a client or colleague. The more personal touch of individual meetings over coffee may work better because they tell the other party you care about them and want to develop a relationship. Sometimes, you may also be asked to deliver a presentation regarding a product, so being prepared to do so also demonstrates interest and ability to the recipient.

One final issue to appreciate is technology's ability to allow us to create visually stimulating presentations using PowerPoint, Prezi, and even Skype. In 2013, former Federal Reserve Chairman Ben Bernanke used technology to deliver prepared remarks to attendees at the RISE Forum hosted by the University of Dayton in association with the United Nations Global Compact.

However, just because technology allows us to use mediated images and messages in the manner Ben Bernanke did does not mean we should do so because images are no substitute for individual attention and actual content. Regardless of whether you are speaking to one person or one thousand, you need to actually present a logical well-developed message.

All in all, how you choose to engage another person sends a very important message about your feelings regarding the relationship. Mediated avenues create an aura of interest and intimacy, but be judicious in choosing when to use them and especially careful in how you deliver messages through them.

THE RHETORICAL SITUATION

rhetorical situation
....
the context of a rhetorical act, made up (at a minimum) of a rhetor (a speaker or writer), an issue (or exigence), a medium (such as a speech or a written text), and an audience.

One framework that might help us as we think about the context of our communication with others is Lloyd Bitzer's concept of the *rhetorical situation*. In 1968 Bitzer published an essay that proposed a specific relationship between rhetoric and situations.[11] Specifically, he said that situations called rhetoric into being. Put another way, each moment in which you find yourself invites you to speak using a specific vocabulary. When you respond to a situation what you say alters the reality of the moment. By way of an example he argued that when presidents are inaugurated they confront a situation that invites them to speak. They do so, thereby changing the reality of the moment, redefining it for the audience and themselves.

exigence
....
a decisive point at which a response is invited or required

Each rhetorical situation compels rhetoric in a particular way. If a speaker does not respond to the situation, the moment is lost, and a new opportunity will need to be discovered. If the speaker responds but does not respond appropriately to what the situation demands, then his or her rhetoric will not be adapted properly to the situation, and its effectiveness will be diminished. According to Bitzer, any rhetorical situation has three elements: the exigence, the audience, and the specific set of constraints that the situation imposes. The *exigence* is that part of the situation that demands a response from those within it. Something happens, and it invites or even requires action. Suppose, for instance, that you are scheduled to give a presentation to a group of neighborhood youth to talk about a community-building effort in which you would like to invite the youth to participate. However, just a day before you give your presentation, you learn that there was a tragic shooting just a few blocks away, in which a couple of youth in a nearby neighborhood died. You could go on with your talk as you planned it and not acknowledge in any way the event that just happened, as it is not directly related to your topic. However, to do so risks not addressing something in the present situation that is potentially quite compelling to the people in it. Some of your audience members might have known the youth who died, their friends, or their families. Some of them might even have been there when it happened. Some of them might be thinking about the safety of their own neighborhood and whether something similar might happen there. Some of them might be asking themselves some weighty questions about their own lives that relate directly to the incident that happened. In this way, the exigence creates a decisive point for those who are in the situation, which often gives the situation a sense of urgency. If you are

SPOTLIGHTING THEORISTS: LLOYD BITZER & RICHARD VATZ

Lloyd Bitzer

Lloyd Bitzer, a longtime professor at the University of Wisconsin, published several important pieces of rhetorical scholarship, but none more controversial or widely read than his 1968 piece "The Rhetorical Situation." For Bitzer, situations hold inherent meaning that speakers identify through their responses. Situations essentially call rhetoric into being.

This position posits that rhetoric is a reaction to situations and that the power of meaning lies with context and not the speaker. Speeches are essentially predetermined responses to existing situations. They are descriptions of meaning and are not meaningful in and of themselves. As an example he wrote that presidential inaugurations are situations that invite a specific form of speech from a president. The inauguration is why they speak and what they speak about.

Bitzer's essay has been widely cited and used as a foundation for rhetorical studies since its publication, but not everyone agrees with its propositions.

Richard Vatz

In 1973 Richard Vatz, a professor at Towson State University in Maryland who primarily studies the intersection of rhetoric and psychiatry, published a response to Bitzer's essay entitled "The Myth of the Rhetorical Situation." Vatz contended that situations do not invite rhetoric, but rather rhetoric creates situations.

For Vatz meaning is created by the speaker through his or her speech, not through the situation. Situations therefore, lack meaning until it is defined for them by the speaker. Speakers, according to this position, hold the power to use rhetoric to define situations.

To illustrate this point, Vatz points to crises. He says that there is not a crisis until the situation is defined as such by a speaker. He also points to the fact political candidates often seek to "control the agenda," implying speakers define the campaign and not vice versa.

Scholars often cite Vatz's essay as an attempt to spur debate over the concept of the rhetorical situation.

Implications of Bitzer vs. Vatz

Bitzer takes a passive view of rhetoric, arguing that it merely describes situations. Vatz believes rhetoric has a more active role and is not simply derivative of situations. In fact, Vatz goes so far as to call the rhetorical situation "anti-rhetorical." The National Communication Association still convenes panels to discuss the debate between these two scholars, with the most recent at the 2008 annual meeting in San Diego.

a speaker, then you do well to identify the exigence in the present situation and create a message that addresses it in some way, so that your message is timely, relevant, and connected to what is compelling people in the situation to act in some way.

The second element of the rhetorical situation is the audience. The particular audience before a speaker compels rhetoric in a particular way. As we learned earlier in the chapter while considering the six components of the context, who the audience is and what they know about you and the topic are defining elements of the situation in which communication occurs. For Bitzer, speakers who wish to be convincing must craft a message that meets the expectations of the audience. This includes even the language with which they speak. A speaker could give a talk on a given topic to a group of seventy year olds and could give a talk on the same topic to a group of seven year olds. The particular terminology that one uses, the stories that one tells, and the facts that one gives would need to be different in each case, for rhetoric to be successful. Such considerations, as we learned in Chapter 1, relate to what Cicero called style in his five canons of rhetoric.

The third element of the rhetorical situation consists of the constraints that limit the speaker's ability to act within the situation at hand. No speaker has unlimited freedom when she or he communicates with others. The situation always imposes obstacles, demands, expectations, and barriers that either must be navigated in some way. Some of these constraints are material, relating perhaps to the physical location in which communication occurs or the medium that is being used. Others are social or psychological in nature, relating to expectations or protocols that make-up the occasion in which rhetoric occurs. Some constraints can be overcome. Others are non-negotiable. If the speaker wishes to be convincing, then she or he must determine what the constraints of the present situation are, find ways to navigate those that can be overcome or avoided, and adjust his or her message in ways that take into account those that cannot be.

Bitzer saw meaning as inherent to the situation and understood rhetoric as discovering the meaning within the situation and responding appropriately and effectively to it by essentially describing what is already there. Not everyone agreed with this static view of situations. Richard Vatz, for instance, argues that meaning is not inherent in the situation; meaning only exists when rhetoric provides it.[12] That is to say a crisis is not actually a crisis until someone calls it a crisis. We do not find meaning; we create it through our speech. For Vatz, situations are defined by the speaker; the situations do not define the speech. This perspective essentially takes a position completely opposite that of Bitzer, but also puts more of an emphasis on the power of language to define and create meaning for audiences, events, and contexts.

The view advanced by Vatz allows us more creativity in defining the scope and impressions of our interactions with others. With the advent of Facebook, the way we communicate the meaning of a relationship changed. People now do not see themselves as "in a relationship" unless their Facebook page says they are. You, as an individual, have the power to name your relationship and thus make it official, The situation does not demand you do so, as Bitzer would argue, but rather you have the power to name the situation as a relationship or not. In not making a relationship Facebook official, you might believe you could date other people, but in giving it that label you close off that action. The key thing to remember is that, for Vatz, you are not in a relationship until you say you are.

We will now discuss how we can analyze our audiences in any setting and adapt our messages to them and the context in which the conversation happens. This adaptation, coupled with the appreciation that we can create an understanding of that context through our messages and statements—or define the rhetorical situation, rather than be defined by it—is an important tool for successful communication in any venue with any audience, large or small.

ADAPTING YOUR MESSAGE TO YOUR AUDIENCE

When you know the makeup of your audience it becomes much easier to construct appeals to them. Speaking in terms your listeners know, using examples designed to resonate with them, and referencing statistics they are more likely to care about becomes easier when you know who they are, what they care about, what they believe in, and what motivates them. After all, why talk to an audience of senior citizens about buying a cell phone when your research tells you they are resistant to new technology? It makes no sense. Understanding your audience can help you create a more effective message.

This section talks about two ways to make use of audience analysis information. The first is through verbal appeals, or the specific construction of what to say so you can better identify with your audience. The second strategy is through how to say it, or the organizational structure of your message. Both the content and structure of any missive can be modified and magnified based upon information from an analysis of the audience.

Content Strategies

There are three main ways of making use of your knowledge about an audience to augment your ability to successfully appeal to them.

- The first involves using the data as part of a strategy for identifying with your listeners, or making you seem as though you are one of them.

- The second thing audience analysis information allows you to do is incorporate knowledge of the audience into your message.

- Third, you can use clear descriptive statements. This allows you to choose more appropriate examples, statistics, or testimonials for the context in which you find yourself.

Each of these builds upon the others to help you establish a strong rapport with your conversational partners.

Identifying with your audience is possibly the most important result of conducting audience analyses. The information you found can help you understand who your audience is and when you know that you can find things you have in common with them. Once you determine what you have in common you can immediately stress those common bonds, thus making you appear similar to the the other party. Such an approach enhances your ethos, or credibility, and strengthens your ability to appeal to them.

For example, Anya is a 21-year-old college senior at New York University with a major in sociology. She plans to go to law school so she can eventually work in the district attorney's office in St. Petersburg, Florida, where she grew up. When she was younger she watched the riots of 1996 that followed the death of a black man after a routine police traffic stop, increasing gang violence. She decided to pursue a career that would enable her to prevent those things from happening again. Now, as valedictorian of her senior class, she is addressing commencement on her campus. She is at a ceremony celebrating graduation at a school in a different area of the country than where she grew up, so how can she identify with her audience immediately? There are several ways.

First, like her audience, she is graduating and thus roughly the same age as many of them. Second, she knows that many of those in the audience live in New York City, which is no stranger to occasional social unrest. This information can help her develop a presentation that celebrates the joy of graduation while also calling on her audience to help improve society. This can be done quickly in the speech by telling an abbreviated version of her story and linking it to New York. She could, perhaps, cite examples from the class's days at the school when fellow students may have been victims of crimes, or just mention they have all watched the news about crime in the city for the last four years. By making such references in her speech, Anya becomes more credible when calling on her audience to be more socially conscious. Audience analysis helps you find strategies for connecting with your audience in a very real way.

Think of the information you glean from audience analysis as contributing to the relationship between you and your audience. Picture a triangle where you are one corner of the triangle, the audience is another corner, and the message is the third corner (see Figure 3.1). You need to find a way to connect with the audience, and the best way to do that is through the message. The audience also wants to find a way to connect with you, and that also occurs through the message. The stronger your message appeals to the commonalities between you and your listeners, the stronger the connection between you both.

There is another way to identify with your audience through the use of words, but it can only happen after you establish common ground with your

Figure 3.1
Connecting with the Audience

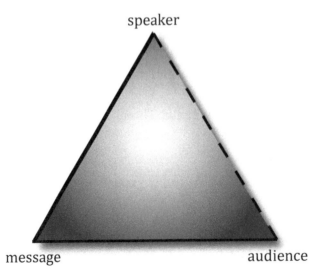

speaker

message

audience

listeners. "*We*" language allows you to speak as if you are a member of the group, and once you establish a connection between yourself and your listeners this type of language should be used often. Instead of saying "I," say "we." Instead of saying "me," say "us." This approach enhances your connection to the audience, but if you use it too early without creating common ground, it will actually diminish your credibility. People need to know how you are one of them before you declare that you are one of them. This approach to language works in small groups as well as larger settings. Be careful not to assume a "we" when it has not been demonstrated.

A second way to use audience analysis information to enhance your connection with the audience is *through incorporating what you know about your listeners into the message*. We do this in daily conversations with each other when we state that we know what other people like or believe. Be sure when you do this, however, that you actually do know it as true and are not making an assumption based upon little evidence. In interviews this tactic helps establish that you sought information about the interviewer by demonstrating some knowledge about what they do, produce, or are otherwise interested in. In larger settings, speakers often will use one person as a representative of an entire group in the audience to help make a point. Using knowledge about the audience within a message helps build bridges between people; just make sure what you use is positive in nature and meant to help create rather than damage your association with the other party.

Another way to incorporate information about your audience into the speech is through descriptive statements. At graduation and convocation, University of Dayton President Eric Spina might describe the demographic characteristics of the graduating or incoming class. This illustrates knowledge about the group to whom he is speaking and demonstrates that he cared enough about the group to "do his homework." Citing statistics alone probably will not do much, but creatively incorporating this information into a message can go a long way to establishing a bond with an audience.

The third and final strategy for using audience analysis information to enhance the content of your speech involves the selection of stories, statistics, and examples that will resonate with your listeners. When you know who your audience is it becomes easier to reference things that are familiar to them. The more you appear to know about them, the more you appear as one of them. For example, if a roommate comes to you and tells you her grandfather just passed away, and you recently lost someone in your life, you might tell that story to help comfort your roommate. You also might remind your roommate of some experiences they may have had with her grandfather to help her feel better as well. Narratives, stories, and examples help us craft messages that connect us with others so long as we know where to build those connections. Even Aristotle would recommend you select the appropriate inartistic proofs so that they help enhance your ability to connect with the audience.

Information about your audience helps you make informed choices about the content of your message. It ultimately helps you find ways to identify with your audience members through incorporating that information into your message through the use of specific examples, statistics, and stories that are more likely to appeal to your listeners. Content, however, is not the only area where this information can help improve your communication skills.

Organizational Strategies

Knowledge of the audience can influence the way you organize your messages, specifically the order in which you present main points in a speech or discussion and whether you reference members of the audience as well. The organization of points is one of the most important parts of the developmental process, and information about your audience can help you choose the best arrangement for your information. Traditionally there are three ways to organize points. You must use knowledge about your audience to decide which one will be a better fit for your situation.

One way to arrange main points for maximum effect involves delivering your strongest point first. Each point that follows builds off the foundation of the first main item. This allows you to draw your audience in immediately with a strong start and then build your case from there. In some ways this method serves as a "backup" or secondary attempt at gaining the attention of the audience. This organizational approach typically works best when an audience is not already prone to believing or agreeing with you. A strong first point then helps draw them in and helps them realize that you have a valid argument worth hearing out. So, when you determine there is initial dissonance between you, your audience, and/ or your topic through audience analysis, consider arranging the points so that you deliver the strongest first. In a conversation this may also help convince people quickly, rather than having to present more data and evidence later.

Quintilian taught his students to both make their strongest point first as well as to treat the strongest points in great depth. In other words, spend more time on the strongest arguments than the weaker ones. In fact, he advised students to ditch the weakest parts of the argument if need be. This approach to crafting and delivering points makes as much sense today as it did when Quintilian lived.

crescendo
....
an organizational pattern in which the strongest point is placed at the end and is built up to by smaller main points

Another traditional way of organizing points places the strongest at the end of the body of the speech. This pattern puts less powerful points at the beginning and builds toward the most important main point in a *crescendo* pattern. Such an organizational approach could enhance the pathos of an appeal by building excitement, interest, and emotional attachment to the argument made by the speaker. This approach typically works best when you know the audience already agrees with, or is prone to agree with, the position. Crescendo patterns can also be useful in debate settings as a strategy for holding your strongest claim until the last possible moment so the other side cannot or does not have the time to adequately respond to it.

In addition to a strong organizational pattern, knowing who, how and when to reference audience members can also be helpful. Carefully planned references, and even the occasional impromptu nod while speaking, can augment the appeal of your speech. If certain points within a speech will be magnified by relating them directly to the listeners, or to a characteristic of a larger group, then it makes sense to do so. Only when you are aware of those characteristics through survey information, or know members of the audience by working the room and interviewing, can you make proper use of this technique.

Creating your message is not simply an effort in putting words to paper, but it also involves using audience analysis to choose the proper words to put to paper. When time allows, analyzing the audience before delivering a message is an invaluable tool for any speaker. There is one approach to audience analysis, however, that does not involve extensive advance preparation and is, in fact, available to every speaker in every communication situation.

ANALYZING THE AUDIENCE DURING THE INTERACTION

In any interaction we can watch, learn, and adapt to the statements, actions, and reactions of those involved. There are also several tactics you can employ to maximize your ability to connect with and influence an audience based upon that constant feedback. This section details two ways you can analyze the audience while speaking, and offers some suggestions as to how to adapt to them based upon that information.

Observing the Audience

As we illustrated in Chapter 1 with the models of communication, we play the role of both message deliverer and message receiver during an interaction, and so in some ways we are also an audience. A majority of the time speakers do not listen to verbal responses while they are speaking, but receive nonverbal messages from the audience. They can then use that nonverbal feedback to change their delivery and measure the effectiveness of those changes.

One key nonverbal activity you should be attuned to is eye contact. Not only should speakers themselves make significant eye contact with their audience, they also should monitor the amount of eye contact they receive from their conversational partners. If the audience or other person is looking away, at a wall, or reading, then chances are they are not paying attention. Speakers can then make adjustments to regain the audience's focus.

Audience members may also shift in their seats, look at their watches or move around during an interaction. Sometimes this may be due to the discomfort of the chairs they are sitting in or the need to be somewhere very soon, but other times it may indicate boredom. Be attuned to both the potential restlessness of your conversational partners as well as the very real possibility that they need to move on to something or be somewhere else. Be judicious when asking people to give of their time and only expect them to give as much as you might in a given situation. Knowing how long you spent with a person or group may help tell you if the movement you see is boredom or an indicator that time is up.

Polling the Audience

Another useful way to gain information about an audience is through impromptu polling. The results are not scientific, nor are they generalizable, but they do provide immediate information for you and your listeners. We poll people in interpersonal contexts when we ask friends or family if they know something or if they have been someplace before. We also poll people in business settings and public speaking situations to gather targeted information useful to making a sale or identifying with a new group. For example, a supervisor may start a meeting by asking how many people are familiar with the policy change under discussion.

Polling in this manner can also help you learn about whether or not the other people comprehend the information which you provide them. Oftentimes, stopping to ask listeners if they understand or if they need something repeated or said in a different way can be a useful tool. It allows the audience to consider the information they have been given, determine if they need clarification, and play an active part in the interaction. In short, it encourages the audience to be interactive. Polling can occur in small groups where you may just be asking everyone you are with for their thoughts on something, or it might occur in a more formalized setting such as in a speech or classroom.

Many classrooms are moving in the direction of incorporating electronic polling to gauge student understanding and interest, and yours may even be one of them. They use classroom response systems, or clickers, which are two-part devices. The first part includes clickers that audience members (students in this case) use to answer questions posed through PowerPoint presentations. The second component is the software that allows for tabulation of the poll results so the presenter can gather immediate feedback on audience comprehension, agreement, or even enjoyment regarding the speech or portions of the speech.

As you can see, audience analysis can and should be conducted during any interaction. Just as preparatory audience analysis allows you to design messages for maximum impact, audience analysis during a speech or conversation also allows you to make adjustments in an effort to maintain attention and even increase your ability to identify as one of the group. We now turn our attention to methods of adapting to audience feedback during a communicative event.

Adapting to Feedback During Delivery

Audience analysis during your interactions with others can help you determine how to proceed. Those adaptations can occur immediately or later, after you come to a realization about something, but it is important to be aware of what you can do to increase the impact of your messages based on the audience's reaction to them. There are also two things you can do from the very beginning to increase the likelihood that others will pay attention and not get distracted or bored when you speak.

The first thing you can do in reaction to the audience's behavior at the beginning of the interaction is make sure you effectively use the space in which you are speaking.

- make sure there is adequate seating to seat everyone in the meeting, if not, try to find more seats or an alternative space that has the necessary number of places to sit.

- make sure tables are relatively clean and clear so that people can use the space by them to take notes or lay out materials.
- make sure the lighting is appropriate, and that the place where the interaction takes place is accessible to disabled people if necessary.

Space usage responsibilities extend to the audience as well, so when you are listening to someone or even attending a movie, it is not civil to "reserve" more space than you need by placing your items on seats so no one takes them. Of course, if you are in a group and you will be using the seats, then that is different, but "clogging" space just so you can have more is rude.

The second action a speaker can employ either at the outset of the speech or at some point during the meeting, involves eliminating a barrier between you and your listeners. To increase the intimacy of the speaking environment, and to demonstrate your comfort among the audience (thus increasing your ability to appear as one of them):

- move out from behind your seat
- walk amongst the group
- call for a break so people can get up and interact with each other in a more relaxed manner.

These actions can make an audience feel more at ease with the other people in the room, making them more receptive to the messages of others.

Other adaptation strategies work better when you are speaking. If, for instance, you notice people look confused or seem to be lost, stop and ask them if they understand, or if they need something repeated and/or clarified. Revisit points through the use of impromptu internal summaries of the information if the group appears not to understand a connection you made.

Sometimes people can seem bored or uninterested, and in this case it becomes important to vary your actions. Remember, people's attention spans are not very long, so you need to change things up every once in a while to "restart" their attention span. This can involve changes in the rate or tone of your speech, a noticeable change in the volume of your voice, going off on a short but interesting tangent, or inviting comments and questions from others at the table. It may also indicate people need a break. These surprising changes will work to counteract negative audience behaviors you may notice. Adapting to the audience based on how they react to you as speaker is an important element of being a successful and effective communicator.

Summary

This chapter explained the importance of audience analysis before and during an interaction. We also discussed the different types of information you can and should try to find about your audience and provided several methods of gathering that data. Finally, we learned about what to look for in your audience and how to adapt to their reactions. Remember, there can be no message without an audience and no effective communication without understanding who the audience members are, where they come from, and what they care about.

Key Terms

context 63	fixed-response questions 68
crescendo 78	open-ended questions 68
demographic 63	rhetorical situation 72
exigence 72	stereotyping 64

Review Questions

1. What do demographic data consist of?
2. What are some useful methods for researching demographic psychographic data?
3. What audience characteristics would lead you to consider placing the most important main point first? Last?
4. What are some ways of measuring audience responses during a speech?
5. What adjustments can you make at the outset of a speech to help you identify with an audience and increase their attention?
6. What were some of the challenges Mary Church Terrell faced when speaking?

Think About It

1. Is there a difference between audience analysis and stereotyping? If so, what is it?
2. Are there any ethical considerations for audience analysis?
3. Do we rely on survey information too much when developing speeches in today's society?
4. How could an unethical speaker use audience analysis to his/her advantage?
5. Is it possible for a speaker to overuse audience analysis?

1. Once you have a speech topic in mind and you know where you will deliver your speech, devise a list of questions regarding demographic and behavioral or attitudinal beliefs. Format these into a survey for your audience to take in advance. Use a Likert scale for attitudinal questions, and phrase them as statements rather than questions.

2. Go to a website for a popular dating service, such as http://www.match.com or http://www.eharmony.com, and look at a handful of profiles. Take a look at the questions the site asks and the options from which people can select their answers. Determine if these are demographic or attitudinal questions.

3. Watch a few films where characters deliver speeches, such as *The Contender, City Hall, Remember the Titans,* or *Mr. Smith Goes to Washington*. Listen to the speeches in these films and identify how these speeches are designed to reach the audiences in the film. Do they employ inclusive language such as "we" or "us"? Do they use a crescendo pattern to conclude the speech? What is done to make the speeches effective? This also can be done with contemporary speeches, but films are fun and effective to look at in this manner.

ENDNOTES

1. Michael Grunwald, James Carney, & Michael Scherer, "A Right Fight," *Time*, February 18, 2008, 37.

2. June Kronholz, "Will McCain Make Nice to the Right?" *Wall Street Journal*, February 6, 2008, eastern edition, sec. A.

3. Ivy J. Sellers, "CPAC 2007 Hosts Record Crowd of Enthusiastic Conservatives," Human Events, March 19, 2007, http://findarticles.com/p/articles/mi_qa3827/is_200703/ai_n18755647 (accessed May 23, 2008).

4. Robert Novak, "Fred Thompson's Progress," Human Events.com, July 21, 2007, http://www.humanevents.com/article.php?id=21616 (accessed May 23, 2008).

5. Mary Church Terrell, "What It Means to Be Colored in the Capital of the U. S.," www.americanrhetoric.com. http://www.biography.com/articles/Mary-Church-Terrell-9504299 (accessed June 11, 2011).

6. Ibid.

7. Ibid.

8. Ibid.

9. John Medina, *Brain Rules* (Seattle, WA: Pear Press, 2008), 156–158

10. Lloyd F. Bitzer, "The Rhetorical Situation," *Philosophy and Rhetoric* 1 (1968): 1–14.

11. Richard Vatz, "The Myth of the Rhetorical Situation," *Philosophy and Rhetoric* 6 (1973): 154–161.

12. http://marshallmcluhan.com/biography (accessed May 10, 2010).

13. Ibid

Interteaching Session

Dialogue

In July 2017, President Trump was the keynote speaker at the National Boy Scout Jamboree. President Trump spoke to a crowd of thousands of Boy Scouts and their leaders. At the beginning of the speech, the President said that he was not going to bring politics into the presentation:

> Tonight, we put aside all of the policy fights in Washington, D.C., you've been hearing about with the fake news and all of that . . . We're going to put that aside. And instead we're going to talk about success, about how all of you amazing young Scouts can achieve your dreams, what to think of, what I've been thinking about. You want to achieve your dreams, I said, who the hell wants to speak about politics when I'm in front of the Boy Scouts? Right?[1]

However, as the speech continued, the President made multiple comments of a political character. For instance, he said,

> "You know, I go to Washington and I see all these politicians, and I see the swamp, and it's not a good place. In fact, today, I said we ought to change it from the word 'swamp' to the word 'cesspool' or perhaps to the word 'sewer.' "[2]

Referring to Secretary of Human Services Tom Price, he said,

> "Dr. Price still lives the Scout oath, helping to keep millions of Americans strong and healthy as our secretary of Health and Human Services," Trump began. And then: "And he's doing a great job. And hopefully he's going to get the votes [Tuesday] to start our path toward killing this horrible thing known as Obamacare that's really hurting us."[3]

Other comments included criticisms about the news media:

> "By the way, what do you think the chances are that this incredible massive crowd, record-setting, is going to be shown on television tonight?" Trump said. "One percent or zero? The fake media will say, 'President Trump spoke'—you know what is—'President Trump spoke before a small crowd of Boy Scouts today.' That's some—that is some crowd. Fake media. Fake news."[4]

They also included reflections on his electoral win:

> "And you know, we have a tremendous disadvantage in the Electoral College. Popular vote is much easier. We have—because New York, California, Illinois, you have to practically run the East Coast. And we did. We won Florida. We won South Carolina. We won North Carolina. We won Pennsylvania. We won and won. So when they said, there is no way to victory; there is no way to 270. You know I went to Maine four times because it's one vote,

1 Helen Regan, "Read the Full Transcript of President Trump's 2017 Boy Scout Jamboree Speech," Time, July 25, 2017, http://time.com/4872118/trump-boy-scout-jamboree-speech-transcript/

2 Helen Regan, "Read the Full Transcript of President Trump's 2017 Boy Scout Jamboree Speech," Time, July 25, 2017, http://time.com/4872118/trump-boy-scout-jamboree-speech-transcript/

3 Helen Regan, "Read the Full Transcript of President Trump's 2017 Boy Scout Jamboree Speech," Time, July 25, 2017, http://time.com/4872118/trump-boy-scout-jamboree-speech-transcript/

4 Helen Regan, "Read the Full Transcript of President Trump's 2017 Boy Scout Jamboree Speech," Time, July 25, 2017, http://time.com/4872118/trump-boy-scout-jamboree-speech-transcript/

and we won. We won. One vote. I went there because I kept hearing we're at 269. But then Wisconsin came in. Many, many years. Michigan came in. So—and we worked hard there.

"You know, my opponent didn't work hard there, because she was told . . . she was told she was going to win Michigan, and I said, well, wait a minute. The car industry is moving to Mexico. Why is she going to move—she's there. Why are they allowing it to move? And by the way, do you see those car industry—do you see what's happening? They're coming back to Michigan. They're coming back to Ohio. They're starting to peel back in.

"And we go to Wisconsin, now, Wisconsin hadn't been won in many, many years by a Republican. But we go to Wisconsin, and we had tremendous crowds. And I'd leave these massive crowds, I'd say, why are we going to lose this state? The polls, that's also fake news. They're fake polls. But the polls are saying—but we won Wisconsin."[5]

The crowd seemed to respond favorably to the President's speech, as many people cheered, laughed, and responded with favor and enthusiasm to his comments. Observing the crowd's reaction, White House Spokesperson Sarah Sanders said, "I saw nothing but roughly 40,000 to 45,000 Boy Scouts cheering the president on throughout his remarks and I think they were pretty excited that he was there."[6] However, after the Jamboree, the Boy Scouts of America received negative feedback from many parents about the partisan character of the speech. In fact, in an open letter published on the official website for the Boy Scouts of America, the head of the organization Michael Surbaugh apologized to the members of the organization for the "political rhetoric that was inserted" into the National Jamboree by President Trump: "I want to extend my sincere apologies to those in our Scouting family who were offended by the political rhetoric that was inserted into the jamboree. That was never our intent."[7] Some parents defended the speech with claims that the reaction was overblown and argued that exposure to political speech in all forms was an important part of a Scout's development.[8]

1. Consider the rhetorical situation as defined by Bitzer. Analyze the rhetorical situation in which President Trump spoke at the Jamboree in terms of the three elements that Bitzer identifies: exigence, audience, and constraints.

5 Helen Regan, "Read the Full Transcript of President Trump's 2017 Boy Scout Jamboree Speech," Time, July 25, 2017, http://time.com/4872118/trump-boy-scout-jamboree-speech-transcript/

6 Jonathan Allen, "Boy Scouts of America apologizes for Trump's 'political rhetoric,'" Reuters, July 27, 2017, https://www.reuters.com/article/us-usa-trump-boyscouts/boy-scouts-of-america-apologizes-for-trumps-political-rhetoric-idUSKBN1AC2WX?utm_source=applenews

7 Jonathan Allen, "Boy Scouts of America apologizes for Trump's 'political rhetoric,'" Reuters, July 27, 2017, https://www.reuters.com/article/us-usa-trump-boyscouts/boy-scouts-of-america-apologizes-for-trumps-political-rhetoric-idUSKBN1AC2WX?utm_source=applenews

8 Jonathan Allen, "Boy Scouts of America apologizes for Trump's 'political rhetoric,'" Reuters, July 27, 2017, https://www.reuters.com/article/us-usa-trump-boyscouts/boy-scouts-of-america-apologizes-for-trumps-political-rhetoric-idUSKBN1AC2WX?utm_source=applenews

2. Analyze the situation in terms of the six components of context:

   - Who is the audience?
   - What does the audience know?
   - Where is the meeting taking place?
   - When is the meeting taking place?
   - Why are you meeting?
   - How are you meeting?

3. In your opinion, how well did President Trump respond to the situation? Justify your answer.

Performance

You are part of a group of students who is going to be presenting to a committee of faculty members, administrators, and staff regarding the topic of Saint Patrick's Day on campus, which has been convened by the President of the University. The committee to whom you will be presenting is made up of 15 individuals from across the college. Your group's goal in this presentation is to explain major concerns that students on campus have about St. Patrick's Day, which the committee can take into consideration as it makes recommendations to the President about how the University should approach St. Patrick's Day during this coming March.

1. What do you know about the demographics of faculty, staff, and administrators at the University? What information is available through the University's website? How else might you acquire such information?

2. What assumptions can you make about the members of the committee that can guide you as you prepare your presentation?

3. Suppose that you were to attempt to gain some insight in advance from the committee members about their current perspective regarding St. Patrick's Day. Create a ten-question survey that uses both fixed-response and open-ended questions that you could give to the committee members prior to your presentation to learn about their views.

4. Share with the class how you would approach your interaction with the committee, including the survey that you created.

Explaining Complex Ideas to Non-Experts

CHAPTER OVERVIEW

- Discusses the foundations of effective explanations in a variety of contexts
- Details the components of explanations that facilitate understanding by an audience
- Provides tips and suggestions for delivering effective explanations in multiple speaking situations

Practically SPEAKING

On March 8, 2014, Malaysia Airline Flight 370 disappeared while en route from Kuala Lumpur to Beijing, China. The story captured the attention of the globe as it took weeks for investigators to determine where to search for the plane. Ultimately, the search narrowed to a remote portion of the Indian Ocean off the coast of Australia. Even still, search teams encountered tremendous challenges while looking for signs of the plane's whereabouts and news media covering the story quickly turned to experts in fields like mathematics, aeronautical engineering, terrorism, oceanography and computer science to help explain the intricacies of this mystery to the viewing public. All of these experts were tasked with talking about complicated equations, concepts and ideas from their fields of study in terms non-experts in the audience would understand—and to do so in only a few minutes!

For example, The Royal Aeronautical Society convened a panel of experts that included pilots, manufacturers, policy regulators and airline executives in London on April 2, 2014 to help explain the potential utility of the myriad theories about how the plane could have gone off course and disappeared. This group went through six possible explanations for the diversion and disappearance and analyzed them all. They determined that, of the six, there were three possible scenarios (depressurization, deliberate sabotage, terrorism) but one of them (terrorism) was increasingly less likely. To help explain both the theories and their evaluation of them the panelists needed to relay complex information in a way the audience could understand.[1]

When the search turned to a more restricted, albeit deep, part of the Indian Ocean and it became clear the plane's black box was no longer sending out a location signal, the authorities turned to a specialized submersible vehicle called the Bluefin-21 to help them scour the ocean floor. The unmanned submarine is a product used by the US Navy that runs missions as long as 24 hours, mapping the ocean floor and using sonar to look for objects. The Bluefin-21 is an enormously complicated machine, but nevertheless experts in its use and development needed to help audiences understand what it was, what it did, and how it would help locate the remains of the plane.[2]

This example illustrates that explanation of complicated objects or concepts to non-experts is a central task regardless of what field you are in. There is no way we can understand everything in our own field of study, let alone things that emanate from another discipline, so it is important to develop the skills to help others understand things with which they may not be familiar. In this chapter we will help you acquire these skills by first discussing the foundations of explanation and how they are intertwined with how every individual makes sense of the world around them in different ways. Finally, we provide some practical and useful tips for explaining complicated subjects to non-experts in a way that helps listeners remember what it is you explained to them.

---

1 "Experts give six reasons to explain disappearance of MH370, says report," TheMayasianinsider.com, (April 2, 2014), http://www.the-malaysianinsider.com/malaysia/article/experts-give-six-reasons-to-explain-disappearance-of-mh370-says-report, Last Accessed April 29, 2014.
2 Xu Geng, "Experts explain how Bluefin-21 works in search for MH370," CCTV.com, (April 16, 2014) http://english.cntv.cn/2014/04/16/VIDE1397600401238183.shtml, Last Accessed April 29, 2014.

PREP QUESTIONS

Part 1: Key Concepts

1. List four principles for explanation that help listeners to understand the information that a speaker is giving to them. Explain how each facilitates understanding this information.

2. List three principles for explanation that help listeners to remember the information that a speaker is giving to them. Explain how each helps a listener to remember this information.

3. Identify two tools for adding clarity to an explanation. Give an example of how you might use each in an explanation.

4. Identify three tools that make unfamiliar concepts relatable to an audience. Give an example of how you might use each in an explanation.

5. Give the three steps in the three-part structure for explaining a point.

6. What is a summary question? Describe what to do and what not to do in creating an effective summary question.

Part 2: Application

1. Imagine it is one year ago today. You may have been thinking about going to college. You may have visited a couple of universities. You may have even decided to go to UD. Think about the schema that you had regarding college life, living on your own, coursework, friends, social life, etc. Describe one of these schema that you had regarding college life. List several beliefs that you had about college life and how it was supposed to be. Have these schema changed today?

2. Choose a concept from your field with which others outside your field might not be familiar. Create a short explanation of this concept that you could give to someone outside your field that uses the three-part structure from the book. Make sure that you incorporate at least one tool for adding clarity and one tool for making unfamiliar concepts relatable to the listener.

FOUNDATIONS OF EXPLANATION

Explanation is a process of making information clear to a person who previously did not understand it. The ability to explain clearly is an essential element of almost every job, as well as a key tool for communicating in social contests as well. Although you would be hard-pressed to find a job for which explanation was never necessary, there are many careers where people's success is *especially* tied to their ability to explain complex ideas to non-experts. The STEM fields (science, technology, engineering, and math) are one group of professions for which explanation is critical. In each of these professions, people with specialized scientific knowledge must coordinate their work with, or advocate ideas to, those who lack the same expertise in order to successfully obtain funding, receive support, facilitate implementation, or allow others to use the products of one's work. An engineering firm has to explain a proposal it entered in a competitive bid for a contract; a pharmaceutical researcher might need to explain a proposed project to supervisors to receive approval to do research on a drug; and a geologist may need to explain to a city planning commission how roads and buildings could be affected by an earthquake.

explanation
a process of making information clear to a person who previously did not understand it

But the STEM fields are not the only professions for which explanation is an essential job skill. In education, the ability to explain ideas is one of the primary tasks for a teacher on a daily basis. In other professions like business, politics, and law, people's job success often hinges on the ability to explain ideas to those lacking specialized knowledge. A financial analyst must explain to managers the impact of a proposed fiscal plan; an elected official will need to explain the effects of a change in regulations, and an attorney must be able to explain how the law applies to a policy an organization is considering adopting. In short, the ability to explain complex or advanced ideas to non-experts is important in the majority of professions.

The most important point about explaining new ideas is the goal of the activity— it is to *elevate the listener's understanding, not to dumb-down the message.* In that regard, explaining ideas is the act of teaching the listener some new information. To do this well, the speaker needs to know the audience's level of knowledge on the topic, understand how people learn, and then apply principles of communication that will help listeners easily process and understand content. Explanation is a listener-focused activity, not a speaker-centered task. To put it another way, explanation is a transactional process, not a linear one.

Because explanation requires that listeners learn new information, we must first offer a basic introduction to how people understand the world around them. This topic is far bigger than could be covered in a chapter, course, or even undergraduate degree program, so we will focus on one particularly useful concept—the *schema*.

Schemas

schema
a mental representation that organizes information about a subject

A *schema* is a mental representation that organizes information about a subject. We use schemas to make sense of the information we encounter. We *have* to use schemas because our brains are bombarded with more information than we could make sense of without a guide to process it. Schemas give us a template for processing all the information we encounter. They allow us to know exactly what to do with the majority of information we encounter, and to respond to it with little cognitive effort. Without them, we would have to actively consider and evaluate every sensory input we encounter, and that would overwhelm our cognitive abilities.

Stop reading and take just a few seconds to consider your environment right now: What do you see? What do you hear? What do you feel, smell, or even taste? The details you could report would fill many pages. Now consider this: Does all this information challenge your ability to make sense of it? The answer, as you sit in a familiar location reading a textbook, is probably not. It is likely that virtually everything you are sensing fits so nicely into a schema, you don't even feel like you're being exposed to anything that requires cognitive effort.

Elaboration Likelihood Model (ELM)
a theory that proposes two primary cognitive processing paths we use to make decisions

Schemas are very helpful with regard to processing information. One theory that helps detail this is called the *Elaboration Likelihood Model (ELM)*. Developed in the 1980s by Richard E. Petty and John Cacioppo, ELM proposes two primary cognitive processing paths we use to make decisions. The *peripheral path* is quick, relying on schemas and prior experience to guide expectations and decisions. We typically use the peripheral path when we have little interest in a topic or are already positively disposed to it. The *central path*, on the other hand, involves careful thinking and evaluation of the messages we receive. When an issue is unclear but relevant to us, we tend to employ the central path. Although Petty and Cacioppo used ELM to explain persuasive messages, the same routes apply to receiving, evaluating and understanding explanations. We will be more apt to rely on schemas and prior experience when the topic being explained is of little interest to us, while we will pay much closer attention to explanations about things that affect us.[1]

Consider this story from the mid-1990s. A few days after a man moved to a new town, he heard a radio contest on a classic rock station while driving home from work. In the contest, listeners had to name a Led Zeppelin song being played by another group, such as a marching band, and the winners would get tickets to a Led Zeppelin tribute band. Led Zeppelin was a staple on classic rock stations at that time, and listeners of that station should have had little difficulty identifying their well-known songs. The listeners, however, did not do well. The next day, the DJ announced that he was repeating the contest but making it easier. Again, he asked listeners to name the song. This time he played a lengthy excerpt from Led

Zeppelin's greatest hit, "Stairway to Heaven," a song about as familiar to classic rock fans as "Happy Birthday" is to the average American. The contest was now ridiculously easy, but caller after caller guessed the wrong song and in several cases they weren't even guessing songs by Led Zeppelin and others weren't even guessing classic rock artists. What made the whole thing truly bizarre was that the DJ did not seem surprised at these outrageous answers. What was going on? The man had just moved from a major city to a smaller town in a different region of the country. Was there something about this place he didn't know about? He became so perplexed by the time the third caller guessed an artist who hadn't even had a hit in the same decade as Led Zeppelin that he actually pulled over. This situation was so inexplicable that for a few seconds he couldn't make sense of it and drive at the same time.

What explains the man's confusion? People have many schemas that help them understand all the information their senses provide—what the objects you see are used for, how people interact with each other, how objects should be arranged (e.g., chairs and podium in a classroom), and an endless list of other things. Most Americans have a schema for a call-in radio show. In one common form, the DJ asks a question, people call in with their best attempt to answer, and the winner gets a prize. In some variations, the winner must be a certain number caller, or DJ's playfully make fun of wrong answers. But when the contest asked listeners to guess the Led Zeppelin song, and fans of that music fail so miserably, the information cannot be explained with any schema a person is likely to have—particularly when the DJ reacts as if the responses are to be expected. Unable to explain this situation with an available schema, the observer has to abandon the shortcut to making sense and evaluate a wide range of possibilities. That generates enough of a cognitive load that it interferes with other active cognitive processes, like driving a car.

What does a schema look like? In general, they may best be thought of as networks of association. Imagine a web of ideas, concepts, and attributes that are linked based on association. Your schema for a college class probably includes elements like listening to a professor talk, having a class discussion, reading a textbook, writing a paper, and taking tests—but not, dancing, eating snacks, and playing loud music. Likewise, you have a schema for what makes a good birthday party, Thanksgiving dinner, or attractive outfit. The filing system for documents you have on your computer's desktop is a type of a schema—it is a schema for classifying the types of documents you regularly save.

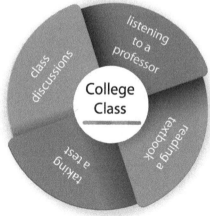

Figure 4.1
Example of a schema

Scripts

Sometimes a schema includes a sequence of behaviors. This type of schema is called a *script*. Scripts include both the activities associated with an event, and

script
when a schema includes a sequence of behaviors

also the order in which they should be done. The script for dinner at a sit-down restaurant includes being seated by a host, getting drinks and a menu, ordering food, receiving a check, and paying the server before leaving. Think about a restaurant experience you may have had where it did not follow this script. Perhaps the server forgot to offer you drinks before taking your order, or delivered the bill before the meal. If this happened, you likely had an averse reaction because it did not follow the script that typically occurs in these situations.

Many schemas are unique to each individual. Throughout your life you have created your own understanding of the world and developed your own schemas. Characteristics of an ideal romantic partner form a schema that is different for each person. However, many schemas are shared among members of a culture. Proper behavior at an orchestra concert, what to do at a church service, or what should be served at Thanksgiving dinner are all schemas widely shared among Americans. Scholars have documented many socially shared schemas and scripts, such as ordering at a restaurant and even what happens on a first date.[4] Part of becoming a member of a culture, whether as a child growing up or as an adult moving to a new country or region, is learning those socially shared schemas.

Because many schemas are shared among members of a culture, they provide shared understanding for those people, but, they can also be confusing to outsiders, because their schemas are likely to be somewhat different. For example, every culture has a schema for family, but, the exact nature of that schema varies across cultures. Many cultures consider family to be based on a husband and wife, but there are polygamous cultures whose schema for family includes the possibility of multiple married partners. In American family schemas most children are of similar status, while many Eastern cultures specify different status levels based on age or sex. These differences in status may determine how the family members are to interact. So, while some schemas are widely shared, the more diverse your listeners' cultural background is, the greater the chance that audience members won't always share identical schemas. Assuming the audience shares your schema can often inhibit effective explanation.

It is also worth noting that socially shared schemas often change over time. The increasing prevalence of single-parent or unmarried-parent families and growing acceptance of gay and lesbian marriage is challenging the expectation of married heterosexual parents in many western cultures. Sometimes schemas vary across generations. For instance, the millennial generation may, in general, have a different schema than their parents for the qualities of a good job. Experts have noted, "This new crop of employees is far more motivated by their mission than by the money they make. They want to transform a broken industry, save the planet, feed the starving, etc."[5] For today's college students, making a difference may be a more significant part of the schema of "a good job" than making a lot of money.

EXPLAINING IN A WAY THAT SUPPORTS UNDERSTANDING

Prior to formulating an explanation, speakers need to attend to two tasks: Establish a clear purpose, and learn about the audience. The former is necessary, because speakers must have clear boundaries on what exactly they are explaining.

Without a clear purpose and scope, the explanation will likely wander and confuse the audience.

Audience analysis is also essential. Imagine you are an accountant and have been asked to offer some basic financial principles to an audience. Do you think you know what you might say? Without knowing what the audience knows and doesn't know about your topic, you probably cannot offer an answer to that question. If your audience is a kindergarten class, your points are likely to be simple comments about making sure you save some of your money instead of spending it all the day you get it. If your audience is a group of college students, you might wish to offer some guidance on how to pay off school loans. If your audience is a group of accountants, you might explain how a new legal ruling will affect how their company should handle certain receipts. In each instance the purpose, scope and even strategies for explaining the issue are very different.

In some cases, you can reasonably guess what your audience knows just by looking a few simple demographics like age and education, or perhaps you might know the other person well to begin with (i.e. family and friends). But for others, you may need to do some specific analysis before speaking. Having a chance to survey audiences or find other ways to learn about their knowledge prior to offering an explanation may allow you to do a much better job.

When a person understands an explanation it means they have learned it, but unfortunately there is no one way to guarantee learning occurs in a listener. That said, although different people seem to learn better with different methods, some fundamentals of learning apply the same to almost everyone. In particular, presenting information in a manner that helps people cognitively process it tends to increase understanding for almost everyone. Here are four tips for presenting information in a way that helps audiences process what you are saying as accurately as possible.

Start with the Big Picture

One of the most important things a speaker can do to help the listener understand a new idea is to begin by presenting a brief, easy-to-follow overview of the big picture. This approach essentially provides a general schema for understanding all the details to follow. When people begin by jumping right into details, the audience has no sense of how those elements relate to each other or the larger concept being explained, and that makes it difficult to process that information.

Suppose a speaker wants to explain some basic exercises people should do, and then begins to give lots of specific instructions on each move. The audience could easily be confused. But, if the speaker first organizes the information by letting the listeners know there will be exercises for the upper body, legs, and core, and then offers some general principles about doing all of these moves, the listener now has a mental framework into which they can easily put the specifics. Until people know what to do with information, they have to store it in their short-term memory, which is very limited in space (only about three to seven items). When they try to put too much in, earlier information gets pushed out to accommodate newer information, and it is lost forever. This overload makes learning difficult.[6]

It is important when presenting the big picture that you make it as simple as possible, leaving out all non-essential information. You can fill in the important details later, but the big picture should present a simple framework so everyone gets that part right. Extraneous information is often interesting, but it can actually decrease learning. Bits of interesting information associated with your topic, but not part of it, are called *seductive details*. Researchers have found that people are often so fascinated with seductive details that audiences focus on them, rather than the idea you are trying to explain.[7] While interesting information or stories can have an appropriate role in an effective explanation (such as grabbing a listener's attention at the start of a presentation), speakers just need to be careful not to place them in a location where they cause a distraction.

Pace Information Appropriately

In addition to structuring information in a manner that makes it easy to process, it is also important to present the information at an optimal speed for the audience. This "Goldilocks zone" of information flow should be neither too fast, nor too slow. If you present too much information too quickly people cannot keep up, and even those trying their hardest to follow will eventually be overwhelmed and lose track of your point. On the other hand, if you present information too slowly, people will start to lose focus and think about other topics. Their minds will often be elsewhere when relevant information is presented.

The trick is to present a steady flow of information, and keep it within the limits of what people can process. A few techniques can help keep you from going too fast. First, if a point or a question will require some time to think about (perhaps because audience members lack a schema to process it), pause briefly to allow the listeners to think. The same is true if listeners are trying to take notes so they can follow or retain information. Second, appropriate repetition of core information can be helpful in pacing, because it can buy the listener time to process existing information while emphasizing an important point. Repetition should not be over-used, because it can reduce information flow to a point that is too slow, but strategically repeating a main point can allow time for it to sink in and can signal to the audience that this information is especially important. Plus, repetition by itself can enhance retention of information, and if that information is central or foundational, you will want to be sure the audience retains that point.

Choose a Manageable Amount of Information

Related to pacing, consider the total amount of information that a listener will be able to process in the time you have allocated to explain something. While the human brain is an amazing device, it still has limits on how much it can add to its storage at one time. So, when explaining something, you need to consider not just how quickly people can absorb the information, but also the total information that can be retained at one setting. Exceeding that limit by trying to cram too much information into one message is a common cause of people forgetting.[8] The over-exertion of trying to follow too much information may even cause a *reduction* in learning, compared to what a person could retain if trying to learn a more manageable amount.

Here is the important implication: *You need to begin by deciding what is most important, and make sure you present only that information.* If time permits elaboration on some of those ideas, you can then select the next most important information and add that layer. But you're better off picking a smaller amount of information and have the audience retain all of it, than to try to cover too much and have them retain little or none of it. Aside from hurting your audience's ability to retain information, presenting too much information can obscure what is really important. When a person is exposed to too much information it can be difficult to know what is most significant, and that person may focus effort on retaining material that is not the most important. When explaining a subject to another person or group of people it is imperative you know what you want them to understand when you are done, and not obscure that information from them under layers of interesting, but tangential information.

Use Presentational Aids When Possible

When helping someone understand a new idea, speakers need to consider all channels of communication. While our spoken language can convey amazing amounts of information in a fairly concise form, many ideas are better understood if they are not just heard, but also seen, smelled, tasted, or felt. Are you trying to help the audience recognize important smells, like a natural gas leak? Much better to let people smell it than just try to describe it. Do you want your audience to know how much fish sauce to put into Vietnamese soup? Let them taste too little, too much, and the right amount. Do you want them to be able to find a location? Showing a map will make it easier than just describing it.

Presentation aids can be used in a variety of settings and are not simply restricted to PowerPoint or Prezi. Home Interior Designers, which can be found independently or in stores like Lowes, use engineering programs to draw scale pictures of designs for rooms in a house requested by clients. You might then explain the very same design to a friend at lunch and sketch it on a napkin. The napkin and engineering software program are just as much presentation aids as a PowerPoint, and just like PowerPoint, if they are not necessary they will detract from understanding. Consider drawing on a napkin when the person you are speaking to already understands what you are drawing. That could come across as doodling and be perceived as rude by the other person. So, presentation aids take many forms, but should only be used when they are needed.

Don't waste time preparing presentational aids if they aren't necessary, but if any other senses can help people understand what you're explaining, then engage those senses in addition to offering a verbal explanation. The added layer of stimulation will enhance the probability that you effectively explained the subject to the audience.

HELPING LISTENERS REMEMBER YOUR INFORMATION

Have you ever forgotten something important that you knew you should have remembered? Perhaps you had even heard it more than once, and still forgot. Your answer is sure to be "yes," because all of us forget things we wish we'd have remembered. On the other hand, are there things that you remember well, even if they aren't that important or you haven't heard them in a long time? Again, your answer should be "yes," because latching onto certain memories is a universal human experience.

Brothers Chip and Dan Heath asked the question, "Why do we remember some ideas but forget others?" They found six principles that account for much of why certain ideas stay with us better than others, and presented them in a book called *Made to Stick*.[9] Although they were not asking how to explain complex ideas to non-experts, it turns out that these are overlapping questions—people better recall information they easily understand, and retaining information on a topic helps people better understand complex ideas. Three of the principles they suggested are particularly useful in helping people process new ideas.

Making it Simple

In order for something to be memorable, it must be easy to comprehend. To do this, a speaker must find the core of the idea, and present it in a compact manner that listeners understand when hearing it for the first time. So, a simple message has two qualities: *Core* and *compact*.

This concept is easily illustrated with corporate mission statements. If you look up an organization's mission statement, you'll normally find long complicated sentences, full of abstract language and big concepts. As an illustration, take a look at the UD Mission statement:

> As a vibrant academic department in the College of Arts and Sciences grounded in the Catholic and Marianist character of the University of Dayton, we actively serve our various and multiple communities, we produce high quality scholarship within the broad contours of our discipline. We provide an academically rigorous, critical, intellectually diverse, and praxis-oriented set of educational degree programs in political science, human rights studies, and public administration intended to properly educate and equip our students for life-long learning, faithful citizenship and positions of conscientious leadership and service to their professions, community, and the world.

After reading such a statement several times carefully, see how much you can recall an hour later. Odds are, not much. These statements cover a lot of ground, but they rarely present a core idea in a compact manner.

In contrast, consider one of the more successful US-based airlines, Southwest. They have made a point of summarizing their mission in one sentence: "We are THE low-fare airline."[10] That simple presentation of mission has more impact than an entire page of fancy lingo because it is easy to understand and recall.

For Southwest, that simple idea has guided decisions and actions for over three decades to great success. Hearing that sentence, you immediately understand the business plan of Southwest Airlines.

How do you make an idea simple? Heath and Heath explain, "'Finding the core' means stripping an idea down to its most critical essence. To get to the core, we've got to weed out the superfluous and tangential elements. . . . The hard part is weeding out ideas that may be really important, but just aren't *the most important* idea."[11] Speakers often want to pack a lot of information into a presentation, but trying to cram too much in prevents simplicity, and makes a message hard to understand and retain.

Contained in Heath and Heath's procedure for making a message simple is an important truth: *Clearly explaining an idea requires that you have thought and planned carefully before speaking.* Achieving clarity isn't something you can do off the cuff. You need to understand what is most important, because that determines the starting point of your explanation. Then, you can start to fill in other important information that supports that core idea. A common cause of confusing explanations is trying to describe something that has not been carefully thought through. People often fail to start with a clear presentation of the core, mix important and tangential information together, present information in illogical sequences, use wording that sounds contradictory, and often run over their allotted time—all because they tried to talk before fully thinking about and planning their message.

One final but important note about making explanations simple bears mentioning. Just because you are making the explanation simple, does not mean the topic is itself simple. Remember, complex things which people do not understand require explanations they can understand in order to learn the subject. The explanation must be simpler than the subject and placed into terms the audience understands, but it does not mean the topic's importance or core need to be dumbed down.

Making it Concrete

Consider an important research article on how people think, which leads with this sentence: "A fundamental tenet of all recent theories of comprehension, problem-solving, and decision-making is that success in such cognitive arenas depends on the activation and appropriate application of relevant pre-existing knowledge."[12] Read that again. Was it easy to understand? Will you remember it tomorrow? Unlikely. There are many reasons this sentence is difficult to understand, but one is that the language is so abstract. Now consider that it could have been said this way: "People understand more and make better decisions when they use schemas properly." You likely found that easier to follow.

Heath and Heath use the product Velcro to explain why we process and recall concrete ideas better than abstract ones. Velcro has two sides—one with lots of loops, the other with lots of hooks. When you press the two sides together, the hooks slip into the loops to form its grip. Memories seem to work that way as well—the more hooks they have, they more easily they are retained. Try to recall this information: (a) The house you spent most of your childhood in, and (b) the definition of "satisfaction." Which was easier for you to remember? Which brought multiple thoughts to your head at once? Most likely it was your childhood home. That residence offers lots of memories—events, smells, sights, sounds, and more. These are all hooks that make something memorable. You might be able to think of some words to define satisfaction, but it is probably harder to do as there are fewer "hooks." Concrete ideas seem to have better hooks than more abstract ideas. There is more there for us to mentally "grab hold" of.

When explaining complex ideas to non-experts, if you begin with—or rely heavily on—abstract ideas, your listeners will probably not fully grasp your ideas. The more you can offer explanations grounded in concrete ideas, the more effective you are likely to be. One of the best ways to provide hooks for your loops and engineer effective explanations is to tell stories.

Using Stories

Finally, one of the most important ways we can help people understand an idea is to share a story that illustrates the idea. While we often think of stories just as a fun diversion, they are actually much more important. Some experts go so far as to suggest that stories are one of the more common ways people make sense of the world around them.[13] While meaning is partially created by knowing the definition of words being used, much more of meaning is made by understanding the story in which those words play out. For example, your religious faith is a story which not only guides your actions, but also helps you make sense of events you experience. In a sense, a story becomes a schema for events you experience.

Stories have substantial impact on understanding ideas. Consider Aesop's fables, such as the boy who cried wolf. The story makes an important point (don't ruin your credibility), and it offers an easier way to understand and remember than an abstract statement of ethical theory would do. Stories need to be used appropriately when supporting an explanation. Used poorly, they can run on too long, contain ideas irrelevant to the core (likely to be seductive details), or be so emotional that they distract cognitive processes. But, if a story is told sharing only elements that are related to the point being made, it can offer insight that would otherwise be missed. When telling a story, it is essential that you clearly state how the story sheds light on the point you are explaining. If you don't do that, people might enjoy the story, but won't connect it with what you want them to understand.

Stories also capture the attention of listeners, and thus present an opportunity to reach an audience with a memorable way of understanding a key point in your message. Stories, though, should be focused, short and concrete. You also should tell the listener the point of the story explicitly either before or after telling the tale, or else they may very well take a meaning from it that is not what you intended.

Stories are also not necessary for every explanation, but if a story truly enhances a listener's ability to understand the idea you are explaining without distracting from the main point, then including it can add impact what would otherwise be missed.

SPOTLIGHTING THEORISTS: CHIP AND DAN HEATH

The authors of the *New York Times* bestseller, *Made to Stick: Why Some Ideas Survive and Others Die,* Chip and Dan Heath have contributed much to our understanding of how to explain complex subjects to audiences of one, one hundred or one thousand people. While neither is a communication scholar, they understand the way in which ideas from different disciplines like Business and Psychology intersect and influence how we can construct effective explanations.

The brothers have also co-authored two other popular press books that take academic research and explain it in a way the general public can understand. In 2010 they released *Switch: How to Change Things When Change is Hard*, which debuted as #1 on both the *New York Times* and *Wall Street Journal* bestseller lists. Recently, they completed another book, *Decisive: How to Make Better Decisions in Life and Work*. All three of their books help people understand how both their own minds and the minds of audiences work when processing complicated information in an effort make good decisions.

Both brothers have strong pedigrees. Chip is a professor at the Stanford Graduate School of Business, while Dan is a Senior Fellow at Duke University's CASE Center, which focuses on social entrepreneurs, and also the founder of Thinkwell, an innovative publishing company. Chip has done extensive consulting with companies such as Google, Gap, and the American Heart Association. Dan previously worked as a researcher for the Harvard Business School, where he earned his MBA. Together, their works have been translated into 28 different languages.[14]

TOOLS FOR EFFECTIVE EXPLANATION

The principles discussed above offer some general approaches to explanation. People understand best when presented with a schema to organize the information they encounter, and with a manageable amount of information to process in the time allotted. They understand better when the message appeals to the appropriate senses, and, they understand better when information is simple, concrete, and illustrated with a story. These principles alone provide useful guidance for decisions you will make in crafting an explanation. There are also some basic techniques that you can use when applying those principles that make implementing them more effective.

This first pair of techniques add clarity to an explanation. In a situation where explanation is needed, the audience has less understanding of the topic than the speaker, and so listeners will not understand important information if it is not provided clearly. Two techniques are especially useful in providing the information listeners need: Definition and vivid description.

Definition. Any time a word is used which a listener might not know—especially if that word has a specialized meaning in that instance—then the speaker needs to define the word. Imagine a company's Chief Financial Officer (CFO) is presenting a financial report to employees. In the report, she talks about *operating margins, beginning net assets, hedge fund investments, real assets*, and *private equities*. Will the audience know what the financial figures mean? They are likely to understand the math, which is very simple, but without definitions they are unlikely to know what those numbers mean. Thus, she will fail in her goal of explaining the company's financial situation. If the CFO offers a definition of each concept that is easy to understand, her explanation of the company's financial situation has a good chance of being clear to the audience.

Vivid description. If a listener needs to visualize something in order to understand it, then a vivid description may be necessary. Such a description includes a wide range of details, perhaps relating to many different senses, which allows the listener to understand better. If you have ever watched a TV show about food, you know that a talented host will describe food using vivid descriptions that appeal to sight, taste, feel, and sound. Andrew Zimmern and Adam Richman use vivid descriptions, full of concepts the viewer understands to describe foods that viewers may never have eaten. For example, what do you think kangaroo tail soup tastes like? If you have no idea, Andrew Zimmern describes it in *Bizarre Foods:* "It smells like beef and barley . . . Winey, deep, and aromatic . . . Kangaroo tail tastes like braised beef. It's kind of crunchy and smooth, all at the same time." Getting a better idea? More description could give you even a better idea . . . if that sounds like something you'd want to eat. For another example of the power of vivid description, look at the testimony given by Fannie Lou Hamer in 1964 on racial injustice in the Speaking of Civic Engagements box in this chapter.

The next set of tools are important techniques you can use to help listeners understand ideas they are not currently familiar with: comparison, contrast, and metaphor. These each involve creative uses of language to make concepts more relatable for audiences. Like stories, description and definition, the key is knowing when they are appropriate to employ, and what comparisons and metaphors will work best with a given audience in a specific context.

comparison
connecting new information with something a person already knows

Comparison. One of the more common ways people learn is by connecting new information with something they already know. Comparing something new with what is known allows a person to use all or parts of an existing schema. That means that the information that is part of that schema can be applied. So, an apt *comparison* allows a lot of information transfer to happen at one time. For example, if you want to explain the experience of being stung by a jellyfish, comparing the experience with sensations a person might have experienced will make it easier to understand. Comparing a complicated idea or item to a more commonly understood concept helps people appreciate the foundation of the more complicated subject by identifying characteristics it shares with something they already know.

Contrast. In some cases it is what is *different* between the new information and what is known that is most important. For example, piloting a large sailboat has some similarity to driving a car, in that both use a wheel of some type, but that's where the similarities end. When sailing a boat, there is enough lag time between moving the ship's wheel and the vehicle response that beginners overdo almost every steering move. Steering a boat requires small movements and patience, plus knowledge of how much a steering adjustment will move the craft. Likewise, changes in speed happen very slowly using the sails, not quickly like they do with an accelerator or brake pedal. So, while driving a car and commanding a sailboat both involve controlling speed and direction, it is the contrast, not the comparison, that helps explain the experience and process to the listener.

Comparison and contrast are often most effectively used when paired together. Because few things are identical in every regard, a comparison of what is similar followed by a contrast of what differs may offer the most helpful route to a more thorough understanding. Explaining how to drive a riding mower might involve a more balanced presentation of comparison and contrast from driving a car than the example of a sailboat. But, both pairings (car-boat, car-mower) can benefit from comparison and contrast in the explanation.

Metaphor. In the chapter on Language we will define metaphor and provide you with different types of metaphors that could be employed in a message. For the purposes of our discussion here, know that metaphors are very effective and efficient tools for explaining complicated subjects to listeners. In fact, they are so prevalent in our everyday language you probably don't even notice you use them. Metaphors help us extend meaning to things with which people are not familiar by connecting them to things they know very well. In fact, one of the most common ways to expand our language is to develop new meanings through the metaphorical extensions of existing words. Computer technology provides an obvious example.

With the invention of new technology, we suddenly needed language to describe a lot of new hardware and software. Most of those words were metaphors. Consider the origins of words like *mouse*, *tablet*, the *web* (on which you can *surf*, so how is that for a mixed metaphor!). These words, along with hundreds of others, are metaphors used to make new complicated concepts and things familiar. Our brains are wired to understand new ideas as metaphorical extensions of existing knowledge, providing us with a useful and creative shorthand for making new things understandable for an audience.

PREPARING AND TAKING NOTES

Language skills are not the only elements of an effective explanation. In professional settings where explanations are called for, such as a team meeting, briefing on a policy, or performance review, it is immeasurably helpful to prepare notes before the meeting. Taking notes helps you organize the explanation before having to provide it.

Comments Before the Credentials Committee
by Fannie Lou Hamer

Delivered August 22, 1964, at the Democratic National Committee, Atlantic City, New Jersey

Fannie Lou Hamer, the granddaughter of slaves, was born in 1917 in Mississippi. She became a sharecropper on a plantation, and in 1962 when members of the Student Nonviolent Coordinating Committee (SNCC) came to town to hold a voter registration meeting, Hamer didn't even know that she had a constitutional right to vote. Once she knew she could, she volunteered to help register others to vote and was later jailed, beaten, and driven from the farm where she was a sharecropper as result.[3]

Hamer went on to become secretary of the SNCC and traveled to various places registering people to vote, spoke about voting rights, and cofounded the Mississippi Freedom Democratic Party (MFDP). The Credentials Committee of the 1964 Democratic Convention asked her to speak about racial injustice.[4]

Hamer told the committee about the treatment she had received from the police, how the plantation owner had pressured her to withdraw her registration request, and that when she refused he told her to leave his property. She also recounted the resistance at registration drives and how she and others with her were not allowed to eat in some restaurants or use restrooms.[5] She told of black prisoners ordered to beat her with blackjacks and of the terrible names the police called her. Here is an excerpt from her informative and emotional testimony:

"I was carried out of that cell into another cell where they had two Negro prisoners. The State Highway Patrolmen ordered the first Negro to take the blackjack. The first Negro prisoner ordered me, by orders from the State Highway Patrolman, for me to lay down on a bunk bed on my face. As I laid on my face, the first Negro began to beat me. And I was beat by the first Negro until he was exhausted."[6]

Preparing Your Speaking Notes

As the sender, notes allow you to recall the important points of the explanation without having to rely on memory. Notes also can provide you with multiple ways of explaining a particular point, depending on how well the other party seems to understand your explanation. For instance, consider a doctor explaining the survival rate of a particular cancer to a patient. They might begin with talking about the data on how many people survive for a particular period of time, but the patient may not understand what this means for their specific case. So, the doctor then might resort to telling a story or comparing the numbers to something that might make the data more understandable. Now, if the patient understands the numeric information the doctor initially explained, these other methods of explanation are not necessary—but it's good to have them in case you do need to employ other ways to unpack complex information for the other person.

Now, what do good notes look like for an explanation? First, because the explanation takes place in a conversation not a speech, the notes need to be somewhat structured. This means that the important takeaway points need to be clearly delineated, while the relevant supporting information and the methods you might use to explain that information appear under the each point. In general, three steps are needed when presenting information that helps to explain an idea. These steps do not need to be enumerated or labeled in the speaking notes, but they should all be present:

1. State the point that you want your listener to understand.

2. Present relevant information using the principles and tools in this chapter.

3. Make the connection between this information (Step 2) and the take-away point (Step 1).

Each point that you intend to share with your listener should have these three elements. If we return to the above example of the doctor explaining the survival rate of a particular cancer to the patient, the doctor's notes might look something like this for the first point in the conversation:

1. **State the Point:** The survival rate for patients with this particular cancer is high when diagnosis and treatment can occur early.

2. **Supporting Material:**

   a. **Evidence**: 90% of patients survive this cancer when diagnosis and treatment happen early.

   b. **Story**: Another patient in my office had a similar diagnosis last year and because treatment occurred early, the cancer is in remission.

   c. **Visual Images**: a graph that shows survival rates corresponding with time when diagnosis and treatment occurred

   d. **Analogy**: Similar to finding a water leak in a roof. If identified early and a fix can be made, the roof's integrity can be preserved. If identified too late and the fix comes after a long while, the damage is too great, and the structural integrity of the roof might be beyond repair.

3. **Connect Supporting Material Back to Point**

In any given explanation, you likely do not have only one point that you want to communicate to your listener but many points. For this reason, you will need to prepare multiple talking points in your notes. How many points do you need to prepare? There is no one answer to this question. The number of points that you need to prepare depends on many factors, including the complexity of the concept or idea that you want to explain, the time that you have available for the explanation, and the needs of the listener.

Let's look at another example: a performance review by a boss. The supervisor has evaluated the employee according to three categories. Accordingly, the conversation in which the boss explains her evaluation to the employee might have three points, each one corresponding with one of the categories. For each category, the boss might have multiple pieces of evidence to support the overarching point that she wants to make about the employee's performance in that category. She also might think of a few different tools that she might use to explain this evidence, such as contrasting the employee's current performance with his same performance last quarter, using a metaphor to explain how the employee's performance fits into the larger system of performance in the workplace, or providing definitions of key performance standards. She might not have the time to explain all of this, and once the explanation is underway, the conversation might unfold such that she does not feel that there is a need to talk about all of these pieces of evidence or to use all of these tools. Nevertheless, she puts this material into her notes, in case she does need it.

An effective explanation has three segments, each of which has its own requirements and accordingly must be planned with some care:

- **A brief introduction** that leads into the talk by introducing the topic and purpose of the conversation, building rapport with the listener, gauging her or his familiarity with the topic, and establishing the speaker's credibility

- **The body of the talk**, in which the speaker presents the different points that she or he wishes to communicate, shares information about those points, and includes different tools for explaining that information to the listener

- **A brief conclusion** in which the speaker reinforces the main ideas from the talk - often by asking the listener to give a summary of what she or he understood and then reaffirming or clarifying key ideas - expresses gratitude to the listener, and brings the conversation to an end.

In some ways, the conversation resembles a job interview. In the introduction of the interview, the interviewer briefly welcomes the listener, builds rapport perhaps by engaging in some small talk, and orients the listener to the purpose of the interview. In the body, the interviewer asks the questions that pertain to the topic at hand, often by focusing on particular aspects or dimensions of the topic for periods of time before moving to new aspects or dimensions of that topic. In the conclusion, the interviewer brings the interview to a close by summarizing any key points relating to the topic and expressing gratitude to the listener.

We have included an example of the speaking notes for an explanatory talk about an important concept in the social sciences: ideology. You can imagine an instructor meeting with a student in his or her office and giving a short explanation of this concept after the student expresses some confusion about this topic and asks for help. You can use this sample as a model for preparing your own speaking notes. As you examine these notes, consider the following qualities that are typical of speaking notes for explanatory talks:

- The notes are organized into distinct talking points. These points all relate to the concept or idea that the speaker is explaining overall. They are perhaps components, dimensions, factors, causes, or consequences of that concept or idea. They might have an initial order but are organized in a way that allows for adaptation in the middle of the conversation, if necessary.

- Main takeaway points are clearly defined, while supporting information and explanatory tools are designated under each.

- Each talking point offers several different explanatory tools that the speaker can use to explain the overarching takeaway point and the supporting information, even though not all of these tools might be used during the talk when it occurs.

- The notes have a distinct introduction, body, and conclusion.

- In the conclusion, the speaker has prepared a summary question, an open-ended question that she or he can ask to prompt the listener to give a brief account of what she or he has understood as the main points of the talk.

- The notes contain citations for relevant information, so that the speaker can note from where she or he took this information. Citing one's sources orally in this manner is called verbal attribution and will be covered in Chapter 5. In class, you will be expected also to provide a list of references that give the full citations for the sources that you cite in the text of the notes.

- The notes are extemporaneous, which means that they contain no full sentences except direct quotations that the speaker might share with the listener. They do not function as a script to be read, but rather a rough sketch that helps the speaker to remember key elements of the talk.

The semi-structured, flexible nature of speaking notes allows for the speaker to adapt to the listener's knowledge and needs as the conversation unfolds. A key means whereby the speaker can learn about the experience and understanding of the listener is by asking questions throughout the conversation, some at the beginning, some during the talk, and some as the talk comes to an end.

ASKING QUESTIONS TO CHECK UNDERSTANDING

Asking questions is a primary way of learning about what a listener already knows about the topic, gauging how clearly she or he is understanding the explanation once it begins, and determining what points might need to be reinforced before ending the talk. Often, complex information takes a few minutes to unpack for a listener—even when the explanation is clear. The appropriateness of questions relates both to their timing and how they are worded. A poorly timed question may come across in a way that insults the other person, too many questions may detract from the explanation, while a poorly worded question may not get you the information you seek.

There are three periods of an explanation when you might ask questions of the listener: near the beginning, in the middle and towards the end. The goals of each of these questions are slightly different, but all should provide you with information that helps you adjust the explanation in a way that makes it clearer for the other party.

Asking early questions: Near the beginning of an explanation you might want, or need, to ask the other person what they know regarding your overall topic.

The answer to this question will help you gage where to begin the explanation, because if a person is not familiar with the topic you might need to provide a little more information than if they had some idea of what you are talking about. These questions should be specific, because just asking a "yes or no" question does not tell you what the person knows. Therefore, you should ask them to briefly explain what they know about the topic.

If you walk into a situation where the overall concept is something you believe the other party has some understanding of at the start, you don't need to ask a question early on. Take the case of the aforementioned performance review. The supervisor does not need to find out what the employee knows about the categories or performance review process, and so they can just get started explaining the review. They might, however, need to ask questions in the middle of the explanation.

Asking questions in the middle of the explanation: These are the most common questions that take place during an explanation. Their goal is to make sure a main point is understood, and these questions can be either planned or prompted by the listener's behavior. Sometimes when the topic is pretty complex and unfamiliar to the other person you might want to plan a question to gage their understanding after explaining a key point. If the person does not seem to get it, you can try another method of explaining the same point to help them understand.

Other times it may seem from the nonverbal behaviors of the other person that they either have stopped paying attention or do not understand the material you have explained. In this scenario you would ask a question to see if they are, in fact, paying attention and understanding the content. The box to the right

> Shaking head from side to side
>
> Looking down or away from the speaker
>
> A furrowed brow
>
> A frown
>
> Shrugging shoulders

contains some nonverbal behaviors that might hint that the other person is lost or does not understand what you are saying.

Just like questions you might ask at the outset of an explanation, these questions should not be of the "yes/no" variety. Rather, they should ask for a specific response from the other person that demonstrates understanding. One of the best ways to do this is to ask them to apply the content to something else and have them relay it back. Here are some examples of good perception checking questions in the middle of an explanation:

- Can you give me an example of this from your life?
- What does this sound like to you?
- How might you explain this point to someone else?

These types of questions force the other person to demonstrate their understanding by verbalizing a coherent application of the material you just explained. If they do so accurately, you can move on to the next key point—if they do not, you need to *both* correct their misperception and explain the material in a different way to ensure understanding. When we ask someone questions like "Do you understand this?" and "does this make sense to you" the other person will most often say "yes" even if they do not and thus no understanding is achieved.

Asking questions at the end: The third period of an explanation where questions are helpful. Whereas questions at the beginning are used to help identify where to begin the explanation and those in the middle serve to identify understanding of a specific complicated key point, questions near the end of an explanation help to pinpoint how well the other party understands the topic now that you have explained it. Ideally, these questions give the other party an opportunity to extend the conversation by asking them to think about issues which the topic might relate to now that they understand it.

Take the case of a student explaining hydroponic farming to a friend. After detailing the reasons why it is becoming more popular and relaying the ways in which is can be beneficial to the environment the person may ask the listener to think of other ways this type of farming might help. Or they may ask them what they see as the potential drawbacks or benefits to hydroponic farming. The answers to these questions will help the explainer see how well the other party now understands the concept by seeing if they can now think more deeply and critically about the subject.

One type of question that is especially helpful to ask as the conversation draws to a close is called a *summary question*. A summary question prompts the listener to give a brief synopsis or list of the main points that the talk covered. Such a question creates an opportunity for feedback from the listener and adjustment to the message on the part of the speaker. An effective summary question is open-ended. Fixed response questions, especially questions that ask for a yes or no response such as "Do you feel that you understand the topic?" or "Do you have any questions about the topic?" do not tend to elicit a summary from listeners. As such, they do not make effective summary questions. Speakers also should avoid questions that focus on the listener's opinions, such as "How do you feel about this topic?" or leading questions that seek agreement with the speaker's general orientation towards the topic. An open-ended, fact-seeking question such as "What do you see as the main takeaways from our talk?" tend to elicit a brief summary from the listener, which provides the speaker with feedback about how the listener understood the content of the talk. At this point, the speaker should affirm the listener's summary, if it reflects the points that the speaker wished to communicate, or offer further clarification about what the speaker intended to share. If the listener's summary diverges to a considerable extent from what the speaker intended, then the speaker can say something like "You and I seem to have understood our conversation in different ways. The points that I intended to communicate are…

summary question
a question that prompts the listener to give a brief synopsis or list of the main points that the talk covered

Asking appropriate questions at the right time during an explanation is key to facilitating understanding. It is also not as easy as it might seem because knowing when to ask questions and phrasing those questions in a way that provides you with actionable information takes practice and requires paying attention to the context in which the communication takes place. In addition to language skills and questions there is one more strategy we will discuss that aids in achieving understanding in an explanation.

VISUAL SUPPORT FOR EXPLANATION

When you prepare an explanation, you should consider not just the words you use, but also what other means of communicating information will help. Presentational aids—especially visual aids—are one element you should always consider in advance. Guidelines for how to prepare and use them effectively are presented later in the book. However, sometimes in the course of an explanation, you discover that some visual representation might be helpful, for reasons you could not have foreseen before speaking.

What can you do to be most effective when using visual aids on the fly? There is no simple or complete list of rules, because each situation is different. However, we offer a few general principles here that are worth keeping in mind. In all cases, the question is *"What will help the listener understand, without becoming a distraction?"* The guidelines presented below are often useful, but always go back to this question rather than mindlessly following a rule. And the more you know about how listeners process information, the better you can answer this question.

Keep your visual aid simple and as neat as possible. Drawing or writing while speaking takes time and focuses audience attention on the visual element. Adding tangential information takes additional time away from your message—giving listeners' minds time to wander—and can be confusing. Listeners will naturally try to understand why each detail is there, so unnecessary information becomes a distraction. Fun, but seductive, details are also distracting, and can take listeners' minds away from your point.

While you want to write or draw quickly so as to keep audience members attentive to your points, going so quickly and sloppily that your audience cannot read your writing or understand something you've drawn undermines the point of having done it in the first place. So, only go as quickly as you can write legibly.

Maintain visual contact with the audience. When writing on a board, the natural position is to turn your back to the audience—which is one reason why speakers should always prepare visuals in advance when the need can be anticipated. However, if the need to produce a visual on the fly comes up, speakers should write and then turn back to the audience as soon as the writing or drawing is done. Always talk to the audience, not to the presentation aid.

Explain what you write or draw. A list, chart, drawing, or some other visual aid may be essential to your explanation, but just putting it out by itself may create more questions than it answers. Always be sure to offer a clear explanation of what your visual is and how it contributes to understanding the point you're making.

Be attuned to the listener's response. If you have discovered the need for unplanned visual support of an explanation, you have now moved "off the script" and are engaging the audience directly on something that you just discovered is causing difficulty in understanding. Take care to watch their nonverbal and listen to verbal responses to gauge whether or not the visual aid helped them overcome their confusion. Head nods, smiles and raised eyebrows can indicate they have achieved understanding, while shrugs, furrowed brows and open mouths can indicate they still do not get it. Watching your listeners' reactions allows you to make sure the audience understands the important point the visual conveyed before you move on.

SUMMARY

In this chapter we discussed explanation and its various components. We illustrated that in order to effectively explain something to someone you must first appreciate the fact you and the other person have different schemas that help make sense of the world. We provided some principles for explanation that, if followed, help enhance audience understanding and retention of key information in the explanation. We provided practical tips for helping others remember information, and for how you can construct effective explanations. Finally, we offered some guidelines for effectively employing presentation aids in explanations that occur in a variety of different contexts.

KEY TERMS

comparison   104

Elaboration Likelihood Model (ELM)   94

explanation   93

schema   94

script   95

seductive details   98

summary question   111

ENDNOTES

1. John T. Cacioppo and Richard E. Petty,"The Elaboration Likelihood Model of Persuasion", in NA - Advances in Consumer Research Volume 11, eds. Thomas C. Kinnear, (1984) Provo, UT : Association for Consumer Research, Pages: 673-675.

2. Mary Claire Serewicz & Elaine Gale, "First-date scripts: Gender roles, context, and relationship," *Sex Roles, 58,* (2008) 149-164.

3. Brian Halligan, "How Millennials think, and what to do about it" *Inc.* (July 3, 2013), http://www.inc.com/brian-halligan/how-millennials-think-and-what-to-do-about-it.html, Last Accessed April 29, 2014.

4. Sarah Blissett, Rodrigo B. Cavalcanti, & Matthew Sibbald, "Should we teach using schemas? Evidence from a randomised trial," *Medical Education, 46*(8), (2012) 815-822.

5. Shannon F. Harp, & Richard E. Mayer, "How seductive details do their damage: A theory of cognitive interest in scientific learning," *Journal of Educational Psychology, 90,* (1998) 414-434.

6. Donald A. Bligh, *What's the use of lectures?* San Francisco: Jossey-Bass (2000).

7. Chip Heath & Dan Heath, *Made to stick,* New York: Random House (2000).

8. Heath & Heath.

9. Heath & Heath, p. 28.

10. Rand J. Spiro, Walter P. Vispoel, John G. Schmitz, Ala. Samarapungavan, & A.E. Boerger, "Knowledge acquisition for application: Cognitive flexibility and transfer in complex content domains," In B. K. Britton & S. M. Glynn (Eds.), *Executive control processes in reading* (pp. 177-199). Hillsdale, NJ: Lawrence Erlbaum, (1987).

11. Fisher, Walter R. (1984). "Narration as Human Communication Paradigm: The Case of Public Moral Argument." in *Communication Monographs* 51. pp. 1–22.

12. Injuries Related to Texting and Walking Increasing," *Claims Journal,* (March 5, 2014), http://www.claimsjournal.com/news/national/2014/03/05/245467.htm Last Accessed April 29, 2014. See their website for even more information: http://heathbrothers.com

Interteaching Session

Dialogue

How would you explain college life at UD to a senior in high school who is thinking about going to college here? Identify a couple aspects of college life here at UD that someone unfamiliar with the campus might not understand. Plan a short explanatory talk in which you explain each of these points to your listener. Make sure that you use the three-part structure from the chapter for each point and at least two explanatory tools for each point, one that adds clarity and one that makes an unfamiliar concept relatable to the audience. Your explanation as a whole should last no more than three minutes. Be prepared to give your explanation to someone in another group in the class, as though they were your listener.

Performance

Find a video clip from a documentary, such as *How the Universe Works* or *Nova.* Your clip should last no more than three or four minutes. After you watch the clip with your groupmates, analyze the explanation in terms of the following:

- Four principles for explanation that help listeners to understand information
- Three principles for explanation that help listeners to remember information
- Two tools for adding clarity to an explanation
- Three tools for making an unfamiliar concept relatable to an audience

Be prepared to share your clip and your analysis with the class in a short presentation that lasts no more than five minutes or so.

Research and Preparation

Practically SPEAKING

Students today typically react to the necessity of venturing to the library with a mixture of dread, loathing, and reluctance; however, that has not always been the case. In fact, there was a time when libraries held an exalted status and represented more than simply storage facilities for the printed word. In the ancient world, libraries were castles of learning and homes to schools, zoos, museums, and the brightest minds of the day. They were, in point of fact, the backbone of empires and kingdoms.

The most famous library in history was located in Alexandria, Egypt, and its history is a mixture of both fact and myth. King Ptolemy I (Soter) and his son King Ptolemy II (Philadelphus) commissioned the Great Library at Alexandria and modeled it after Aristotle's Lyceum in terms of mission, but the Alexandrian library dwarfed the Lyceum in terms of size, structure, and content. This model, however, occurred for good reason.[1]

Ptolemy I was one of Alexander the Great's generals, and after the death of his leader and subsequent partition of the empire, Ptolemy ruled Egypt. Alexander was a student of Aristotle's, and so he made sure his generals were schooled in the same vein. Additionally, through his conquests Alexander attempted to Hellenize the world by spreading the value of the *enkyklios paideia*, or rounded education, which tiered instruction into the trivium (grammar, rhetoric, and logic), and quadrivium (arithmetic, geometry, music, and astronomy).

The Ptolemys sought to create a universal library, one where knowledge of all things could be found, not just a localized culture-specific repository of knowledge. The Great Library also contained a museum. Together they represented one of the greatest achievements in all of antiquity.[2] The Great Library and Museum worked in tandem to store and develop the wisdom of the ages. Scholars from around the known world lived and worked tax-free at the Library copying scrolls secured by the government. On several occasions, Ptolemy and his successors even brought scrolls on loan from Greek city-states and copied them only to keep both the original and the copy! It was the epicenter of scholarship and innovation because many of those holdings were original Greek works and translations of non-Greek texts of religious, poetic, and political significance.[3]

Unfortunately, nothing much remains of the Great Library and Museum and the histories of it are the product of researching letters and writings that reference it. No one is sure how it was destroyed, but destroyed it was, and many writings contained there are now lost forever. Ironically, we know about the ancient world's research mecca only through research, as it no longer exists and its documents are long gone.

Nowadays we think of libraries simply as places where knowledge is stored, and the university as a whole fits the model set forth by the Great Library. Nevertheless, the Greeks and Romans recognized that libraries and research skills are central to the development of a critical mind, and we should learn from that example.

In this chapter we will explore the very nature of research, and illustrate the importance of becoming information literate. We will discuss different types of sources and how you can find the ones most appropriate to your project. Finally, we will detail the importance of properly citing sources you use and provide three examples as to how you can do so.

Prep Questions

Part 1: Key Concepts

1. What are the three characteristics of an effective research question? Create a research question for a topic that you are considering for your upcoming explanatory assignment that has all three characteristics.

2. List the five characteristics of information literacy. Explain briefly how information literacy is necessary for quality scholarship as defined in the chapter.

3. Define the three types of information that you might seek as you do research on a topic.

4. Identify the five criteria for evaluating information that you find through research, reflected in the acronym C-R-A-A-P. Explain what a researcher might consider in applying each criterion to evaluating a source.

5. Name and define the three types of plagiarism.

6. List and define the six components of Toulmin's model.

Part 2: Application

1. Find one example of each of the following types of sources relating to a topic that you are considering for your upcoming explanatory assignment:

   - a news article
   - a scholarly article in an academic journal
   - a book
   - a documentary or video clip

   Create a full citation using proper APA style for each of these sources, such as what you would include in the references page for your speaking notes.

2. Now create an oral citation for each of these sources. Write what you would say if you were to provide verbal attribution for information from each of these sources in an explanatory talk. Make sure that your oral citation has all of the elements that the chapter describes as necessary.

3. Create a factual argument relating to a topic that you are considering for your upcoming explanatory assignment, using the three primary components of Toulmin's model. State the claim that you want to make about the topic. Provide some specific evidence to support that claim. Then give a brief explanation of the warrant: that is, how the evidence that you have given supports the claim that you are making.

5

THE INVENTION PROCESS

When you set out to prepare a message such as an explanatory talk, you must make some important decisions. One of these decisions is what topic you will address. You also will need to decide how you will begin exploring that topic through research. The research that you do might lead to further refinements of your topic.

You may recall from Chapter 1 the story of Cicero. One of Cicero's major contributions to the study of rhetoric was his five canons of rhetoric. Cicero's canons can provide a framework for you as you prepare for an upcoming talk. The first of his five canons was invention. Invention, as Cicero understood it, involves choosing the best possible arguments for your case. In an explanatory talk, you are not trying to convince anyone to change their attitude about a given topic or to take action in a particular way, yet you are still making an argument, albeit a factual one. You are offering claims about a particular topic and giving factual evidence to support those claims. However, before you begin constructing this argument, you need to determine what specifically will be the topic of your talk.

Choosing a Focus

There is no single formula for how a speaker should choose a topic. Often, a speaker's topic is given to him or her by others who have invited or appointed him or her to speak. In such cases, the speaker might exercise some discretion about what specific aspects or dimensions of this overarching topic to address, yet the general subject of the talk has already been determined. Sometimes, the speaker has a wide latitude for choosing a topic and very few, perhaps even no parameters have been given for this decision. Whatever the case might be, it is helpful to think of the selection of a topic as part of a larger process of invention, as Cicero envisioned. A speaker might choose an initial topic, but once she or he begins researching that topic and thinking further about the context in which communication will occur, the topic of the communication might evolve.

At the earliest stages of the invention process, there are some methods that the speaker can use to get some preliminary ideas. One of these methods is brainstorming. Brainstorming is a method for generating a pool of ideas by creating a list of alternatives. While most people are familiar with the concept of brainstorming, there are some concrete guidelines that can help make brainstorming effective:

1. **Generate as many ideas as possible.** The goal of brainstorming is quantity not quality. You can concern yourself with the quality of the ideas later.

2. **Give yourself enough time to create an adequate pool of alternatives.** It might be helpful to set a time frame for the brainstorming process, such as a couple of days or even a week. If you are working with a shorter timetable overall, then you can set a shorter time frame, such as an hour or a day. The point is that idea generation takes time.

3. **Don't critique the ideas that you create until brainstorming is completed.** Because the goal of brainstorming is the generation of ideas, one does well to suspend any concerns about the quality of specific ideas until idea generation is over. Critiquing ideas while they are being generated tends to result in a smaller pool of alternatives.

4. **Keep the flow of ideas moving.** This is especially important if you have a shorter time frame. It is easy when brainstorming to allow your creativity to become frozen if no quality ideas are coming to mind. Resist this tendency by writing down any idea that comes into your thoughts. The important thing is to keep the creative flow moving. Even a silly or impractical idea can be the basis for other ideas that could be worthy of consideration in the end.

One variation of brainstorming that might help you to generate some ideas is brainstorming using categories. With this method, before you begin brainstorming, you create several categories that can give some shape to the generation of ideas. Some common categories that you might use include:

People	Events
Places	Concepts
Objects	Organizations
Processes	Technologies

With this method, you follow the same basic guidelines for brainstorming, yet instead of generating ideas in a completely open-ended fashion, you generate ideas within each of the categories. You can brainstorm across all of these categories at once, placing ideas within the most appropriate list as they come to you. Alternatively, you can focus on each category, one after another. In either case, by the end, you should have a fairly substantial list of alternatives from which you can think further about a topic.

A third method for generating possible topics is called mind mapping. When you create a mindmap, you construct a diagram of topics and subtopics as these relate to each other. You might start with the name of a particular topic at the center of your page, often something quite broad, such as "community." From this topic, you begin drawing branches reaching outwards on the page, representing other topics that might relate to this first one. Some might be subtopics to this first one, such as "religious communities" or "neighborhoods." Others might be topics peripherally related, such as "civility" or "trust in others." The specific relationship between the different topics is less important than that you are creating a map or web of many different ideas, any of which singly or in combination could form the basis for a talk. For each of these branch topics, you also create other topics branching outwards from it. For instance, radiating outwards from "religious communities," you might write several other ideas, including "congregations," "cults," "denominations," "initiation rites," and "excommunication." Any of these topics, in turn, might become the center of even more topics radiating outwards. When you have reached a suitable stopping point, you can review your map and see what ideas or clusters of ideas might lend themselves to further development as a topic for your talk.

A final method that might help you in choosing a topic is web browsing. By entering a few search terms in your browser, you can see what sites appear. By perusing these sites, you might get some ideas about what you would like to explore further. There is no one best way to explore ideas in this manner. The main thing is to see what inspires you and what captures your interest at this early stage, as you think about the talk that you will be giving. One advantage of this method is that, by searching the internet for ideas and visiting particular sites, you might get a headstart on your research. Some of the sites that you visit might be worth revisiting once you begin diving further into a topic that you have chosen.

At some point, you will need to choose a topic to investigate further. The open-ended creativity of generating alternatives cannot continue forever. Otherwise, you would not be able to develop your talk further. While there is no formula for how a speaker must settle on a particular topic from among the many alternatives, a speaker does well to keep certain considerations in mind. One primary consideration is the context in which the communication will occur. In Chapter 3, we explored six components of the context, each in the form of a specific question. These questions can be helpful in giving shape to the selection of a topic, for ultimately whatever a speaker chooses to address must be adapted to the context. Otherwise, the speaker is not likely to be successful in communicating with the audience. We also explored Bitzer's model of the rhetorical situation. Analyzing the situation in which communication will occur can help the speaker to focus the topic of the talk. Who is the audience? What exigency exists in the current situation that is demanding or inviting a response? What constraints must be taken into consideration as communication unfolds?

While context is a key consideration, your interests as a speaker also are important. With all of the challenges that you might need to overcome in giving your talk, you do not need to add to them the challenge of speaking on a topic in which you have little interest. Choosing a topic for your talk about which you are passionate not only can make the communication more enjoyable for you, but your commitment to what you are saying can strengthen ethos for you as a speaker. People are more likely to be moved when they are listening to someone who cares deeply about what they are saying. As you choose a topic, you should consider not only the audience's interests, but also your own.

Crafting a Research Question

research question
....
the question about
your topic you seek to
answer

Once you determine your topic, you need to focus your research around a question about that topic. This question is called your *research question*, and it guides you through the discovery process. Regardless of whether you are delivering a speech or participating in a discussion about an issue, a research question is essential for providing you with a focus for your efforts. It allows you to keep attention on the issue and not get sidetracked with extraneous information. There are three characteristics of every quality research question.

Bob Dylan

First, a research question is an open-ended question and cannot be answered with a simple "yes" or "no." The answer to the question is complex and requires a level of detail and description that is not necessary for a "yes" or "no" question. If the general topic of discussion is about a famous musician, and the specific topic is Bob Dylan, then your research question might be "What inspired Bob Dylan to write his song "Hurricane"?" Answering such a question calls for you to explore who Bob Dylan was, some history of the song, background on its topic, and even perhaps some cultural issues at play during the time he wrote the song. Of course, you could craft a myriad of different research questions from the specific topic of Bob Dylan, and each would need different data and information to answer, but any question you seek to answer must be open-ended.

In addition to being open-ended, a research question must be tailored to the topic. In other words, it must be relevant to the general and specific topic under consideration in some way. Using the Bob Dylan example again, some other successful research questions might be "What was Bob Dylan's childhood like?" "Why did Bob Dylan choose music as a career?" or even "How has Bob Dylan

Rubin "Hurricane" Carter

influenced contemporary musicians?" What would not work in the framework of this general and specific topic would be a persuasive question like, "How can I convince people to listen to Bob Dylan?" or an informative question unrelated to the topic like, "Who else was a successful speaker at the time of Bob Dylan?" This question, though it mentions Dylan, is not about Dylan, thereby violating the specific topic and creating a tangent for the discussion.

Finally, the answers to strong research questions will inevitably become the thesis statement or argument you present to others. Look at the Dylan example from a few moments ago. Let's say that your research indicates that Dylan wrote his hit song "The Hurricane" because of a personal sense of social justice, the desire to right a wrong perpetrated on a minority, and to shed some light on the situation in which Rubin "Hurricane" Carter found himself. That presents a strong thesis about the song and how it reflected the plight of Carter, a former boxer who was accused, convicted, and later exonerated for the murder of three people at a bar in Paterson, New Jersey in 1966. This topic is obviously complex and warrants further explanation, hence the need for a longer discussion built on the foundation provided by the answer to your initial research question. See Table 5.1 for some examples of poorly and properly worded research questions.

Table 5.1

Wording Research Questions	
Poorly Worded Research Questions	**Properly Worded Research Questions**
Who is Barack Obama?	What is the history of Barack Obama's political career?
Is it easy to pass Calculus 1?	What are some study strategies to successfully pass Calculus 1?
What is an easy way to break up with someone?	What is an ethical method to end a romantic relationship?
Why do service learning?	What benefits can students receive from engaging in service learning?
Are you a healthy eater?	What are the factors to consider for a healthy diet?
Why did Germany start WWII?	What were the historical, economic, and social events that contributed to Germany's military aggression leading to WWII?
Why play video games?	How can playing video games improve hand and eye coordination?

Refining Your Topic

As you search for the answer to your research question you also must adapt to the results of your research. To do this, you must be prepared to refine your specific topic and even your research question to better guide you on your quest for information. First and foremost, when you begin you must be prepared to discover that the focus when you finish researching may very well not be the focus you wanted, or thought you had, when you began. This is only natural, and is the result of good research skills.

One of these skills is note-taking. Good researchers have a method of note-taking that works best for them. This may involve note cards, photocopying information to better write margin notes, keeping a research notebook, or even using Post-it notes to label where you found information. Regardless how you do it, you need to develop a categorizing system that makes sense to you so when it comes time to organize the information you found into meaningful points you can easily do so. Taking good organized notes while you research will help you refine your topic and focus your thoughts.

Good researchers seek information with an open mind, and do not simply look for data that supports their original idea. It is important to allow contrary information to count as much as material that supports your ideas. There are multiple interpretations of a variety of different data, from statistics, to events, to even the lives of people, and good researchers find as many of these as possible to better balance their results. The more relevant information you collect, the stronger your position will become. Let the information be your guide, rather than you guiding the research.

It is tempting for any student to simply go and locate the minimum number of sources to complete the assignment, but that defeats the purpose of expanding your knowledge base and contributing to the research field. If you research properly, sometimes it can take you to places you never thought about. If you research properly, sometimes it can introduce you to a new area of interest. Remember, those who used the Library at Alexandria lived there; they did not just visit. Follow the information, don't simply collect it, and you might just find the experience enjoyable and enlightening. Approach research with a spirit of discovery and adventure, rather than as a chore to be completed.

One final tip for conducting research and developing your topic is to think big initially and then reduce your topic to something more precise. As we have explored in this section, you might begin with an initial topic after using one or more methods for generating ideas, thinking about the context of the communication, and reflecting on your own interests. Afterwards, you might create a research question that allows you to learn more about the topic that you have chosen by referring to various sources on the topic. As you continue to research, your thoughts about what you want to address might continue to evolve. As you gather more information, you can fine tune your focus and make it increasingly specific. A key consideration at this stage of invention is the amount of time that you have for the upcoming communication. A particular topic might be well-suited for the context, something of interest to the audience, and something about which you as a speaker care deeply; however, it might be simply too broad for the available time frame. Often in the professional world, messages must be delivered within very short spans of time. You might only have five minutes to explain a concept to a colleague as you are talking between appointments. You might have only three minutes within a meeting with a group of clients and suppliers to explain the process whereby a certain part of the project on which you are working will unfold. Time is money in the business world. Knowing how much time you have and adapting your topic to fit that time frame is a crucial skill for those who participate in public discourse, especially in the professional world.

A final part of refining your topic is articulating the particular stance that you are taking with regard to your topic. Your topic is the subject matter of your talk. You can describe your topic to your audience in a sentence or two, but this description is only a statement of the topic. It does not tell either you or your audience what you want the audience to understand about that topic. In written communication, we call a statement that communicates not just the topic but what you want your audience to understand about that topic, your *thesis statement*. Oral communication too is strengthened when a speaker articulates clearly yet succinctly what she or he wants the audience to understand. In Chapter 4, we explored the notion that each talking point in an explanatory talk should begin with a statement of the overarching idea that the speaker wants the audience to take away from that part of the conversation. The thesis statement is, in essence, the takeaway point for the entirety of the talk. It states in a single sentence the overarching idea that the speaker wants to communicate to the listener. As you move further into preparing the argument that you wish to present, you do well to have a clear and succinct thesis statement, which you can give to your audience in the introduction of your talk, reinforce throughout the body of the talk, and reiterate at the end of the talk before you close. Creating your thesis statement might not make sense until you have explored your research question in considerable depth, for initially, you might not know enough about your topic to decide what you want your audience to understand about it. However, as you draw to the end of your research, you are likely to have a more precise understanding of what you want to communicate to your audience. In many cases, the answer to the research question is the thesis statement for a talk. For instance, if your research question at the start of your project was "How can playing video games improve hand and eye coordination?" then your thesis statement could be a one-sentence answer to this question, which summarizes what you learned from your research and now want your audience to understand about this topic.

thesis statement

a clear and succinct one-sentence statement of the overarching idea for the talk, what the speaker wants the audience to take away from the communication as a whole; it is often the answer to the research question that guided the project

STRENGTHENING YOUR CAPACITY FOR SCHOLARSHIP

As you explore the particular topic on which you are focusing your communication, you are engaging in a process of scholarship. Scholarship is not something that only professors and other professional researchers do. It does not refer only to the publication of textbooks or articles in academic journals. Certainly, the work that people in these occupations do is one meaning for the term. However, understood more broadly, *scholarship* refers to the pursuit of knowledge by anyone who wishes to deepen or expand their understanding and the production of works by people for others to consider as they participate in and contribute to that same pursuit. To engage in scholarship means to be part of the great human effort to investigate truth, however we or others might define it, and to engage each other in a discourse that allows claims to be made, investigated, tested, refined, and sometimes rejected as people strive to ascertain what is true. The advancement of any society and the welfare of its citizens depend on this process of investigation. The Common Academic Program (CAP) of our University, which is rooted in the Catholic Marianist tradition, identifies scholarship as one of the seven habits of inquiry that all students are encouraged to develop as they pursue their respective degrees. Many of the ethical principles that we studied in Chapter 1 help to create an environment in which people can advance this great investigation of truth and provide a foundation for collective inquiry as people explore particular questions. Building capacity for scholarship is a primary goal of this course, and understanding the work that you and your fellow students are doing in creating

scholarship

the pursuit of knowledge by anyone who wishes to deepen or expand their understanding and the production of works by people for others to consider as they participate in and contribute to that same pursuit your explanatory talks, your persuasive presentations, and the dialogues in which you later will participate as scholarship is a part of its vision.

One of the challenges of engaging in scholarship in today's world is the wealth of available information. On one hand, that such a vast pool of information is available to people who wish to research a given topic is a great strength, a bounty that defies estimation. The information that people can reference in their desire to learn about a subject has increased exponentially over the last century, let alone the last few decades since the internet became accessible to the public in the 1990s. On the other hand, the availability of such a prodigious amount of information on any given topic creates its own difficulties. Encountering apparently endless sources of information after a quick internet search can be quite dizzying. Moreover, not all of the information available on a given topic is accurate, some of it being wholly false, even to the point of being dangerous to those who would make use of it.

Furthermore, in today's world, as much of the public discourse about science becomes increasingly politicized and the inner workings of institutions, including the influence of partisan agendas on their operations, have become more transparent to the public, faith in the institutions that have been entrusted conventionally with the charge of advancing the frontiers of human knowledge has deteriorated. The erosion of confidence in universities, news sources, scientific organizations, religious institutions, and government has inspired many social commentators to argue that we now live in a "post-truth society," one in which facts become less important in the positions that people take and for which they advocate in their interactions with others than how they feel or what they want to believe about particular topics.[1] Indeed, so widespread is this trend that, in 2016, the Oxford Dictionaries designated "post-truth" as the Word of the Year.[2] They defined the term as "relating to or denoting circumstances in which objective facts are less influential in shaping public opinion than appeals to emotion or personal belief."

If people are not going to give in to this trend, then they must develop those capabilities that allow them to engage in scholarship in today's information society. The term *information literacy* refers generally to the ability to read information. Specifically, it consists of four competencies:

1. The ability to identify the type of information that one needs
2. The ability to find that information
3. The ability to evaluate that information
4. The ability to use that information to produce new knowledge for others.

Literacy refers to the ability to read, while information literacy is the ability to read information. Specifically, information literacy is the ability to figure out the type of information you need, find that information, evaluate it, and properly use it. There are five characteristics of an information literate person, and in this part of the chapter we will explain each of them, paying particular attention to understanding the issues regarding the use of information. We will then differentiate between three different types of information researchers encounter and eventually use.

Just as literate people can read properly, information literate people can successfully research material they need. The five characteristics of information literate people include first the ability to determine what they need information for. They are also able to go out and find that information. Third, they can evaluate the information for accuracy, bias, and relevance to their purpose. Next, they can use the information they find to create new knowledge for themselves or others. As they use information, information literate people also appreciate the ethical and practical need to cite the sources from which they have acquired their information and thereby to avoid committing plagiarism.

Identifying the Type of Information You Need

When you have a topic and purpose you then begin to research, but for what? Good researchers take an intermediate step between determining the topic and researching the material. They determine their information need. Are they seeking background information? A strong anecdote for an attention getter? Or evidence for their claims? Knowing the type of information you need will determine where you look, because not all types of information can be found in the same place. Depending on your need, you will look at different sources to find the information that best suits your need.

Information contributes to messages in a variety of ways. Researchers sift through the data they find and determine if and how that material can be used. One way information can be used is to provide background for the topic. Another way it can help is by "adding flavor" or color to the message. The third and final form of useful information is evidence, or information that supports main points.

Background information provides context for your topic. It covers things such as definitions of key concepts, dates of events, and the key players or moments related to the topic. This type of information helps you further narrow your topic and point you in the direction of evidentiary information for your topic. Despite the fact you will undoubtedly not use all of the background information you gather, you should hold onto it as it may be useful later.

background information
material that provides context for a topic

A second form of useful information is that which may capture the audience's interest. This type of information may be only slightly related to your topic, but is nevertheless interesting and can be used to draw an audience in through use as an attention getter. It also includes tangential anecdotes that can be used to illustrate a point. The more popular forms of *tangential information* include startling statistics, famous quotations, and unique stories; all should be related to the topic under consideration in some way, but not necessarily directly linked to the topic. Each of these may not support main points you make, but they do help make the message more creative, interesting, and effective by adding unique data.

tangential information
evidence used to provide background and capture an audience's interest

The third, most common, and most important use of information is to support main points. *Evidentiary information* is information that supports main points you make and is directly related to the topic. It allows you to bring the voices of experts to bear through building on their research findings. Without evidentiary information there would be little support for any points you make, thus turning

evidentiary information
information that supports main points within a speech and is directly related to the topic

your statements into speculative opinions, rather than informed judgments. It is essentially the "meat and potatoes" of any message. This information can take the form of personal accounts, newspaper stories, or statistics, but all of it has to be directly connected to the main point it is intended to support. One example of effective use of evidentiary information in a speech can be seen in an address given by Reverend Billy Graham to the Empire Club in Canada in 1996 (see the box on page 132).

So far we have discussed both how to create a research question and what type of information we seek to help provide answers to those queries. In the next part of this chapter we will cover how to find information, because knowing how to find information is an essential characteristic of an information literate researcher.

Finding the Information You Need

Finding information is no longer as difficult as it was during the days of the Great Library of Alexandria. Advances in technology and access now allow researchers to gather plenty of materials for projects without even leaving the comfort of their own office. In this section of the chapter we will discuss three places the contemporary researcher can explore when seeking information: libraries, personal correspondence, and the World Wide Web.

Libraries

Even with the advent of the Internet the library still represents the largest and most reliable source for research materials. Every college and university still maintains a library, and many towns and cities also have public libraries that are easy to access. Libraries store books according to the Dewey Decimal System or a similar system, and many allow for searches according to that classification system or by identifying other search criteria. Libraries also typically hold subscriptions to many different research databases that can also help researchers find information they seek. Above all, the most practical and useful tool in a library for assisting in research is the staff. Library staff can answer questions about your research in a variety of ways, such as email, phone, text, and in person.

Dewey Decimal Classification System
the coding system for books, magazines, and journals used in libraries

Libraries catalog and store books, magazines, and journals using either the *Dewey Decimal Classification System* or the Library of Congress Classification System. Depending on the country, other classification systems are used, such as S. R. Ranganathan's Colon Classification System in India (see the Spotlighting Theorists for this chapter). The Dewey Decimal Classification System has been revised 22 times since it was developed by Melvil Dewey in 1876. The Library of Congress Classification System was developed in the late nineteenth century and early twentieth century to organize the Library of Congress book collection. It is the most widely used library classification system in the world and is used here at the University of Dayton's Roesch Library. Classification systems like these allow for researchers to locate several sources related to the same subject just by initially finding one. Now, libraries allow users to search for materials via library websites or online catalogs according to keyword, subject, author, and more.

SPOTLIGHTING THEORISTS: S. R. RANGANATHAN

Shiyali Ramamrita Ranganathan (1892-1972)

Library scholar, mathematician, and philosopher S. R. Ranganathan was born in Shiyali, India and brought a fresh perspective on librarianship to India and beyond. He wanted to be a mathematician, and earned his BA and MA in mathematics in his home province. He became the University Librarian for the University of Madras despite no prior experience or training in library studies or stewardship. He devised the Acknowledgement of Duplication which states that any system of classification necessarily implies a given item can be classified in in at least two different categories. For instance, a book on the history of China could be categorized under "China" and "history."

He also devised the Colon Classification Scheme in 1933, which uses subject units as the basis for organizing information. This is different from the system used in the United States and the system devised by Melvil Dewey. By 1947, he was known for successfully turning the university library at Madras into a modern research facility. His Five Laws of Library Science help frame the principles behind the management and organization of libraries. According to Ranganathan, the Five Laws of Library Science are:

1. Books are for use, not simply storage and preservation.

2. Every reader his [or her] book, or every patron should be able to obtain what they need.

3. Every book its reader, which suggests each book in the library has a person who would find it useful.

4. Save the time of the reader through business methods that improve customer service.

5. The library is a growing organism and thus must accommodate a growing staff and collection.[1]

Roesch Library is constantly updating its study spaces and accessibility of research sources in order to fit the needs of students, faculty, and staff. Although not a communication scholar, Ranganathan's theories inform the way libraries consider the relationship between the researcher and the sources they need.

1. McCrimmon, Barbara. Encyclopedia of Library History, 1st ed., s.v. "Philosophies of Librarianship." New York: Garland Publishing, Inc., 1994.

Getting Research Help at Roesch Library

Email: ref@udayton.edu
Text: 937-369-OLIB (0542)
Chat: udaytonlib (Google Talk)
Phone: 937-229-4270
Twitter: @roeschlibrary

Visit the Information or Roesch Help Desk on the first floor of Roesch Library for in-person assistance. Library staff will assist you in finding sources for your speeches and other coursework.

The same types of searches are also available for databases to which a library subscribes. These databases allow for specified searches of discipline or source specific material. For example, databases such as *JSTOR* allow a researcher to explore only academic journal articles related to politics. *Communication/Mass Media Complete* allows the same for journals and mainstream references related to communication and journalism. While those are examples of discipline specific databases, *Lexis-Nexis* is a source specific database available to many researchers. Lexis-Nexis allows people to sift through newspaper and magazine articles from publications around the world, thereby limiting its reach to newspaper and magazine sources. There are many, many more databases of which researchers can avail themselves, and the best way to find out which one best fits your needs is to make use of the most approachable tool in the library: librarians.

Even with the advances in organization and technology that revolutionized the research process, it is important to remember that librarians still remain one of the best resources for locating information. Librarians know where to go to find information on many different topics, and the chances are high they know how to help you as well. They also have that human knack for thinking on their feet and trying different tactics if initial lines of thought do not prove fruitful. It is important to talk to librarians when starting your project because they will be able to cut down on your research time and assist you in finding the most accurate, unbiased and relevant information for your project. They also will counsel you on how to find information from more places than databases and the full-text information found there. They will open doors to print sources that are not uploaded on the web, but are just as relevant to your project, sometimes even more so.

Personal Correspondence and Interviews

Libraries often carry special collections of materials previously owned by private citizens. Within these collections are personal correspondences such as letters and diaries. These materials, as well as more structured personal correspondence like surveys, make up yet another potential resource for researchers. Additionally, communications such as interviews and emails also can be used for background or evidentiary information, and can sometimes be used to provide a colorful anecdote or clever attention getter.

Researchers survey groups of people to find out their moods, feelings, or characteristics. These surveys can take two forms, the first being formal surveys. *Formal surveys* employ scientific methods to ensure random sampling, reliability and validity. These take time to administer, and oftentimes in preparing for a formal presentation, a person will not conduct an original survey, but rather find the results of one conducted by someone else that provides insight into the topic on which they are speaking. The second form of surveying is an *informal survey*, whereby the researcher asks a handful of people their opinions on a topic to add context to their work. These surveys are not reliable or valid, but can still yield useful information.

Informal surveys sometimes morph into another method of gathering information, especially when conversations become deeper than the planned survey questions.

This method, *interviewing*, allows for more information from an individual than a survey, which aggregates group responses. Interviews follow a specific format that respects both the needs of the interviewer and the rights of the interviewee.

interviewing
a direct method of gathering information from a human source that allows for questions to adapt to responses

When conducting an interview it is important to first identify what you hope to learn from the interview. After developing these goals, set out to find the person to interview who will best help you achieve those information gathering goals. Once the person is contacted and agrees to the interview you develop the questions in advance for the interview. During the interview, you must allow for the possibility of asking questions you did not initially plan for based on the responses provided by the interviewee. Following the interview it is important to take your notes from the conversation and translate them to source material as quickly as possible, because memory fades and becomes unreliable the longer you wait to record information.

One ethical issue related to interviewing concerns undercover interviewing. *Undercover interviewing* is when the interviewers either disguise themselves or their purpose in an effort to trick interviewees into sharing more information than they might have if they knew to whom they were speaking. Many reporters and researchers use this technique to gather information, but it raises ethical questions. Is it right to disguise your motives or identity to gather information? Are there other, more honest, options available to get the information you seek? Researchers must weigh these questions when thinking about hiding their identity and/or purpose during an interview.

undercover interviewing
when the interviewer disguises either himself or his purpose in an effort to trick someone into sharing more information than they may have if the interviewee knew to whom he or she was speaking

Interviews are not limited to face-to-face interactions, and can take place through email or letters; however these, especially emails, must be approached with care. Research indicates emails are often read with a negative bias, and that plays a role in how a researcher may interpret information received through email. People also write emails in a more informal style than letters, where letters typically follow proper rules of grammar. Some emails also contain disclosure notices at the end that may prohibit researchers from using the information contained within the message. It is important when sifting through such messages that you take care to see if this is the case with an email you consider using.

Internet

Email occurs on the Internet, but websites are far more commonly used as sources by researchers than email correspondence. Unfortunately, for the many benefits the Internet affords researchers, there are still many pitfalls of which a researcher must be aware. There are different types of websites, each providing information on various subjects with varying degrees of accuracy. Credibility, therefore, is a significant issue when it comes to using the Internet to find information on a topic. Researchers must take care when evaluating information found on websites.

The Library Tutorial prepared by the University of Dayton's Libraries Staff covers in depth some of the sources that you might find while you do internet research. A key skill that you must develop to find information effectively on the internet is keyword searching. In this course, the CMM 100 Research Guide also can give

Leadership in the Third Millennium by the Reverend Billy Graham

Delivered June 6, 1995

The Reverend Dr. Billy Graham presented an invited speech to the Empire Club in Toronto, Canada.[5] Reverend Graham is a well-known author and evangelical Christian minister who has promoted a message of redemption through Jesus Christ since the late 1940s. In this address Graham spoke of the importance of leadership in a world fraught with challenges. Graham utilized multiple sources of information to support the main points in his speech—all of which emphasized what he saw as the five attributes needed for contemporary leaders: integrity, personal security, sense of priority, sacrifice, and commitment.

Graham quoted numerous people throughout the address, ranging from Alexander Solzhenitsyn and George Washington to Queen Elizabeth. He quoted the Bible several times, particularly passages in the New Testament. Additionally, he quoted writers and reporters, as well as data on suicide rates in Canada. All of these various forms of evidentiary information provided data in support of his claims.

Graham's conclusion included a quotation from Sir Edmund Hillary, the famous mountain climber, who during a London speech when he reflected on his latest attempt to climb Mount Everest stated: "'I tried to conquer you once and you beat me. I tried to conquer you the second time and you took the lives of two of my best friends. But Everest, you will not be victorious. I will be victorious because you can't get any bigger, but I can." This piece of information fit perfectly with Graham's message of what it takes to be a leader in the third millennium and serves as an example of how speakers can wield information in different ways to maximum effect within a speech.

you a headstart on finding internet sources that relate especially to the theme for the course. We recommend that you see the Library Tutorial and the CMM 100 Research Guide as key supplements to the material in this chapter and that you spend some time exploring the content of each. The librarians in Roesch Library also can help you as you look for sources. These experts are trained in library science and can assist you in developing strategies and skills for finding information relating to your chosen topic.

Evaluating Information

When you find information that relates to your topic, as an information literate researcher, you must evaluate it, for much of the available information on any given topic might not be advisable to use as you build the message that you intend to communicate to others. The credibility of the information that you give matters for a number of reasons. First, the information that you give to your audience can affect *your* credibility in their eyes. If you use sources that they perceive to be inaccurate, outdated, or biased, then they might see you as a less credible speaker and might not be as receptive to the arguments that you are making. Second, you as a speaker have an ethical obligation to present quality information to your audience. The National Communication Association's credo on ethics suggests that speakers have some responsibility for the short- and long-term consequences of their communication with others. It also identifies "truthfulness, accuracy, honesty, and reason" as ethical values to uphold in communication with others. Providing inaccurate information to an audience can lead to actual harm to that audience, if the audience tries to make decisions on the basis of that information. Giving biased information to an audience as though it were impartial contributes further to the general uncertainty and distrust that seem to be characteristic of a post-truth society. If you wish to live in a world that is not characterized by these qualities, then you must strive to provide the most accurate and unbiased information that you can provide to your audiences.

There are several criteria that you should consider as you evaluate the information that you find, whether you find it in a published book, an article in an academic journal, or a web page. One of these criteria is *accuracy*. Accuracy refers to the correctness or truthfulness of the information in the source. Another criterion, *bias*, refers to the attempt to unfairly influence someone or the perception of something. The information in a source can be accurate, but presented in a manner that unfairly influences how one side is perceived. A key part of evaluating bias is determining the purpose for which the information was created and why it is being communicated in the particular source in which it now appears. A third criterion is *relevance*. The information in a given source might be highly accurate and relatively free of bias yet it does not relate to the topic that you have chosen except perhaps in a peripheral manner. Such information, if you were to include it, could become a distraction or otherwise might dilute the focus of your message. A fourth criterion is *currency*. Currency relates to the timeliness of the information. In general, the more recent the source of information, the more useful it is, as you design your message. If you are not careful, you might use outdated statistics, quotations, or data. Information, especially on the internet, changes quickly, so even a source that is only five or six years old might be outdated, relative to other available information. In some cases, you do not want the most recent information, but the information that is most recent to the time of an event or occurrence that you are researching. For instance, if you are discussing the 2008 Presidential Election, blogs and postings from the time of the election itself might be more useful to you than those from today. When one is researching a historical event, the most current sources are not always the most desirable ones. A final criterion is *authorship*. Knowing who wrote the source and what that person or organization's credentials are can be helpful in determining whether using the information from that source is advisable. The author might not have adequate qualifications for making the claims that she or he is making. She, he, or they also might have a reputation in the eyes of certain people that might lead your audience to question the credibility of the source.

accuracy
the truthfulness or correctness of a source

bias
presenting information in a way that unfairly influences someone's perception of something

relevance
information that is connected to the topic

currency
timeliness of the information

authorship
who wrote the information and are they credible

The Library Tutorial provides a list of questions for each of these criteria that you can use to make critical judgments about the advisability of using information from any given source. It also provides an acronym to help you to remember these five criteria for evaluating sources: C-R-A-A-P. If you are trying to determine whether a source is credible, then subject it to the C-R-A-A-P test:

- Is the source **current**?
- Is the source **recent**?
- Is the source **accurate**?
- What do you know about the **author**?
- What can you determine about the **purpose** of the source?

Often students want to use encyclopedic sources when doing research, probably due to the quick concise synopsis that an encyclopedia can give on a topic. There are online encyclopedic sources as well as written ones. Wikipedia is a common online encyclopedic reference. While there are certain advantages to using such sources, they are not acceptable for providing evidence to the claims that you make in any formal communication message that others will be scrutinizing. First, they are not primary sources, but rather summaries of information available on a given topic, including other works written on the topic. For information that you are going to provide as evidence, you should find the primary sources written directly by authors with expertise on the subject in question, such as the original research articles on the topic. Also, in the case of online encyclopedic articles, entries on these websites can be unreliable. Anyone can post, edit, or delete information within entries on sites such as Wikipedia. One has reason to question the veracity of the content found there. An information literate researcher will not use these sources as references but rather as a place to go to get ideas for potential topics, research questions, or background information that can direct you to other more credible sources.

Table 5.2

Using Wikipedia and Other Online Encyclopedias	
Improper Uses	**Proper Uses**
Citing in paper or speech	Background information that can direct you to other sources
Believing its accuracy is always reliable	Ideas for speech topics

Using Information to Create New Knowledge for Others

The fourth component of information literacy, so integral to scholarship as defined earlier in this chapter, is using the material garnered through research to create new knowledge for others. Information literate researchers use the information that they discover to educate and enlighten not only themselves, but also others around them. They combine new and old information to create fresh perspectives on topics. They may also provide valuable information about something to a group of people who were unaware of what they needed to know about it.

One way in which you can share your own research and learn from the research of others during your time here at the University of Dayton is through participation in the Brother Joseph W. Stander Symposium. The Stander Symposium, which takes place every April at UD, is designed to recognize student learning through faculty-mentored undergraduate and graduate research, scholarship, and artistic accomplishments from all academic units at the University of Dayton. The Stander Symposium represents the Marianist tradition of education through community and is the principal campus-wide event in which faculty and students demonstrate our mission to be a "community of learners." More information on the Stander Symposium can be found at http://stander.udayton.edu. Building new knowledge from old research and information is one of the primary aims of research.

Creating an Argument

To produce new knowledge for others using the information that you have found, you need to create an argument. An *argument* is essentially a claim that you are making about a given topic that you support with evidence and reasons. While the term argument is often associated with persuasion, one can make factual arguments that set forth claims about what is true or real and provide evidence and reasons that support those claims. In general, arguments of this sort form the main part of messages that have the general purpose of explaining something to others, while arguments that focus on questions about the value of something or that urge a particular form of action typically form the main part of messages that have the general purpose of persuading an audience. In other words, both explanation and persuasion involve making arguments; they differ with respect to the arguments that the speaker makes.

argument
a claim that you are making about a given topic that you support with evidence and reasons

Any complex message in communication is typically made of many arguments, not just one. Each point in an explanatory talk, for instance, is essentially an argument. In each point, you make a claim that you want your listener to accept as true. To support that claim, you offer information that functions as evidence or support for that claim, and that evidence connects with the claim through reasoning that you as a speaker might or might not make explicit to the listener. If your listener challenges the argument that you have made, then you might need to provide additional support that shows the soundness of your reasoning. When you feel that you have made a convincing argument, you move to the next talking point and begin crafting a new argument focusing on different claim.

claim
the conclusion that the speaker wants the audience to accept as true

British philosopher Stephen Toulmin provides a model that identifies the basic components of arguments as people make them in the course of their everyday communication with others. Toulmin's model has three primary elements. The *claim* is the conclusion that the speaker wants the audience to accept as true. While the audience might accept the claim at face value, often they demand some evidence that supports the claim. This evidence is called the *grounds* of the argument. The grounds of an argument can take many forms. Some common forms of evidence that people give to support claims are statistics, examples, expert testimony, and stories about particular illustrative or exemplary cases. The third primary element of an argument in Toulmin's model is the *warrant*.

grounds
evidence in the Toulmin model

warrant
explains why the grounds support the claim and makes that connection clear to the audience

The warrant is the statement that allows for movement from the grounds to the claim. In order for the audience to accept that the grounds that the speaker has provided do indeed support the claim that she or he has made, the warrant must be accepted. Often, the speaker does not state the warrant explicitly; it remains unspoken. However, if the audience were to question the connection between the grounds and the claim, then the speaker might need to provide the warrant directly.

For example, suppose that you are talking with a group of people who live in your area about ways of improving the community. As the participants in the conversation discuss different ideas for strengthening the community, you make the suggestion, "Offering a program that helps middle school aged girls to cope with depression would strengthen the community." One of the other participants is intrigued by your suggestion and gives you an expression of curiosity. You respond, "Depression is a major problem for many adolescent girls even when they are preteens. Did you know that the National Institute of Mental Health that says that over 3 million adolescents in 2015 admitted to suffering from a major depressive episode—that is 12.5% of the population of adolescents ages 12 to 17. Between the sexes, the number was considerably higher in girls than in boys. Approximately 20% of girls admitted to suffering from a major episode of depression: that is 1 in 5 girls." The other participants look at you as if they would like you to explain your idea further, so you explain, "If depression is a major problem for many middle school aged girls, then a program that provides girls with coping strategies for depression can help girls who participate to have better mental health. Having such a large percentage of the youth population of a community to have better mental health will help the community as a whole to improve."

In this brief example, one can see all three primary elements of Toulmin's model.[3] You as the speaker put forth a claim that you want your listeners to accept: offering a program that helps middle school aged girls to cope with depression would strengthen the community. When your listener seems to require support for your claim, you provide some evidence in the form of a factual statement about the seriousness and incidence of depression for girls who fall into that age range, drawn from a research report from a well-known, highly reputable source. This is the grounds for the argument. When your listener seems to want further explanation, you make explicit how your evidence supports the claim. You explain that the girls who go through the program can learn how to cope with depression better. This will lead to their having improved mental health. Having half of the youth population in a

Figure 5.1
Toulmin model

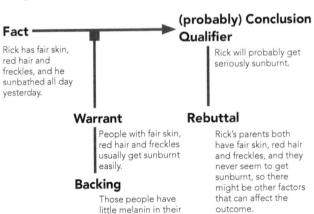

community to have better mental health will benefit the community as a whole. Initially, your reasoning that connects the grounds to the claim is unspoken, but you then make it explicit. Once you make it explicit, that you are essentially using causal reasoning becomes clear: the program will cause better mental health for girls, which in turn will cause the community to benefit. In explaining your reasoning connecting the grounds to the claim, you provide your audience with the warrant of the argument.

Toulmin's model also recognizes several secondary elements of an argument that, in any given case, might be incorporated into the argument. Often, the audience will accept the argument as a speaker gives it, and the speaker can move onto the next argument. However, in some cases, the audience does not accept the argument, even after you explain your reasoning. If the audience rejects the warrant, then you might need to provide support for the warrant itself. In Toulmin's model, this support is called **backing**. Suppose one of the participants challenges your reasoning and says, "You don't know that a program like that will actually benefit the community in the end. How do we know that giving girls coping strategies will actually help them when they suffering from depression?" You might respond with an additional statement of support for the reasoning that you previously offered. For instance, you might respond, "I've seen it work firsthand. My former middle school worked with some local child psychologists and professors at the university to create a program like this. They offered it in the local area over a period of two years. Over 100 girls went through the program and reported a much lower incidence of major depression than the national average and also among girls in a neighboring community where the program wasn't offered."

backing
support for the argument

Sometimes a speaker can make a stronger argument by anticipating the objections that someone might raise against the argument and offering statements that overturn these challenges. In Toulmin's model, such statements are called a **rebuttal**. For instance, in making the argument about creating a program in the community that helps adolescent girls to cope with depression, you might anticipate a counterargument that "such programs only work if the participants remember those strategies once they leave the program and have to face the realities of their everyday lives." Accordingly, when you first make the argument, you might acknowledge that potential objection and explain that the program has an element of accompaniment built into it, whereby the girls continue to have contact with a psychological professional and a peer group in their area after they complete the initial training, with whom they meet periodically, remember the strategies they have learned, and reflect on how their efforts to cope are going.

rebuttal
a refutation or contradiction

Finally, a speaker can introduce a **qualifier** into the argument to characterize the degree of certainty with which she or he is offering the argument. A qualifier is a word or statement that indicates the level of probability for the argument to bear out as given. For instance, the claim "offering a program that helps middle school aged girls to cope with depression *will* strengthen the community" expresses a greater degree of certainty than the claim "offering a program that helps middle school aged girls to cope with depression *probably* will strengthen the community." In some cases, a speaker might not want to offer the claim with absolute certainty, but rather express a conditional or limited degree of certainty.

qualifier
a word or statement that indicates the level of probability for the argument to bear out as given

As you craft the message that you wish to deliver to your audience, you can use Toulmin's model to ensure that you have the three principal elements of an argument as Toulmin has defined it. If you wish, you can introduce any of the three secondary elements as well.

Citing Using APA Style

Producing knowledge for others to consider as people investigate truth often takes place within a community of scholars. Sometimes these communities have their own conventions about how people ought to present their work for others. These conventions often include specific expectations about how to reference the sources from which the information that one has used in making one's arguments. Referencing one's sources is important for a number of reasons. First, it gives credit to those people whose work is the foundation for one's own work. Giving credit to these others is a way of showing appreciation for them and not claiming as one's own original work what they produced. When one presents information and does not cite a source, one implicitly sends the message to others that the information came from one's own original research or firsthand experience. If this is not the case, then one is falsely claiming to be the source of this information. Second, citing sources allows others to examine the foundations of one's arguments. When one is part of a community of people who share a commitment to investigating truth, making the sources that have shaped one's thinking as transparent as possible is a way of enabling others to consider those sources for themselves and possibly to confirm one's interpretations of the information that they provide or to offer alternative explanations. Third, citing one's sources builds one's own credibility. It sends the message to the audience, "I've done my homework on this topic" or "I have prepared myself to make the claims that I am making."

American Psychological Association (APA)
....
preferred reference manual for social science communication scholars

Within the field of communication there are two preferred forms for references, each one slightly different from the other. Most who conduct rhetorical research follow the Chicago Manual of Style (CMS), while those who utilize a social science approach to exploring communication follow the *American Psychological Association (APA)*. You may also encounter a third citation style, that of the Modern Language Association (MLA), when you do research in other fields within the liberal arts and humanities. In addition to formal written bibliographies and in-text citations, students must also verbally attribute their sources when speaking. Because CMM 100 uses APA style as a requirement, in this section, we present a basic overview of APA style.

APA uses in-text parenthetical citations in a paper or an outline. These occur at the end of sentences or after an author's name that is referenced in the sentence. In the event the source does not have an identifiable author then it is referenced using a truncated form of the title and the year of publication. In this section we will offer some brief guidance for some common reference types using APA style.

First, let's look at some examples of in-text citations using APA:

- One author, not directly quoted: (Smith, 1990)
- Multiple authors, not directly quoted: (Smith, Jones, & Thompson, 1998)

- One author, directly quoted: (Johnson, 1981, p. 242)
- Multiple authors, directly quoted: (Smith, Jones, & Thompson, 1990, p. 461)
- Website with author, not directly quoted: (Stevens, 2008, December 1)
- Website with no author, not directly quoted: ("The sky is blue," 2003, April 2)
- Website with author, directly quoted: (Morris, 2001, June 1, para. 2)
- Website with no author, directly quoted: ("Great sea," 1991, February 2, para. 1)
- Personal interview: (Peter Hong, personal communication, April 27, 2015).

There are some idiosyncrasies to keep in mind as well. For instance, if a work has more than six authors, you should use the last name of the first author and then the phrase "et al." to refer to the rest of the authors. Additionally, if the author's name is written in the sentence then the parenthetical citation needs only to have the year or the year, and page number if it is directly quoted from the source. Finally, when a work's author is credited as "Anonymous," cite the word "Anonymous" followed by the date in the parenthetical citation.

In addition to the in-text citations, APA calls for a "References" page, which provides a list of all sources that the author has cited in the text of the paper or outline. The References page is organized alphabetically and contains only the sources referenced within the project. Sources not cited in the paper or outline are not included in the References page. If there is no author, the title is treated as author when it comes to placing it in the proper alphabetical spot in the works cited list. Additionally, if the entry runs onto a second line, then that next line, and all subsequent lines for the entry are indented. This is called a hanging indent.

The following are the APA forms for some types of sources commonly included in papers and outlines:

Journal Article in Print:

Author Last Name, First Initial. Middle Initial. (Year of publication). Article title. *Journal Title, Volume* (Issue), starting page-ending page.

Smith, J. (1993). Studies show bibliographies are easy to do. *European Journal of Communication, 19*(1), 89–114.

Christians, C. G., & Fortner, R. S. (1981). The media gospel. *Journal of Communication, 31*, 190-199.

- Lead with the last name of the author, followed by first initial and middle initial and then the year of publication in parentheses. If there are multiple authors, list authors' names sequentially in this format, separating the last two authors' names in the list with the "&" symbol, not the word "and."

- Capitalize only the first letter of the first word in the article title, as well as in any subtitle. All other words are not capitalized.

- Proper nouns are an exception. Capitalize them always.

- Capitalize the first letter of all words in the journal title except prepositions (of, in, for) and articles (e.g., a, an, the, that)

- Include the issue number only if the journal is paginated by issue. Otherwise, only include the volume number.

Journal Article from an Online Database with a DOI Assigned:

Author Last Name, First Initial. Middle Initial. (Year of publication). Article title. *Journal Title, Volume* (Issue), starting page-ending page. doi:0000000/000000000000 or http://dx.doi.org/10.0000/0000

Brownlie, D. (2007). Toward effective poster presentations: An annotated bibliography. European *Journal of Marketing, 41*, 1245-1283. doi:10.1108/03090560710821161

Wooldridge, M.B., & Shapka, J. (2012). Playing with technology: Mother-toddler interaction scores lower during play with electronic toys. *Journal of Applied Developmental Psychology, 33*(5), 211-218. http://dx.doi.org/10.1016/j.appdev.2012.05.005

- Format the citation for the journal article as you would for the same article in print.

- If a DOI has been assigned to the article that you are referencing, then include it after the page numbers after "doi:" or with the "http://" designation. The DOI System provides an identifier for managing information on publications in digital databases. When a DOI identifier has been provided for an article, this identifier can be used as a link to access the article.

Journal Article from an Online Database with No DOI Assigned:

Author Last Name, First Initial. Middle Initial. (Year of publication). Article title. *Journal Title, Volume* (Issue), starting page-ending page. Retrieved from http://www.website.com

Smyth, A. M., Parker, A. L., & Pease, D. L. (2002). A study of enjoyment of peas. *Journal of Abnormal Eating, 8*(3), 120-125. Retrieved from http://www.articlehomepage.com/full/url/

- Format the citation for the journal article as you would for the same article in print.

- If you are referencing a journal article that appears online and no DOI has been assigned, then include the URL for the website from which you have retrieved the article. Do not include a period at the end of the URL.

Book:

Author Last Name, First Initial. Middle Initial. (Year of publication). *Book title: Book subtitle.* **City, State: Publisher.**

Deetz, S. A. (1992). *Democracy in an age of corporate colonization: Developments in communication and the politics of everyday life.* Albany, NY: SUNY Press.

Lead with the author's last name, followed by first and middle initials. If there are multiple authors, separate the authors' names with the "&" symbol, not the word "and."

- Italicize book title and the subtitle, if one is given.

- Capitalize only the first letter of the first word in the book title and the first letter of the first word in the subtitle, if one is given.

- Proper nouns are an exception. Capitalize any proper nouns in the book title.

- Separate title and subtitle with a colon.

Chapter or Essay in an Edited Book or Volume:

Author Last Name, First Initial. Middle Initial. (Year of publication). Chapter or essay title. In Editor First Initial. Middle Initial. Last Name & Second Editor First Initial. Middle Initial. Last Name (Eds.), *Title of edited book or volume* **(pp. starting page-ending page). City, State: Publisher.**

Whedbee, K. E. (2008). In other's words: Plagiarism as deceptive communication. In R. L. Johannesen, K. S. Valde, & K. E. Whedbee (Eds.), *Ethics in human communication* (6th ed., pp. 283-292). Long Grove, IL: Waveland Press.

- Lead with essay or article author(s)—last name, then first initial and middle initial, if middle initial is given—followed by year of publication.

- Capitalize first letter of first word in chapter or essay title and subtitle, as you do for a journal article.

- After the word "In," give names of editors for the book or volume in which the chapter or essay appears. Unlike you did for the author's name, write the editor's name, beginning with the first initial, then the middle initial (if one is given), and the full last name. Separate the names of multiple editors with the "&" symbol, not the word "and." Afterwards, place the designation "Ed." in parentheses to designate a single editor and "Eds." in parentheses to designate multiple editors.

- Capitalize first letter of first word in edited book or volume title and sub-title.

- Italicize book or volume title.

- If you are citing a specific edition of the book or volume, then include the edition number followed by "ed." in parentheses.

- Include page numbers in parentheses—the same as the edition number, if applicable—after the abbreviation "pp." Use "p." if the essay or chapter spans only one page.

Website:

Author Last Name, First Initial. Middle Initial. (Year Published, Month Date). *Article title.* **Retrieved from URL.**

Simpson, H. (2007, April 1). *A letter to John Smith.* Retrieved from http://www.xgtsfjmnouiyh.com/jstr/ htm/070908

- Lead with author last name, followed by first initial and middle initial (if given).

- If the website has a corporate author, give the name of the organization in place of the name of individual author(s).

- Give publication date in parentheses, beginning with year published, then the month and day. If no publication date is given, use the abbreviation "n.d." to designate that "no date" was provided.

- Italicize website title.

- Capitalize only first letter of first word in the title and also in subtitle (if present).

- Capitalize all proper nouns, e.g. John Smith in the above example.

- If the website that you are referencing contains more than one web page, use the URL for the homepage or start page. Do not put a period at the end of the URL.

Online Video:

Author Last Name, First Initial. Middle Initial. [Screen name]. (Year, Month Day). *Title of video* **[Video file]. Retrieved from http://xxxxx**

Apsolon, M. [markapsolon]. (2011, September 9). *Real ghost girl caught on Video Tape 14* [Video file]. Retrieved from http://www.youtube.com/watch?v=6nyGCbxD848

- Lead with author last name, followed by first initial and middle initial (if given). Then give screen name in brackets.

- Provide title of video in italics. Capitalize only the first letter of the first word in the title – and in the subtitle, if given – with the exception of proper nouns.

- Follow title with the words "Video file" in brackets.

- Give URL after the words "Retrieved from" with no period at the end.

In the case of a Youtube video, sometimes the screen name of the person who posted the video appears without the real name of the person. In this case, use the screen name in the author position without brackets. For instance:

Screen name. (Year, Month Day). *Title of video* [Video file]. Retrieved from http://xxxxx

Bellofolletti. (2009, April 8). *Ghost caught on surveillance camera* [Video file]. Retrieved from http://www.youtube.com/watch?v=Dq1ms2JhYBI&feature=related

- If the poster of the video is an organization, use the organization's name as the screen name.

Newspaper Article Retrieved from an Online Source:

Author Last Name, First Initial. Middle Initial. (Year of Publication, Month Day). Title of article. *Title of Newspaper.* Retrieved from http://www.someaddress.com/full/url/

Parker-Pope, T. (2008, May 6). Psychiatry handbook linked to drug industry. *The New York Times.* Retrieved from http://well.blogs.nytimes.com/2008/05/06/psychiatry-handbook-linked-to-drug-industry/?_r=0

- Lead with the full last name of the author of the newspaper article, followed by the first initial and middle initial (if given). If there are multiple authors, separate the last two authors in the list with the "&" symbol, not the word "and."

Data Sets:

Author, First Initial. Middle Initial. (Year). *Title of data set* [Data file]. Retrieved from URL

Corporate author. (Year). *Title of data set* [Data file]. Retrieved from URL

United States Department of Housing and Urban Development. (2008). *Indiana income limits* [Data file]. Retrieved from http://www.huduser.org/Datasets/IL/IL08/in_fy2008.pdf

- Lead with author last name, followed by first initial and middle initial. Then give year in parentheses. If citing a corporate author, then given the name of the organization in place of the names of individual authors.
- Italicize the title of the data set. Capitalize only the first letter of the first word in the title – and in the subtitle (if present). Follow the title with the words "Data file" in brackets.
- Give the URL after the words "Retrieved from" with no period.

Graphic Data:

Name of organization conducting research. (Year). [Explanation of type of data is given and the form in which it has been given]. *Project Name.* **Retrieved from URL**

Solar Radiation and Climate Experiment. (2007). [Graph illustration the SORCE Spectral Plot May 8, 2008]. *Solar Spectral Data Access from the SIM, SOLSTICE, and XPS Instruments.* Retrieved from http://lasp.colorado.edu/cgi-bin/ion-p?page=input_data_for_ spectra.ion

- Lead with name of the organization conducting the research, followed by the year in parentheses. In the event that individuals have conducted the research, lead with their names in this position, using the format that you have used for the authors of other types of sources.

- In brackets, give a brief description of the type of data that is provided and the form in which it has been given.

- Italicize the name of the project. Capitalize all words in the title except articles or prepositions, as you would capitalize the title of a journal.

- Give the URL after the words "Retrieved from" with no period at the end.

Interviews or Emails:

Personal interviews or emails do not need to appear in APA reference pages, but must be cited in-text by listing the initials and last name of the interviewee and as exact a date as possible for the interview.

Citations allow readers and audience members to know where you found the information you used so they can verify it, or even use it for their own work. It also is designed to give proper credit to the person whose ideas you are using.

If you have questions about citing types of sources other than those that we have listed in this chapter, we recommend that you consult the Style Manual for the American Psychological Association (6th edition). You also can find some information about formatting in-text sources and the references page at the Purdue Online Writing Lab at https://owl.english.purdue.edu/owl/section/2/10/. Many of the examples that we have given here in this chapter appear at that site.

Verbal Attribution

verbal attribution
the act of citing sources orally when you give information that you have taken from those sources

You not only need to cite sources within your manuscript or outline, but you must orally cite those sources during the presentation or talk as well. This is much easier than it sounds, and citing your sources helps you to build credibility with your audience or listener. Similar to citing sources in your written work, you must cite the source for any information that you give that you did not acquire through original research or other firsthand experience. The act of citing sources orally when you give information that you have taken from those sources is called *verbal attribution*.

An effective oral citation includes the following information:

1. The name of the author
2. A brief statement of the author's credentials
3. The title of the work in which the author gives the information in question
4. The date of the publication of the work in which the author provided the information

Giving the credentials of the author is necessary, especially if the author is likely to be unfamiliar to the audience. The description of the author's credentials need not be lengthy. Mentioning the official title or position that the author holds, such as a governmental, administrative, or academic position, or some formal certification that the author holds, such as a doctoral degree in a relevant field, is sufficient. If what qualifies a particular author to make the claims that she or he is making is not necessarily the position that she or he holds or some formal credential, but rather is a particular life experience that she or he has had, then you should describe briefly the experience when you cite the author.

Usually the oral citation begins with a phrase such as "According to…" or "So-and-so states…" For instance,

- "According to Dr. Geoffrey Stone, the Edward H. Levi Distinguished Service Professor of Law at the University of Chicago Law School, in his book *Perilous Times*, published in 2004…"

- "Many major league baseball players used steroids in the 1990s, as stated in the Mitchell Report produced by former Senator George Mitchell and his investigative team, published in 2007…"

Once you have stated the full oral citation once for a source, you do not need to say all of the information that you gave during the initial citation, if you refer to that source again. Referring only to the author will suffice, as you have already given the audience the information that they need, if they wish to take a look at the source on their own.

PLAGIARISM AND INTEGRITY IN SCHOLARSHIP

In addition to the four characteristics we just discussed, information literate individuals understand the gravity of the issues involved with information use. The most important of these issues is that of giving credit where credit is due. Not to give credit to people whose work you use in a report or speech is *plagiarism*, or to present another person's work or ideas as your own. It is important to understand that intent is irrelevant with plagiarism, so it is better to over-cite sources than not cite them enough.

plagiarism
to present another person's work or ideas as your own

Plagiarism comes in three different forms, but all are equally wrong. The first is *incremental plagiarism*, or failing to give credit for pieces borrowed from a source. Incremental plagiarism is the most common form of plagiarism, as many people fail to reference statements or information they paraphrased or even lifted from a source. In 2005 Republican Nevada Congressman Jim Gibbons ran for governor and delivered a speech that seemed to rail against liberals. In this speech

incremental plagiarism
failure to give proper credit for parts of a speech that are borrowed from others

he delivered fifteen paragraphs that were taken directly from a speech delivered by Alabama Auditor Beth Chapman two years earlier.[4] This is a perfect example of incremental plagiarism. Another example is when students use paragraphs from sources in their presentations or papers, change only a few words, and fail to cite the source.

patchwork plagiarism
....
stealing ideas from two or more sources without referencing them

Another form of plagiarism is called *patchwork plagiarism*, or stealing ideas from more than one source and pawning them off as your own. Patchwork plagiarism involves lifting whole sections of information from several sources and linking them together without referencing any of them. This may appear to involve using various forms of information to build new knowledge, but it is not, as there is little to no integration of the sources into a coherent argument. This type of plagiarism occurs most often when students list information within a project without referencing where the data came from. Verbally citing your sources is an important component of being an ethical and civilly aware speaker. It also improves your credibility as a speaker.

global plagiarism
....
taking an entire speech from a single source and pawning it off as your own

The final form of plagiarism, *global plagiarism*, is the one most people are familiar with. Global plagiarism involves stealing an entire speech or paper from a single source and calling it one's own. Global plagiarism takes many forms, from cutting and pasting, to having someone write a speech for you, to even buying a paper off a website. All of these do not give credit to the source of the ideas and information that became the project and as such represent plagiarism.

Perhaps the greatest problem with plagiarism, aside from the fact it is an ethical and moral affront, is the fact it destroys the fruits of researching. No longer are you able to learn about something, build new ideas, or expose yourself to things you may never have explored if not through research. You lose the opportunity to expand your own knowledge and help others do the same. Plagiarism attacks the very heart of a university's mission, and as a result is typically punished harshly; it is the worst academic crime possible. Information literate researchers are aware of all of this and avoid plagiarism at all costs by properly citing the information they find when researching.

ghostwriting
....
to write for and in the name of another person

There is one exception to the rule when it comes to presenting someone else's ideas as your own—but it does not apply in the classroom. *Ghostwriting*, or writing for and in the name of another person, is a fairly common practice among politicians and business leaders. In fact, presidents employ an entire speechwriting staff to write their speeches because they simply do not have the time to write their own speeches. Business executives also have staff researchers who write many of their presentations because of time constraints.

The difference between ghostwriting and plagiarism is that ghostwriters are professionals who still abide by the rules of research and expectations for citations. They also allow the speaker to take credit and accountability for what is eventually said in the presentation, and most importantly, know that their participation in the speech's development is not hidden from the audience. In short, we all know the president uses speechwriters, but in the case we discussed earlier about Jim Gibbons of Nevada, there was no ghostwriter and the material was appropriated from a source without letting the audience know from whence it came.

Ghostwriting is not a new phenomenon. In classical Greece citizens often hired professionals to help them write speeches. The Sophists whom we mentioned in Chapter 1 sometimes fulfilled this role, and made a pretty penny doing so! Clients often sought out professionals to help them write speeches to use in assemblies or in court, much the same way those business leaders and politicians use ghostwriters today.

SUMMARY

Research and preparation are the most important steps toward developing successful and ethical messages. Proper research skills come from being an information literate person. Information literate people know what they need information for, where to go and find it, how to use it properly, and the ethical implications of information use. It is important to make use of all of the research tools at your disposal, from librarians to the Internet, when seeking different types of sources and information. It is equally important to use a consistent and accepted citation style when referencing material you gathered from other places.

KEY TERMS

accuracy   131

American Psychological Association
   (APA)   138

argument   135

authorship   133

background information   127

backing   119

bias   133

claim   135

Communication/Mass Media
   Complete   130

currency   133

Dewey Decimal Classification
   System   128

evidentiary information   127

formal survey   119

ghostwriting   146

global plagiarism   146

grounds   135

incremental plagiarism   145

informal survey   130

information literacy   126

interviewing   119

JSTOR   130

Lexis-Nexis   130

patchwork plagiarism   146

plagiarism   145

qualifier   137

rebuttal   137

relevance   133

research question   122

scholarship   125

tangential information   127

thesis statement   125

undercover interviewing   131

verbal attribution   119

warrant   135

REVIEW QUESTIONS

1. What are the five characteristics of the information literate researcher?
2. What are the three primary forms of information?
3. What are the three main places to find source material?
4. What are the three major citation styles?

THINK ABOUT IT

1. Is it ever ethical to employ undercover interviewing?
2. How do you determine if you need to cite a piece of information?
3. Which reference style is better? Why?

ACTIVITIES FOR ACTION

1. Sit down with a group of friends, classmates, or colleagues and brainstorm topics for speeches. Each time a person introduces a statement about a topic they are interested in reframe it as a research question. By the end of this discussion you should have a list of potential speech topics that are written as research questions rather than topic statements.

2. Find a partner and go on a scavenger hunt for the following items: a magazine article, a newspaper article, a government document, a peer reviewed journal article in communication studies, a documentary film, a news page from microfiche records, a survey result, a blog entry, and an interview transcript. To complicate this activity, give yourself a topic that each item must relate to. For instance, find one of each item related to the topic of the "Beatles musical invasion."

ENDNOTES

1. Francis Fukuyama, "The Post-Truth Society," https://news.stanford.edu/2016/10/04/post-truth-society/, 4 Oct 2016, using citation style consistent with rest of citations in book.

2. Amy B. Wang, 'Post-truth' named 2016 word of the year by Oxford Dictionaries, Washington Post, 16 Nov 2016, https://www.washingtonpost.com/news/the-fix/wp/2016/11/16/post-truth-named-2016-word-of-the-year-by-oxford-dictionaries/?noredirect=on&utm_term=.c998d143fcb2

3. Russell T. Church and Charles Wilbanks, *Values and Policies in Controversy: An Introduction to Argumentation and Debate*, Scottsdale, AZ: Gorsuch Scarisbrick, 1986.

4. Edward Alexander Parsons, *The Alexandrian Library* (Barking, Essex, England: Elsevier Publishing, 1952), 83–106.

5. Ibid.

6. Roy MacLeod, "Introduction: Alexandria in History and Myth," in *The Library of Alexandria: Centre of Learning in the Ancient World*, ed. Roy MacLeod (New York, NY: St. Martin's Press, 2000), 4–7.

7. Erin Neff, "Gibbons's Speech Plagiarism: 15 Paragraphs Came from Copyrighted Talk by Alabama Woman," *Las Vegas Review Journal*, March 4, 2005.

8. http://speeches.empireclub.org/61435/data?n=2 (accessed May 28, 2011).

Interteaching Session

Dialogue

Review the definition of a post-truth society from the chapter. Then watch the video clip of Stanford University political scientist Francis Fukuyama as he talks about the concept of a post-truth society, available at https://news.stanford.edu/2016/10/04/post-truth-society/.

1. How does Fukuyama describe a post-truth society?

2. What does he suggest as key factors that have led to the creation of such a condition today?

3. Do you agree with his assessment of today's society? If so, give some examples of post-truth conditions in today's world. If not, give an argument regarding why his assessment is false.

4. What challenges does a post-truth society present to scholarship?

Performance

With your groupmates, choose a topic that one could address in your upcoming explanatory assignment in light of the course theme for this semester. Do some preliminary research on this topic with the purpose of finding evidentiary information. Find two sources: one that you deem to be a credible source of information for your explanatory talk and one that you deem to lack credibility. Prepare a short explanation that you can give to the class regarding how each source does or does not meet the various criteria of the C-R-A-A-P schema.

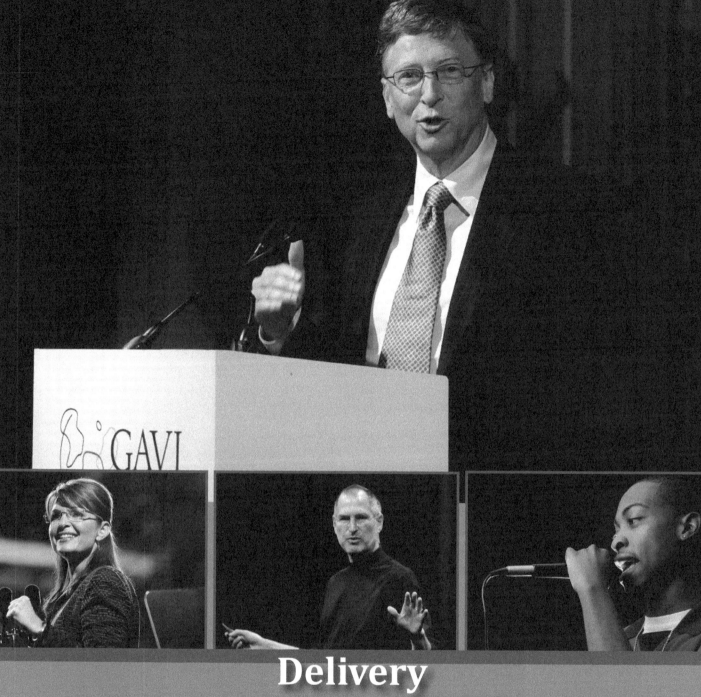

Delivery

Practically SPEAKING

In the 1986 movie *Ferris Bueller's Day Off*, the economics teacher, played by Ben Stein, went on a tirade about the economy when his students did not respond to questions.[1] Using a lethargic delivery, Stein woefully made his potentially vibrant points seem irrelevant, boring, and hard to focus upon. Stein used the term "Anyone?" fourteen times during the entire scene. While he was speaking the students in the class predictably fell asleep, put their heads down on desks, and stared off into the distance, daydreaming. Stein's portrayal of the dreadfully boring teacher emphasizes the importance of vocal and physical delivery when addressing an audience.

The combination of word repetition, vocal emphasis, and proper posture and gestures can add force and meaning to words, but when delivered in a monotone with no energy, the rhetorical effect is minimal. In addition to no vocal variety Stein's posture was lethargic, making him appear as bored as his students. He lacked presence, despite having content.

Verbal delivery works in tandem with nonverbal delivery. The verbal content of Stein's message is clear, but the repeated begging for "anyone" to answer did nothing to get the audience's attention. His leaning posture and pleading facial expressions underscored his poor verbal delivery and worsened matters. As illustrated by Stein, verbal and nonverbal delivery can display the speaker's attitude toward themselves and the audience.

Too much focus on delivery, however, can also produce problems. A powerful delivery can detract from content if the audience members focus more on delivery than content. Good delivery comes through practice and balances a desire to gain and maintain attention with the need to keep the audience focused on the message. Audiences do not notice good delivery; rather they remember the content conveyed without saying much about how the speaker conveyed it.

A speaker may have great ideas, a new way to do something, or a way to improve life on campus, but if the speaker mumbles, does not project their voice, fails to make eye contact and does not present themselves well the ideas will likely be lost upon the audience. All of us have seen, or delivered, a message in an awkward manner. This not only makes the speaker feel uncomfortable, but can also cause anxiety and even mental pain in the audience, which makes it doubtful that the audience will believe the information or take the action advocated by the speaker.

This chapter will cover the basics of good delivery, both verbal and nonverbal, discuss how the two work together, and provide some commonsense ways to improve delivery. We will then focus on the public speaking context and discuss the four distinct ways a speaker can deliver a speech to an audience in this format.

Prep Questions

Part 1: Key Concepts

1. Define the terms pronunciation and articulation. Explain how they differ.

2. Define vocalics. Identify four vocalics that are listed in the chapter.

3. What are kinesics? List some nonverbal behaviors that belong to this category of behavior.

4. List the five functions of effective nonverbal communication.

5. Define each of the three modes of delivery. Give an example of time when each mode might be required of you as a speaker.

Part 2: Application

1. Consider the five functions of effective nonverbal communication. For each of the functions, give an example of how a single nonverbal behavior or combination of nonverbal behaviors could perform that function at some point during your upcoming explanatory talk.

2. Think about a time when you experienced nervousness or anxiety when communicating with someone. Why were you nervous? What did you do in terms of nonverbal behavior to conceal your communication apprehension? Do you think that the other person or people knew that you were feeling the way that you felt?

VERBAL ELEMENTS OF DELIVERY

The most obvious component of presenting any message is verbal delivery. Mastering verbal delivery takes lots of practice even when you understand the fundamentals. Those fundamentals include pronunciation and articulation, which contribute to the development and use of different dialects and slang. In this part of the chapter we will cover these aspects of verbal delivery and how to use them when delivering messages to others.

Pronunciation and Articulation

Proper word *pronunciation*, the accepted standard of how the word sounds, is very important to a speaker. In formal presentations, mispronouncing words can hurt your credibility. Would you trust a doctor who couldn't pronounce the name of your illness? You might take this mispronunciation as a sign that your doctor isn't prepared or educated. Even in casual conversation consistently mispronouncing words can create the perception that you do not know what you are talking about. In any situation, this can damage your credibility with others.

pronunciation
the accepted standard of how a word sounds when spoken

We mispronounce words for a variety of reasons. Sometimes we learn how to say a word incorrectly from hearing others say it that way. Other times we try to speak too quickly, resulting in slips of the tongue on more complex words. Sometimes we believe using words with which we are unfamiliar makes us look smarter or more eloquent to others. Whatever the reason, speakers need to correctly pronounce words. Mispronunciation damages credibility, the heart of a speaker's ethos. Mispronunciation of words or names in certain situations can make a difference in getting a job or making a sale.

Table 6.1

Most Commonly Mispronounced Words	
The website yourdictionary.com lists 100 of the more commonly mispronounced words on its website.[2] Do you make any of these errors? The left column notes how these incorrectly pronounced words would be spelled.	
Common Mispronunciation	**Correct Pronunciation**
anartic	Antarctic
aks	ask
calvary	cavalry
fedral	federal
hiarchy	hierarchy
irregardless	regardless
jewlry	jewelry
libel	liable
libary	library
nucular	nuclear
perogative	prerogative

articulation

physically producing the sound needed to convey the word

blending

one of the more common articulation errors, and it occurs when speakers intermingle two words together

Closely related to pronunciation is *articulation*, or physically producing the sound needed to convey the word. In many cases we commit articulation errors by picking up bad habits from others through modeling; in other instances we are just plain lazy. *Blending* is one of the more common articulation errors, and it occurs when speakers intermingle two words together. For example, "I don't know" becomes "I dunno," "give me" is reduced to "gimme," or "would have" transforms into "woulda." There are more egregious articulation errors, such as running three words together like when "I bet you" becomes "Ibetcha." A speaker may get away with sloppy pronunciation and articulation in some casual situations, but professional settings often demand correct speech. It is important to practice good articulation in all interactions, and don't expect to just "turn it on" when it might appear to matter. One suggestion for improving your ability to articulate words is to consciously work to pronounce the final consonant of each word. This practice method has the added benefit of slowing down your rate of speech and making your message more understandable for an audience.

Dialects and Slang

Different people from around the United States sound different when speaking, yet speak the same language and communicate with general success. Anyone who travels to Boston will hear people articulate their "a's" as "ah's," and anyone who goes to states below the Mason-Dixon line find people saying "y'all" rather than "you all." The latter of these two examples is often referred to as southern drawl due to the slower speech pattern. Other recognized variations of Standard English include Ebonics and Gullah, both of which have produced literary products of high regard.

So, what are these differences and how do they occur? They are called *dialects*, or aspects of articulation, grammar, vocabulary, and pronunciation that differ from Standard English. The term *dialect* comes from the Ancient Greek term *dialektos* meaning a tongue, or the language of a particular group of people that makes them distinct. The phrase "speaking in tongues" grew out of this understanding of the word.

dialect
....
aspects of articulation, grammar, vocabulary, and pronunciation that differ from Standard English

A dialect is a sort of subgroup of a language, and can result in some miscommunication between a people when the receiver is either unaware of, or cannot decipher, a speaker's dialect. As Sarah Trenholm notes, "Problems occur when one dialect is defined as the standard and given greater status than other dialects." The important thing to remember is that dialects are regionally accepted forms of articulation and/or pronunciation, and one is not any better or more accurate than another.

Those who speak a particular dialect sometimes develop additions to the general standard vocabulary. In the case of Standard English, certain regions develop words and phrases that are understood by those who reside there, but not by those who hail from elsewhere. Over time these words are appropriated by the general population and become part of mainstream culture. When this happens the terms become *slang*, or words derived from dialects that most people understand, but yet do not use in professional writing or speaking.

slang
......
words derived from dialects that most people understand but do not use in professional writing or speaking

Cultures usually develop their own forms of slang. Watch an old gangster movie and you will hear actors using terms such as *heater, roscoe, piece,* or *rod* when referring to a weapon used to *bump off, ice,* or *whack* an enemy. If caught the shooters might find themselves in "the big house." Each of these terms grew from a small part of society and infiltrated mainstream culture. The terms represented the language used by a subsection of Americans, and eventually they were immortalized in the movies and through other cultural experiences. The words no longer belonged to a particular group, but rather they became part of the general lexicon.

Take the case of the word *ain't*, which until recent versions of the Webster's Dictionary was not considered a word, but rather a slang pronunciation of the term *isn't*. The use of the word *ain't* can even be seen in some landmark speeches in American history, such as the one delivered by Sojourner Truth at the Women's Convention in 1851. When used by Sojourner Truth the word was understood as a form of slang; however, today it is part of the general lexicon.

As such, slang is not cemented in society; that is to say some terms may die over time. Think about the gangster example from the previous paragraph. Do you hear about people being sent to "the big house" for "bumping off someone" at the same level you might have fifty or sixty years ago? No, and the reason is that the usability of the terms as slang is dying out. Now you might hear that someone is "in the can" for "dusting someone off." This phrasing, too, may leave common vernacular if it hasn't already!

Slang, although common, is not recommended for professional settings. Because slang is not common vernacular, and we live and work in a globalized society, the risk of an audience not understanding your use of slang is increased, thus creating

Ain't I a Woman?
by Sojourner Truth

Delivered in 1851 at the Women's Convention in Akron, Ohio

Born Isabella Baumfree, Sojourner Truth was raised in slavery. She worked the fields as men did and suffered many physical abuses, including beatings at the hands of more than one slave master.[3] Truth eventually became a free woman and well-known minister. One memorable speech she delivered in this role was entitled "Ain't I a Woman."

The speech was short, especially by the standards of the day, clocking in at only 356 words, but nonetheless compelling. She made use of repetition in her address, specifically a phrase that included grammatical slang. The inclusion and repetition of that slang phrase enhanced the delivery of the speech. Take a look at the following excerpt:

"And ain't I a woman? Look at me! Look at my arm! I have ploughed and planted, and gathered into barns, and no man could head me! And ain't I a woman? I could work as much and eat as much as a man—when I could get it—and bear the lash as well! And ain't I a woman? I have borne thirteen children, and seen most all sold off to slavery, and when I cried out with my mother's grief, none but Jesus heard me! And ain't I a woman?"[4]

In this speech Truth brought issues such as race and gender to the forefront of her audience's minds. Given that it took place in 1851, these issues would remain important for the American public for years to come. When one considers the lack of rights that all women had at this time and then considers her race, Sojourner Truth's speech was certainly remarkable.

problems for communicating ideas to others. It also shows a lack of appreciation for an audience, and so sticking with Standard English is a much better route when speaking in professional settings.

Nonverbal Elements of Delivery

In addition to verbal delivery, or the words you use, nonverbal delivery also aids in the transmission of messages and can, in fact, play a much larger role in the success of accurate reception of that message. Nonverbal delivery can be broken down into two distinct areas: nonverbal elements related to voice, and nonverbal characteristics of the body. These aspects of your delivery serve several purposes when it comes to speaking, and a successful communicator incorporates good nonverbal delivery with strong verbal delivery. In this part of the chapter we will discuss the two types of nonverbal delivery and the functions of nonverbal delivery.

Vocalics

When people think of the nonverbal aspects of speech they often focus on the body, but actually most nonverbal behaviors emanate from the voice. When we focus on how loud a person is, whether the speaker's voice is dull or nasally, and how fast or slowly he or she speaks then we are looking at nonverbal actions. Think about it this way: are any of these things associated with pronunciation, articulation, or vocabulary? No, so therefore they are not categorized as elements of verbal delivery. We call these things *vocalics*, or anything that contributes to the creation or maintenance of sound in a person's voice.

vocalics
anything that contributes to the creation or maintenance of sound in a person's voice

One vocalic is the volume of a person's voice. Volume refers to how loud or soft a person's voice is when he or she speaks, and controlling it is trickier than you may realize. Volume can be augmented or reduced based on environmental factors, such as the acoustics of a wall. The distance between the sender and reciever can also influence volume. If a voice is too loud then the audience may leave, too soft and they may not receive the speaker's message. In casual conversation if someone is too loud or too quiet their conversation partner will often let them know. There are also situational expectations for volume, like sitting in a movie theater. Generally, you are asked not to speak during a movie, but if you had to then you should use a lower voice so as not to disturb others. Outside of this context, however, a lower volume may send a different message.

All of us, at one time or another, have been an audience member when someone was speaking and had to strain to hear what the speaker was saying. At its best this is a distraction, but it may also be considered either lazy or rude. Low volume can show shyness, anxiety, a lack of preparation, being unsure, or a speaker's lack of interest in being there. In all of these cases, if an audience cannot hear a speaker then the credibility of that speaker is damaged.

That does not mean that the speaker should shout at the audience. Rather, the speaker should use sufficient volume so that the person farthest away can hear with ease. The size of the room can often influence your decision on how loud you must speak. If you are in a large crowded room it might be necessary to simply ask if the people to whom you are speaking can comfortably hear you. If not, perhaps you speak more loudly or move closer to them to make sure everyone can hear you.

Volume alone does not constitute vocalics. Another element is *tone*, or the syllabic emphasis on a sound that expresses emotion or meaning. Think about our example from the beginning of the chapter. The tone of Ben Stein's character illustrates how speech that has no tonal inflection or variety can quickly lose an audience by conveying a lack of interest in the subject, audience, and occasion. Monotone deliveries can also quickly bore other people and distract them from the purpose and goals of the interaction. If you are excited about what you have to say it will be conveyed in your tone and make the message all the more interesting to listen to for the audience.

tone
the syllabic emphasis on a sound that expresses emotion or meaning

Tone also expresses different emotions when you adjust it for specific words. Sarcasm is often conveyed through the use of a different tone of voice when making a statement that otherwise might mean something else. Think about the inflection in someone's voice when they respond to the question "How are you doing today?" If they respond "fine" it could mean they are doing ok, but it can also imply that they are not if the word is given a sharper, more cutting edge to it. This is when we might hear someone say that they "heard" some emotion in the person's voice. Tone is a nonverbal vocalic that expresses emotion.

Another aspect of vocalics is the rate at which you speak. The rate, or pace, of your speech can be the result of a variety of things. The average rate of speech in the United States is 150 words per minute. This rate may vary by region. For example, people often observe that individuals from the Northeast speak much faster than people from the rest of the country, so culture can play a role in speech rate. It is also quite normal for a nervous speaker to speak at a more rapid rate than someone who is comfortable. In any communication situation you need to make sure you speak at a pace the other people involved can follow, or else your message will be lost. It is important to note, as well, that when delivering a public presentation your pace will naturally increase over the rate with which you practiced or speak in casual conversation. If you need to time yourself, make sure you prepare for this adjustment.

When speaking publicly, if you are worried about your rate of speech there are a few things you can do. You might want to audio record yourself in a normal situation speaking, or practicing your speech. If you have a concern that you might get caught up in the moment and begin to speak rapidly, you might want to put visual cues in your notes, such as a hand-drawn slow or stop sign on your speaking outline to remind you not to speak too fast. You can also practice formal presentations in front of an audience of friends and colleagues to gather feedback.

In meeting scenarios, your rate of speech increases for potentially different reasons. Sometimes you may feel rushed due to time or the need to get a lot of information out that you have been waiting to say for some time. In these instances, jot down notes before you speak so that you can use them to guide your statements when it is your turn to speak. Also, remember to breathe and give people time to digest what you are saying.

One final element of vocalics is pausing. Pauses are normal and necessary, and in many circumstances are useful tools. Professors use this tactic quite often to quell students talking among themselves in class. Pausing can be effectively used, as when you stop after making a point you want the other person or larger audience to consider. They also can be effective for allowing listeners to catch up, to permit yourself to catch a breath, and even to recognize and subdue an unruly or rude audience. Look at this scenario: some students are chatting among themselves during class, and the professor pauses and looks at the students until they stop. They stop because the students feel that the whole class's attention is on their conversation, resulting in them ending the rude behavior.

Pauses can also be a powerful tool for any speaker, as they can help emphasize something of importance. After providing a compelling statistic or story, a pause of a few seconds will alert the listener that something dramatic was just said. As with all other vocal qualities the pause must seem natural, and timing them is crucial. Using pauses effectively is a skill you learn with practice, and they can be a distraction if you are not careful. Awkward pauses make speakers look unprepared, unsure, or nervous, but effective pausing can be an equally positive interaction device.

Sometimes speakers feel pressure to speak all the time, and thus do not pause. Instead they fill the perceived void with a noise like *er, um, ah* or *uh* when they speak. These utterances have a variety of names, but generally they are called *vocalized pauses*. Even polished speakers can fall prey to this speaking irregularity. We have all seen speakers stammer and overuse these annoying pauses and inflections, and we realize how much they hurt delivery. Kept at a bare minimum they may not be much of a problem, but as a speaker you should strive to limit their interfering with your delivery. Vocalized pauses infect everyday interactions as well, and nothing makes a person seem less coherent or intelligent than repeating vocalized pauses like *y'know, like,* and *for sure*. These overused phrases serve no purpose in most messages.

vocalized pauses
utterances that are not words and have no place in a speech, but are done instead of pausing the delivery of the speech

Kinesics

Your voice, although an important element, is not the only nonverbal aspect of your delivery. Your body also conveys information about credibility and emotions to others through facial expressions, gestures, posture, appearance and eye contact, otherwise known as *kinesics*. These nonverbal behaviors are often the hardest to control, but when you learn to do so they can significantly impact your delivery and presence.

kinesics
nonverbal behaviors related to movement

The face is often the first thing people notice about you in any situation, and speaking is no different. Your face expresses emotions and sends messages to the audience in a way that can either aid or damage your ability to get your message across to an audience. If you try to say something you do not believe in, your facial expressions will often give you away, but when you do believe what you are saying then your expressions can illustrate your sincerity to the audience in a way no amount of evidence or list of credentials ever could. How you handle your facial expressions is important, but not nearly as challenging a question to answer as what to do with another part of your body.

One of the things people often struggle with when interacting with others is what to do with their hands. Hands can be effective tools, but they also can become unwanted distractions if not treated properly. Hands are the primary source of *gesture*, or physical movements used to convey a message. Skilled speakers use their hands to complement their messages, pointing to people when they are mentioned, if possible, or making forceful motions to emphasize a point.

gesture
a physical movement used to convey a message

In addition to gestures, your posture is also important when trying to convey a message to others. *Posture* refers to the position of your body, and it means more than simply facing the audience. If you lean toward someone over a table, or slouch in your chair your posture conveys a negative impression to others, just as it does when you stand rigidly and do not move. The key to good posture in

posture
the position of your body

delivery is being comfortable, yet confident. See the examples of good and bad posture in Figure 6.1.

Having a comfortable and confident posture is connected with effectively using gestures. To maintain the ability to gesture effectively you should not keep your hands in your pockets, folded in front of you, or even held behind your back. These positions all negatively impact your posture by making you appear uncomfortable.

Figure 6.1

Examples of Bad Posture (top) and Good Posture (bottom)

Good posture is relaxed and allows you to make use of your hands when needed.

The next aspect of nonverbal communication we will discuss is appearance. Some professors require students to "dress up" when speaking while some do not. Some high schools also have dress codes for students, borne from the idea that if students dress well they will behave well. Even if you are not expected to wear more formal clothing you should always dress neatly with your hair in place. If you do not respect your own appearance, then people will not respect you and you will never be able to get your message across to them.

Appearance also can boost your self-confidence and help you feel successful even before you say a word. Consider how you feel when you have on your best clothes. We all feel more competent and confident in what we do. Research shows that when you dress professionally for a presentation it often results in better actual and perceived performance. Appearance is especially important for speakers who address an audience who is unfamiliar with them, because the first impression the speaker makes on the audience is based on the speaker's appearance. See Table 6.2 for appearance tips.

Table 6.2

Appearance Tips
• Dress neatly • No baseball caps • Hair combed or brushed • Better to overdress than underdress

The last category of nonverbal action we will discuss is eye contact—perhaps the most feared nonverbal action during a formal presentation. Novice speakers often get nervous when they realize they need to look at the audience during their presentation. This is understandable, but eye contact conveys confidence and interest in the audience, making it an indispensable aspect of any speech. One way to minimize the pressure created by eye contact is to look at a speech as a series of conversations. Instead of a speech being you talking to a group of, for example,

25 people, view it as 25 individual one-on-one conversations. To do this, select one person to look at in the audience and speak directly to them until you reach a new idea or point, then move on to someone else in another part of the room. We typically are not afraid of individual conversations, and yet we make eye contact with the other participant, so taking the same perspective on larger speaking engagements might help. In any event, eye contact, gestures, and posture all play a role in the delivery of a message to an audience.

Functions of Nonverbal Communication in Speech

As individuals we send more nonverbal messages than we do verbal. As such, it is important for communicators to understand the various purposes their gestures, posture, and eye contact can serve with regard to how they present themselves. In this section we will look at the five positive ways nonverbal messages can influence perceptions of your speech, and the one negative role they could play in your delivery if you are not careful.

One way nonverbal actions can influence your message is by allowing you to reiterate your verbal message without saying it. When physical actions restate verbal messages in this manner then nonverbal behaviors *repeat* their verbal counterparts. You can make use of this function by pointing to people in the audience as you reference them, or using your fingers to count along when listing certain items or points.

repeat
when physical actions restate verbal messages

Nonverbal messages can also amplify, or *accent*, your desired message. For example, when you wish to emphasize a point you can pound on the podium or table at the end of stating the point. When you get excited about something you are saying, you can raise a fist in a mock sign of triumph. Not only do these behaviors support your message, but they increase its power and the likelihood the audience understands your point.

accent
nonverbal behaviors that augment a verbal message

Nonverbal actions are most effective, however, when they *complement* the verbal message. This occurs when the nonverbal message is the same as the verbal message. A perfect model of this occurring is when speakers laugh at jokes they make. By laughing, they display the action associated with the verbal content of the joke.

complement
when the action demonstrates the message contained in the verbal content

Facial expressions and body movement also can *substitute* for verbal content on occasion. A person who smiles after being introduced does not necessarily need to state her enjoyment at being there as the smile conveys that message. When asked a question to which you do not know the answer, you may follow with a simple shrug of the shoulder instead of saying "I don't know." Waving to someone you know on the street is another example of a nonverbal behavior substituting for a verbal message.

substitute
physical actions that take the place of verbal messages

One other positive function nonverbal messages perform is *regulating* an interaction. During normal conversations nonverbal actions such as pauses and hand gestures can cue responses and comments from the other person. During speeches they serve much the same purpose—allowing an audience to know when they can ask questions, when they should clap, and when they should cheer.

regulate
nonverbal actions that help govern the course of a speech or interaction

These types of gestures help regulate, or direct, interactions so that receivers know when messages have been completed and it is their turn to speak.

conflict
....
nonverbal cues that convey a message that contradicts the verbal statements of the speaker

On the downside, ***conflicting*** nonverbal cues can negatively influence your ability to get your message across. These occur when your message says one thing, but your body sends the opposite message. If you are not pleased to be doing something, but tell people you are, most likely your nonverbal actions tell the truth. It is extremely difficult to hide your true feelings about something because of the prevalence of nonverbal communication in any interaction.

MODES OF DELIVERY

Delivery encompasses more than verbal and nonverbal skills; it also refers to the style speakers use to deliver their messages to their audiences. Different contexts allow speakers the opportunity to bring varying amounts of notes and preparation with them. To quote the Greek philosopher Demosthenes, "The three most important parts of speaking are delivery, delivery, and delivery." You will encounter three primary modes of speech delivery in CMM 100 and your other courses. In this part we will define and discuss each of them.

Manuscript Speeches

manuscript speech
....
when a speaker has an entire speech written out word for word in front of him/her as s/he speaks

Most students welcome the chance to deliver a ***manuscript speech***. Manuscript speeches are commonplace today, although they may not seem to be so. Politicians frequently deliver them. When the president gives an address before Congress he speaks directly off of a teleprompter; when he speaks from the Rose Garden he does so with the script right in front of him; and, when the president of the University of Dayton, Dr. Eric Spina, speaks at convocation or graduation he reads from a manuscript. Just because it is acceptable for a variety of occasions, however, does not mean it is the only, or even best, form of delivery.

Speaking off a manuscript carries with it many positives for a speaker, particularly a newcomer to public address. You do not have to fear the freeze as you might with a memorized presentation. Your speech will come off as organized, or at least as organized as you made the manuscript. The opportunity to jump off the manuscript is possible, but it is constrained by the need to stay on message. Finally, manuscript style speaking allows you to note where you need to make gestures and employ different nonverbal actions at moments during your speech. No wonder first-time speakers prefer the manuscript style!

Despite the enormous benefits afforded by manuscript style addresses, the form is not a panacea. Making adjustments to audience feedback, though possible, is extraordinarily difficult without experience. Additionally, there is a temptation to stare directly at the manuscript, reading off of it to the audience, which makes you appear distant and uninterested in the audience—not to mention unable to gauge their reaction to what you say. Manuscript speeches invite speakers to focus on their script, and not the audience or their own gestures and reactions, making it hard to successfully incorporate effective and positive nonverbal communication into the presentation.

SPOTLIGHTING THEORISTS: DEMOSTHENES

Demosthenes (384–322 BC)

Considered one of the greatest of the Attic orators in ancient Greece, Demosthenes reportedly gave his first speech in court arguing to receive what was left of his inheritance. He became a speechwriter and lawyer in Athens, and eventually became one of the leading voices in opposition to Philip II of Macedon and his son Alexander the Great. Demosthenes, like Socrates and Cicero, eventually died in the service of his principles. He took his own life rather than be arrested by Alexander's supporters. Many of his contemporaries lauded him and his contributions to oratory.

Praise for Demosthenes came from many corners of the ancient world. Cicero, the father of the five canons of rhetoric, proclaimed Demosthenes to be the "perfect orator" and

Quintilian stated Demosthenes was "by far the most excellent" of the Greek orators. Like Cicero, Demosthenes believed that speakers should be educated on what they talk about, and therefore often declined to speak on subjects he had not studied before. Additionally, Demosthenes valued delivery (gestures) above rhetorical flourish and style, believing that these elements of a speech contributed more to its success.

To that end, stories tell of Demosthenes practicing his own speeches in unique fashion. One story tells that he practiced his speech in front of a roaring waterfall in order to work on projecting his voice. Another speaks of how he would practice his presentations with pebbles in his mouth to concentrate on improving pronunciation and articulation of words. For Demosthenes, delivery truly represented the most important aspect of any speech.

The main reason beginning speakers relish manuscript speaking is that it eliminates the freeze factor; however, it can also create a much less energetic speech and ultimately distances the speaker from the audience. There is a middle ground, however, between manuscript and memorized speeches and we will discuss that style next.

Extemporaneous Speeches

Since instructors do not normally expect memorized speeches, and yet typically do not allow students to deliver manuscript speeches, how then are most student speeches delivered? The answer, most student speeches are *extemporaneous speeches*, or speeches delivered with notes in front of the speaker. Extemporaneous speaking requires practice, but also allows for speakers to have organized references in front of them in case they lose their place during the presentation. Extemporaneous speeches much like manuscript speeches, have positive and negative qualities of which every speaker needs to be aware.

extemporaneous speech
a speech delivered with notes but not the entire speech in front of the speaker

The primary benefit of using notes instead of a full manuscript is that you will have a more natural and fluid delivery. You can adapt to audience feedback and expound on or eliminate examples and points based upon the audience's reaction to what you are saying and how you are saying it. Your vocal inflections and

 physical gestures are not planned, and therefore do not risk coming across as rigid and robotic as in the other styles of delivery. When you stress an inflection of a word or syllable, or gesture in support of a particular statement it comes from your emotions, not your guide, providing your audience with a perception of authenticity.

A secondary benefit of extemporaneous speaking related to the ability to have a natural delivery is improved eye contact. With only notes in front of you it becomes possible to make more eye contact with the audience, increasing your connection and identification with them, thus making you appear more believable. Eye contact is an essential part of any successful speech, and extemporaneous speaking allows you to make eye contact with the audience while also being able to check your notes if you lose your place.

As you can probably imagine, extemporaneous delivery depends on two things: adequate practice and a strong organized set of notes. To deliver a believable address with only notes you must spend a significant amount of time practicing the speech. First you practice with a full text draft, but over time you reduce it to a speaking outline where only direct quotations appear in full text form. This speaking outline comes from paring down a full sentence outline, and still retains the same structural format of the original, just with far fewer words and phrases. The process of drafting, practicing, and then constructing a speaking outline for use during the actual presentation takes a lot of time, but the payoff when you speak more than accounts for that investment.

The most significant obstacles to a successful extemporaneous speech involve creating an effective speaking outline and keeping your notes organized. Some people who deliver speeches off of notes use bulleted lists or even note cards in their speech. Bulleted lists are dangerous because they are not structured, and thus you can easily lose your place when staring back and forth at the list. Note cards can be problematic, especially if they are not numbered, because you might drop them or put them in an incorrect order, causing you to lose your place or get flustered when delivering the speech. But these problems can be minimized and even eliminated through extensive practice and preparation for the presentation. There are, however, some speeches that allow for little to no preparation.

Impromptu Speeches

At one time or another in your life you will need to speak without any preparation, research, or notes. These unplanned unprepared presentations are called *impromptu speeches*, and they can be as short as a minute or as long as ten, depending on the topic, speaker, and situation. These may also be the most nerve-racking of any speech because even the most experienced orator will feel a bit jittery when called on to speak about something without any preparation.

impromptu speech
a presentation done with little or no preparation

When called upon to deliver impromptu remarks it is best to first collect your thoughts and quickly develop a mental outline of what you wish to say. Just because these speeches have no preparation time does not mean they should not be organized or logical. Two topics are always handy when asked to deliver such remarks: the situation and the audience. Connecting your comments to both provides an easy way to focus your remarks.

One of the most common places where you may deliver impromptu remarks is during a celebratory event honoring someone or something. No one will warn you that you might speak, you will not have prepared for the moment, and you might be surprised at the opportunity, but remember to identify with the audience and the event. It may also behoove you to reference the fact that you had no idea you might be speaking, thus acknowledging to the audience the impromptu nature of the address. These are high-stress speeches, but also often are very short. Audiences typically have lower expectations for performance of impromptu speeches than they do for a planned presentation.

SUMMARY

Delivery is a complicated and important element of communication, and it is also the one part that engenders the most fear in people. Delivery is divided into three components, each with equal importance. The first is verbal delivery which focuses on correctly speaking the language. The second part of delivery involves nonverbal actions from vocal variety to physical gestures and posture. Finally, the style of presenting the material in a public speaking setting allows for reading off a manuscript, using limited notes, or delivering unplanned remarks. We must remember that presenting the message is just as important (and complex) as planning it.

KEY TERMS

accent 163

articulation 156

blending 156

complement 163

conflict 164

dialect 157

extemporaneous speech 165

gesture 161

impromptu speech 167

kinesics 161

manuscript speech 164

posture 161

pronunciation 155

regulate 163

repeat 163

slang 157

substitute 163

tone 159

vocalics 159

vocalized pauses 161

REVIEW QUESTIONS

1. What are the two fundamentals of verbal delivery?

2. What is the difference between dialects and slang?

3. What are the two major categories of nonverbal delivery?

4. What are the four functions of nonverbal delivery?

5. What are the three types of speech delivery?

THINK ABOUT IT

1. How would you define great delivery?

2. Which of the nonverbal characteristics of delivery is most important?

3. How do you determine the proper relationship between nonverbal and verbal delivery?

ACTIVITIES FOR ACTION

1. Write down two sentences of average length about any particular topic; the content does not matter for this exercise. Then, take a sheet of paper and cut it into six pieces. On each sheet of paper write one of the following emotions: angry, happy, sad, confused, excited, depressed. Then, on the back of each sheet write a different emotion from the one on the front. Ask a friend to pick a sheet of paper, then give him or her the sentences you wrote and ask your friend to say those sentences using the emotion on the top of the paper selected. Finally, ask him or her to convey the emotion on the other side of the paper without speaking. See if you or others in the audience can accurately identify the emotions.

2. Try saying the following tongue twisters as many times as you can in a row without any errors in pronunciation or articulation: "Sally sells sea shells by the seashore." "How can a clam cram in a clean cream can?" "The thirty-

three thieves thought that they thrilled the throne Thursday." "Picky people pick Peter Pan peanut butter." And, if you really want a challenge: "Out in the pasture the nature watcher watches the catcher, while the catcher watches the pitcher who pitches the balls. Whether the temperature's up or whether the temperature's down, the nature watcher, the catcher, and the pitcher are always around. The pitcher pitches, the catcher catches, and the watcher watches. So whether the temperature rises or the temperature falls the nature watcher just watches the catcher who's watching the pitcher who's watching the balls."

3. We all know the challenge presented by vocalized pauses and the importance of limiting their occurrence. To practice speaking without using a vocalized pause have a friend time you speaking on any given topic as long as you can until you use a vocalized pause. The larger the audience the better for this exercise, as everyone starts listening for the vocalized pauses. The person who goes the longest wins.

ENDNOTES

1. *Ferris Bueller's Day Off*, written and directed by John Hughes (Paramount Pictures, 1986).

2. http://www.yourdictionary.com/library/mispron.html (accessed June 10, 2008).

3. http://www.lkwdpl.org/wihohio/trut-soj.htm

4. http://www.feminist.com/resources/artspeech/genwom/sojour.htm

Interteaching Session

Dialogue

Watch a videorecording of a speech or interview from a famous person, such as a politician or social leader. Afterwards, explore the delivery of the speaker in a conversation with your groupmates.

1. How did the speaker use vocalics? Give an example of a particularly effective or ineffective use of vocalics.

2. How did the speaker use kinesics? Give an example of a particularly effective or ineffective use of kinesics.

3. How would you describe the dialect of the speaker? What about other aspects of her or his verbal delivery, such as the use of slang, articulation, or pronunciation?

4. Find another videorecording of a speech or interview from this same speaker. Do you observe the same patterns in his or her delivery in this recording? How might this person's delivery in public communication be a factor—positive or negative—in the image that this person has created and the appeal that he or she has in the eyes of the public? Be prepared to share your thoughts with the rest of the class and to listen to theirs.

Performance

Take turns with your group members delivering the following paragraph as though you were reciting it in a speech. As you do, have one of your groupmates make a videorecording of you:

> Social pressure is another reason people get nervous speaking in front of an audience. There is a certain status quo that we all live up to. If we make a mistake, we often believe that it will damage our reputation. We cannot pretend we don't get nervous and we can't avoid the fact that we all get nervous and we cannot allow our nervousness to take us over. So, how can we manage anxiety? Let's break it down. Before we begin, remember this: accept the fear and make it work for you. Most people cannot see your nervousness, so don't even mention that you are. Use this adrenaline rush of nervous energy by turning it into enthusiasm in your delivery.

Now watch the video. What aspects of your delivery were effective and you should continue to incorporate into your delivery when you give your explanatory talk? What aspects of your delivery were not as effective and you should not incorporate into your explanatory talk? Repeat this process for each of your groupmates.

Go through this process again, but this time, instead of reading a script, tell a story about a particularly memorable trip that you had with your family or other loved ones. As you tell the story, have one of your groupmates to make a videorecording. Consider the same two questions about your delivery. Repeat this process for each of your groupmates.

After you have finished, discuss the advantages and disadvantages of using the two different delivery styles, manuscript and impromptu. How does extemporaneous delivery incorporate some of the strengths of manuscript delivery while incorporating also strengths of impromptu delivery?

Types of Persuasion

PracticallySPEAKING

On June 12, 1994, police discovered the bodies of Nicole Brown Simpson and Ronald Goldman in the courtyard of Nicole Brown Simpson's Brentwood, California, residence. Simpson and Goldman died from excessive stab wounds, and immediately suspicion fell upon Simpson's ex-husband, former NFL star turned actor O. J. Simpson. On June 13th authorities informed Simpson of the murders while he was on a business trip in Chicago. Upon his return, police took him into custody for questioning and he retained Robert Shapiro as his legal counsel. Within a few weeks a grand jury and judge decided that there was sufficient evidence to prosecute O. J. Simpson for the murders of his ex-wife and Goldman. On July 22, 1994, before presiding judge Lance Ito, O. J. pled not guilty to the crimes, and one of the most famous trials in American history began.

The trial opened on January 24, 1995, after a brief holiday recess. During the trial the defense managed to get admissions of procedural errors from members of the police department regarding the collection of DNA and other evidence. Additionally, detective Mark Fuhrman came under fire for supposedly making racist comments during the investigation. Eventually, after various legal maneuverings by both the prosecution and defense, the trial began to wind down.

On September 26–27, 1995, over a year after the deaths of Nicole Brown Simpson and Ronald Goldman, the prosecution and defense delivered their closing arguments.[1] Deputy District Attorney Marcia Clark and Prosecutor Christopher Darden delivered their closing argument first, making specific mention of the perception that Detective Fuhrman was a racist: "It would be a tragedy if, with such overwhelming evidence, you find the defendant not guilty because of the racist attitudes of one officer." Immediately following their presentation, the defense, represented by Johnny Cochran and Barry Scheck, made its case to the jury, with the former referring to Fuhrman as a "lying, perjuring, genocidal racist," and the latter referring to a "cancer" at the heart of the investigation into the murders.[2] Ultimately, the arguments made by the defense proved to be more persuasive than those offered by the prosecution, and on October 3, 1995, the jury acquitted O. J. Simpson on both counts of murder.

The speeches made by both the prosecution and the defense in the O. J. Simpson trial are examples of one type of persuasive speech but as we will discover in this chapter, there are other categories of persuasion.

Prep Questions

Part 1: Key Concepts

1. Define stasis. List and explain the four forms of stasis in Quintilian's theory.

2. What are the three types of persuasive questions? Provide an example of each that could serve as the focus of a persuasive speech relating to the course theme.

3. Compare and contrast refutation and rebuttal.

4. List the four stages of the persuasive process. Explain what happens at each stage.

5. What are four ways to build credibility during communication? Distinguish which three of the four came from Aristotle's work on rhetoric and which modern social scientists identified.

Part 2: Application

1. Consider the theme for the course. Give an example of each of the four forms of stasis that relates to this theme. For each one, explain what specifically is under dispute among people.

2. Give an example of a time when someone succeeded in persuading you about some topic. Explain briefly what happened that allowed this person to persuade you at each of the four stages of the persuasion process.

FORMS OF PERSUASIVE MESSAGES

In this section of the chapter we will identify the different types of persuasive messages using both classical and contemporary terms. At the heart of any persuasive attempt is what classical philosophers referred to as the issue in dispute, or what contemporary scholars call the question. Quintilian, the Roman philosopher and teacher, wrote extensively about the different ways we dispute a persuasive argument. We will discuss four.

After examining Quintilian's work we will demonstrate the three forms of persuasive messages people use today. We will then define the two types of persuasive messages proposed by Aristotle and how they relate to the issues in dispute. Finally, we will discuss how to use persuasion to respond to arguments made by another person.

Quintilian and Stasis Theory

All persuasive attempts revolve around an issue that is disputed. The speaker thus attempts to persuade listeners that they should agree with the speaker's interpretation of the issue in dispute. This central focus is called *stasis*, the object or idea that people argue over. Quintilian provided four different types of stasis, or disputed issues, that may exist in a persuasive situation. In this section of the chapter we discuss each of them.

stasis
the basic issue in dispute between one or more speaking parties

The first form of stasis is *definitive stasis*, or a dispute over the meaning of a term. When two sides define a term in two different ways, there is definitive stasis. One arena where this occurs is in politics, where terms and phrases are defined differently by each candidate or party. Take, for instance, the issue of marriage. Some define marriage as a contractual agreement only between a man and woman. Others, however, do not define it that way, and interpret it as a contractual bond between any two consenting adults, regardless of sex. When two sides apply different definitions of marriage, then the central issue of their disagreement is an example of definitive stasis.

definitive stasis
when the issue in dispute is the meaning of a term

A second form of stasis is what we saw at play during the O. J. Simpson trial we discussed in the opening of the chapter. *Conjectural stasis* exists when the central issue of disagreement is whether or not something occurred. The issue at stake in

conjectural stasis
when the issue in dispute is whether something occurred or not

the Simpson murder case was whether or not O. J. killed Nicole Brown Simpson and Ronald Goldman. All criminal court cases address issues of conjectural stasis.

qualitative stasis
········
when the issue in dispute involves the morality, ethicality, or value of an action

When the sides in an argument seek to persuade an audience about the moral or ethical nature of an action, the central issue of discussion involves *qualitative stasis*. Debates about issues of qualitative stasis also include those that cover what is best in a given situation. Remember when we mentioned that the district attorney's office decided not to seek the death penalty in the O. J. Simpson case? Arguments for whether or not to seek the death penalty in the Simpson case exemplify an issue where the topic is a matter of qualitative stasis. Would it be right to kill Simpson as punishment for murdering his ex-wife and Ronald Goldman? At the heart of such a question is the morality of capital punishment, thus making the issue of disagreement one of qualitative stasis.

translative stasis
········
when the issue in dispute is the competency of the judge or arbiter

Finally, Quintilian proposed a type of stasis that occurs when both sides debate the competency of the judge in the dispute; in effect, both sides make judgments about the judge. *Translative stasis* involves disputing the competency of the judge or arbiter.

In 1989 when New York mafia leader John Gotti was on trial, news accounts reported the judge, John Reis Bartels who was 91, and whom President Dwight D. Eisenhower appointed in 1959, fell asleep during the proceedings. Both the judge and the lawyers in the case disputed those stories, arguing that the judge merely closed his eyes during long witness testimonies. The lawyers felt Bartels was competent to serve as judge in the case, while the newspaper reporters questioned his ability to oversee the trial.[4] The debate over the competency of the 91-year-old Bartels was an example of an issue of translative stasis.

Whenever speakers attempt to persuade an audience to change their beliefs or values, or even to act in a particular way, there is a central issue in dispute between the two sides. That disputed issue can be over whether something actually occurred, how to define a specific term, determining if an action is right or wrong, or deciding if a judge is competent to make a decision. These different issues represent what Quintilian referred to as stasis, because the issue the two sides argue over never changes. It is important to you as a speaker and audience member to know which issue is in dispute. This knowledge allows you to maintain your focus and identify the key points to the argument, thereby enabling you to come to a reasoned conclusion. Today we commonly refer to stasis theory in a simpler way, and categorize the central issue in dispute as a *question*.

Contemporary Persuasive Questions

What Quintilian and his Roman colleagues called stasis theory we now refer to as the issue in question. Today, we identify three different types of questions, but each has its roots in stasis theory. These questions, just like stasis, identify the focus for the persuasive appeal, allowing both the speaker and the audience to avoid going off on tangents. The key element of any successful ethical persuasive appeal is that it remains focused on advocating an answer to one of these three persuasive questions.

SPOTLIGHTING THEORISTS: QUINTILIAN

Quintilian (35–99 BC)

Quintilian was the last of the great classical rhetoricians produced by Greece or Rome. He followed in the footsteps of Cicero and Isocrates and attempted to expand Cicero's work by proposing reforms to educational practices throughout the Empire. Quintilian began his career in much the same way as other famous Greeks and Romans—as a lawyer—but did not choose fame and fortune in the political arena.

Quintilian made his mark as a teacher, not a lawyer or politician. He received a grant from the Emperor Vespasian and worked at a school subsidized by Vespasian. Quintilian's resistance to corruption in politics and the prevailing standards of Roman education at the time were not overtly noticeable, but rather emerged through more subtle actions. Unlike people from other schools of his time, Quintilian frowned on physical punishment as a means of teaching his students, instead attempting to foster a family dynamic between himself and his charges.

Like Isocrates, Quintilian felt that students should be well read on a variety of subjects in order to master both concepts and language. His school, therefore, emphasized more reading than repetitive performance exercises. Quintilian famously stated that education should produce "the good man speaking well." This "good man" combined all the positive attributes of a Platonistic speaker who committed himself to seeking the truth, with the Ciceronian and Isocratean emphasis on developing public virtue and character in the service of society.

Quintilian's lone surviving work is the *Institutio Oratorio*, or the *Institutes of Oratory*. This massive project was divided into twelve books, each dealing with a different aspect of the speaking process and education in general. Book One lays out the ideal curriculum and talks about early childhood education; Books Two and Three discuss stasis theory at length; Books Four through Six develop Cicero's concept of invention; Book Seven addresses arrangement; Books Eight and Nine deal with Style; Book Ten identifies the "right" authors a speaker should emulate; Book Eleven covers memory, delivery, and decorum; and Book Twelve covers the character of the perfect orator, or "the good man speaking well."[5]

When speakers seek to persuade people about how to interpret facts they are addressing a ***question of fact***. Whenever the reliability, veracity, or interpretation of something is in doubt, a question of fact exists. Questions related to whether or not something exists are questions of fact. A persuasive message about a question of fact is different from an explanation because a speaker seeks to persuade people, not teach them. This type of persuasion is similar to what Quintilian termed conjectural stasis. To explain, let us look again at the O. J. Simpson example. The jury entertained serious doubts about whether O. J. committed the crime or not. The trial and the closing arguments made by the lawyers, attempted to persuade an audience (the jury) that their answer to a question of fact (did O. J. kill his ex-wife and Ronald Goldman?) is correct.

question of fact
when a speaker seeks to persuade people about how to interpret facts

question of value
a persuasive speech about the rightness or wrongness of an idea, action, or issue

The second type of question a persuasive message addresses is similar to what Quintilian referred to as qualitative stasis. Today, this kind of question is referred to as a *question of value*. The focus of a message involves whether something is right or wrong or advocates valuing one thing over another. Questions about value are not limited to moral and ethical questions, but also include disagreements over prioritizing certain items, as one does in a budget. When you prioritize, you are valuing certain items or ideas more than others. This kind of message also might advocate that one thing is better than another, such as when you attempt to persuade a friend to take a particular class because you feel it is a more interesting one than the class selected by your friend.

question of policy
when a speaker takes a position on whether an action should or should not be taken

The third type involves *questions of policy*. With a policy question, speakers take a position on whether an action should or should not be taken. Like questions of value, questions of policy share some characteristics with qualitative stasis, but also contain some qualities not thoroughly explained by Quintilian's definitions of issues in dispute. Questions of policy focus on action, and often disputes over answers to what action to take occur in deliberative bodies such as governments and organizational committees. A union might hold a meeting where members discuss whether or not to go on strike. Legislators may dispute whether or not to vote for a bill that raises taxes to pay for more teachers. This also takes place on campus, when the UD administration recently debated changes to housing policies in the student neighborhood responding to student celebrations during the 2014 Elite Eight run of the Flyer basketball team. When a problem requiring a specific action to solve it exists, there exists a question of policy.

Notice that Quintilian's stasis theory does not really address questions of policy directly, nor does the contemporary approach address definitive or translative stasis directly. Instead, under the contemporary structure definitive and translative stasis are included in questions of fact, as the definition of a term or the competency of a judge can be considered questions of fact. Quintilian would most likely argue that questions of policy address issues of qualitative stasis, or whether taking such action is right or wrong. The important thing, however, is to see that how we talk about persuasion today developed from the classical understanding and approach to persuasion and argument. In the next part of this chapter we will explore the two different situations in which Aristotle noted that persuasion occurs.

ARISTOTLE ON PERSUASIVE SPEAKING

Stasis theory focuses on the issues and central ideas of a persuasive message, but as we hope to illustrate in this chapter and this book, a communication event is more than its subject; it also includes the situation and the purpose. So, in this section we discuss the difference between the two forms of persuasion proposed by Aristotle and where the issues in dispute can be found in each.

Aristotle's Two Types of Persuasion

People sometimes try to persuade others to take action regarding an issue currently in dispute, or as a response to something that might occur in the future.

These types of messages occur most often in decision-making bodies such as the floor of Congress, but also occur when small groups try and determine a way forward to accomplish a task. The speakers deliberate over problems and issues while proposing solutions to them. These messages are what Aristotle referred to as *deliberative messages* and they often attempt to answer questions of policy or questions of value as they try to prioritize problems and propose solutions to those dilemmas.

deliberative messages
one of two forms of persuasive speech proposed by Aristotle; it often takes place in legislative settings and focuses on discussing policies and actions to be taken

One example of deliberative persuasive advocacy occurred during the 2008 financial crisis, when members of the House of Representatives, Senate, and Bush administration spoke about the fiscal emergency and how to properly approach solving it. Some advocated a large federal investment, while others felt the market should be left to correct itself. A third group debated the size of the federal investment that should be made, proposing even more spending than other groups. The messages in support of these various positions were typical of deliberative persuasive appeals. Deliberative, however, is only *one* form of persuasive speech.

forensic messages
arguments where speakers debate the facts of a case and attempt to answer questions of justice

Aristotle recognized that not all persuasion is deliberative, such as in the case of courtroom arguments. Arguments in a courtroom, where speakers debate the facts of a case and attempt to answer questions of justice rather than policy, are examples of what Aristotle called *forensic messages*. Unlike deliberative messages in which the parties advance arguments concerning the most effective way to manage resources and debate action to be taken, forensic messages contain a *kategoria*, or accusation, and an *apologia*, or defense against the accusation. *Forensic oratory focuses on defining the past rather than proposing a path for the future.* In order to craft an effective forensic message, you should be familiar with what your audience values as well as how to wield evidence in the construction of a reasoned argument or position regarding the issue at hand.

kategoria
a forensic speech that makes an accusation

apologia
a forensic speech that makes a defense against an accusation

Forensic messages are most common in courtrooms, but that is not the only place they occur. Any time we take a position or present an argument to interpret something in a specific way, we are making a forensic argument. For instance, in the summer of 2006 actor and director Mel Gibson was arrested for drunk driving and subsequently went on a tirade during which he made anti-Semitic remarks. A short time later he issued a public apology for those remarks and offered an explanation for what he said and why he said it. That explanation was a forensic argument because he presented an interpretation of the events and his feelings afterward to ask for forgiveness. The apology was ultimately accepted by the Anti-Defamation League and Gibson has been able to move on from the incident.

Situation and purpose influence persuasive appeals as much as topics. Certain topics are limited to, or better suited for, certain situations. Both play a role in focusing persuasive messages and are therefore important tools. As a speaker you need to stay focused on the issue in dispute, while providing a reasoned rationale for your argument. As an audience member you need to remain tuned to the issue a speaker presents so you can then follow the argument. In the next section we will discuss one type of persuasive message that does not necessarily address a question per se, but rather seeks to respond to an argument made by someone else. It is also one of the most common forms of advocacy we engage in, as we do so during conversations with friends, family members, faculty, and others.

Refutation

As you know by now, where there is persuasion there is dispute, and where there is a dispute there is a response. In fact, even the Greeks and Romans recognized that often persuasion is not simply advocating for a position in a vacuum, but rather involves responding to the argument of another individual in an attempt to prove their message—or at least a part of what they are saying—wrong or to make their position less appealing. There are two types of persuasive messages that respond to an argument presented by another person. In this section we will detail these two types.

rebuttal
....
a speech that involves overcoming the opposition's argument by introducing other evidence that reduces the appeal of the opposition's claims

The first type of response is a *rebuttal*, which involves overcoming the other person's entire argument by introducing other evidence that reduces the appeal of their claims. In a rebuttal, you use evidence not cited by the other person to illustrate how that argument is incomplete or misleading, thus casting doubt on their entire position. This type of response often takes place in academic and political debates where the person who speaks second seeks to minimize the strength of the arguments made by the person who speaks first. A rebuttal's purpose is always to persuade the audience that the opposition's argument is incomplete and not as strong as it appears. Essentially, a rebuttal does not claim the other person's argument is false, but rather that it is not as strong as they originally made it out to be.

Let's look at an example of a rebuttal. Kane and Jacquelyn were discussing whether Las Vegas should build a new stadium to attract a professional sports team to the city. Kane argued that the city of Las Vegas should use tax revenue to accomplish this goal. He emphasized how much money it would bring to the city in the long run, how many jobs it would create in the short term, and how a sports team would give the city its own image. Jacquelyn did not agree with Kane, and thus issued a rebuttal.

Jacquelyn made several points that did not disprove Kane's argument, but rather made them seem less appealing. She said that yes, there would be short term benefits in terms of jobs created to build the stadium, but to fund such an operation would mean a tax hike on current residents. Further, she said the long range benefits would only be seen if a professional sports team came to the city, and pointed out there was no guarantee that would happen, which might leave the city with a big expensive arena and no team to use it. Finally, she pointed out that Las Vegas already had an image, and that a sports team would not help or change it much. Each of the points in Jacquelyn's rebuttal minimized the effect of Kane's original argument, but did not disprove it entirely. Still, her message was persuasive, as her specific purpose was to illustrate that Kane's argument was not as appealing as he made it sound. As you can see, to issue a clear and effective rebuttal you need to listen closely to the messages of others.

A second kind of response is a *refutation*. A refutation is slightly different from a rebuttal in that it does seek to prove that the opposition's argument is wrong, or false. When refuting an argument you might focus on the faulty reasoning or lack of support provided by the other speaker. The specific purpose, then, for refutation is to persuade the audience that the opposition's argument is wrong or false. Let's look at an example.

refutation
a speech that seeks to prove the opposition's argument is wrong, or false

Caitlin presented an argument to her class that global warming needs to be addressed. She pointed out that temperatures are rising due to increased carbon emissions resulting in the melting of the polar ice caps. She then pressed for increased fuel efficiency standards and called on people to take public transportation whenever possible. Corey responded by refuting Caitlin's claims and citing scientific studies that counter the idea of global warming. He argued that those studies showed the temperature changes Caitlin spoke about are actually cyclical patterns in the Earth's temperature and are not caused by carbon emissions and global warming. Thus, he said people should not feel undue pressure to carpool, ride the bus, or force a change in the way cars are built. In his message, Corey refuted Caitlin's argument by claiming it was false, or erroneous.

Unlike in the case of Jacquelyn and her rebuttal, Corey did not accept certain elements of his opponent's argument, but rather pointed out faulty data by presenting contradictory evidence. The primary difference between a rebuttal and refutation is that a rebuttal takes issue with the conclusions, whereas refutation disputes the entire argument and the evidence presented by the opposition. Like rebuttals, refutation requires careful listening and knowledge of a wide array of topics. You cannot effectively refute an argument with hearsay or innuendo, as you need verifiable data to make others accept your refutation of an original message. It doesn't matter, however, if you are refuting, rebutting or proposing a position; persuasion is a very complex process. To remove some of the mystery surrounding persuasion, we will attempt to "unpack" how that process works in the next section.

Table 7.1

Rebuttals and Refutations	
Rebuttal Characteristics	**Refutation Characteristics**
Introduces evidence that lessens the impact of the evidence presented by the other person	Seeks to prove the opponent's argument is wrong or false
Uses evidence not cited by the other person	Focuses on the opponent's reasoning
Shows that the evidence you are rebutting is incomplete	Points to a lack of supporting material

The Persuasive Process

Persuasion does not take place simply because there is a topic on which two or more sides disagree. In fact, the persuasive process is much more involved. Additionally, persuasion almost always takes time, and its effectiveness often must be measured in degrees. In this section of the chapter we will discuss the four stages of the persuasive process, the development and importance of credibility in that process, and how to avoid unethical behavior when persuading others.

Stages of Persuasion

Persuasion is a psychological process. When you attempt to persuade someone you are asking for someone to make a decision based on a logical argument

SPEAKING of **CIVIC ENGAGEMENT**

Television and the Public Interest
by Newton Minow

Delivered May 9, 1961, to the National Association of Broadcasters

In 1961, newly elected President John F. Kennedy selected Newton Minow to be the Chairman of the Federal Communications Commission (FCC), the governmental agency responsible for governing television and radio.[5] Some were surprised at Kennedy's choice of Minow as he had been critical of television and lacked extensive experience with communication law or the media industry.

As FCC chairman, Minow challenged the content on television and asked for reform.[6]

In his speech Minow raised eyebrows, especially with this statement:

"But when television is bad, nothing is worse. I invite each of you to sit down in front of your television set when your station goes on the air and stay there, for a day, without a book, without a magazine, without a newspaper, without a profit and loss sheet or a rating book to distract you. Keep your eyes glued to that set until the station signs off. I can assure you that what you will observe is a vast wasteland."[7]

These words of Newton Minow became famous, or infamous depending on the audience. In fact, some felt his comments were elitist, and so they even named the S.S. Minnow of Gilligan's Island fame after him as an expression of criticism for his stance on the media industry.

Although Minow never achieved significant broadcast regulation, he did raise awareness of content and the impact of the "vast wasteland." After he retired from the FCC he became a partner in one of America's most powerful communication law firms.[8]

regarding an issue in dispute. Persuasion is different from other less ethical ways to gain agreement from an audience. In this part of the chapter we will discuss the four elements of the persuasive process and then demonstrate why persuasion, when employed correctly, is the most appropriate and ethical means for gaining agreement from an audience.

The persuasive process has four stages, each of which is equally important. The first step in the persuasive process is called *issue awareness*, and we have already begun to discuss it. Issue awareness occurs when you alert other people about the existence of an issue requiring their attention. This stage occurs immediately in the introduction of your message because it is what you use to motivate other people to listen. The issue should be couched in a manner that conveys its importance to the lives of the listeners so that they feel a personal connection with the topic, thus making them more likely to listen. For example, if you are talking to your friends and trying to convince them to eat a gluten-free diet, thus giving up things like pretzels and beer, they likely will not see a reason to do it. However, if you begin by explaining you have a way to increase their energy and help them avoid certain cancer risks, you make the issue that much more relevant to them, thus increasing the likelihood they will listen to you.

issue awareness
the first step in the persuasive process whereby the speaker alerts the audience to the issue requiring its attention

Another concrete example of raising issue awareness in an audience can be found in the case of Newton Minow, who President John F. Kennedy named as chairman of the Federal Communication Commission. Minow made increasing the quality of content on television a priority of his term on the FCC, and when addressing Congress about the lack of good television challenged anyone to watch it for a day and see if they too did not come to see television programming as a "vast wasteland." His comments, and specifically that phrase, made the issue of television content an issue of public concern for decades to come.

Once you engage the attention of your listeners by making them aware of the important issue, you move to the second stage in the persuasive process: *comprehension*. In the comprehension stage, you provide a context for the issue in dispute so the audience understands what you are talking about. Continuing with the gluten-free diet example, this part of the process might involve a discussion of what glutens are and how they impact a person's digestive system in negative ways. The comprehension stage then continues by laying out your position on the issue and why you feel others should share your view. This part of the persuasive process allows you to provide the foundation of your argument and then move to the third stage in the persuasive process.

comprehension
the second step in the persuasive process in which the speaker provides context for the issue in dispute so the audience understands what the speaker is talking about

The third and fourth steps focus less on the speaker and more on the audience. After you establish a context and make your case, it is up to your listeners whether or not they accept your position. *Acceptance* of your message is the third stage in the persuasive process. After carefully considering the facts you presented, the people to whom you are speaking could decide not to agree with you. On the other hand, they may very well be convinced that you are right. Knowing whether or not the audience truly agrees with you after hearing you speak is difficult to determine, but understanding your goals as a speaker enables you to have some

acceptance
the third step in the persuasive process in which the audience decides whether or not to agree with the position for which the speaker advocated

idea as to whether or not your appeal was successful. A little later we will return to this discussion of measuring the effectiveness of your appeal.

If members of the audience ultimately accept your position on the issue in dispute the persuasive process moves to its fourth and final stage: *integration.* Long after the lights have dimmed and your listeners have moved on to other activities, they begin to integrate that position into their daily lives. It becomes a part of their identity and their own personal philosophy. It is easiest to see after a call for immediate action, because people will either do what was proposed, or not. When listeners act in the way suggested by the speaker, they have integrated the speaker's point of view into their own lives.

So, let us summarize the persuasive process. When attempting to persuade an audience you need to make them aware of *what* you are speaking about. Then, you must ensure that they *understand* the issue. This is especially important when speaking about a complex topic. Third, the audience needs to *decide* whether or not they will accept your argument. Finally, if they do accept your ideas, they need to *integrate* them into how they now see things. This process can take place very rapidly, or may take hours, days, weeks, or even years to accomplish. In the next section we will discuss how to determine your expectations for persuasive appeals as a speaker, and how to determine their success after you make them.

integration
the fourth stage in the persuasive process in which the audience makes the speaker's position a part of its own personal philosophy and worldview

Figure 7.1
Stages of the Persuasive Process

Issue awareness	Understanding the issue	Acceptance of the issue	Integration into viewpoint

BUILDING YOUR CREDIBILITY

Whether or not we accept a person's argument often depends upon how credible he or she seems to us. Credibility represents a large part of what you will remember Aristotle called ethos, and it is an extremely important element of the persuasive process. As we mentioned earlier, speakers enter a communication situation with a certain level of credibility based on their own background and reputation, their perceived competence or expertise on the topic on which they are speaking, and even their appearance. In this section we revisit how credibility can be maintained and built during any communication event, and we will discuss how your credibility can also be damaged. To effectively persuade other people in any situation you must first establish your credibility, and then build upon it.

Credibility During the Communication Event

initial credibility
the level of believability a speaker has before beginning his or her speech

Initial credibility. You will recall we all bring a certain degree of credibility into any situation, and this is called our initial credibility. In persuasive messages, establishing credibility is just as important, if not more so, than for explanatory messages because you are asking an audience not only to trust what you have to say, but to follow your advice and direction. You are asking them to believe in you and take a leap of faith. You should make every effort to maximize your initial credibility in every persuasive situation. Keep in mind that your initial credibility will vary with different groups for different reasons.

Derived credibility. Credibility can be difficult for any student because the topics discussed in class and researched for term projects in many classes are often not something you have much experience with, and your audiences have no knowledge of any previous work you may have done.

derived credibility
the level of credibility during a speech that comes from what you say and how you say it

Our suggestions for enhancing your credibility during your speech are not new. Aristotle actually laid out three ways to build credibility, and contemporary scholars have given us a fourth way. The first is *good character,* which Aristotle defined as the state of being virtuous. You may recall from Chapter 1 that Aristotle understood virtue as qualities of moral excellence, which make one capable of performing outstanding deeds. Examples include courage, honesty, generosity, and fairness. For Aristotle, virtue consists of the mean between extremes. Courage, for instance, is neither foolhardiness nor cowardice. Persons of virtuous character occupy a state of being in which they have learned to have an appropriate emotional response to situations, and they avoid excessive displays that are unsuitable to the moment. Persons of good character tend to have a balanced response to situations and stay "calm under fire." For Aristotle, this ability defines good character. Good character may manifest itself through not attacking another person, yelling, screaming or attempting to inappropriately play upon negative emotions. It is, in short, behaving ethically and civilly by respecting the other people.

Aristotle's second way to derive ethos is through *sagacity,* or the demonstration of reasonableness and sound judgment. Reasonableness and judgment are demonstrated through the proper citation of important and relevant information and evidence. By verbally attributing sources, you not only fulfill your ethical obligations, but also demonstrate that you did research to ensure your competence to speak about the topic. It also means demonstrating a willingness to compromise and recognize strengths in the arguments put forth by others.

Finally, Aristotle proposes that you can derive credibility through demonstrating your *goodwill* toward the audience and the topic. Aristotle defined goodwill as the speaker's unselfish disposition that seeks the good for others regardless of what is good for the speaker. It means placing the good of others above your own desires. Goodwill toward others requires that we not hide our intentions or try to deceive the audience for personal gain. When persuading someone, you derive more ethos by making your motives clear and honestly assessing the benefit of the appeal for the others involved.

dynamism
a social science term for strong delivery that creates the impression with the audience that the speaker has practiced and thus cares about what he is talking about

Aristotle, however, was not the only one to provide us with ways to enhance our ethos during a speech. Social scientists today have added the concept of dynamism as a way to increase our credibility during a speech. *Dynamism* is a strong, confident delivery that convinces the listeners you are engaged in the topic and in their welfare. The more you speak, the more confident you will get, and that confidence translates into a better performance, thus increasing your credibility.

Terminal credibility. By the end of any interaction, you will likely achieve a new level of credibility as a speaker on your topic. The credibility with which you leave the situation is called terminal credibility. Where you end up, however, is largely influenced by how you established and built your credibility throughout your presentation. In any situation we walk away with an impression of the credibility of the other person, and sometimes, as in the case with first impressions of roommates, friends, business associates or even romantic interests, this can make or break the development of a relationship. Unfortunately, there are ways you can take steps back, and so we should consider the ways credibility and your reputation could be damaged.

Ways to Lose Credibility

There are three unethical behaviors that can irreparably damage your image and credibility with people. The first of these is *lying*. There are several different ways in which you can lie. The first occurs when you willfully present false evidence to another person. Creating new facts out of thin air just to advance your argument is not persuasion, it is *lying by commission. Lying by omission,* on the other hand, occurs when a speaker willfully chooses *not* to acknowledge facts about an argument that might damage its effectiveness. Both of these behaviors are unethical and can destroy a person's credibility.

Instead of leaving facts out, you should acknowledge them as a rebuttal, as it lets the other people know you did your research and have thought through potential problems with your position. Such a tactic actually tends to increase your credibility with an audience. Ignoring these problems, or trying to hide them, makes it appear you are serving a selfish interest and are not out for the good of the community.

A second behavior that can cause significant harm to your credibility is *manipulation*. Manipulation is the deliberate misrepresentation of facts and evidence so that listeners will see what you want them to see, rather than presenting them with a reasoned argument and trusting their ability to come to a careful conclusion. An example of the use of manipulation by a speaker involved former President Bill Clinton when he made statements regarding his relationship with an intern, Monica Lewinsky. President Clinton misrepresented the nature of his association with Lewinsky by stating that he did not have "sexual relations" with her, when, in fact, he did have sexual contact with her. The term Clinton used misled the audience by inferring he had no sexual relationship with Lewinsky. In this example he did not, strictly speaking, lie to the American people in that he did not have intercourse with Lewinsky, but he did mislead them as to the nature of their association.

Finally, you can damage your credibility by using the *threat of force* instead of reason to obtain agreement from your audience. *Coercion* is the use of threats or pressure to get listeners to do something against their will, and it can manifest itself in both physical and psychological ways. The least likely is physical, in that no one expects you to put a proverbial gun to the heads of your listeners to make them agree with you. It is possible, though, that you could coerce your listeners by threatening them with negative consequences if they do not agree with you. For instance, you might be coerced into taking an extra shift at work by a boss who threatens to fire you if you do not comply. A more common version of coercion is the "guilt trip" in which someone tries to elicit a feeling of guilt in you in order to get you to do something, thus expunging the guilt. Psychological coercion involves making others unduly afraid of what will happen if they do not agree with you. Using such tactics will damage your credibility by making you appear to be selfish or a fear-monger, rather than someone who can construct a rational plan to which people might agree.

coercion

the use of force or threats to make someone do something against his or her will

Your credibility, or ethos, is an essential part of every message you deliver. If your listeners think you will tell the truth, then they are more likely to pay attention to your argument and give you a fair hearing. The trust others have in you is something you should protect by trying not to lie, manipulate, or coerce them into agreeing with your position. If your position is right, and you present a well-reasoned argument, your listeners should come to the same conclusions you do about the issue in dispute. If they do not, then at least you allowed them to make the choice on their own while making the best case you could. It also bears noting that a rejection of your appeal does not mean a rejection of you as a person, because if you handled yourself civilly and ethically then there will be another opportunity in the future to engage in persuasion with the same individuals. If, however, you did not, then you may not be able to discuss matters with them in the future. Always remember that true persuasion leaves a choice for the audience.

SUMMARY

Persuasion takes place when there is an issue in dispute, or as Quintilian called it, an issue of stasis. Over the years stasis theory developed into what we now call persuasive questions. These issues in dispute are part of larger categories of persuasive appeals, identified by Aristotle as deliberative or forensic in nature. Regardless of the issue in dispute, or the form of persuasion you undertake, it always follows the same process: issue awareness, comprehension, acceptance, and integration. In order to successfully implement the persuasive process you need to come across as credible on the topic which you speak about, logically craft your speech, and construct appropriate emotional connections between the audience and your speech topic.

KEY TERMS

REVIEW QUESTIONS

1. What are the four types of stasis proposed by Quintilian?
2. What are the three forms of questions that a persuasive message could address?
3. What are the two types of persuasive messages proposed by Aristotle?
4. What are the three types of credibility a speaker has or can have?
5. What are the three ways you can irreparably harm your own credibility?
6. What does dynamism add to our understanding of credibility?

THINK ABOUT IT

1. Are there any types of issues in dispute not covered by the four forms of stasis proposed by Quintilian?
2. Are there any other ways you can damage your credibility? Enhance it?
3. If it is so unethical, why do people often manipulate data or lie to audiences to achieve their goals?
4. Could dynamism not be a factor in credibility?

ACTIVITIES FOR ACTION

1. Look at the stages of the persuasive process in this chapter. Think about how you have had your mind changed in the past, and identify how that process unfolded for you. Then, if there are differences, devise an alternative method for explaining how the persuasive process worked in your example. Are there different stages? Fewer? More?
2. Imagine a politician who has been caught cheating on his spouse, has been arrested for drunk driving, and has a tax lien on his property. If you were his political consultant, what would you suggest he do to increase his credibility? What might he do to re-establish his credibility?

ENDNOTES

1. The timeline of events can be found at: http://www.law.umkc.edu/faculty/projects/ftrials/Simpson/Simpsonchron.html (accessed October 16, 2008).

2. CNN, "OJ Simpson Trial: Marcia Clark, Johnny Cochrane Deliver Closings," http://www.cnn.com/2007/US/law/12/11/court.archive.simpson11/index.html (accessed October 16, 2008).

3. Thomas Morgan, "Competency of Judge, 91, in Gotti Case Questioned," *The New York Times* (April 20, 1989). Available: http://query.nytimes.com/gst/fullpage.html?res=950DEFDC173CF933A15757C0A96F948260 (accessed October 17, 2008).

4. Patricia Bizzell and Bruce Herzberg, *The Rhetorical Tradition: Readings From Classical Times to the Present,* 2nd Ed. (Boston, MA: Bedford St. Martin's, 2001), 38–39.

5. http://www.museum.tv/eotvsection.php?entrycode=minownewton (accessed June 1, 2011).

6. Ibid (accessed June 1, 2011).

7. http://www.americanrhetoric.com/speeches/newtonminow.htm (accessed June 1, 2011).

8. http://www.museum.tv/eotvsection.php?entrycode=minownewton (accessed June 1, 2011).

Interteaching Session

Dialogue

Choose a character from a favorite movie, TV show, graphic novel, comic, or book. With your groupmates, prepare a short persuasive presentation that accuses, blames, or otherwise holds that character responsible for something in the story: what in forensic persuasion is called the kategoria. Make sure that the outcome or event for which you are holding the character responsible is clear, and that you present your reasons why you believe that character is responsible for this outcome or event. Be prepared to make your argument to the class.

After you have presented your argument, listen to any counterarguments that your classmates might offer in defense of the same character: what in forensic persuasion is called the apologia. Explore with others in your class the reasons that they have offered in their defense and, if you wish, rebut or refute the arguments that they have made. Be prepared for them to do the same.

Performance

Suppose that you are wanting to study overseas in a study abroad program administered through the Center for International Programs here at the University. You are worried that you will not be able to pay for the cost of the trip, so you have decided to talk with your parents and ask them for assistance. As you prepare for this conversation, you give some thought to how you can convince your parents to believe in you, regardless of what they might think about what you are proposing: what Aristotle called ethos. For each of the following, identify one strategy that you could employ in your conversation to convince your parents to believe in you:

Sagacity:

Good character:

Goodwill:

Dynamism:

Be prepared to make your case to two of your classmates in a short roleplay, as if they were your parents in this conversation.

Using Evidence and Logic in Persuasion

- Describes classical models of reasoning
- Differentiates between deductive and inductive reasoning
- Details common reasoning fallacies that damage an argument and a speaker's credibility

Practically SPEAKING

For the last 50 years the Harvard Law School Forum has invited domestic and international celebrities to speak to the campus on a host of different issues. Included among the speakers who have come to the Forum in the past are Fidel Castro, Gerald Ford, and even sex therapist Dr. Ruth. No speaker in recent years, however, caused more of a stir than former head of the National Rifle Association (NRA) and Oscar-winning actor, the late Charlton Heston.[3]

On February 16, 1999, Heston addressed a crowd of about 200 people, consisting of students, faculty, conservatives, and liberals. The speech, entitled "Winning the Cultural War," inspired much debate around the campus for about a month after he delivered it, and if it wasn't for one event it probably would have faded into obscurity (For a transcript of Heston's speech, see: http://www.americanrhetoric.com/speeches/charltonhestonculturalwar.htm). On March 15, 1999, almost a month to the day after he gave the speech, popular conservative talk show host Rush Limbaugh read Heston's speech word for word on the air. After his rendition, thousands of people sought copies of the speech transcript, flooding both the Harvard Law School Forum and Limbaugh's radio station with requests.[4] The now immensely popular speech had only one problem: its argument.

Within the speech itself Heston attempted to make a logical argument; however, he was not very successful, despite the fact people loved the speech. He employed many of the logical fallacies later explained in this chapter to make his case. The unfortunate outcome of this was the wide support for his point of view coming from an audience that did not critically examine the message itself. In this chapter we will discuss models of reasoning and constructing an argument, which Heston did not use. Finally, we will use examples from his "Winning the Cultural War" speech as well as other texts to illustrate the different types of logical fallacies employed by speakers. By the end of this chapter the differences between correct and proper logic and improper appeals will be clear and easy to identify.

Prep Questions

Part 1: Key Concepts

1. Define syllogism. List and explain a syllogism's three component parts.

2. Explain how an inductive argument as understood by Aristotle differs from a deductive argument.

3. Define reasoning by analogy. Give two types of analogies that can be proposed.

4. Define reasoning by cause. Contrast the two types of causes that can be proposed.

5. List and define the ten logical fallacies identified in the chapter.

Part 2: Application

1. Construct a syllogism of one of the three types in the chapter that you could include in a persuasive presentation regarding a topic that you are considering for your upcoming persuasive assignment. Be sure that you identify the type of syllogism that you are creating and that you are labeling clearly all three parts of the syllogism.

2. Construct an inductive argument that you could include in a persuasive presentation on the same topic. Identify each of the three primary elements of Toulmin's model as they are reflected in your argument: the claim that you are making, the grounds that you are offering in support of the claim, and the warrant, which when explained, makes clear the reasoning that you are using to connect these grounds to this claim.

3. Create either an argument from analogy or an argument from cause that you could include in a persuasive presentation on this same topic. As before, identify each of the three primary elements of Toulmin's model as they are reflected in this argument: the claim, the grounds, and the warrant. Explain the reasoning that you are using, so that the way in which you are connecting the grounds to the claim is clear.

USING EVIDENCE AND LOGIC

In the last chapter, we explored the process of persuasion and different types of persuasion in which one can engage. We also examined one of the three components of rhetoric that Aristotle identified: ethos. We will now consider another of his three components, what he called logos. Logos consists, in part, of the evidence and reasoning that a speaker gives in support of her or his arguments. In general, we construct ethical and effective arguments by providing clear evidence that supports our claims. When we demonstrate the connection of the evidence we provide to the claims that we make, we demonstrate sound reasoning. In this chapter, we will explore some classical forms of reasoning, how we can use Toulmin's model to structure arguments in the persuasive messages we create in personal and professional contexts, and specific logical fallacies, or errors in logic, that we must avoid.

Classical Forms of Reasoning

Among Aristotle's many achievements relating to philosophy, science, the arts, and rhetoric, he established some of the most fundamental structures of formal logic. While these structures are not typically used explicitly by speakers when they strive to persuade others in everyday contexts, they do provide a way of understanding the essential structure of people's arguments. Everyday talk is often messy, disorganized, non-linear, and incomplete; the same is true for the arguments that people make in their interactions with others. Training oneself to think through arguments in a way that uses the structures that Aristotle identified can strengthen one's overall capacity to think logically. It also can enhance one's capacity to test the logic that others are employing when they construct arguments that they intend to be persuasive. Indeed, in certain professions, such as judges, attorneys, criminal investigators, and scientists, the soundness of arguments can make the difference between whether someone lives or dies, or is incarcerated or goes free. In these occupations, the structures of formal logic that Aristotle provided can strengthen a speaker's capacity to persuade in consequential ways. This is true for anyone who makes arguments to persuade others, although in everyday communication today, people seldom structure their arguments with the formality that Aristotle advocated.

Deductive Arguments

deductive argument

an argument that reasons from known premises to an inevitable conclusion

syllogism

the basic structure of a deductive argument that comes to an absolute conclusion

major premise

the first part of a syllogism, consisting of a general statement about the subject of your argument

minor premise

a statement about a specific case related to the general characteristics of the major premise

conclusion

a statement that follows logically from the application of the generalization or factual statement included in the major premise to the specific object or case identified in the minor premise

categorical syllogism

a syllogism in which the argument is based on membership in a group

Aristotle proposed two basic forms of logic: deductive and inductive. A *deductive argument* is based on generally accepted principles or known facts, which are then applied to a specific situation or case to an inevitable conclusion. The conclusion is inevitable because, if one accepts the general principle or known fact as stated and then applies it to the specific case, the conclusion logically follows. One can say that the conclusion is already contained within the terms of the argument.

The basic structure for deductive logic, for Aristotle, is the *syllogism*. As a structure of formal logic, syllogisms always contain three parts. The first is called the *major premise*. The major premise is a statement of a general principle or known fact about a particular subject or topic. The second part is called the *minor premise*. The minor premise is a statement that identifies a specific case or instance that relates to the subject or topic. This case has, in some way, the characteristics identified in the major premise. If the major premise states a generalization about an entire category or class of objects, then the minor premise might identify a particular object that has the same characteristic that the major premise attributes to that class or category. The final part of a syllogism is the *conclusion*. The conclusion is a statement that follows logically from the application of the generalization or factual statement included in the major premise to the specific object or case identified in the minor premise. The conclusion is the "therefore" that results when the major and the minor premise are brought together.

A well-known example of a syllogism that traces back to Aristotle's own writings, slightly modified to reflect contemporary language conventions, is:

Major premise:	All human beings are mortal.
Minor premise:	Socrates is a human being.
Conclusion:	Therefore, Socrates is mortal.

As you can see in the example, this syllogism contains a major premise that puts forth a general principle or statement of general fact, in this case about an entire class of objects: human beings. It presents the generalization that all human beings are mortal, which then functions as a general principle within the argument. The syllogism also includes a minor premise, which presents a specific case or object: in this instance, Socrates. Moreover, the minor premise identifies Socrates as a specific instance or case that has characteristics reflected in the major premise: that Socrates is a human being, that he belongs to the class or category that the major premise establishes. The conclusion follows logically from the application of the major premise to the minor premise. If we know that all human beings are mortal and we know that Socrates is a human being, then we know that he too is mortal. We do not need to look anywhere outside the two premises to find the conclusion. It is already contained in the premises; to arrive at the conclusion, we need only to bring the two premises together. The conclusion is inevitable insofar as its follows logically from the premises.

We can categorize syllogisms according to their components parts. The first type of syllogism are *categorical syllogisms*. Categorical syllogisms are based on membership in a category. The major premise in a categorical syllogism consists of a statement of general fact or principle, as it does in all syllogisms. However, unlike in other syllogisms, in a categorical syllogism, the major premise establishes some fact about an entire category, class, or group of objects. The previous example regarding Socrates is a categorical syllogism because the major premise identifies a particular class or category of things and establishes that something is characteristic of that group of things: in this case, that all human beings are mortal. The minor premise in a categorical syllogism presents a specific instance or case, as it does in all syllogisms. However, unlike in other syllogisms, in a categorical syllogism, the minor premise identifies the specific instance or case as being a member of this general class or category of things. The conclusion follows inevitably from the major and minor premises: if X is true about such-and-such class of objects, and Y is a member of that class, then X is true about Y. One need not look beyond the two premises to derive the conclusion; it flows from bringing these premises together.

The second type of syllogism is a *disjunctive syllogism*. A disjunctive syllogism contains two or more mutually exclusive alternatives. The alternatives are mutually exclusive insofar as only one of them can be true, not both. If one of them can be shown to be true, then the other must be false. In a disjunctive syllogism, the major premise presents as a general principle or statement of fact that two alternatives exist. The minor premise focuses on the specific instance of the present situation by eliminating one of the two alternatives. Consider the following example:

disjunctive syllogism
a syllogism in which the major premise includes two or more mutually exclusive alternatives

> *Major premise:* Either my CMM 100 class is in Miriam 205 or it is in Zehler 101.
>
> *Minor premise:* My CMM 100 class is not in Miriam 205.
>
> *Conclusion:* Therefore, my CMM 100 section is in Zehler 101.

As it does in other syllogisms, the conclusion follows logically from bringing together the two premises: if either X or Y must be true, and we know that X is not the case, then Y must be true.

conditional syllogism
a syllogism in which the major premise contains a hypothetical condition and its outcome

The third type of syllogism we will examine is a *conditional syllogism*. In a conditional syllogism, the major premise presents a hypothetical condition and establishes what its outcome will be, using an "if-then" statement. The "if" portion of the major premise is called the *antecedent*, while the "then" portion of the statement is called the *consequent*. This "if-then" statement functions as a general principle or statement of fact. The minor premise in a conditional syllogism focuses on the specific instance of the present situation by affirming that the antecedent is indeed the case. The conclusion follows inevitably from the two premises, as it does in other syllogisms. Consider this example:

antecedent
the hypothetical condition in the major premise of a conditional syllogism

consequent
the outcome of the hypothetical condition in the major premise of a conditional syllogism

> *Major premise:* If we increase revenue, then we will not need to downsize.
>
> *Minor premise:* We increased revenue.
>
> *Conclusion:* Therefore, we will not need to downsize the workforce.

The conclusion follows logically from bringing together the major and minor premises: if X occurs, then Y will be the result, and we know that X has occurred; then we can know that Y will be the result.

A couple of concepts are useful when one is trying to assess the logic of a syllogism. The first is a *valid argument*. The concept of validity, on its own, has no relationship to the truth of the premises or the conclusion that make up the argument. An argument is valid when the conclusion follows logically from the premises. For example, one might put forth the argument, a conditional syllogism:

Major premise: If knowing how to communicate effectively is something that everyone knows how to do, then I don't need to take CMM 100.

Minor premise: Everyone knows how to communicate effectively.

Conclusion: Therefore, I don't need to take CMM 100.

This argument is valid because the conclusion follows inevitably from the two premises. If one accepts the major premise that there is no need to take CMM 100 if communicating effectively is something that everyone knows how to do, and if one accepts the minor premise that everyone indeed does know how to communicate effectively, then the conclusion that there is no need to take CMM 100 follows logically from these premises. The syllogism is valid, not because the statements are true or false, but because the conclusion does indeed follow from the premises. When one assesses the validity of a syllogism, one *assumes* that the premises are true and then tests whether the conclusion can be guaranteed to be also true, given what the premises state. If the premises are assumedly true and the conclusion can be shown to be assumedly true solely on the basis of the premises, then the argument is valid. If the premises are assumedly true yet the conclusion that ostensibly follows from them is false, then the argument is invalid.

Here is an example of an invalid argument:

Major premise: If knowing how to communicate effectively is something that everyone knows how to do, then I don't need to take CMM 100.

Minor premise: Some people know how to communicate effectively.

Conclusion: Therefore, I don't need to take CMM 100.

The argument is invalid because if we assume that the premises are true, they cannot guarantee the conclusion. In other words, the conclusion does not follow inevitably from the premises. We can assume that if knowing how to communicate effectively is common sense, then I don't need to take CMM 100. However, suppose that upon investigation, we come to the belief that knowing how to communicate effectively is something that some people, but not all know how to do. If we assume the truth of this statement, then we can't assume that the conclusion is true based on these two premises. We can't conclude that I don't need to take CMM 100 because, upon bringing the minor premise and the major premise together, I can't assume that I don't need to take CMM 100. After all, I might be one of those people who don't know how to communicate effectively, for the minor premise only established that some people know how to communicate effectively, not everyone as the major premise stipulated.

A valid argument is not necessarily a *sound argument*. In order for a syllogism to be a sound argument, two conditions must exist. First, the argument must be valid. The conclusion must follow logically from the premises. If we assume that the premises are true, then the conclusion also must be true. Accordingly, the premises must be able to guarantee the assumed truth of the conclusion. Second, the premises must be *actually* true. When assessing validity, one *assumes* the truth of the premises as they are stated, and then determines whether the conclusion is an inevitable consequence of applying the major premise to the minor premise. One does not determine whether the premises—and thus the conclusion—are, in fact, true. To call an argument sound, one must satisfy this additional condition of determining whether the premises are indeed factual. If they are false, then the argument is not sound, even if it is valid.

sound argument
a valid argument that has true premises

Stereotypes are examples of syllogisms that are valid but not necessarily true. Consider, for instance, this example:

Major premise: All communication instructors lack competence in math and science.

Minor premise: Teresa is a communication instructor.

Conclusion: Therefore, Teresa lacks competence in math and science.

This argument is a categorical syllogism. It also illustrates the pattern of many common stereotypes. It asserts a major premise, which sets forth a general principle or statement of fact about an entire class, category, or grouping of things: in this case, communication instructors, to whom it attributes the characteristic of lacking competence in math and science. It follows with a minor premise, which identifies a specific case or instance that belongs to the aforementioned class or category of things: in this case, it identifies a person named Teresa who is a communication instructor. The conclusion results from applying the major premise to the minor premise. The argument is valid because if we assume the truth of the premises, then the stated conclusion does follow inevitably from the premises. If we assume that all communication instructors lack competence in math and science, and we assume that Teresa is indeed a communication instructor, then it follows logically that Teresa lacks competence in math and science.

To be sound, the argument would need to be not only valid, but also actually true. To determine this, we can start with the premises. Do all communication instructors lack competence in math and science? Communication instructors, like all people, might vary in the level of competency in math and science, but it would be false to say that they as a category of people lack competency. In fact, if we consider the educational training that any given communication instructor would have needed to complete, the opposite seems to be true: that communication instructors as a category have a considerable degree of competency in math and science. Communication as a field is considered to be a social science at many universities, including at the University of Dayton. To teach a college-level communication course, an instructor would need to have a Bachelor's degree or be working on an advanced degree in Communication or a related field. Most Masters programs in Communication require at least one core course in statistics and scientific methods, if not additional courses. Many instructors have a doctorate; these instructors have potentially even additional training in scientific methods and the use of quantitative methods in social science. Some communication instructors conduct their own quantitative social scientific research and publish multiple articles every year in reputable journals. Some even teach courses in which others learn how to conduct scientific studies and to perform complex statistical procedures. While none of this is absolutely true for every communication instructor, we can find many instances in which communication instructors certainly have competence in math and science. Accordingly, the major premise is demonstrably false. If either of the premises is false, then the conclusion also cannot be true. Although the argument is valid, it is not sound. If stereotypes are constructed in a way that has validity, then an audience might be disposed to accept them because the premises and the conclusion hang together logically. However, a valid argument is not necessarily a sound argument. If any of the premises, upon further investigation can be shown to be actually false, then the argument is not sound.

enthymeme
. . . .
a syllogism missing one or two of its parts

One final term relating to syllogisms is noteworthy. In his study of deductive arguments, Aristotle highlighted a specific way in which a syllogism could be presented to an audience, which he called an *enthymeme*. The term enthymeme refers not so much to a type of syllogism, such as the three types that we examined earlier, but the form in which it is presented. Enthymemes are truncated syllogisms. They are syllogisms that are missing one or two of their essential components. When the syllogism is delivered to an audience, the speaker leaves out a part of the syllogism, either one of the premises or the conclusion. Often, the part that is left out is so commonly accepted that it need not be put into words. Nonetheless, despite the missing component, the enthymeme is convincing. Why? Because the audience fills in the missing piece, and no one is likely to be more convincing to an audience than they themselves!

Consider the example from earlier in the chapter regarding Socrates. The speaker can construct this argument in a formal sense, in which case it would take the form of the syllogism that we have already seen. However, when the time comes to engage the audience, the speaker could state the argument this way: "Socrates is mortal, my friends. How do I know this? Because Socrates is a human being." In this case, the argument is stated as an enthymeme. The argument has a conclusion, which in this case, the speaker says first: "Socrates is mortal." It also has a minor premise, which the speaker provides as a basis for the conclusion: "Socrates is a human being." What piece is missing? The speaker has left out the major premise: "Human beings are mortal." In this particular case, the premise is so accepted that it does not need to be said. However, there is another reason not to state this premise. By not stating the premise, the speaker creates an opportunity for the audience themselves to provide it. The argument is likely to be more convincing to them because they themselves are contributing to it. They are helping to construct the very argument through which the speaker is trying to convince them!

Inductive Arguments

The other form of argument that Aristotle explored are *inductive arguments.* An inductive argument begins with observations regarding specific instances and moves towards a general principles or statement of fact that identifies a pattern across those instances. In this sense, its logic moves in a direction opposite to that in which a the logic of a syllogism moves. An inductive argument moves from an observation of specific cases to a conclusion that expresses a general principle or statement of fact; whereas, a deductive argument moves from a general principle or statement of fact to a conclusion regarding what that principle or statement of fact implies about a specific case, including perhaps the present situation.

inductive argument
••••••••••••
reasoning from individual observations or events to conclude a general principle

An inductive argument has the following structure:

> Specific Case 1: My cat Louis likes milk.
>
> Specific Case 2: My parents' cat Biscuit likes milk.
>
> Specific Case 3: My daughter's cat Callie likes milk.
>
> Specific Case 4: My son's cat Frisk likes milk.
>
> [Additional Cases, if Warranted]
>
> Conclusion: Therefore, cats like milk.

The argument rests on several examples that share some characteristic or commonality: in this case, four different cats, all of which like milk. The conclusion generalizes the shared characteristic or commonality to the category of things or conditions that the specific instances exemplify: in this case, cats. Based on the examples that are available in the argument, a conclusion is drawn about all things that belong to that class of objects or conditions relative to that characteristic.

The strength of an inductive argument depends upon the number and the representativeness of the specific cases or instances relative to the general principle. If only a few examples have been given, then the argument might not be convincing to the audience. In the aforementioned example, a generalization about all cats is made on the basis of four cats. The audience might ask how such a broad generalization can be made for the billions of cats in the world from such a small number and decide that we simply do not know enough about the class or category of things or conditions identified in the conclusion by looking at these few examples. For this reason, a rhetor should consider offering many examples to convince their audience. How many examples are needed? There is no single answer to this question. The number of examples that a speaker must give depends ultimately on what the audience will find to be convincing. In general, the more examples a rhetor gives, the more compelling the inductive logic of the argument will likely be, though she or he must take into account a number of other considerations, including the available time, the experience and disposition of the audience relative to the topic, and other factors relating to the context, some of which we examined in Chapter 3.

This concern regarding the number of examples relates to the second concern: their representativeness. The more "typical" the examples in an inductive argument are relative to the class or category of objects or conditions identified in the conclusion, the more compelling they will likely be to the audience. In a given argument, even if numerous examples are given to illustrate the point that a speaker is trying to make, if those examples are highly unusual or anomalous to the general class of objects or conditions about which the speaker is drawing a conclusion, then the audience is likely to question the argument.

Scientists today often use inductive logic when they make generalizations about social interaction and other human behavior across large populations of people. When they conduct research about a particular population of people, for instance, in most cases, they cannot ask, observe, or otherwise acquire information from every person in that population. The population that they are studying in a given research project might consist of thousands or even millions of people. In such cases, engaging every individual in the population would require exorbitant amounts of time, energy, and resources, if it was possible at all. Rather than try to engage every individual in the population, scientists often create a sampling of people that is smaller in number but highly representative of the population as a whole. To create such a group, the researchers often employ methods that reduce as much as possible the statistical likelihood that the population will over-represent certain groups within the population and under-represent others. The sample also must be large enough to make generalizations about the population; a sample of three people is not an adequate basis for making generalizations about a population of 30,000 people. Accordingly, both concerns of the size and representativeness of the observed cases must be taken into account in creating the sample. After creating such a sample and conducting their research, scientists then use inductive logic to offer generalizations regarding the population that the sample is meant to represent. If the scientists observe something as being true about a considerable number of the people in the sample, then they might make a generalization about the population as a whole. Much scientific research today depends on this sort of inductive logic.

Creating Arguments Using Toulmin's Model

Aristotle's two forms of formal logic and the structures that he identified can help you to think logically about the arguments to convince others that you want to make and the arguments that others make as they attempt to convince you, especially if these arguments involve deductive or inductive logic. However, as you begin crafting those arguments and considering how they might fit within the overall organizational structure of the message you want to present, we encourage you to use Toulmin's Model, which we examined in Chapter 5, as a guide.

If you recall from Chapter 5, Toulmin's model depicts any argument as having three primary elements and possibly one or more secondary elements. The three primary elements are the claim, the grounds, and the warrant. The claim is the statement that you as the speaker want your audience to accept; it is, in essence, the conclusion to which you are leading your audience. The grounds are the evidence that you provide in support of that claim. The warrant consists of those statements, often unspoken, that must be accepted if the audience is to accept the grounds as convincing evidence for this claim. In some cases, you as a speaker might incorporate other elements into an argument. These elements might include backing, or additional support for the warrant; a rebuttal, or an attempt to convince the audience that certain counter arguments that the argument might evoke are not tenable; or a qualifier, which is a statement or phrase that expresses the degree of certainty of the argument that the speaker is offering. If you use Toulmin's model as a framework for creating the arguments that you intend to make, at minimum, you need to determine the specific claim that you are making in each, the grounds that you are providing in support for that claim, and consider the warrant that holds the two together logically. We already have studied in some depth in Chapter 5 the claim and the grounds. In this section of the chapter, we will look more closely at the warrant.

One way of thinking about the warrant in an argument is that it expresses the reasoning that makes the connection between the grounds and the claim logically defensible. Often, speakers do not state the warrant explicitly, but if one looks closely at the argument, one can bring to the surface the particular reasoning whereby the connection between the grounds and the claim "makes sense" for the speaker - which is what she or he is trying to get the audience also to see. We will consider four fundamental types of reasoning, any of which might be an integral part of the warrant of an argument.

Reasoning from Principle or General Statement of Fact

The first of these four types is deductive reasoning, or reasoning from principle or general statement of fact. We have explored already syllogisms as the basic structure of deductive reasoning. We also looked at how speakers, when they deliver deductive arguments, often leave out one of the premises or the conclusion and create what Aristotle called an enthymeme. When you wish to create an argument using deductive reasoning, you can create a syllogism as Aristotle explained. However, if you wish to use a more informal style for making your argument, Toulmin's model can be helpful.

Table 8.1

Tips for Using Deductive Reasoning
• Make sure the premises of your argument are actually true.
• Provide evidence to demonstrate the accuracy of your premises.
• Consider mapping out the deductive logic of the argument in the form of a syllogism
• Test the validity of the argument: does the conclusion follow inevitably from the premises?
• Give evidence to demonstrate the accuracy of the conclusion.

You might begin by making a claim that you want to convince your audience to accept. For instance, you might say, "No matter how much nostalgia people feel for this little world, Pluto is not a planet." Next, you would present the grounds for your claim. Continuing with this example regarding planets, you might provide a definition of what a planet is, from recognized experts, in this case the International Astronomical Union, along with a factual observation about Pluto:

Women's Rights Are Human Rights
by Hillary Clinton

Delivered September 5, 1995, at the United Nations 4th World Conference on Women in Beijing, China

First Lady Hillary Clinton advocated for the rights of both children and women during her husband's time in office. In 1995 she traveled to the 4th United Nations Conference on Women in China. It is also a nation that allows little political dissent.

As First Lady she had significant prior ethos and initial credibility, and she derived more by noting her involvement on the issue of women's rights:

"Over the past 25 years, I have worked persistently on issues relating to women, children, and families. Over the past two-and-a-half years, I've had the opportunity to learn more about the challenges facing women in my own country and around the world."[5]

Mrs. Clinton made her case often through the use of enthymemes, or syllogisms missing one or more parts. Take the following passage as an example: "What we are learning around the world is that if women are healthy and educated, their families will flourish. If women are free from violence, their families will flourish. If women have a chance to work and earn as full and equal partners in society, their families will flourish. And when families flourish, communities and nations do as well."[6]

Mrs. Clinton uses this parallel structure to enthymematically argue for better treatment of women around the world. It is an enthymeme because it is a syllogism missing a part. If it were a syllogism it would look more like this: Communities and nations wish for their members to flourish. Women are members of communities and nations. Therefore, communities and nations wish for women to flourish. The enthymematic argument sounded a lot easier on the ears than the syllogism and also got the point across more creatively and effectively.

"Pluto does not meet all of the characteristics that the International Astronomical Union, at their website, identifies in their definition of what constitutes a planet: 'A celestial body that (a) is in orbit around the Sun, (b) has sufficient mass for its self-gravity to overcome rigid body forces so that it assumes a hydrostatic equilibrium (nearly round) shape, and (c) has cleared the neighbourhood around its orbit.' Specifically, Pluto has not cleared the neighborhood around its orbit."

The warrant in this argument is what one must assume to be true in order for the grounds to support the claim.

In this particular argument, the warrant involves deductive reasoning. That reasoning could be represented with the following syllogism:

Major premise: A planet is a celestial body that (a) is in orbit around the Sun, (b) has sufficient mass for its self-gravity to overcome rigid body forces so that it assumes a hydrostatic equilibrium (nearly round) shape, and (c) has cleared the neighbourhood around its orbit.

Minor premise: Pluto does not have all of these characteristics.

Conclusion: Therefore, Pluto is not a planet.

This syllogism is a categorical syllogism. It works by presenting a general principle regarding a class of objects, in this case a statement of characteristics that define a whole category of things called planets. It makes an observation about a specific case relative to the category in question: that Pluto as a specific body lacks all of these characteristics. It then draws a conclusion by bringing together the definition and the observation about the specific case. The conclusion follows logically because the specific case does not have all of the characteristics that are required for things belonging to the category in question.

The syllogism is not stated with all of its premises and its conclusion, but if the audience were to challenge the argument as given, it could be laid out for the audience and explained. The actual argument, as delivered to the audience in a talk or presentation, might sound like this:

> *No matter how much nostalgia people feel for this little world, Pluto is not a planet. Pluto does not meet all of the characteristics that the International Astronomical Union, an association of professional astronomers from around the world, at their website dated 2018, identifies in their definition of what constitutes a planet: "A celestial body that (a) is in orbit around the Sun, (b) has sufficient mass for its self-gravity to overcome rigid body forces so that it assumes a hydrostatic equilibrium (nearly round) shape, and (c) has cleared the neighbourhood around its orbit." Specifically, Pluto has not cleared the neighborhood around its orbit.*

The audience could challenge this argument in a number of ways. They could question the definition of a planet that has been given as evidence. They might do this by questioning the specific characteristics that the International Astronomical Union identifies in its definition. For instance, they might ask why a celestial body must clear the neighborhood around its orbit to be a planet? They also could question the credibility of the source for this evidence: who is the International Astronomical Union that we must take their definition over the alternatives that other experts have offered? The audience could question the statement that Pluto lacks the characteristics of a planet, which also serves as part of the grounds for the argument.

If you are going to employ deductive reasoning in making an argument, then you might keep in mind certain tips. Make sure that the premises on which you are basing your argument are actually true. To demonstrate the accuracy of these premises, you might need to cite additional evidence or provide additional explanation. Test the validity of your reasoning. You might consider mapping out the logic of your argument in explicit formal terms in the form of a syllogism, as Aristotle described, and then examine whether the conclusion follows inevitably from the premises. If the premises are true and the argument is valid, then the conclusion also will be true. However, because there is no guarantee that your audience will accept the argument, you might provide evidence to demonstrate the accuracy of your stated conclusion as well.

This is one advantage of using Toulmin's model: it highlights the need to support any claims that you make with evidence. Syllogisms, in themselves, do not necessarily incorporate evidence. In Aristotle's time, syllogisms often were employed to address philosophical questions that had a more abstract nature. Moreover, the classical worldview of the society in which Aristotle lived did not have the same empirical orientation that the contemporary world has, in which truth claims at the heart of public discourse are often subjected to scientific testing and verification. The two premises constitute statements of assumed fact, one of which functions as a principle and the other that describes a specific situation or case. The conclusion follows logically from the premises. At no point does the structure of a syllogism require a speaker to provide actual evidence. Using Toulmin's model can remind a speaker that as long as the premises on which one's argument rests are not universally accepted, one will need to provide evidence of some kind to convince the audience to accept them as true.

Reasoning by Example

reasoning by example
the process of inferring general conclusions and making general claims from specific cases

The most common form of reasoning involves taking specific cases and making general conclusions based on their characteristics. The process of inferring general conclusions and making general claims from specific cases is called *reasoning by example* and it is a form of inductive reasoning. On rare occasions only one case or example allows you to make a generalization, but more often than not you will need to use multiple cases to strengthen your ability to make a general claim. Additionally, there are several important elements you must pay attention to when choosing the examples that support your claim.

First, the examples must be relevant to the case you make. The more closely you can tie the examples to the claim the stronger your claim. You also must provide a reasonable number of examples to support your case. Relying on just one may make it appear that there is not enough evidence to support your argument. The examples you use must also be typical and represent that larger population of which they serve as a sample. Finally, you must be sure that the examples you choose do not contradict your argument.

SPOTLIGHTING THEORISTS: ISOCRATES

Isocrates (436–338 BC)

As one of the ten greatest orators of Ancient Greece, otherwise called the Attic Orators, Isocrates taught rhetoric to many Greeks and influenced the work of Cicero, Quintilian and many other Roman rhetoricians. He was born into a wealthy family that provided him with an opportunity to receive a good education. Unfortunately, following the Peloponnesian War his family was stripped of its money, forcing Isocrates to find gainful employment.

His early efforts to make a living involved work as a logographer, or courtroom speechwriter. Later, around 392 BC, he opened his own school to teach rhetoric where he charged a much higher fee than most schools at the time. He still amassed many students and eventually reconstituted his family's fortune.

Isocrates focused on practical speaking in situations where finding absolute truth was not possible. He believed that the ideal orator was someone who not only possessed talent in delivery, but also was well learned in a variety of different areas. Additionally, he felt they needed to be virtuous in intent, value

freedom—or at least the Greek notion of it—and practice self-control. A good Isocratean speaker, therefore, could knowledgeably speak on a variety of different topics, in a variety of different situations, and do so in an ethically sound manner.

One of the most influential concepts in rhetoric most linked to Isocrates is that of kairos. Kairos is the notion of timing, so it was said "Kairos is all," or as we now say it, "Timing is everything." Kairos is the speaker's ability to adapt to any occasion and deliver a speech fit for that moment. This is relevant to all speaking situations, including those for which epideictic address is necessary.

A good ceremonial speaker can adapt to the audience, the moment, and the topic to deliver a knowledgeable, ethical, and practical speech that balances the importance of the moment with the emotion of the audience. Proper attention to kairos enables someone to speak well at any event. Kairos is all.

Tips for Reasoning by Example	**Table** 8.2

- Ensure the example is relevant.
- It is wise to have more than one example.
- Make sure the examples are typical of the issue.
- The example should not contradict the point you are making.

Reasoning by Analogy

reasoning by analogy
when you compare two similar cases in order to argue that what is true in one case is also true in the other

literal analogy
when the two cases being compared are classified the same way

figurative analogy
when the two cases being compared are from completely different classifications

A third form of reasoning you may use when creating a persuasive argument involves making a comparison. *Reasoning by analogy* is when you compare two similar cases in order to argue that what is true in one case is also true in the other. Analogies can be constructed in two ways. A *literal analogy* occurs when the two cases being compared are classified the same way. For instance, if you argued that a certain crime prevention program would work in Los Angeles because it also worked in Houston, you are making a literal analogy between two real cities. The other form of analogy, a *figurative analogy*, occurs when the items are from completely different classifications. These analogies employ similies, such as this example: *The art of compromise is a lot like modern art.* Compromise and modern art are not in the same classification; however, the analogy allows you to take characteristics of one and ascribe them to the other.

When reasoning by analogy you must be aware of several things. First, the items in the comparison must have significant points of similarity, and those points must be crucial to the association you are making. You may need to explain those connections, but as long as you can in a cogent manner then you should be fine. You also need to recognize that all analogies have points of difference, but so long as these points of difference are not critical or important to your comparison then the analogy should hold. Also, you must remember that as effective as figurative analogies are, they cannot be used for making a logical proof for your argument; rather they are best suited for explanations. To employ an analogy for a logical proof you must instead rely on literal analogies. Analogical reasoning is an effective way to make a point because it allows you to use more concrete language and make your point using items with which your audience may be more familiar.

Table 8.3

Tips for Reasoning by Analogy
• Points must be similar.
• Points need to be crucial to the case.
• Be prepared to explain connections.
• Be aware that all analogies have differences.
• Figurative analogies cannot be used for proof.
• Figurative analogies can be used for explanation.

Reasoning by Cause

reasoning by cause
arguments that claim one event or factor produces an effect

A final form of reasoning is called *reasoning by cause*, and it refers to arguments that claim one event or factor produces an effect. Almost all causal reasoning is based on probabilities. Here is an example of one such case: *Obtaining a college education will allow students to get better paying jobs when they graduate.* The cause is a college education and the effect is a better paying job; however, we all know it is not a guarantee that a college degree will get you a better paying job. It merely increases the probability that such an effect will come to pass. Causal reasoning can be very persuasive with an audience, but it must be carefully constructed.

Much like the other forms of reasoning we have discussed so far, causal reasoning also must be conducted with several things in mind. First, the cause you discuss must be relevant to the effect you describe. For example, you could claim that chewing a new piece of gum during every inning of a baseball game caused your team to win. These two events are completely unrelated, and the gum chewing almost certainly does not have any bearing on the result of a baseball game. A second aspect of the relationship you must be aware of is whether the cause you discuss is the only possible cause for the effect in your argument. Almost always more than one cause contributes to an effect, and recognizing this in your argument is important. Also at issue is whether the cause is actually capable of producing the effect you discuss. For instance, generally people believe that receiving a college degree will cause them to get a job when they graduate. Although the idea of college degrees helping students get jobs upon graduation has some merit, other factors are also at play, such as how well the applicant interviews, how the student performed while in school, and a whole host of other variables.

Tips for Reasoning by Cause
• Cause must be relevant to the effect.
• Are there other possible causes?
• Is the cause really capable of producing the effect?

Table 8.4

Finally, and most importantly, you must determine if the cause you present is necessary and sufficient. A *necessary cause* is a condition that must be present for the effect to occur. A temperature of less than 32 degrees Fahrenheit must be present for freezing to occur. A *sufficient cause* is a condition that automatically produces the effect in question. For example, a broken spine is a sufficient condition for paralysis. Academically, plagiarism is a sufficient cause for failing a class, but it is not a necessary cause for failure as other things can also cause someone to fail a course. The necessary cause for failing a course is not completing the work assigned in an acceptable manner. When sufficient conditions are known, they can be brought together to ensure an event's occurrence. See Figure 8.1 for additional examples.

necessary cause
a condition that must be present for the effect to occur

sufficient cause
a condition that automatically produces the effect in question

Necessary Cause Examples	Sufficient Cause Examples
• People need water to live. • Oxygen must be present for fire to burn. • Metal will expand when the temperature becomes hot enough.	• A gunshot wound to the head is sufficient to cause death. • Stealing at work is a sufficient cause to be fired. • Lack of fertilizer is a sufficient cause for a plant to die.

Figure 8.1
Examples of Necessary Cause and Sufficient Cause

Knowing how to carefully craft arguments using each of these reasoning processes will help make your speech that much more effective. One key to constructing the most persuasive argument possible in any given context, be it a conversation with a boss or friend, or a sales presentation to a larger audience, is appreciating the context in which you find yourself. Your ability to find examples or choose analogies that resonate with a given listener, and the careful timing of delivering those reasons may determine success or failure in your effort. For example, approaching a friend to ask a favor may not work when he or she just received a bad grade on an exam, no matter how strong your case may be. Waiting until the most opportune time is essential for maximizing your potential for successful persuasion. This idea of timing was first discussed at length by the Greek philosopher Isocrates, who proposed that "kairos is all." *Kairos*, or a person's ability to adapt to any occasion and deliver a message fit for that moment, is best understood as timing. Today, we paraphrase this important principle taught by Isocrates as "Timing is everything."

kairos
a person's ability to adapt to any occasion and deliver a message fit for that moment

It is important to understand that the classical models as well as more contemporary approaches can be very effective at making a successful persuasive appeal. You don't have to limit yourself to the classics if you find other methods and styles that work well for you. As the Greeks, Romans, and many others have noted, creating a reasoned argument is not easy. In fact, the "easy road" to argument often involves using improper modes of argument known as logical, or reasoning, fallacies. In the next section we will discuss ways in which the reasoning process we have discussed so far can be damaged or perverted through the use of such fallacies.

REASONING FALLACIES

Making a reasoned argument may seem like a simple task, and we all may believe that we use reason properly all the time, but in fact many times we use fallacious, or erroneous, reasoning. There are ten common fallacies that distort the reasoning process by only *appearing* logical when, in actuality, they are not. In this section we will discuss these ten different reasoning fallacies and illustrate how they damage your ability to make an ethical and effective persuasive claim.

Types of Fallacies

begging-the-question fallacy
when a speaker presumes certain things are facts when they have not yet been proven to be truthful

The first of the reasoning fallacies is dangerous because it presumes truth without proof. The *begging-the-question fallacy* occurs when someone presumes that certain things are facts when they have not yet been proven to be truthful. This fallacy is easy to identify as it involves making statements that begin with things like "Everyone knows that" and "It should go without saying." These phrases assume that the statement that follows is an absolute indisputable truth, even though that is almost always not the case. When seen as a truth, the information then becomes false grounds upon which the remainder of the argument rests.

At the beginning of the chapter we told the story of a speech given by Charlton Heston at Harvard in 1999. We mentioned that the speech included quite a few logical fallacies, and the begging-the-question fallacy was one of them. At one point Heston stated:

> "Americans know something without a name is undermining the nation."[7]

example: begging-the-question fallacy

This statement presumes that every American believes there is something wrong with the country, while he provides no evidence to back up this likely erroneous statement. Accepting the implicit argument in this statement, however, is the foundation of the speech and without analyzing it for what it is, the audience simply accepts it and moves closer to agreeing with Heston. Begging-the-question is faulty logic that depends on audiences accepting broad assumptions with no support.

A second form of reasoning not based on logic is the non sequitur, from the Latin phrase for "does not follow." A *non sequitur fallacy* occurs when you make an unwarranted move from one idea to the next. Often this happens because you do not provide evidence or fail to clearly connect your evidence to your claim. The evidence you provided does not relate to the claim you made. If the relationship between the evidence and your argument remains unclear and you still move to the next point, you have committed a non sequitur.

non sequitur fallacy

when you make an unwarranted move from one idea to the next

Heston also included non sequiturs in his speech. Take this passage, for example:

> "As I have stood in the crosshairs of those who target Second Amendment freedoms, I've realized that firearms are not the only issue. No, it's much, much bigger than that. I've come to understand that a cultural war is raging across our land, in which, with Orwellian fervor, certain acceptable thoughts and speech are mandated."[8]

The passage starts with a discussion of firearms and the Second Amendment, but then suddenly moves to freedom of speech, which involves the First Amendment. He provides no evidence for the move from one issue to the next, except to say it involves a larger problem.

Non sequiturs can sometimes be confused with a third type of logical fallacy. The *slippery slope fallacy* is a logical fallacy that assumes once an action begins it will follow, undeterred, to an eventual and inevitable conclusion. Whereas the non sequitur makes leaps from claim to claim without evidence, the slippery slope assumes a predetermined path for events simply because the first stage occurred. Again, Heston's speech at Harvard provides us with a perfect example:

slippery slope fallacy

a logical fallacy that assumes once an action begins it will lead, undeterred, to an eventual and inevitable conclusion

> "What does all of this mean? It means that telling us what to think has evolved into telling us what to say, so telling us what to do can't be far behind."[9]

Here, Heston assumes that people are being told what to think and say. Additionally, since that is happening, people will inevitably be told what to do. There is no evidence for any of these stages; there is a presupposition they are true, and more importantly, he assumes a direct causal connection between each that eliminates the possibility of other contributing factors or the occurrence of a change in the process he outlined. In other words, he presents the appearance of an inevitable series of events, thus fitting the description of a slippery slope fallacy.

A fourth logical fallacy also involves erroneously assuming causal connection between two events. The *post hoc, ergo propter hoc fallacy* comes from the Latin for "after this, therefore because of this" and assumes that because one event happened after another, then the preceding event caused the event that followed. Many superstitions grew from this fallacy, like the black cat walking across your path brings bad luck. As if the color of the cat that walks in front of you causes bad things to happen to you! In persuasive arguments such as the one presented by Heston at Harvard, however, it is much more seductive.

In the final segment of his speech Heston attempted to demonstrate a point regarding the power of social activism. He described his attendance at a stockholder meeting for Time/Warner, which at the time produced an album by rapper Ice-T entitled "Cop-Killer." At the meeting he read the lyrics of two songs, one depicting acts of violence against police and another about sodomizing two 12-year-old nieces of Al and Tipper Gore. After these renditions, he claimed:

> "Two months later Time/Warner terminated Ice-T's contract."[10]

example:
post hoc, ergo propter hoc fallacy

This statement assumes that his actions caused the termination of Ice-T's contract, yet that most likely is not the case. It may have contributed to it, but it is very doubtful, without specific statements corroborating the claim, that Heston's speech at the stockholder meeting caused the ensuing termination. He erroneously assumed that since Ice-T was fired after his speech, then his speech must have been the cause.

Another common logical fallacy involves options and ultimatums. Speakers often present their audiences with only two alternatives, as if there were no other options. This type of argument is indicative of the *either-or fallacy*, where you present two options and declare that one of them must be correct while the other must be incorrect. Many candidates in elections operate with this faulty reasoning, declaring that "you will vote Republican, or you will vote Democrat." Such reasoning presents a false image of the political landscape and the choices every voter has. There are multiple parties they can vote for, and they can also choose not to vote.

A sixth fallacy of reasoning attempts not to present an image of fewer alternatives than actually exist, but rather to divert attention from the issues and arguments at stake. The *red herring fallacy* exists when a speaker introduces an irrelevant issue or piece of evidence to divert attention from subject of the speech. Red herrings begin with a topic under discussion, then introduce something else as if it is relevant to the original topic, and ultimately they disregard the initial topic altogether. Here is an example of a red herring at work:

example:
red herring fallacy

> "I believe we need to increase enrollment requirements for undergraduate education. With fewer students, we can help solve the budget crisis we face today."

The budget crisis, although seemingly related to increased admission standards, is actually not related to the requirements for entry into college, and thus serves as a red herring. To avoid this fallacy it is important to make sure your evidence directly supports your claims.

The next reasoning fallacy we will discuss is also concerned with the evidence you provide for claims within your speech. Sometimes individuals feel that they should do something because everyone else does it, but as speakers we must avoid using this type of reasoning as a justification for agreeing with our argument. When we attempt to persuade people by arguing that our position is reasonable because so many other people are doing it, or agree with it, we are employing the bandwagon, or *ad populum fallacy*. Many magazine advertisements, beer commercials, and speeches employ this fallacy by trying to convince you of the popularity of an item, event, or idea. Many messages fall victim to this fallacy by relying on too much qualitative evidence and peer testimonials and not enough hard data to support claims and conclusions.

Appeals to the masses are not the only types of appeals that are illegitimate and invalid. Sometimes the reason people provide for their argument relies entirely on their ethos or the credibility or venerability of a tradition because it has significant authority. An appeal for persuasion based on higher authority or tradition is emblematic of the *ad verecundium fallacy*. Again we return to the Charlton Heston speech at Harvard for an example of this fallacy at work.

One of the main claims advanced by Heston was a call for his audience to:

> "disobey social protocol that stifles and stigmatizes personal freedom."[11]

He explained that disobedience is justified and honorable because of the fact people like:

> "Gandhi, Thoreau, and Jesus and every other great man who led those in the right against those with the might" did it before. He went on to say that "disobedience is in our DNA."[12]

Such appeals justify disobedience based on the authority and tradition of the action, not for any other reason. Other more common examples of the ad verecundium fallacy include when your parents told you to do something "because I am your mother/father." There is no logical connection between the action advocated and the reason provided for you to act.

When logic fails them, individuals sometimes revert to attacking their opponent in a debate instead of criticizing their ideas in a reasonable manner. When speakers attack the person making the argument, and not the argument itself, it is representative of the *ad hominem fallacy*. Ad hominem attacks often exist under the guise of attacks on a speaker's credibility, but in truth they are irrelevant to the argument and do not justify claims about the topic of debate. For instance, when an attorney in a court case argues that a prostitute's testimony should not be admitted because prostitutes are not trustworthy or reliable sources, it is an example of an ad hominem attack. In this case, the credibility of the individual making the claim is not in question, nor is the content of her testimony; instead,

ad populum fallacy
when we attempt to persuade people by arguing our position is reasonable because so many other people are doing it or agree with it

ad verecundium fallacy
an appeal for persuasion based on higher authority or tradition

example: ad verecundium fallacy

ad hominem fallacy
when speakers attack the person making the argument and not the argument itself

the prosecutor makes her seem unreliable by attacking her profession through stereotypes. An interesting thing to keep in mind about ad hominem attacks is that the more frustrated or angry we get in a conversation with those who do not agree with us, the more likely we are to devolve into using these types of claims. It is thus important to keep a cool head and focus on the issue, even when we are upset.

We can look to references made by Heston for examples as well. In his speech he claimed that as a result of his support for the NRA the public attacked him. At one point he said:

> "I ran for office, I was elected, and now I serve ... I serve as a moving target for the media who have called me everything from 'ridiculous' and 'duped' to a 'brain-injured, senile, crazy old man.'"[13]

Now, Heston himself did not use an ad hominem, but he pointed out that others used that line of reasoning against him by attacking him and not his position on guns.

straw man fallacy

when a speaker ignores the actual position of an opponent and substitutes it with a distorted and exaggerated position

The tenth and final common reasoning fallacy we will discuss most often occurs in the rebuttal section of a speech. The *straw man fallacy* occurs when a speaker ignores the actual position of an opponent and substitutes it with a distorted and exaggerated position. He or she then proceeds to attack the incorrect position because it is easier to defeat, although the process itself is illogical because it does not accurately respond to the original position.

Think about a political debate over funding the defense department, specifically the development of a missile defense shield in Europe. Candidate X wants to cease funding the research behind this project, and Candidate Y responds by saying "I cannot believe you do not support protecting the American people." First, the original position specifically called to question one program, not the entire goal of defense. Second, Candidate Y substituted that one program with a more exaggerated position that was easier to use as an attack. The equation of opposing a missile defense shield with not protecting the American people is illogical and erroneous based on the statements made here, and are thus illustrative of the straw man fallacy.

The sheer fact that there are ten common logical fallacies should serve as a reminder to you to be careful when you construct messages. Your claims must be well supported and the evidence you use must relate to those claims. These ten fallacies are seductive in their simplicity, but destructive in their effects. They damage your credibility as a speaker and also potentially take advantage of your audience. Although it involves more effort and work, the payoff of taking the time to construct a proper speech that avoids these fallacies far outweighs the consequences of using them. Conversely, being able to identify them when used by others also makes us better critical consumers of messages. See Table 8.4 for a summary and additional examples of these ten fallacies.

Chart of Fallacies and Examples			Table 8.4

Fallacy	The Error in Reasoning	Example
Begging-the-question	When a speaker presumes certain things are facts when they have not yet been proven to be truthful	"Oh, everyone knows that we are all Christians."
Non sequitur	When you make an unwarranted move from one idea to the next	"Well, look at the size of this administration building; it is obvious this university does not need more funding."
Slippery slope	Assumes that once an action begins it will follow, undeterred, to an eventual and inevitable conclusion	"If we let the government dictate where we can pray, soon the government will tell us we cannot pray."
Post hoc, ergo propter hoc	Assumes that because one event happened after another, then the preceding event caused the event that followed	"Every time Sheila goes to a game with us, our team loses. She is bad luck."
Either-or	Presents two options and declares that one of them must be correct while the other must be incorrect	"We either raise tuition or massively increase class size."
Red herring	When a speaker introduces an irrelevant issue or piece of evidence to divert attention from the subject of the speech	"Why do you question my private issues, when we have social problems with which to deal?"
Ad populum	When we attempt to persuade people by arguing our position is reasonable because so many other people are doing it or agree with it	"Why shouldn't I cheat on this exam? Everyone else cheats."
Ad verecundium	An appeal to persuasion based on higher authority or tradition	"If the president of Harvard says it is a good idea, then we should follow suit." Or, "That is how we have always done it."
Ad hominem	When speakers attack the person making the argument and not the argument itself	"We can't believe anything he says; he is a convicted felon."
Straw man	When a speaker ignores the actual position of an opponent and substitutes it with a distorted and exaggerated position	"Oh, you think we should agree to a cut in our salaries. Why do you want to bleed us dry?"

SUMMARY

This chapter provided you with various ways to construct a well-reasoned, ethical, and effective argument. Whether you choose to employ the classical mode of argument or a more contemporary model, you now have a blueprint for crafting a solid persuasive message. It is also important to remember that any one message can use different types of reasoning to accomplish its goals. The classical approach includes three different ways to reason involving different types of evidence. The classical models that Aristotle examined provide structures for formal logic that you can use to create your own arguments and to test the arguments that others make, and Toulmin's model provides a framework for you to create arguments using evidence that are based on any of four types of reasoning: deductive reasoning, reasoning from example, reasoning by analogy, and reasoning by cause. Whichever route you take, you must take good care to avoid logical fallacies, no matter how attractive it may seem to use them.

KEY TERMS

ad hominem fallacy   199

ad populum fallacy   217

ad verecundium fallacy   217

antecedent   201

begging-the-question fallacy   214

categorical syllogism   200

conditional syllogism   201

consequent   201

deductive argument   200

disjunctive syllogism   201

either-or fallacy   220

enthymeme   204

figurative analogy   212

inductive argument   205

kairos   214

literal analogy   199

major premise   200

minor premise   200

necessary cause   213

non sequitur fallacy   215

post hoc, ergo propter hoc fallacy   216

reasoning by analogy   212

reasoning by cause   212

reasoning by example   220

red herring fallacy   216

slippery slope fallacy   215

straw man fallacy   218

sufficient cause   199

syllogism   200

REVIEW QUESTIONS

1. What are the three types of syllogisms proposed by Aristotle?
2. What is the difference between an enthymeme and a syllogism?
3. What are four types of reasoning that can be used to connect evidence to the claim that one is making in an argument?
4. What are the ten logical fallacies?

THINK ABOUT IT

1. Are there any circumstances under which ad hominem attacks are acceptable? When?

2. What are some enthymemes you are exposed to every day through advertising?

3. How ethical are the persuasive appeals in advertising and political campaigns today? Do they employ logical fallacies? If so, which ones?

4. How can you as avoid argument fallacies?

5. As an audience member do you have an obligation to voice concern about a speaker's fallacies?

ACTIVITIES FOR ACTION

1. Find a copy of the text for the "Winning the Cultural War" speech by Charlton Heston mentioned in the opening of this chapter. Look through the text closely and see how many logical fallacies you can identify. Then, have a friend read the speech and see what his or her initial impression is. After your friend tells you, point out all the logical fallacies in the speech to him or her and see if your friend changes his or her mind.

2. One evening, while watching television, pay close attention to the commercials. As you watch, refer to the reasoning fallacies described in this chapter, and see how many you find. As you note them, think about whether the advertisements that used the fallacies were interesting or effective. Did the fallacies have anything to do with the success of the ad?

ENDNOTES

1. Harvard University, "The Early History of Harvard University," http://www.hno.harvard.edu/guide/intro/index.html (accessed November 7, 2008).

2. Harvard Law School, "Alumni News and Publications," http://www.law.harvard.edu/alumni/news/index.html (accessed November 7, 2008).

3. "Winning the Cultural War" (February 16, 1999), http://isocracytx.net/hp-org/hestonlaw.html (accessed November 7, 2008).

4. Ibid.

5. http://www.americanrhetoric.com/speeches/hillaryclintonbeijingspeech.htm (last accessed: June 6, 2011).

6. Ibid.

7. Ibid. para. #6.

8. Ibid. para. #4.

9. Ibid. para. #11-12.

10. Ibid. para. #23-27.

11. Ibid. para. #19.

12. Ibid.

13. Ibid. para. #3.

Interteaching Session

Dialogue

Find the transcript of a speech from a famous person, such as a politician or social leader. After you read the transcript, identify by type any logical fallacies that you find in the arguments that the speaker is making:

- Begging the question

- Non sequitur

- Slippery slope

- Post hoc, ergo propter hoc

- Either-or

- Red herring

- Ad populum

- Ad verecundium

- Ad hominem

- Straw man

Share at least two of these examples with the class, as well as your reasons for believing that each exemplifies the particular type of logical fallacy that you have identified. Take a position about the ethicality of the argument that the speaker is making, given these fallacies. Be prepared to listen to the views of your classmates, especially those that differ from your own.

Performance

Suppose that you and your groupmates have been hired by the University to create a promotional video that can be shown to high school students by campus recruiters to persuade them to apply to UD. Create a short 3–5 minute video with your groupmates that you can share with the rest of the class. Make sure that your video includes at least two arguments, each of which illustrates a different type of reasoning: deductive, inductive, analogical, or causal. Share your video with the class and see if your classmates can identify the two arguments and the type of reasoning that each incorporates.

Appealing to Emotion in Persuasion

CHAPTER OVERVIEW

9

- Defines meaning and details the characteristics of language
- Relays some basic forms of language that help construct messages
- Provides guidelines for determining the most effective language choices when constructing messages

Practically SPEAKING

In the United States, as in many democracies, there is a fundamental right to free speech for every citizen, but even that right is not absolute. For instance, we cannot falsely yell "fire!" in a crowded theater because that speech may result in the creation of a harmful situation. For the longest time, curse words could not be uttered on prime time television, although now that is hardly the case. Language is controversial because it is powerful. It can move people to action, convey a sense of identity for the speaker, or conjure one for the audience. Because language is powerful, even the right to free speech is curtailed. One famous legal case that underscores the power of language and illustrates society's desire to control it in some way involved the late comedian George Carlin.

Around 2:00 p.m. on a Tuesday afternoon in 1973, WBAI (FM), a radio station in New York City, aired a 12-minute segment from a monologue delivered by Carlin. The monologue, entitled "Filthy Words," was initially recorded before a live audience in California and concerned the words a person could not say on public airwaves. Carlin listed the seven words that fit that category and then discussed them in detail. Right before the station broadcasted the words, it warned its audience that the monologue included language that might offend some listeners. Unfortunately for the radio station, not everyone heard the warning. One man complained to the Federal Communications Commission (FCC) and that government agency quickly responded.[1]

The FCC ruled that Carlin's satirical presentation was indecent because it depicted sexual acts and bodily functions, calling his presentation "obnoxious" and stating it reduced humanity to its "bodily functions." It further pointed out that the radio station was at fault because it aired the satire at a time when children would hear it.[2] The case eventually found its way to the US Supreme Court. It ruled that the FCC did not censor the station because it did not edit it in advance or prohibit the broadcast from airing. For the Court, reviewing content after airing is not an issue of censorship.[3]

The Supreme Court's opinion, written by Justice John Paul Stevens, discussed why Carlin's monologue was not subject to the protection of the First Amendment. He wrote that Carlin's monologue was offensive and lacked literary, political, or scientific value and was not related to the marketplace of ideas. Additionally, Stevens claimed that time of day, content of communication, and the medium used are all important considerations when defining obscene and indecent language.[4]

Language is a primary means through which a speaker can evoke emotion in an audience. In the case of Pacifica and Carlin, language proved to be inappropriate for some audiences. The words, in effect, endangered the standards and practices of society. Carlin attempted to point out what he saw as the silliness of language choices, but in so doing illustrated the reverence and power we accord language. In this chapter we will explain how you may tap into that power and enhance your speech. First we will discuss the basic building blocks of meaning to illustrate the source of language's power. We will then examine several different types of language strategies that can help you enhance the appeal and effectiveness of your message. Finally, we will offer some concrete guidelines for choosing these words when putting together a speech.

Prep Questions

Part 1: Key Concepts

1. Identify the four steps to creating an emotional appeal as described in the chapter. Explain what a speaker would do in each of the steps.

2. What are the four characteristics of language? Explain what each characteristic implies about how language works.

3. Identify and define the two single-word approaches to using language identified in the chapter.

4. Identify and define the two word-cluster approaches to using language identified in the chapter.

5. Define the four techniques for structuring language identified in the chapter.

6. Identify and define the elements of Burke's Pentad.

Part 2: Application

1. Give an example of a story that someone recently told to you. Analyze your response to that story in terms of Fisher's two criteria of narrative coherence and narrative fidelity.

2. Reflect on a presentation that you have seen recently, perhaps in one of your classes, that has involved visual aids. To what degree was the speaker successful in creating pathos through the use of these visual aids? Why was she or he successful or not successful? Justify your answer by referring to at least two of the guidelines in this chapter for using images to create pathos.

9

Developing Emotion in Persuasive Appeals

Ethos and logos, otherwise called credibility and logic, are two of the three dimensions of persuasion and speech identified by Aristotle. The third, pathos, also must be addressed because it complements both ethos and logos in the persuasive process. It is important to remember that employing pathos alone in a persuasive appeal distracts listeners from the issue at hand in an effort to have them make a decision based purely on emotions and not evidence or information. Such a message design is unethical, even if the goal is ethical. So, let's take a moment and discuss the proper place for pathos in advocacy.

Pathos is concerned with the audience's emotions, sympathies, and imagination and is used to connect those feelings and images to the topic of the message in a way that increases the likelihood of achieving your purpose. Pathos can help make abstract concepts and statistical data more palpable and real for an audience. Ultimately, however, proper use of pathos depends on knowledge of to whom you are speaking.

Four Steps for Creating an Emotional Appeal

Pathos is primarily accomplished in four different steps. The first step is to determine the emotion that you want to produce in your audience. Do you want to make your listeners angry? Excited? Do you want them to feel pity? Compassion? The emotion you want to create is the goal of the particular pathos appeal, and therefore what tools you choose to use to achieve that goal must have the emotion at the core.

Once you determine the emotion you wish to create in the audience, you need to connect it to an object. That object can be a person, place, or thing, but it must be real and recognizable to the audience. It is the thing for which you want the other people to feel the emotion and to which you want them to connect. As a general rule, people connect better to singular specific objects than large masses of things. Thus, people feel pity when the advertisements of the American Society for the Prevention of Cruelty to Animals (ASPCA) depicts one dog that has been injured or abandoned, but they would not feel that way if the pictures were of multiple dogs at once. The same principle applies for advocacy messages: connect the emotion to a concrete singular object to which the person or people to whom you are speaking can relate.

Step three is the use of language or images that evoke the specific emotion you wish to encourage the audience to feel. Pictures and strategic language choices help to accomplish this, and this stage is where you make the decisions about when and how to describe the object and the emotion. Different words can convey different emotions, and can elicit different responses as well. For instance, when describing a policy you could choose to label it "moronic" or "ill-advised." What emotions does each trigger? How does that emotional reaction enhance or damage the perception those listening may have of you? These are important considerations for you when crafting your message. You need to make sure your emotional language choices are not the primary driver for persuasion, but rather that they complement the evidence you use and reinforce your goodwill and virtuous character to the audience.

In today's mediated environment, we can also use visual imagery to capitalize on pathos in our persuasive appeals. A moment ago we talked about the ASPCA advertisements, and the pictures of dogs to help give an audience an object with which they can connect. Visual images in this respect can be powerful vehicles for pathos appeals because they provide the audience with a specific object on which to focus their attention, while the narrator provides the verbal message containing the emotional dimension sought by the use of the image.

The final step of incorporating pathos into persuasive messages involves the story, or narrative, you provide about the object. The story uses the vivid language in stage three while also connecting the emotion to the overall logic of the persuasive appeal. The story needs to be connected in some way not just to the emotion, but to the overall topic. If you are seeking to help the ASPCA, for example, you might tell a vivid story about a golden retriever who was abandoned and found half-starved walking the street in front of your home sniffing around garbage bags for food. This quick anecdote used vivid language in telling a story related to your purpose in a way that was designed to create a feeling of pity for the dog. That dog then becomes an analogy for all dogs helped by the ASPCA, thus helping to provide people with both a logical and an emotional reason for acting on your message.

Pathos is a powerful persuasive tool when used appropriately. It can enhance your credibility as a speaker as well as augment the power of the logic behind your appeal. It involves four important steps, beginning with determining what type of emotion you want to have your audience feel. You should then connect that emotion to a singular object, and use vivid language to tell the story about that object in a way that connects it with the larger purpose of your message.

USING LANGUAGE TO EVOKE EMOTION

Language is a powerful means through which you can evoke an emotional response from an audience. In the four-step method that we examined earlier, after you have decided what emotion you want to evoke and connected that

SPOTLIGHTING THEORISTS: MARY HAAS

Mary Haas (1910–1996)

During the 1930s the most renowned linguist of the era, Edward Sapir of Yale, trained a small number of graduate students. One of those students, Mary Haas, went on to become a renowned linguistic researcher and teacher in her own right.[6] Her dissertation concerned the Tunica Indians, a tribe once located in present-day Louisiana, and she earned her Ph.D. in 1935. She also did linguistic work on several other Southeastern America Native American languages, including the Choctaw, Alabama, and Creek.

Prior to World War II she worked with the Thai language assisting in the preparation of training materials to be used by the Armed Services. In 1942–1943 she taught Thai at the University of Michigan. In 1943 Haas began teaching Thai in the Army Specialized Training Program at Berkeley. After the war she became a permanent member of the Berkeley faculty.[7]

Haas was a faculty member at that university until 1977. During that time she directed the Survey of California Indian Languages. She is credited with leading students in doing valuable work on languages that have nearly become extinct.[8] Mary Haas died in 1996 at the age of 86.[9] The scholarly journal *Anthropological Linguistics* published a memorial in its 1997 Winter issue.[10]

emotion to a specific object, you must begin crafting the emotional appeal that you eventually will deliver to the audience. A key building block from which you will construct this appeal are the words that you choose. Your choice of language also is a principal feature of the style of your message, what Cicero identified as the third of his five canons. Your words must be adapted to the context, including the specific audience to whom you will be speaking. If your words are not well-adapted to the needs and expectations of your listeners, then you are not likely to evoke the emotional response that you hope to elicit from them as they hear your message. Before we look at specific techniques and devices for using language to persuade others, let us explore how language in general works, by focusing on four characteristics of all language, regardless of how it is used.

Meaning, as we have pointed out in earlier chapters, can be expressed both verbally and nonverbally. In both instances we exchange meaning through symbols. In that respect, symbols are the building blocks of how we understand the world. Language is a common way in which we communicate meaning to others, and the symbolic base of language is letters. Letters are, for all intents and purposes, symbols that mean something when connected to form words. Words also are symbols that represent objects, thoughts, values, feelings, and ideas, and they are the foundation of communication. When we share an understanding of what symbols mean we are able to connect with each other in meaningful ways about the world around us. In this section of the chapter we will explore the four characteristics of any language.

Who's on First?
by Abbott and Costello

Delivered many times as a comedy skit.

Bud Abbott and Lou Costello were popular on the burlesque comedy stages of America, and joined together to become a popular comedy team in 1936. That year they performed their classic signature skit, "Who's on First," on the Kate Smith Radio Hour and were "hurled to stardom, and to Hollywood."[12] The comedy routine is based on trying to determine the name of the player on first base whose name happens to be *Who*, but due to the ambiguity of language the name causes confusion and consternation for both Abbott and Costello, but lots of laughs for generations of audiences.

Through their routine, Abbott and Costello left an indelible mark and made a lasting impact on comedy and its role in American culture. In fact, their often, imitated and duplicated routine served as a model for many comedians to comment on social and cultural practices through their work. In 1999 *Time* magazine named the *Who's on First* routine the Best Comedy Sketch of the century. This illustrates that civic engagement also takes place through comedy rooted in our cultural practices, norms, and beliefs. Here is an excerpt from their routine:

Costello: Well, then, who's on first?
Abbott: Yes.
Costello: I mean the fellow's name.
Abbott: Who.
Costello: The guy on first.
Abbott: Who.
Costello: The first baseman.
Abbott: Who!
Costello: The guy playing –
Abbott: Who is on first!
Costello: I'm asking YOU who's on first.
Abbott: That's the man's name.
Costello: That's who's name?
Abbott: Yes.
Costello: Well go ahead and tell me.
Abbott: That's it.
Costello: That's who?
Abbott: Yes.

This continues on for several players, all with names that can be confused with days and questions. You can view this video at http://www.americanrhetoric.com and see the frustration the ambiguity of language can cause during dialogue.

Language Characteristics

All languages share four characteristics, regardless of their cultural, ethnic, or regional origins. The first characteristic of a language is that it is *arbitrary*, or that the symbols used to represent things are not intrinsically connected to those things. Since meaning is arbitrary it can change over time as different groups ascribe different definitions and purposes for words. The word "hot," for instance, formerly only meant raised temperature, but now also refers to the attractiveness of something ("she/he is so hot") or the success of an action ("he's a hot hitter right now"). We also develop new words every year to the point where the English language has expanded significantly over the past few hundred years. Words and phrases like "affirmative action," "motherboard," and "airline" did not exist until the last century. The arbitrary nature of language illustrates its flexibility, as language changes according to our need to explain the world around us.

arbitrary
symbols used to represent things that are not intrinsically connected to those things

Because language can change and is dependent on constant use to sustain itself, some languages can disappear. When a language is no longer used by a group we call it a dead language, but this does not mean we do not know how to use it or that we cannot read it. For example, Aramaic is considered to be a dead language and yet there are still people who know how to use it and read it—it just isn't a language you will overhear while waiting in line at the DMV! Some scholars focus their efforts on preserving and understanding language and how it reflects a particular culture. One of the more renowned researchers in this area was Mary Haas, who worked on American Indian languages and did important work on the Thai language before World War II. In essence, Haas and other scholars like her focus on trying to understand the arbitrary qualities of language.

The fact that language is arbitrary also can be a bit shocking. Why do we call a cat *cat*? It could have very well been labeled "schmoog," but it was not. There was no reason behind the selection of the symbol "cat" to represent those furry little creatures; it just happened and people implicitly agreed to that meaning for the symbol "cat." It was a completely arbitrary creation of a symbol to represent something in our world so we could communicate about it.

Another component of language is that it is *ambiguous*, or that it's meaning can be interpreted in a variety of ways. When you speak, the language you use doesn't have one precise, concrete or inherent way of being understood by your listener. One name can refer to a plethora of people, one word can mean different things, and without the context in which the word was spoken, there is no way to identify its meaning with any degree of precision.

ambiguous
language that does not have precise, concrete meanings

Cultures imbue words with a variety of meanings, but even within that culture each word has an agreed upon range of potential interpretations and uses. For instance, the term "mean" can refer to the average of a group of numbers or describe a nasty statement or action. Even holidays like Thanksgiving vary in meaning from country to country based on the specific circumstances surrounding that holiday. As a speaker it is always important for you to understand the potential interpretations words can have and use them in the proper context with your conversational partners so that your message is as clear as possible. It is through the ambiguous nature of language that many misunderstandings develop, unless the meaning of the word is made clear.

Movie poster from *Donnie Brasco*

Take, for example, the phrase "friend of mine." For many people this phrase defines a level of association between you and another person; however, different people have different definitions of exactly what a friend is. In the movie *Donnie Brasco*,[5] Al Pacino's character introduces someone he recently met, played by Johnny Depp, to the mobsters for whom he works. On the way over to the introduction he clearly spells out that when he introduces him to his bosses as "friend of mine" it means you are connected but not officially a part of the organization. He further explains that if he said "friend of ours" then Depp's character would have been accorded more respect because it would mean he was a full member of the mob. This example illustrates how ambiguous language can be, and how important it is to make sure the audience knows the meaning of the words and phrases you use. Not everyone understands the meaning of terms in the same way you do.

Another example of the ambiguity of language can be found in the famous Abbott and Costello skit "Who's on First," where Abbott announces he bought a baseball team and tries to explain his players to his friend, Costello. Comedic encounters like this are not uncommon, and oftentimes comedians will take advantage of the ambiguous nature of language in delivering a punch line to a joke. In Abbott and Costello's case, their sketch has had a long lasting impact on comedy, baseball, and language use. This skit, and indeed the nature of language as ambiguous, underscores the importance of clarifying definitions in conversation. When using a word in a specific way that could be understood differently by the listener it is essential to explain how you are using it. If both you and the other person do not operate with the same definitions for complex or unfamiliar terms understanding becomes impossible. Making sure people understand what words mean is a hallmark of communication in the technical professions, such as engineering.

abstract
words are not tangible items; they are only representations

The third component of language is that it is *abstract*. Abstract means that words are not tangible items; you cannot touch them or feel them as they simply represent something else. Language is removed from the actual objective phenomena it represents, thus making it an abstract construct. Words can vary in their abstractness, according to the degree to which they accurately represent the real thing. The tool for identifying and measuring the degree to which our language is abstract is called the ladder of abstraction, a concept developed by Alfred Korzybski and S. I. Hayakawa in the 1960s.[11]

The ladder of abstraction depicts the most abstract term at the top of the ladder and the closest to the objective phenomenon at the bottom. So, in the following example, at the top of the ladder you see "animal." On the level below that, representing a term slightly less removed from the object, is the term "human being." Since there are several billion human beings on the planet we move to the next level and see "musician." Again, even though this term narrows our original term significantly, it is still abstract. The next rung uses the term "pop musician," improving the connection between the term and described object. Finally, on the bottom rung of the ladder of abstraction we see "Taylor Swift," a very specific use of language that is as close to representing the object as possible through words. The more concrete and specific the words we use, the more likely the receiver will accurately interpret our message.

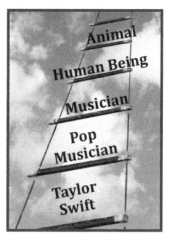

Figure 9.1
Ladder of Abstraction

The ladder of abstraction also is illustrative of the fourth quality of any language. Scholar Kenneth Burke first noted that language, like human beings, is *hierarchical* in nature. That is, it places values of more or less on everything. Think about how we talk about advancing in the workplace. We move *up* from the mailroom when we are promoted. We don't make *lateral* moves. When we go to a hotel we want to stay in the penthouse on the top floor. Language, much like our social lives, reflects a hierarchy in which one thing is more important, or valued more, than another.

hierarchical
language that is structured according to more or less, higher or lower

Math as a Language

Languages come in many forms, and one form not typically thought of as a language is mathematics. Math is a way to transmit meaning between people and fits the definition of language.

First, math is arbitrary. This is not to say that certain numbers can add up to whatever a person wants them to; rather, the symbol of a number has no physical relationship to what it represents. The number one is a symbol, and that symbol can be applied to one hot dog, one dress, or one board game. The symbol "one" only has meaning when used to refer to something else, thus it has no physical connection to what it represents.

Second, math is ambiguous. It is understandable how this might be confusing, but here is an example to illustrate the point. The mathematical equation "x+y" could either be a number itself or a function. Additionally, the more common expression of ambiguity in math is the margin of error, in which a result is plus or minus a certain number, thus giving an ambiguous answer.

Math is also abstract in that it is not concrete or tangible. No one has ever picked up a number and held it. That said, math can be made less abstract when, as we illustrated just a moment ago, it is put in context and related to something else. *Lots of food* is very abstract, whereas *one spear of broccoli* is much more concrete.

Finally, math is hierarchical. This should make sense because numbers are structured to illustrate quantities of something. They illustrate more and less in a hierarchical state so that we all know that one hundred is less than two hundred but more than fifty.

Understanding how math functions as a language helps clarify why there are certain rules to mathematical equations and representations, much like there are rules to the use of other languages in social settings. When someone is not "good at math" it is the same as saying they do not speak Spanish or German very well. Math, however, is the professional language of engineers, financial analysts, and accountants in much the same way English is the professional language for American writers!

Language is arbitrary, ambiguous, abstract, and hierarchical but it is also very useful. Language uses symbols to represent the world around us and serves as the foundation for our ability to connect with each other. In the next part of this chapter we will discuss general forms of language we use in everyday encounters. Understanding what language does for us and how it does it is essential for determining which terms and phrases to incorporate into your messages in order to maximize their effectiveness.

COMMON LANGUAGE DEVICES AND TECHNIQUES

Language can be used in many different ways to send a message. Sometimes, as in casual conversation, single-word strategies are the best way to convey meaning to an audience. In other instances clusters of words form a coherent impression of

"I Have a Dream" Speech
by Dr. Martin Luther King, Jr.

Delivered August 28, 1963, at the Lincoln Memorial in Washington, D.C.

"I Have a Dream" is one of the most, if not the most, referenced and used speech in public speaking classes and other liberal arts classes. It is worthy of such recognition not only because of its historical significance, but also due to its beautiful tone, structure, and use of metaphor, parallelism, and other language devices.

Dr. King used many metaphors in the speech. One in particular stands out.

"In a sense we've come to our nation's capital to cash a check."[14] This statement implies that a check needs to be cashed to fulfill an obligation. Dr. King extends the metaphor further to make his point: "It is obvious today that America has defaulted on this promissory note, insofar as her citizens of color are concerned. Instead of honoring this sacred obligation, America has given the Negro people a bad check, a check which has come back marked 'insufficient funds.'"

This masterful orator also used a form of repetition to emphasize his points:

"Now is the time to rise from the dark and desolate valley of segregation to the sunlit path of racial justice. Now is the time to lift our nation from the quicksands of racial injustice to the solid rock of brotherhood. Now is the time to make justice a reality for all of God's children."[15]

This speech will go down in the annals of great speeches for centuries to come. Reading the speech is one thing, but actually hearing it and even viewing it brings forth the full power of the day and the man who later lost his life due to his efforts to improve the lives of millions of people.

something for people as well. Luckily, in the United States and many other places around the globe, we are free to employ either, both, or neither of these approaches thanks to freedom of speech. In this part of the chapter we first discuss some single-word strategies that permeate our everyday interactions with others. We then detail a few word cluster strategies that also are common in society. Third, we explain a few creative ways to structure language within messages. Finally, we offer some additional best practices for using language, especially to evoke an emotional response.

Single-Word Approaches

In this part of the chapter we will cover three types of single-word approaches to making language meaningful. A *single-word approach* does not necessarily mean that only one word is required for meaning to be transferred, but rather that meaning is derived from specific individual words used in a strategic way. We are all probably quite familiar in some way with the first two of these strategies. We probably can also recognize words that fit into the third category but are unfamiliar with the formal name of that strategy.

single-word approach
meaning is derived from individual words used in a strategic way

The first single-word approach is a broad category that contains a variety of distinct subsets. *Metaphor* is the broad term used to define comparisons that show how two things are alike in an important way, despite being quite different in most ways. We use metaphors often as they add color, flavor, and vividness to our everyday experiences. Take the following phrase as an example: "I will now shed some light on the issue." Obviously, there is no actual light, but a lack of understanding is compared to darkness, and the speaker's intention to provide knowledge is compared to illuminating that darkness through providing light. Another example involves describing a person who is adept at gardening as having a "green thumb." Again, the person's thumb is not actually green, but the color reminds people of grass and plants, thus making the connection and comparison between the activity and the person who enjoys it.

metaphor
comparisons that show how two things are alike in an important way, despite being quite different in most ways

A second single-word approach is often confused with metaphor, but in fact holds one major distinction that separates it in theory and practice. *Similes*, like metaphors, are comparisons between two objects, but whereas metaphors make both objects appear as if they are equal, similes allow each object in the comparison to retain its unique differences. When you use the word "like" or "as" in comparing two objects you are using a simile because the two objects in the comparison are similar but not equal. Here is an example of a simile: "The quarterback threaded that pass like a needle." The needle and the trajectory of the pass keep their distinctive qualities, but the comparison gives the object a reference to which some aspect, such as difficulty, can be ascribed. Another example: "She is strong as an ox." In this example the two objects in the comparison retain their distinctiveness while sharing a specific characteristic.

simile
comparisons between two objects that allow each object in the comparison to retain its unique differences; uses like or as

Similes sometimes need further explanation so their intended meaning can be properly conveyed. Consider this statement: "Her face was like an autumn sunrise." The intention is to convey a comparison regarding beauty; however, more detail of this simile provides greater and more specific meaning for the object. Just like metaphors, similes are very useful tools for enhancing the vivid nature of a message and allowing an audience to visualize a concept or object you might be discussing.

A third single-word approach to conveying meaning was identified by scholar Michael Calvin McGee in 1980. *Ideographs* are essentially ill-defined politically powerful terms and phrases that can push people to action. Examples of ideographs include terms such as *freedom, terror, rule of law, equality,* and *liberty* just to name a few.[13] Each of these has significant cultural resonance in the United States and has served as justification for a variety of different arguments. As recently as 2001 and 2003 President George W. Bush used the terms "freedom" and "terror" to call for military action against Afghanistan and Iraq, respectively. They also have been used to justify actions such as warrantless wiretapping and indefinite imprisonment at Guantanamo Bay. "Equality" was used during the civil rights era to push for desegregation, and has recently appeared again to justify changes in the tax code and advocate for gay marriage.

Ideographs are very powerful because the meaning of the term or phrase is culturally provided, but not everyone in a culture interprets them the same way. Look at the term "fairness," which has been recently applied to tax reform. Liberal politicians argue that higher taxes on those who make more money is only "fair," while conservative advocates argue it is anything but fair because those individuals do not pay the same amount or percentage as others. Regardless of where you sit in this debate, the term "fair" is a perfect example of an ideograph that has an ill-defined but politically powerful meaning within society. You can use such terms like this when you speak, but beware of their ambiguity and potential to activate emotional reactions from others.

Table 9.2

Examples of Ideographs	
Freedom	Terror
Rule of law	Equality
Liberty	Justice

Each single-word approach to conveying meaning we have discussed in this section holds specific power thanks to the arbitrary, ambiguous, and abstract nature of language. You can use them to effectively enhance communication with others by creating more vivid and concrete messages. The more vivid the descriptions you use and the more concrete the detail you provide, the better you will be able to appeal to an audience. Single-word approaches, however, are not the only strategy available to you when making language choices.

Word-Cluster Approaches

Meaning is not only found to be potent in simple words and phrases. In many instances meaning is transmitted through more complex approaches that use language to construct meaning for an event, person, or culture. For the sake of simplicity we will call these *word-cluster approaches* because, unlike single-word approaches, meaning is not contained in individual words used in a strategic way. Rather, meaning is conveyed through more complex structures such as stories. In this section we will explore two different word cluster approaches to conveying meaning: rhetorical history and myth. Any of these tools can be used by you to present information or make an argument in a vivid, creative, and interesting manner.

The first word-cluster approach we will examine involves how we understand and communicate about our past. Think about your past, the country's past, and even world history. Everything you know about these things is only part of the story, but these parts of our past are often used to justify actions in the present. These *arguments from the past* appropriate parts of history to justify present or future actions. Arguments from the past employ stories and explanations to convey meaning. Those stories are interpretations of events that provide the power for arguments from the past.

arguments from the past
....
appropriating historical events, facts, or people to justify present or future actions, or explain events in the here and now

For example, take the events of September 11, 2001, when terrorists attacked the World Trade Center and Pentagon. Immediately following these events people compared the attack to the Japanese sneak attack on Pearl Harbor that precipitated World War II. That comparison imbued 9/11 with certain qualities inherent in Pearl Harbor, thus allowing 9/11 to also become a justification for war against Afghanistan in the same way Pearl Harbor allowed war to be declared against Japan. In this case a past event was used to provide significance to a present situation so future policy could be enacted.

We make arguments from the past in everyday conversations as well. For instance, if you tried to eat sushi once and did not like it but your partner wants to eat sushi for dinner, you need to argue against it. How do you do it? By offering data on the level of mercury in fish? No, you tell the story of your prior experience in an effort to avoid the trip to eat sushi. The story you tell is an argument from the past that may help convince your partner to change his or her mind and go to Skyline Chili instead.

As we have noted, language is imprecise and only somewhat represents an objective reality. History is always incomplete because we were never there and rely instead on the reflections and documents that survive the past. These provide an imprecise understanding of the past because they are incomplete, and because they rely on words—which are ambiguous themselves—to tell the story. Hence it is important to be honest and as accurate as possible when discussing historical events in an effort to explain something or persuade someone. Do not distort the event for your own purposes by leaving something out or embellishing the story; let it speak for itself. Understand, as well, when others use the past to construct an argument that all stories about history are necessarily incomplete.

myth
......
a rhetorical construction that tries to explain natural events or cultural phenomena and is used to identify with a group and justify actions or beliefs

A second word-cluster approach is even more abstract than incomplete stories about our past because it does not need to rely on actual facts. *Myths* are rhetorical constructions that try to explain natural events or cultural phenomena and are used to identify with a group and justify actions or beliefs. Myths carry similar power to arguments from the past. Speakers often use myths to identify with other people that share the values the myth contains, but myths also can be used as justification to preserve a seemingly sacred event, object or institution.

One of the central myths of any culture is the founding or origin myth. Early Mesopotamians portrayed their founding in the story of Gilgamesh, while the Romans looked to the story we now call the *Aeneid* for the myth of their inception. The *Aeneid* allowed Romans to connect their past to the legends of Troy and also served to glorify and legitimize Roman values and practices. Founding myths are useful because when someone tells a version of the myth it allows him or her to connect with others by identifying with their past and the values expressed within the story. The meaning of myths is not inherent in one word or phrase, but is rather a more elaborate and complex use of language.

Simply knowing the characteristics of language and some of the ways in which it can be used to creatively and artfully convey meaning is not enough; in fact, it borders on dangerous. It is also important that you understand the ethical dimensions of using language to convey meaning. In the next part of this chapter we will discuss some of these ethical issues that are only relevant in a society where you have freedom of speech.

Structuring Language

The way you structure your messages can help enhance both your ability to deliver meaning and the audience's ability to understand the meaning. In this section we will cover four specific strategies for creatively structuring language. Strategic use of these structural patterns will greatly enhance your ability to communicate with others, but overuse or inappropriate use will damage your credibility, so be judicious in choosing when to use any of these.

repetition
repeating either the same phrasing pattern for main points, or a phrase you just stated, in order to maximize the audience's ability to receive the information

The simplest structural strategy can often be the most effective at capturing an audience's attention and highlighting an important part of your message for them. *Repetition* occurs in two forms, but both involve repeating the same words or phrases. The first form occurs by using the same pattern of words whenever you introduce a new point. The pattern is not immediately repeated because there is data and evidence between the repeated phrase, but audiences quickly identify the pattern, thus making it easier for them to identify when you introduce another related point. The other version of repetition takes place when you want a specific claim, point, or piece of information to resonate with listeners. Here you simply repeat what you just said. For example: "*Grey's Anatomy* was number one in the ratings last fall. *Number one.*" The number is repeated, emphasizing to the audience that the number was important to know and remember.

alliteration
repeating the same consonant or vowel sound at the beginning of subsequent words

A second structural strategy also involves repeating something, but not words or phrases. *Alliteration* repeats the same consonant or vowel sound in subsequent words. Audiences notice this form of speech because it is unique. Phrases like "peace, progress, and prosperity," or "direct, deliberate, and decisive," repeat the same consonant sound at the beginning of three words that follow each other, making it more pleasing to the ear. Additionally, the words build on and relate to one another, thus underscoring your description of an object.

Repeating patterns of sounds or words is not the only structural way to enhance a speech. We can also use *parallelism*, or the practice of similarly structuring related words, phrases, or clauses. Unlike repetition, parallelism does not require the use of the same words, phrases or clauses, only that the ideas in those clauses are similar. Take for example, the following from a speech by Jesse Jackson at the 1984 Democratic National Convention: "If, in my high moments, I have done some good, offered some service, shed some light, healed some wounds, rekindled some hope, or stirred someone from apathy and indifference, or in any way along the way helped somebody, then this campaign has not been in vain." Here, he uses similar words and phrases like "offered some service," "shed some light," "healed some wounds," and "rekindled some hope" to drive home a point. The ideas of each phrase are the same, and the structure is similar but the words used are different. By structuring different phrases and words in a similar fashion you can emphasize importance and create memorable wording that others are more likely to remember.

parallelism
similarly structuring related words, phrases, or clauses

The fourth and final structural strategy we will cover involves inverting language. *Antithesis* calls for you to take two ideas that sharply contrast with each other and juxtapose them in a parallel grammatical structure. A famous example of antithesis comes from John F. Kennedy's inaugural address: "Ask not what your country can do for you, but what you can do for your country." On the one hand he decries socialism, and on the other he inspires individual effort. These are two ideas that compete with one another but work together to make a point in this statement. This is one of the more difficult structural strategies to employ, but the reward for the effort within the speech is high.

antithesis
two ideas that sharply contrast with each other and are juxtaposed in a parallel grammatical structure

Speech Structure Strategies		Table 9.3
Type	**Example**	
Repetition	"The TV show *The Simpsons* has been running since 1989. 1989!"	
Alliteration	"I want this report clear, concise, and concrete."	
Parallelism	"My hobbies are hiking, boating, and fishing."	
Antithesis	"To err is human, to forgive divine."	

Guidelines for Using Language

As you consider specific words, word-clusters, and language structures that you want to incorporate into the emotional appeals that you create, keep in mind some additional guidelines for using language effectively.

1. **Use Language You Know and Are Comfortable with**: One of the common pressures speakers feel is the misplaced idea that they need to sound smart. Understand that you sound smart by presenting evidence in a logical cogent fashion and making a clear argument, not by filling your speech with big words. In fact, if used too often complex words can lose

an audience and also hinder your efforts to identify with them. You need to sound conversational and natural, not formal and forced. This is true in any setting.

2. **Eliminate Wordiness**: Be economical in your choice of words. Just as every speech has a purpose, so too does every word. Be concise and clear rather than overly intricate and elaborate in your description. Try to avoid using words that are unnecessary in helping you make your point. Excess words take attention away from the points within your speech and can confuse the audience. In conversation excessive wordiness can create the impression that you wish to monopolize the conversation. Be direct and clear so that you respect others and their right to speak.

Online Help

www.merriam-webster.com
www.dictionary.com

3. **Know When to Use a Thesaurus and When Not to**: An essential tool for any speaker also becomes a threat to a speech's success if used improperly. A thesaurus can help you find synonyms for words you may find yourself using quite a bit. However, when using a thesaurus you must be sure that you know the synonym, are comfortable using it, and use it in the proper context. Varying how you say something is a great way to enhance the appeal of your messages and makes it easier for others to pay attention, but using words just because they are different is a bad idea. Remember the first guideline: use language you know and are comfortable with.

4. **Use Active, Rather than Passive, Voice Whenever Possible**: A simple way to inject excitement into any message is to use active verbs. Active verbs depict movement. Passive voice, on the other hand, is boring and easily identified. Avoid writing or speaking with forms of the verb *to be*, such as the following: *was, being, were, is,* and *are*. These all indicate the passive voice. When you correct these constructions look to craft sentences where there is a subject followed by the action it performs, and then the object upon which it takes the action. Think about the following statements:

> Passive Voice: *"Harold and Kumar were driving to White Castle so they could buy a snack."*

> Active Voice: *"Harold and Kumar drove to White Castle to buy a snack."*

Which of these sounds more appealing? Which avoids the passive voice? As the example also illustrates, taking care to use active voice sentence construction also eliminates wordiness.

5. **Use "I, Me, We" Language**: This guideline essentially asks that you take ownership of your ideas and statements. Be clear about what is your language and what is attributed to someone else. Words like *we* and *our* also help you connect with others by making it appear as though you speak as a member of a collective group that includes them. This type of language helps you differentiate between your claims and the data that supports the claims, speak more forcefully without being rude, and enhance your relationship with others in a subtle but effective manner.

That said, when you believe something, make sure you claim it by using "I" or "my" when you speak. Beware, however, that excessive use of "I" statements that ignore the other people involved in a conversation can create the impression that you are self-absorbed and not interested in other people.

USING IMAGES TO EVOKE EMOTION

Images are another powerful tool for evoking an emotional response in an audience. As you create specific emotional appeals to incorporate into the message that you want to communicate to your audience, you do well to think of ways in which you can use visual images, as well as images that appeal to other senses, to elicit the feelings that you want your audience to feel.

As we learned earlier in this chapter while studying the four-step method for creating emotional appeals, as you begin crafting an emotional appeal, you not only must decide what specific emotion you want to evoke, but also must connect it to an object that you want the audience to associate with that emotion. Emotions are especially compelling when they have an object. The more concrete the object, the stronger the association is likely to be for the audience. Abstract concepts such as "freedom" or "knowledge" do not make for effective objects in emotional appeals, for they lack concrete immediacy for the audience. What is "freedom"? What does "knowledge" look like? However, an image of something tangible such as the American Flag or an elementary school classroom is much easier to grasp and thus feel something in association with it.

Accordingly, as you move into the third step of creating an emotional appeal in which you create language and images that can help the audience to feel what you want them to feel, selecting one or more images of the specific object that you want your audience to associate with the feeling in question. The following guidelines can help you as you decide what images to use:

- **Choose images that are visually compelling.** For instance, if you are going to encourage your audience to associate the image of the American flag with the feeling of pride, then don't choose just any image of the flag; choose one that has a strong aesthetic value, is memorable, and emotionally evocative.

- **Don't overwhelm your audience with too many images of the same object.** One or two are sufficient for providing your audience with something concrete to associate with the feeling you want to evoke.

- **Don't focus the emotional appeal on multiple objects in any given appeal.** Having multiple objects can confuse the audience about the connection you are trying to make or dilute the power and focus of the emotional appeal.

- **Be careful about using disturbing images.** When you speak to an audience, you are asking them to trust you enough to open their perspective to what you are saying. If you present images to them that are too gory, inappropriate, obscene, or otherwise disturbing, then you risk the trust that you so far have created with them and might lose credibility in their eyes. If you must use potentially disturbing images to make a point, then you show consideration to your audience if you warn them first about what they are going to see and give them an opportunity to look away if they wish, until the image is no longer visible.

- **Choose images that resonate with the experiences, understanding, and ideals of your audience.** What has an emotional impact on you is not necessarily what has an emotional impact on them. While you must speak from your own standpoint, taking some time to learn about your audience in advance, as Chapter 3 describes, can help you to choose images that can create a bridge between what you want to communicate and what is familiar and impactful to the audience.

- **Give credit to the source of the image.** As you would cite the source of a statistic or piece of expert testimony that you give in a message, you should cite the source for visual images. You do not need to cite the source orally, if you feel that doing so would lessen the impact of the appeal. If you are using a chart or a graph as a visual image, then you are likely to be talking about the specific information in the image; in this case, you should include an oral citation for the source of the data. However, sometimes, such as in the case of photographic images, you might not want to do this. If you do not cite the source of the image through verbal attribution, then you should credit the source in some other way, for instance with a small note at the bottom of the screen on which the image appears.

- **Consider the use of other sensory images as well as visual images.** Visual images are a powerful means of evoking emotion from an audience. However, images that appeal to other senses also can be quite powerful. A sound clip, for instance, can elicit feelings. Though it might require some creative preparation and setup, olfactory, tactile, or gustatory images also can evoke deep and rich emotional responses.

In addition to images of the object that you are connecting to the emotion that you wish to evoke, you also might wish to incorporate other images into your message to create an emotional effect. Speakers in presentations often make use of presentation slides, such as Power Point or Prezi. If you use such slides, we urge you to resist the temptation of using your slides as a vehicle for displaying your speaking notes to the audience, with slide after slide containing bullets of text. While applications such as these can be helpful tools in some respects in creating visuals, having a stream of slides that essentially function as your speaking notes on display does little to create an emotional experience for your audience. Indeed, it is wise to avoid bullet points except when they are absolutely necessary. In most cases, they do not help your audience much at all; rather, they give the audience something to read, which can distract their attention from listening to what you are saying. The popularity of such slides likely comes from the tendency for speakers who might be feeling some apprehension to use these slides as a crutch for their own confidence in front of the audience. No doubt, you have seen presentations like this before, perhaps even in your classes here at the

University. In an educational context, there might be some value in having a set of presentation slides, to which you then can return and use as a reference or study aid. However, in a professional or public presentation, we encourage you to be more selective in what you use as visual aids and to think about pathos as you create slides.

Rather than creating slides that consist of several bullet points of text, one after the other, we recommend that you consider some of these other visual aids, which you can place on a select number of slides over the course of your presentation:

- **Bar graphs**, which can show the magnitude of particular variables or categories of things
- **Pie graphs**, which can show the proportion or percentage of particular variables or components relative to some whole
- **Line graphs**, which can show trends over time
- **Pictograph**, a diagram that represents populations of people or objects using symbols, which can show relative magnitudes
- **Diagrams**, which can show visual representations of objects or parts of a whole
- **Maps**, which can show geographic locations relative to each other
- **Flow charts**, which can show steps in a process or sequence
- **Timelines**, which can show specific events or moments within a particular span of time

While many of these visual aids are especially useful as explanatory devices, they can also be used for persuasive effect. For instance, a pictograph depicting the magnitude of a particular condition or consequence for people in a particular population relative to others can suggest social inequalities, which are themselves manifestations of injustice in society. If coupled with a compelling personal story about someone within that population to give a human face to these injustices, this pictograph can function as a powerful means for creating pathos.

If you use presentation slides, you should only use the minimum number of slides that you need to communicate your message and evoke the response that you are seeking from the audience. The fewer the slides, the more impact each individual slide is likely to have on the audience. Each slide, moreover, requires time to discuss, perhaps as much as a minute to discuss its content in adequate depth. As you prepare your visual aids, you should consider how the number of slides will impact the timing of the communication as a whole.

As you prepare, remember also that the way in which you deliver the message while using visual aids has consequences for the emotional impact that you are trying to create. In Chapter 4, we explored some guidelines for using visual aids to explain a concept or idea. Those guidelines included:

- Keep your visual aid simple and as neat as possible.
- Maintain visual contact with the audience.

- Explain what you write or draw.
- Be attuned to the listener's response.

You should not only prepare your visual aids in advance, but also practice with them prior to the actual communication with the audience. If you deliver your message in a manner that is disjointed, incoherent, uncoordinated, or otherwise poorly rehearsed, then your credibility in the eyes of your audience is likely to decrease. Moreover, with respect to pathos, the impact of your message is likely to be diminished or might even have a different emotional effect than you had hoped to create.

TELLING A STORY

The final step in the four-step method that we have presented in this chapter for strengthening pathos involves telling a story about the object that you have chosen as the focus of the emotional appeal, to evoke the specific feeling that you want the audience to experience. In a sense, the story brings together all of the elements that you have created so far: the object on which you have chosen to focus the appeal; the compelling words, word-clusters, and language structures that you have decided to incorporate into the appeal; and the images that you have selected, all as means for evoking the emotion in question. What is needed before your work is complete is a narrative to bring all of these elements together. In this final section of this chapter, we will explore ways in which telling a story can create pathos by incorporating all of these other components that you have prepared.

First, it might be helpful to consider what makes up an effective story. Storytelling is an important area of study in the field of communication. Scholars in communication and other related fields have developed a number of frameworks for understanding how stories work and the elements that comprise them. We will examine two of them: Kenneth Burke's dramatic pentad and Walter Fisher's narrative paradigm.

Burke's Pentad

The first of these frameworks comes from American rhetorician Kenneth Burke. Among his many other contributions to the study of rhetoric, Burke developed a framework for analyzing the messages that speakers create to influence others called the *Pentad*. For Burke, all human action is drama. When the speaker creates a message and delivers it to an audience, the speaker is essentially dramatizing reality in a particular way.

Pentad
a framework for analyzing the messages that speakers create to influence others

The speaker creates an account of what happened. This account has five component parts: the act, the agent, the agency, the scene, and the purpose. The account contains either an explicit or implicit subject who performs an action. The subject who performs the action in the account is the agent. What the speaker says that the subject is doing is the act. For example, when your mother says, "Take out the garbage," you are the implied agent, and taking out the garbage is the message that she has created. Agency is how the act is performed by the agent, according to the speaker. The speaker might identify particular means, strategies, techniques, or processes through which the agent is performing the act. The scene is the context within which the act takes place, according to the speaker. Looking at the example again, we can see that the agency in your mother's words is that you will take out the garbage through your own labor, and the scene, which is implied, is a dirty house. The purpose is the reason why the act is being performed, according to the speaker. In the above example, the reason for taking out the garbage, which is largely implicit, is to clean the dirty house.

Consider a longer example, an excerpt of a speech delivered by Oprah Winfrey on June 15, 2008, to the graduating class of Stanford University:

> *The world has so many lessons to teach you. I consider the world, this Earth, to be like a school and our life the classrooms. And sometimes here in this Planet Earth school the lessons often come dressed up as detours or roadblocks, and sometimes as full-blown crises. And the secret I've learned to getting ahead is being open to the lessons, lessons from the grandest university of all, that is, the universe itself. It's being able to walk through life eager and open to self-improvement and that which is going to best help you evolve, 'cause that's really why we're here, to evolve as human beings. To grow into more of ourselves, always moving to the next level of understanding, the next level of compassion and growth.*[16]

We can use Burke's Pentad to analyze how Oprah is dramatizing reality through the account that she gives in this speech. In this excerpt, the act that stands at the heart of her account is learning what the universe has to teach. Her use of metaphor, particularly that of the Earth as a school and one's life as a classroom, gives clues about what is happening most centrally in her account. The agents are the graduates. She speaks about her own experiences, but the story is really about the graduates that she is addressing, learning as they move through the world. The clue that they are the agents in her story is in the first sentence of her account: "The world has so many lessons to teach you." This is a story about them, not really her. The agency through which the graduates will learn what the universe can teach them is their openness: they must remain open, to the detours, roadblocks, and crises; open to self-improvement and whatever else will help them to evolve; open to moving to the next level of understanding, compassion, and growth. Oprah's story is primarily about the graduates' learning, and the way that they will do this is by being open to what the universe sets before them. The scene in the story is each graduate's life here on Earth, which is the classroom where this learning will take place in the university that is the universe. Why will all of this learning take place? So the graduates can evolve into better people. This is the purpose in the account. Evolving into better human beings is "really why we're here," according to Oprah, and it is why the graduates will learn what they must learn.

Note that the five elements are always defined according to the speaker's perspective in the account, not what happened in some objective sense. The Pentad helps us to understand how the speaker dramatizes reality by making an account that has these five elements. Another speaker might dramatize the same events in a completely different manner, with a different act, agent, agency, scene, and purpose making up the account. Indeed, one can use Burke's Pentad to analyze the accounts that different communicators use for the same events and exploring why their accounts might differ from each other. This might be an especially useful way to analyze communication if one of these accounts has been more influential than the other, or if each account has been more influential with a different audience than the other.

According to Burke, all five components of the Pentad work together within a message according to a ratio. Ratios are pairings of elements in the Pentad whereby one is understood by the speaker as having a determining effect over another. For instance, the scene-act ratio implies that the scene, or setting, plays a dominant role in determining what actions are necessary. The scene-agent ratio suggests that the scene places particular limits upon or otherwise mobilizes the agent in a particular way. The scene-purpose ratio implies that the setting influences the reasons or motivations behind the act. In the above "take out the garbage" example, for instance, the scene-purpose ratio is central. The account, although brief, revolves around the dirty house as a scene necessitating the motive of cleaning the house. The scene-act ratio also is central, but perhaps is secondary to the scene-purpose ratio. The dirtiness of the house demands that someone takes the garbage out, but there seems to be an overarching motive of cleaning the house that is especially driven by the present dirtiness of the house. Considering particular ratios in analyzing the story helps one to understand which parts of the account as dramatized are more dominant and important in the message.

Burke's Pentad can provide a framework for telling a story as part of creating an emotional appeal, for one must craft an account that dramatizes reality in a particular way. One can begin by identifying what happened, the act. Next, one can identify who performed that act, the agent. Third, one can describe how the act was done, the agency. Fourth, one can tell where the act occurred, the scene. Finally one can tell why the action was done, the purpose. One need not tell the story by addressing these elements in this particular order; one should tell the story in a way that is most likely to evoke the desired emotion from the audience.

Also, telling the story effectively involves more than simply addressing these five points. One must think about how the action in the story develops across time. As British literary critic Frank Kermode explains, stories typically have a beginning, a middle, and an end.[18] Action develops from crisis to victory and to crisis again until a climax is reached, and a resolution occurs. The five components of Burke's Pentad can provide the basic outline or skeleton of the story at a given moment, but as you continue telling the story, you might describe a new action that occurs and complicates the first, with a new act, agent, scene, agency, and purpose. Then, as the action continues to build, another action might take place that resolves this difficulty, only to be thwarted later by another development in the unfolding action. Eventually, the story will reach some sort of climactic moment followed by a resolution, which might illustrate in some way the point that you were trying to make by telling the story.

You as a speaker also want to think about how you can deliver the story in a way that is compelling to the audience, perhaps using some of the language devices and structures that we examined earlier in the chapter. For example, you can see in the story that Oprah told to the graduates at Stanford how Oprah uses metaphor and parallelism as language devices in telling the story. She uses metaphor by identifying each person's life as a classroom within the universe as a university. She uses another metaphor of "walking through" life and another metaphor of evolution in describing how human beings grow. She uses parallelism in the final sentence: "To grow into more of ourselves, always moving to the next level of understanding, the next level of compassion and growth." The repetition of the structure "the next level of _____, the next level of _____" creates a rhythm to the account, which itself can have an emotional impact.

Fisher's Narrative Paradigm

Another framework that can help you as you bring together the various elements of the emotional appeal into a single story is Walter Fisher's *narrative paradigm*. Fisher's narrative paradigm argues that humans are storytelling beings by nature. For this reason, stories are especially effective at making arguments and explaining the world to audiences. Fisher's framework explains what characteristics of a story are likely to result in its acceptance by those who hear it.

narrative paradigm
humans are storytelling beings by nature

According to Fisher, people evaluate stories according to two criteria. The first criterion is that the story has *narrative coherence*, or that it makes sense in the world in which the people who hear the story live. If the people who are listening to the story cannot make sense of what is happening, if they do not comprehend what the characters in the story are doing and why they are doing it, if they cannot follow the story from one point to another, then the story will lack narrative coherence for them. They, in turn, are likely to reject the story. If those who are listening to the story are able to follow what is happening and the story generally makes sense to them in terms of the world in which they live, they are likely to accept the story.

narrative coherence
the degree to which a story makes sense in the world in which we live

For example, suppose a speaker tells a story about two friends who go skiing one afternoon after the public authorities issue a winter storm warning and urge county residents to refrain from any non-emergency travel. While the friends are driving to the ski resort, the inclement weather begins to escalate. The friends' car slides off the road after hitting a patch of black ice and careens into a snow drift. Because no one else is traveling on the road and the friends' accident occurred in a remote area, the two friends nearly die from exposure to the elements until they are discovered by a local ranger passing by on a snowmobile after being stranded overnight. The speaker tells the story as a way of evoking fear and convincing the audience of the need to listen to public authorities whenever they issue safety warnings. Many of the audience members are able to follow what the speaker is telling them. In fact, because some of them have been in similar precarious wintry situations at some point in their lives, the story especially makes sense to them. However, a handful of the audience members come from a part of the world in which there has never been a snowfall on historical record. They have never witnessed snow. They don't know what a ski resort is. These audience members

Kenneth Burke (1897–1993)

Born in Pittsburgh near the turn of the twentieth century, Kenneth Burke remains one of the most influential American philosophers of all time. Unlike many other twentieth century scholars, Burke never received a college degree. In fact, he dropped out of not one, but two, universities. He preferred to write on his own, rather than pursue a doctorate and a career as a professor. He wrote multiple books and essays that influenced a variety of different disciplines.

Burke graduated from high school in Pittsburgh and then enrolled at The Ohio State University. Soon after attending he dropped out and chose to enroll at Columbia University. That experience also ended in his withdrawal from school. His lack of a college degree or formal higher education did not deter him from entrenching himself in academic life, however.

In 1939 he examined speeches by Adolf Hitler, then the chancellor of Germany. In this essay he eerily predicted the problems Hitler would cause in Germany simply by looking at how he managed to use speech to seize power. The essay entitled "The Rhetoric of Hitler's Battle" proposed a process by which Hitler's speech explained away the troubles of the German people by scapegoating people of Jewish descent and purifying what it meant to be Aryan. This work helped future scholars work to identify the ways in which leaders talk about enemies and war, and even apologize for wrongdoings.

Burke also wrote original poetry, fiction, and a plethora of literary critiques that are still considered essential reading for students in many different fields. His early interests in music and poetry led to his later exploration of language and symbols as explanations of the structure of human action. He eventually theorized that all human action is drama.

Although he was influenced somewhat by Marxism, throughout his life Burke never strictly adhered to any ideology or dogma. He also never held a permanent academic post anywhere, preferring to stay as fluid in his career as he did in his works. He passed away in 1993, having left an indelible mark on communication, philosophy, education, and literature.

So influential was Burke that many master's theses and doctoral dissertations employ and/or analyze Burke's criticism and theories. There also is a scholarly organization called the Kenneth Burke Society, and many different English, philosophy, and communication academic organizations have a Kenneth Burke division dedicated to exploring or employing his work.

APPLICATION OF KENNETH BURKE'S PENTAD

The following is an excerpt of a speech delivered by Oprah Winfrey on June 15, 2008, to the graduating class of Stanford University:

"The world has so many lessons to teach you. I consider the world, this Earth, to be like a school and our life the classrooms. And sometimes here in this Planet Earth school the lessons often come dressed up as detours or roadblocks, and sometimes as full-blown crises. And the secret I've learned to getting ahead is being open to the lessons, lessons from the grandest universe of all, that is, the universe itself. It's being able to walk through life eager and open to self-improvement and that which is going to best help you evolve, cause that's really why we're here, to evolve as human beings. To grow into being more of ourselves, always moving to the next level of understanding, the next level of compassion and growth."[16]

PENTADIC ELEMENT	APPLYING THE PENTAD
Agent	Graduates
Agency	Openness
Act	Learning
Scene	Life on earth
Purpose	To evolve into better people

According to Burke, all five components of the pentad work together within a message according to a ratio. The ratio helps an analyst understand which parts of the drama are most dominant and important to the message's success. In our "take out the garbage" example, the most important ratio is the scene/purpose ratio. This pentadic approach is emblematic of how complicated Burke understood language to be, and how he believed language related to thought and action.

do not know what a snow drift or black ice is, nor how either could be a danger. They also have no concept of what a snowmobile is. As the story unfolds, while others are able to follow what is happening and make sense of the story in terms of their world, these audience members feel confused and lost. Most of the time, they are trying to figure out what specific elements of the story are and have little ability to understand the events of the story as parts of a whole. For these friends, the story lacks narrative coherence. As a result, regardless of how artfully the story might have been told or how agreeable the values that it upholds might be, they are likely to reject the story.

narrative fidelity
....
the degree to which a story matches our own beliefs and experiences

The second criterion is ***narrative fidelity***. Narrative fidelity means that the story must match the beliefs and experiences of the one who hears it. It does not refer to whether the story makes sense to the listener, but rather whether the story upholds values that the listener also holds or ones that the listener can appreciate as reflecting what is best in human beings. If the story celebrates values that the listener does not hold or values that the listener cannot appreciate as reflecting what is ideal for humanity in general, then the listener is likely to reject the story.

Let us return to the previous example. As we mentioned, many of the audience members found the story to have narrative coherence, insofar as it made sense to them in terms of the world in which they live. These audience members were able to follow the events of the story and to make sense of these events in light of the story as a whole. However, suppose that some of these audience members were raised in high northern latitudes, in parts of the world where driving in extreme weather is a normal part of life. These listeners might find the values advocated in the story to be in contrast to their own. They might see the blanket caution that the speaker endorses as being too simple and extreme. Against the value of placing trust in the safety warnings of bureaucratic institutions, they might cherish alternative values such as independence, autonomy, personal judgment, and self-reliance. These audience members might hear this story against a backdrop of what is for them an undesirable creep of public institutions into people's private lives, a sphere of life where personal judgment and autonomy should hold primary sway, in their view. For these listeners, if the travelers in the story were to be criticized for anything, they should not be criticized for not listening to the public safety advisory, but for not being better prepared for the weather. These listeners heard in the story many details that indicated to them a level of foolishness on the part of the travelers, for instance, not taking a four-wheel drive vehicle, not having snow tires or even chains on their tires, taking a route that was unnecessarily remote and would not have been a high priority for snowplows, not having proper clothing for the outing that could have kept them warm even during an accident, and not being prepared with a proper a roadside emergency kit, which would have included a way of keeping themselves warm overnight. If the travelers would have been better prepared and more experienced in driving in snowy conditions, then the wintry weather would not have posed such a problem for them. They find the story to be unappealing not because it didn't make sense to them but because it is advocating something that they themselves don't value: abdicating personal judgment and responsibility to public institutions. Whether or not others in the audience would agree with them, for these listeners, the story lacks narrative fidelity.

Fisher's framework highlights the need for speakers to know their audiences well when creating a story and to tell stories that not only make sense to audience members in light of the world in which they live, but also that promote values that they themselves hold or can embrace. Earlier in the chapter, we examined myths and arguments from the past as two word-cluster approaches that speakers could incorporate into their message. Both myths and arguments from the past are narrative in structure. Part of the reason why they are particularly convincing in persuasion is because, if told effectively, they already make sense in terms of the world of the audience members and resonate with the values that they themselves or others close to them hold.

Once you have created a story, it is wise to practice telling it, so that you can become familiar with its rhythm and timing and can adjust your delivery as necessary. Remember to incorporate language and images that evoke the feelings that you want your audience to feel regarding the object that you have chosen as the focus of the emotional appeal that you are creating. Pay attention to your nonverbal delivery, for much of the audience's emotional experience comes from the emotion that you yourself as the storyteller bring to the telling. Keep your story focused, short and concrete. Share only those elements that relate to the point being made; a story that runs on too long or contains ideas irrelevant to the point that you are making will not be as effective. Make sure that how the story sheds light on the point that you are explaining is clear; if you don't do that, people won't connect the story to what you want them to understand. Chapter 4 includes some guidelines for telling stories, which are as applicable to persuasion as they are to explanation. You might revisit that section of the chapter as you prepare your emotional appeals for your upcoming persuasive presentation.

SUMMARY

In this chapter, we have explored strengthening pathos in persuasion. We first explored a four-step method for creating an emotional appeal. We then examined the primary role of language in communication and four characteristics of language whenever we use it. We then looked at specific ways of using language to evoke an emotional response from audiences: single word and word cluster approaches, different language structures, and some specific guidelines for using language as we create emotional appeals. We considered afterwards some ways of incorporating images into our message as we create an emotional appeal. Finally, we looked at Burke's Pentad and Fisher's narrative paradigm as two frameworks for creating a story that can bring together the other elements of an emotional appeal. By using these concepts, techniques, and strategies, you can strengthen greatly your ability to inspire your audience to feel a certain way and thereby to move them to accept what you are trying to convince them to accept.

KEY TERMS

REVIEW QUESTIONS

1. What are the four steps in creating an effective emotional appeal?
2. What are the four characteristics of language?
3. What are the three single-word strategies for enhancing a message?
4. What are the three word-cluster approaches for enhancing a message?
5. What are the four structural strategies for using words to enhance your communication skills?
6. What language tools did Dr. King use in "I Have a Dream"?
7. What are the five elements of Burke's Pentad?
8. What two criteria must a story meet for people to accept it, according to Fisher's narrative paradigm?

THINK ABOUT IT

1. Where did language originate?
2. Are there any other common characteristics of language in addition to the four mentioned in this chapter?
3. Are speech and language different? If so, where is the line between speech and language?
4. How do you see language evolving in the future?

ACTIVITIES FOR ACTION

1. Print out the text of Dr. Martin Luther King, Jr.'s "I Have a Dream" speech discussed in this chapter. Go through and highlight as many metaphors as you can find, and then see if you can determine their type. Think about whether or not those specific word choices and metaphor types he employed made the speech as powerful as it was.
2. Sit down and watch (or read) the famous vaudeville skit "Who's on First?" by Abbott and Costello. What characteristics of language discussed in this chapter contribute to the humor of this classic comedy sketch?

3. Print out a famous speech—it does not matter by whom—and count how many versions of the verb form *to be* appear in the text of the speech. The chances are, it will be quite a small number. These forms include *have, has, was, were, be, and being,* to name just a few of the more common forms it takes.

ENDNOTES

1. Kent R. Middleton, William E. Lee, and Bill F. Chamberlin, *The Law of Public Communication* (Boston, MA: Allyn & Bacon, 2005), 405; T. Barton Carter, Marc A. Franklin, and Jay B. Wright, *The First Amendment and the Fourth Estate: The Law of Mass Media,* 9th Ed., (New York, NY: Foundation Press, 2005), 817.

2. Pacifica Foundation Station WBAI(FM), 56 F.C.C.2d 94, 32 P&F Rad. Reg. 2d 1331 (1975).

3. *Federal Communications Commission v. Pacifica Foundation,* 438 US 726, 98 S. Ct. 3026, 57 L.Ed.2d 1073, 43 R.R.2d 493, 3 Med.L.Rptr. 2553.

4. Ibid.

5. *Donnie Brasco,* directed by Mike Newell (Culver City, CA: Tristar Pictures, 1997).

6. Mary Haas: http://www.sealang.net/thai/haas-uc.htm (accessed June 9, 2011).

7. Ibid.

8. www.britannica.com: http://www.britannica.com/EBchecked/topic/250703/Mary-R-Haas (accessed June 9, 2011).

9. Mary Haas: http://www.glottopedia.de/index.php/Mary_R._Haas (accessed June 9, 2011).

10. http://www.indiana.edu/~anthling/v39-4.html (accessed June 9, 2011).

11. S. I. Hayakawa, *Language in Thought and Action,* 3rd ed. (New York, NY: Harcourt, 1972).

12. Abbott and Costello, "Who's on First?" www.americanrhetoric.com. http://americanrhetoric.com/speeches/abbott&costellowhosonfirst.htm (accessed June 21, 2011).

13. Michael C. McGee, "The Ideograph: A Link Between Rhetoric and Ideology," *The Quarterly Journal of Speech 66* (1980), 1–16.

14. "I Have a Dream," by Dr. Martin Luther King, Jr. www.americanrhetoric.com. http://www.americanrhetoric.com/speeches/mlkihaveadream.htm (accessed June 24, 2011).

15. Ibid.

16. Oprah Winfrey. Commencement Speech to Stanford University, 2008.

17. Kenneth Burke, "The Rhetoric of Hitler's Battle," *The Philosophy of Literary Form,* 3rd ed. (1941; Berkeley, CA: University of California Press, 1973), 191–220.

18. Frank Kermode, *The Sense of an Ending: Studies in the Theory of Fiction,* New York: Oxford University Press, 1967.

Interteaching Session

Dialogue

Find the full text of Dr. Martin Luther King, Jr.'s "I Have a Dream" speech online. If you can find a video recording of the speech, then watch at least a few minutes of the speech to catch a sense of how Dr. King's use of language created pathos for his audience. After reading the text of the speech, answer the following questions with your groupmates:

1. List at least three metaphors that Dr. King uses in the speech. Discuss how each of these metaphors might add to the pathos of the speech.

2. List at least three ideographs that Dr. King uses in the speech. Discuss how each of these metaphors might add to the pathos of the speech.

3. Find an example of each of the following techniques for structuring language, and discuss how each might add to the pathos of the speech.

   • Repetition

   • Alliteration

   • Parallelism

   • Antithesis

4. How does Dr. King use argument from the past or myths in this speech? Find a specific example, and discuss how it might add to the pathos of the speech.

Performance

Suppose that you and your groupmates are giving a presentation to a group of high school students in the local community to persuade them to volunteer at least a few hours each week for participating in a group or organization that does community service. You know that in order to persuade these youth, you will need to affect their hearts in some way: that is, you will need to create pathos. Using the four-step method in this chapter, create an emotional appeal that you could make to these youth as part of your overall effort to convince them. Make sure that you go through all four steps of the method and that you create a narrative that brings together the various elements that you create. Be prepared to present your appeal to the class, as though they were the youth that you are trying to convince.

Crafting a Persuasive Message

10

Practically SPEAKING

In 1924 at a small YMCA in Santa Ana, California, a small group of people met to help each other become better public speakers and have a little bit of fun in the process. Over the years, that small group expanded and became a group called Toastmasters International, a nonacademic leader in helping people develop oral communication skills. This nonprofit organization now boasts nearly 235,000 members at over 11,700 clubs in 92 different countries.[1]

Thousands of corporations, companies, and civic organizations encourage their employees and affiliates to participate in Toastmasters because of the practical benefits gained from the group. Toastmasters use a manual to help members develop certain speaking skills. It focuses on the use of humor, gestures, and eye contact. Upon completion of the manual, members progress to more advanced instruction.

Toastmasters International also contributes much in the way of community service. They promote youth programs designed around developing oral communication and leadership skills. They support "Gavel Clubs" where they bring speech training inside prison walls. They work with community organizations and businesses to help them tell their stories to their communities. Additionally, they offer short courses on crafting effective messages.[2]

A central focus of the Toastmasters International programs is organization. In fact, they make it a point to tell people that one of the ten most common errors in public speaking is lack of preparation and organization. When you do not organize your thoughts in a logical manner, and then try to present them to an audience, it makes it very challenging for your listeners to follow what you are saying and ultimately get anything out of your presentation.

Persuasive messages must be carefully structured to ensure that the speaker achieves the specific purpose. In fact, persuasive speeches were the foremost concern of the Greeks and Romans. This chapter will briefly highlight the methods classical Greeks and Romans taught students to construct persuasive messages. Finally, we will offer organizational patterns you can use for crafting effective persuasive messages.

Prep Questions

Part 1: Key Concepts

1. List the six strategies from the chapter for creating a strong persuasive conclusion.

2. Compare and contrast the problem-solution organizational pattern with the problem-cause solution organizational pattern.

3. Explain how the comparative advantages organizational pattern works. What does each point in the presentation address if you use comparative advantages?

4. List and define the three principles of outlining.

5. How does a speaking outline differ from the preparation outline?

Part 2: Application

1. Create an introduction for a persuasive speech on a topic that you are considering for the upcoming persuasive assignment. Identify how the introduction that you have created reflects each of the four strategies for creating effective persuasive introductions in the chapter.

2. Consider some of the needs that college students have, and choose one. Use Monroe's Motivated Sequence to propose something that can fulfill this need. For each step in Monroe's Sequence, tell what you could argue to an audience of fellow college students.

Constructing Persuasive Introductions and Conclusions

It is often said that you do not have a second chance to make a first impression. This is true, and particularly important when trying to persuade someone. Additionally, it is equally important to leave them with a lasting positive impression of your argument in the hope they will accept it. In this section we will provide you with some strategies for developing effective introductions and conclusions. We will then explore different organizational strategies for the body of a persuasive message. Keep in mind that these categories of introduction, body, and conclusion apply to a variety of communicative formats, and not just public speaking. They are also ways to think about how to structure a conversation, commercial, or any other type of interaction.

Strategies for Persuasive Introductions

The Greeks and Romans noted the uniqueness of introductions and provided several different options for developing them. These observations also illustrate the differences that exist between persuasive and explanatory introductions. That said, there are similarities between the two types. This section will note the similarities while also providing you with ways to effectively construct an introduction appropriate for a persuasive message.

Cicero and Quintilian suggested that the introduction be the last part that you write, and this advice holds with persuasive as well as explanatory prepared presentations. You should not set up the introduction until you know what you are going to say, as well as have an idea of the knowledge level and disposition of your audience. This information is essential to making sure you effectively capture the audience's interest, establish credibility, and focus the audience's attention. When entering a meeting or making a statement to someone, you should also take care to think through the best way to accomplish these tasks, even though you often do not have time to prepare this in advance.

Those three goals of an introduction are the same for when you explain something as well as when you try and convince someone of something. You need to get an audience's attention, but as Cicero and Quintilian noted, be sure to do so without offending the people to whom you are speaking. You must be attuned to the audience's feelings about the topic or the occasion and determine how best to introduce yourself and your argument. You also need to establish your credibility almost immediately by stating why an audience should listen to you on a particular subject. To this end, it is important to develop your skills of observation to quickly identify things in your surroundings that can help you choose the most effective introduction in a given situation. Finally, you need to preview the main points in much the same way you would for an explanation. To prepare your audience to listen to your argument, you should state the thesis that you intend to argue and list the main points that you will cover as you make that argument.

Table 10.1

Tips for an Effective Persuasive Introduction
• Develop the introduction last.
• Preview the main points that you will present.
• Capture the attention of the audience.
• Establish your credibility.
• Focus the audience's attention on the thesis that you will argue.

Introductions need not be lengthy. In fact, in a presentation lasting around five minutes, you only have perhaps a minute to introduce your argument to the audience. This means that you have only enough time to touch briefly on each of the three goals of the introduction. You don't have time to expound at length on any of them. For this reason, we highly recommend that you practice delivering your introduction after you draft it, so that you know how much time it takes to give it. If necessary, you can trim aspects of it, so that it takes less time. However, if you don't practice, you have no way of knowing how long your introduction will run and will risk taking more time for your presentation than what your audience has given to you.

Strategies for Persuasive Conclusions

Just as with introductions, there are elements common to both explanatory and persuasive conclusions, as well as parts that are different. That said, introductions and conclusions do mirror each other in certain ways. For example, while introductions end with transitions, conclusions start with one. In this section of the chapter we will discuss those similarities and differences while also providing tips on how you can create a strong conclusion when advocating for something.

One of the aspects of conclusions shared by both explanations and persuasive messages is the need for a signpost at the opening of the conclusion. Signposts serve the same function for persuasive message conclusions that they do for explanations: they let the audience know the speech or conversation is almost complete.

Similarly, both types of conclusions should summarize the main points and demonstrate how they connect to and support your argument. You should never introduce new evidence or ideas in a conclusion, but rather re-emphasize the fundamental points of your message. This allows the audience to walk away from your presentation understanding your central point and how you got there. Rarely will listeners recall all the specific evidence you lay out, but they will remember main points. With regard to persuasive messages, this summary also enables you to build up your clincher, which can be a much more powerful statement than those used to end an explanation. A key to any good interaction is adequately summarizing key points so that everyone leaves with an understanding of what was said and what is expected or encouraged.

Although both explanations and persuasive messages have clinchers, persuasive messages allow for much more creativity and direct calls to action with their clinchers. The reason for this is simple: the general purpose of a persuasive message is to persuade, which involves some sort of willing change made by the audience.

The success of your effort at advocacy often depends on your ability to channel and incite the proper pathos through this clincher. The clincher should not take long to state, and there are a variety of ways to construct an effective one for a persuasive message. Most importantly, however, it is essential for you to find a way to reiterate what you want from the audience.

A common error that novice speakers make in conclusions is reserving the persuasive effort for the clincher. Do not wait until the last few moments of your time with the audience to persuade them! The clincher should be the last push and should be a logical next step based on the case you laid out throughout the message. In short, the conclusion should feed off of the rest of the message to accentuate your case and its significance for the audience.

One final note about conclusions bears mentioning. Conclusions should not be very long. In fact, in a formal presentation they should take about as long as your introduction, and thus typically account for no more than 20% of the message. If your conclusion rambles on, it loses its effectiveness and you lose your audience. In a conversation if you do not end the interaction after signaling a conclusion the other party may get irritated and impatient and even lose the point of the conversation. If conclusions are too short, your audience may never truly understand the point of your message. Remember that your conclusion is the last chance you have to underscore your case and its importance for your listeners.

Conclusions are essential elements of any good persuasive message. They involve letting the audience know you are almost finished, restating your argument and main points, and clinching your appeal with a call to action. They share some similarities with conclusions for explanations, but there are key differences you must be aware of when approaching the end of a conversation or preparing the end of a speech. The development of strong introductions and conclusions is only part of the process of crafting a successful persuasive appeal. In the next section we will explore methods that you might use to properly organize the bulk of the content to develop your persuasive message.

Table 10.2	Tips for a Persuasive Speech Conclusion
	• Provide a signpost at the beginning of the conclusion.
	• Summarize the main points.
	• Do not present new evidence.
	• Emphasize the fundamental points.
	• Build up the clincher.
	• Do not wait until the conclusion to present persuasive appeals.
	• Accentuate the points in the body and case.
	• Make it approximately the same length as the introduction.

PERSUASIVE ORGANIZATIONAL PATTERNS

The general and specific purposes of a persuasive message differ from those of an informative address, but they too help you determine how to arrange your points. A closing argument in a courtroom is a persuasive message in which the general purpose is to persuade and the specific purpose is tied to the facts of the case. For example, the lawyer for Kelly, who was accused of stealing money from a CVS pharmacy, gave a closing argument where the specific purpose was "to persuade

the jury that Kelly did not steal the money because she had no motive or opportunity to commit the crime." This specific purpose statement encouraged the lawyer to use a particular organizational pattern to accomplish the speaking goals. In this section of the chapter we will detail common organizational strategies that you can effectively employ when advocating for a position to other people. Although these may seem only appropriate for speeches, they still apply to other contexts in which you are trying to convince someone to agree with you. By keeping your purpose in mind when dealing with others in any context, your goals will help tell you which pattern would be most effective.

Persuasive messages have very different general and specific purposes than explanations, but in both cases the specific purpose typically dictates what organizational pattern should be used. Persuasive messages can be directed at a specific problem or the problem's fundamental cause. They also can focus on stating that one option is better than another. Finally, there are persuasive messages that attempt to move people to immediate action. Depending on which of these is your goal, you may choose any one of four potential organizational patterns.

Organizational Patterns for Persuasive Speeches	Table 10.3
• Problem-solution	
• Problem-cause-solution	
• Comparative advantage	
• Monroe's Motivated Sequence	

Problem-Solution Order

If you seek to convince an audience that a specific policy or action will solve an existing problem, the *problem-solution order* might be best. In this arrangement you first must convince the audience that there is a problem, and then make the case that the solution you propose will alleviate that problem. To effectively arrange this message you must first establish a clear specific purpose that states exactly what you want your audience to do. Then you must consider several important questions to evaluate the merits of your case as you develop it and prepare to present it to your audience.

problem-solution order
......
a means of organizing a persuasive speech in which the discussion of the problem is followed by the preferred solution

The first question deals with the definition and scope of the problem. You should establish how you see the problem at hand and convince your audience to see it that way as well. If your listeners disagree with your definition of the problem, then you can never get the them to accept your solution because you will be stuck arguing what you will recall Quintilian called definitive stasis. In short, make sure all parties agree on the definition of the problem. So, before even offering a solution, you need to clearly establish the scope of the problem you plan to address. In explaining the scope of the predicament, you may wish to discuss whether any parties are harmed by the problem and explain how they are damaged. This can help create an emotional connection between the audience and the issue, thus enabling you to add some pathos to your appeal.

Once the dilemma that faces the audience is established, you move on to the solution. The initial part of this portion of your message should answer the question of evaluative criteria. You should clearly establish for your listeners, or with your conversational partners, the particular criteria by which a potential solution to the problem should be judged. When constructing this list of criteria, you should check your proposed solution against it to ensure that what you propose actually resolves the problem you described. If it does not, then your solution will likely not be adopted by the audience. Finally, you need to explain to the others how your solution can be put into effect. The "how" element is important because it is the prescription for action that you want them to follow. It should contain practical and specific steps for the other party to take that will actually enact the solution and solve the problem facing the community.

Consider also these additional tips for presenting your solution. Remember that you are advocating for a solution, not presenting information about multiple options. As a rule, don't present multiple solutions unless you intend to argue how your chosen solution is more advantageous than the alternatives. Presenting multiple alternatives, unless they are elements or steps of a single plan, dilutes the persuasiveness of your argument. You also might explain how the solution has been effective in solving the problem in the past, perhaps by other individuals, groups, or organizations. If no one has tried to implement the plan that you are presenting, then using analogical reasoning, you might explain how a similar plan was implemented and how, because of the similarities between that plan and the one that you are advocating, the solution will be effective in the present case. If your solution has any limitations or weaknesses, then you can acknowledge those limitations or weaknesses and explain to your audience why the plan is

Blood, Toil, Tears and Sweat
by newly elected Prime Minister Winston Churchill

Delivered May 13, 1940, to the British House of Commons

Prime Minister Winston Churchill delivered a terse yet powerful call to action shortly after becoming prime minister of Great Britain in May 1940. As if the war was not a large enough complication for the new leader, outgoing Prime Minister Neville Chamberlain received a boisterous round of applause, while Churchill was greeted with a subdued reaction from members of the House of Commons, thus illustrating the fragile coalition supporting Churchill and his government.[5]

At the time of the address Adolf Hitler's Nazi war machine was crushing opposition everywhere it went. Britons were concerned that their country's safety, freedom, and sovereignty were at risk. Churchill rose to the task of inspiring confidence in both his leadership and the country itself with this brief (only 688 words) address to Parliament.

In his statement of facts, Churchill noted he selected a five-person war cabinet that represented diverse political views. He pointed out that Britain was already fighting in Norway and Holland, that the Mediterranean was a concern, and that the air battle over the remainder of Europe was "continuous." He argued that these facts required that "many preparations have to be made here at home."

Churchill proclaimed the famous line: "I have nothing to offer but blood, toil, tears and sweat"[6] as part of his rebuttal, and aimed it at those who might criticize the swift creation of the cabinet without "ceremony." In fact, his phrase made it seem like he pled with them to accept it because he was essentially trying his best.

In his peroration the prime minister closed with a clarion call to action after admitting the country faced "many, many long months of struggle and suffering." These words, his declaration of a policy of victory, and his concluding statement of, "Come then, let us go forward together with our united strength"[7] all created emotional connections between the initially divided audience, himself, and his policies.

still advisable, despite the possible costs. This is especially important if there are ethical concerns relating to your plan that could lead the audience to reject the solution you are proposing. As you present your solution, support any claims that you are making with evidence. You must convince your audience that the solution will solve the problem. If you have expert testimony, statistics, or examples that can give support to this claim, now is the time to give it. Also, don't forget about pathos! Your audience must feel something, if they are going to have motivation to change their existing behavior and adopt something new. People, in general, are conservative, inasmuch as they generally do not like to change their habits and routines unless they have compelling reasons to do so.

Table 10.4

Tips for Presenting a Solution
• Present and advocate for only one solution. Don't present multiple options, unless you intend to show how your chosen solution is superior.
• Identify specific criteria that a solution to this problem would need to satisfy, and explain how the solution that you are presenting would satisfy those criteria.
• Describe what the solution involves, including specific components or parts.
• Address how the solution will be put into effect, including specific action steps that specific people, groups, or organizations would need to carry out.
• Explain how the solution will solve the problem that you have identified.
• Give examples of past successes with the approach that you are advocating for solving this problem or similar initiatives that worked elsewhere but could work in the present case.
• Acknowledge any weaknesses or limitations of your solution, and explain why the solution you are advocating is still desirable.
• Provide evidence to support your claims where necessary.
• Consider including an emotional appeal to motivate your audience to adopt what you are proposing.

Let's look at the hypothetical case of Lionel to illustrate how a simple problem-solution message might be approached. Lionel is tired of the potholes in the road in front of his house, so he attends the City Council meeting and addresses the members. First he explains that the road in front of his house contains ten potholes in a three block span, and then informs the council that they have caused several thousand dollars in damage to the cars that drive that road in the last month alone. He then proposes to them that they use city funds to fill the potholes with macadam (a mixture of broken stone) to avoid further damage.

Here Lionel detailed the problem and proposed a solution once the problem became clear to everyone. Using the problem-solution order this message would roughly look like the following:

Body

    I. Main point: State of the road in front of the house *(problem)*

    II. Main point: Funding road repairs *(solution)*

This can be an effective way of convincing an audience to support your plan; however, it is not always the most compelling way to propose a solution. Sometimes, you need to do more.

Problem-Cause-Solution

Problems, public or personal, always have a root cause. To effectively resolve the problem you need to address that root cause; otherwise, the symptoms will recur. To this end you must look at the situation and ask what are the causes of the problem, and whether or not those causes can actually be addressed. If they can, then the message needs to recognize the problems faced by the community, but also add a discussion of why the problem exists—its cause. In short, you must convince the others not just of the existence of a problem, but also of why the problem is there in the first place. Addressing that root cause is the most effective way to handle the situation. Let's return to Lionel and see how this works.

Would it make even better sense not to just fix the potholes, but to make sure they don't happen again? This would involve changing the specific purpose and, as a result, the organization of the main points. Lionel's specific purpose would change to reflect his new goal, and it would be something like this: "to persuade the audience to redesign the street where potholes have damaged cars so that they will not occur again."

The goal for Lionel now is to address the problem (potholes) by providing a solution to it and its cause (poor design of the street).

Body

    I. Main point: The state of the road in front of the house *(problem)*

    II. Main point: The poor street design *(cause)*

    III. Main point: Funding for proper road repairs *(solution)*

problem-cause-solution order
. . . .
a means of organizing a persuasive speech in which you discuss the problem first, then its root cause, and then your preferred solution that addresses both the problem and its inherent cause

His arrangement now is ***problem-cause-solution order***, where he first discusses the immediate problem, then explains what caused it, and finally provides a solution that addresses both the potholes and the poor street design.

Comparative Advantages

More often than not, you will not be the only one offering solutions to a problem. In fact, having multiple ideas about how to fix something or address an issue is commonplace. The important thing to remember is to research and evaluate all the other potential solutions that might be offered to solve the problem. After doing so, if you believe yours is the best, then it might be helpful to recognize the fact you are aware of other potential solutions, but that they would not be the best option. This approach looks at the strengths and weaknesses of other solutions and compares them with your own. Such an approach can help increase your ethos with the audience and make your case even stronger.

Continuing with the example of Lionel and the dangerous potholes, perhaps he is not the only one who has brought this issue to the attention of the city council. In fact, the council already knows about and agrees there is a problem and that its cause is poor street design. Let's say that the day before Lionel presents his message, the council comes out in favor of a plan to fill the potholes, but not redesign the street because it would be cost prohibitive to do so. Lionel, aware of this alternate plan, needs a different specific purpose and organizational pattern than in either of the two previous scenarios. Now his specific purpose is "to persuade his audience that paying the money to fix the street now is a better solution than simply fixing the potholes."

He then structures the body of this message by using the *comparative advantage* organizational pattern, in which every main point in the argument explains why redesigning the street is better than just fixing the potholes and not addressing their root cause.

comparative advantage
an organizational pattern that uses each main point to explain why the speaker's solution is better than another proposed solution

> Body
> I. Main point: Fixing potholes is temporary; a proper repair job will be permanent
> II. Main point: Fixing the road will create a smoother surface
> III. Main point: Fixing the road correctly will be less expensive in the long run

The case of Lionel and his topic illustrates several different ways of organizing persuasive messages. Each one helps to establish a strong case for adopting a particular policy.

Comparative advantage is also a very good way to argue for a position in a conversation in which multiple parties suggest alternative solutions. You can listen to the solutions of others and recognize their strong points, but then argue for why your position is better (if in fact it is, after listening to the other solutions with an open mind). If you pay attention to the statements of others, evaluate their evidence, and think critically about your own ideas, it will allow you to make a good case for an effective solution to the issue under discussion. There is, however, one more organizational pattern we need to discuss which is particularly useful when seeking immediate action from an audience.

Monroe's Motivated Sequence

The fourth organizational pattern for main points we will discuss provides a way to effectively arrange a message designed to incite immediate action from an audience. Alan Monroe, a professor at Purdue University, developed *Monroe's Motivated Sequence* in the 1930s. The five-step sequence combines psychological elements with persuasive structure in an effort to move an audience to action. First, Monroe advocated something the Greeks, Romans, and we have emphasized: getting the *attention* of your audience. Then he argued that a speaker should

Monroe's Motivated Sequence
a five-step organizational pattern that combines psychological elements with speech persuasion to move an audience to action

clearly lay out the *need* for change. Once you clearly establish the problem, you propose a solution to the problem to *satisfy* the need. Fourth, Monroe's sequence calls for you to intensify the audience's desire for your solution to the problem by *visualizing* its success. This involves the use of imagery, and asks the people listening to actually see themselves doing what you call for—at least to see it in their mind's eye. Finally, once you state your case and have gotten the people to visualize what life would be when it was successful, using emotionally stirring language you tell them *how to act*.[8]

In a presentation such as the one that you are giving in this class, Monroe's Motivated Sequence can be used to create a speech with an introduction, a body with three main points, and a conclusion. The introduction, with the elements that we identified earlier in this chapter, functions as the attention step of Monroe's Sequence. The first main point in the body addresses the need and accordingly functions as the second step in the sequence. The second main point presents what will provide this need and thus functions as the satisfaction step. The third main point explores the benefits that will come from adopting the proposed plan or solution. As such, it functions as the visualization step. The only step in Monroe's Sequence that remains is the action step. As the speaker gives the conclusion of the presentation, she or he can call the audience to action by suggesting a specific step that they can take to begin implementing the plan or solution that she or he has proposed. This might be done as the clincher of the speech. In this manner, Monroe's Sequence can be translated into a three-point presentation, similar to presentations organized in accordance with some of the other organizational patterns in this chapter.

As an example: A student participating in the School of Business's Business Plan Competition, in which students compete for over $175,000 in prizes each year by developing their own business plans and elevator pitches, needs to find a way to get the judges to select his plan. He composes the following order for his points using Monroe's Motivated Sequence:

Attention:	"Do you have a yard where you have to both mow and edge your grass? Would you love to be able to do both with the same machine, rather than use a lawn mower and edger separately?"
Need:	"Most houses have grass that lawn mowers cannot get to, requiring you to finish mowing most of the lawn before going and getting an edger to complete the job. This takes valuable time, and you need to buy multiple tools to get the job done, increasing the costs." (Pictures would be a good visual aid at this juncture.)
Satisfaction:	"Thankfully I have a product that would enable you to do both tasks without having to buy both tools, saving you time and money."

SPOTLIGHTING THEORISTS: ALAN H. MONROE

Alan H. Monroe

Alan H. Monroe served as a member of the faculty at Purdue University in Indiana beginning in 1924. He was initially hired as an instructor in English to teach basic courses in the English Department. He quickly infused the English curriculum with classes such as Principles of Speech and Debating in English. Today, we recognize these topics as communication rather than English courses. Through Monroe's efforts Purdue University established a strong Communication department known for teaching and research.[9]

In 1927 Monroe became the head of the Speech faculty in the English Department at Purdue, but he was not formally recognized in that role until 1941. Along with other members of the then English Department at Purdue, Monroe led efforts during the 1930s to expand the curriculum, specifically adding courses in oral interpretation, public address, and debate. In 1935 Monroe published the first edition of his book *Principles and Types of Speech*, which is now in its 16th edition, a testament to the ingenuity and importance of what Monroe accomplished while at Purdue.

In 1948 Purdue inaugurated its own Ph.D. program in Speech Communication, largely through Monroe's efforts. Monroe worked using relationships he had developed in the Purdue Department of Psychology to help push the Speech Communication Department toward a Ph.D. program. He resigned as head of the department in 1963, after successfully creating an independent Communication Department, separate from English, with its own robust undergraduate and graduate curriculum.

As a researcher, Monroe is best remembered for the development of the Monroe's Motivated Sequence model for persuasive speeches that seek immediate action. This model is still taught today, and if you look closely you can see it at play in things as varied as commercials and political speeches. Alan Monroe truly made a mark on the campus of Purdue University as well as the discipline of communication and public speaking education.

Visualization:	"This piece of equipment looks like a combination of a lawn mower and a dyson vacuum, in that it is more flexible, with a side compartment of blades to get those hard-to-reach stretches of lawn up against your house." (Visuals of the piece of equipment would be effective here.)
Action:	"All we need is some start-up funds to perfect the prototype and market the LawnWhacker to Lowes, Home Depot, and Menards. So, join with me, and invest in the future of lawn maintenance."

Let's take a moment and look at each one of these elements.

The first step, gaining the audience's attention, is nothing new. It simply employs a rhetorical question to raise awareness of the topic. Any form of attention-getter we covered earlier in the book would be acceptable for this stage of the Motivated Sequence. The second step of establishing need is a way of presenting a problem to the audience, but it differs slightly from the way we discussed it when we explained the problem-solution order.

Of course, the need for the audience can be to solve a problem. In fact, solving a problem is a terrific motivator when the listeners recognize there is a dilemma that affects them which needs to be resolved. That said, establishing a need can also include constructing or illuminating a need of which the audience may not be aware. For instance, in the above example, investors may not have experience with lawn care, either because they live in an apartment or hire a private company to take care of their property. Not all problems that exist are obvious to an audience, and so sometimes speakers need to work extra hard to establish a need before persuading an audience to act. In short, the Motivated Sequence recognizes that a speaker needs to both raise awareness of a problem and create a need to address it.

Once the need is established, you next must produce a way to satisfy the need. It would be tremendously awkward, if not unethical, to tell people there is a problem but not give them a way to solve it! Monroe labels this step "satisfaction" because it is the point in the message where the solution is provided and couched in a way that it firmly satisfies the need. This can be accomplished by proposing a change to a specific policy or through encouraging an audience to take a particular course of action. Here is where you must offer solid reasoning and evidence that illustrates how your proposed solution satisfies the need and is an appropriate and effective remedy for the problem facing the community. We must be mindful, however, that we do not fall into the trap of using reasoning fallacies in an effort to achieve our goal. The means of satisfying the need, and the tools we use to tell the audience about those means, are just as important as the end goal of attaining audience support and action. So, let us look at how we might go about accomplishing the satisfaction step in Monroe's Motivated Sequence.

In the example regarding the new lawn care product, satisfaction is achieved through providing a product that does the work of two items at a lower cost. In this case, the speaker needs to show how the product fulfills the personal need or desire for the audience. If, for example, you tell an audience that bad breath is both unhealthy and unattractive and thus they need to keep it from occurring, then you need to tell them that the path to satisfying that need to avoid bad breath can be fulfilled by purchasing and using Colgate toothpaste, for example.

Monroe's Motivated Sequence does not stop at satisfaction, however, as the next step is getting the audience to visualize fulfilling the need. Visualization uses concrete language and calls upon listeners to actually see themselves as the instruments of satisfying the established need. It helps the speaker further connect listeners with the issue, its solution, and the speaker by getting them to picture a future where the need has been fulfilled. Such efforts employ both emotional and logical appeals to the audience. Ultimately, when listeners can see themselves taking part in an action that effectively satisfies a need for either themselves or the community, it becomes a simple task to call them to action—the final step of Monroe's Motivated Sequence.

All told, Monroe's Motivated Sequence represents a modernized pattern of organization for a balanced persuasive appeal to an audience. It is also more common in everyday experience than you might think. Commercials employ it to craft quick and effective persuasive appeals for products. We also use it when trying to persuade friends and families to do something or go somewhere. Its five steps are easy to follow as both a speaker and an audience. This strategy is also most effective when immediate action is sought.

STRUCTURING YOUR MESSAGE

Outlines are one of the most crucial components of a properly organized speech, and they are not simple things. In fact, most speeches and situations you will encounter call for two outlines. First, you develop a full sentence preparation outline which essentially works as your speech draft. Then, after practicing with this outline until you are comfortable with it, you will reduce it to a much shorter speaking outline. This appendix first provides the principles that guide the creation of an effective outline. It then gives you directions and models for how to format a full sentence outline. Finally, it explains why outlines are much more useful than drafts, and ultimately how you may change full sentence outlines into speaking outlines so you do not read off your materials during your speech. Keep in mind, though, no matter how good your outline, if you do not practice with it your speech will not be as successful as you want it to be.

Three Principles for Outlining a Message

Much like the other aspects of public speaking, the process of outlining is grounded in theory. Many people believe that simply establishing bullet points or jotting down some notes is enough to call something an outline, but that is not the case. Outlines, in fact, are formal structures that organize content, but it is important to remember that the elements of an outline are not a part of the content of a speech. There are three tenets of outlining theory that are important to keep in mind when crafting an outline for a speech: subordination, coordination, and division. In this section we will discuss each of the three principles relevant to developing outlines for speeches, but first detail the symbolization technique to be followed in an effective outline.

Outlines are formal constructs that help organize the elements of a speech through the use of consistent symbolization. The symbols refer to things like main points and subpoints within the three main parts of the speech. As such, those three parts—the introduction, body, and conclusion—are not indicated by symbols. The first level within each part of the speech consists of main points, and these main points are indicated by Roman numerals. The second level, consisting of those subpoints related to the main points on the first level, are indicated by capital letters. A third level might also become necessary if you have a sub-subpoint, or

outline
formal construct that helps organize the elements of a speech through the use of consistent symbolization referring to main points and subpoints within the three main parts of the speech

an item that relates to the subpoint designated by a capital letter. Items on this level are indicated by Arabic numerals. Here is a sketch of how the symbol system for an outline works:

Body (denotes the part of the speech)
    I. Main point
        A. Subpoint (related to main point above)
            1. Sub-subpoint (related to subpoint A above)
            2. Sub-subpoint (related to subpoint A above)
        B. Subpoint (related to main point above)
            1. Sub-subpoint (related to subpoint B above)
            2. Sub-subpoint (related to subpoint B above)
    II. Main point

In this sketch you see how each symbol designates something else, but is related to the level above it. The basics of symbolization also illustrate one of the principles of outlining effectively.

subordination

the organization of a hierarchy of ideas where the most general appear first, followed by subsequently more specific ideas

The idea that what appears on one level is more general than the information appearing in levels under it is called subordination. *Subordination* is essentially the organization of a hierarchy of ideas where the most general appear first, followed by subsequently more specific ideas. In the example above you can clearly see how the subpoints each relate to the main point, and that they each have sub-subpoints that are subordinate to specific subpoints. Subordinating ideas allows for a more clear articulation of logic, as well as a more thorough articulation of the relationship between statements. Additionally, subordination is also indicated by the fact that each time you move from main point to main point, or between parts of the speech, the symbols reset. This is demonstrated in the example above as the sub-subpoints for each different subpoint begin with the number one, and do not go 1-2-3-4, as such an order of numbering would indicate they all were related. The use of ranked symbols allows subordination to occur within an outline, and it also allows you to put into practice another principle of effective outlining.

coordination

the notion that all information on the same level should have the same significance

Using symbols to rank items in an outline also allows for coordination of ideas and concepts. *Coordination* refers to the notion that all information on the same level should have the same significance. So, looking at the template from a few moments ago, all Roman numerals indicate main points, while all capital letters are subpoints. Even though these items will be different in content, their meaning and significance is the same as indicated by their appearance on the same level of an outline. Subordination and coordination are the first two principles of effective outlining, and now we will cover the final principle.

Consider that each time you provide subpoints related to a main point, or even main points to a specific purpose of a speech, you are dividing the information into its component parts. This is important because when you divide something you must have more than one piece after the division occurs. If you divide a dollar between two or three people, all three do not end up with one dollar, right?

Division is the third principle of outlining, and it states that in order to divide a point you need to end up with two or more items. So, in terms of symbols within an outline, there can never be a Roman numeral "I" without there being at least a Roman numeral "II"; there can never be an "A" without at least a "B"; and, there can never be a "1" without at least a "2."

division
principle that states that in order to divide a point you need to end up with two or more items

Now that we have covered the three basic principles of outlining and detailed the symbolization system used within an outline, we can discuss more specifically the components of a full sentence preparation outline and a speaking outline.

Creating Your Preparation Outline

After you conduct research on your topic, identify the types of information you found, and formulate your specific purpose and thesis statement (or argument) you begin constructing your speech. The natural temptation for anyone is to sit down and write a draft in essay format first; however, this is a dangerous proposition. Instead you should outline your speech structure using traditional formatting. The outline you create after gathering and organizing information for your speech is called a preparation outline. A *preparation outline* is an essentially detailed outline that uses full sentences next to symbols in an effort to help you organize the speech. They identify all the main components of an outline discussed in this textbook. They clearly separate the three main parts of the speech: introduction, body and conclusion. In this section of the appendix we will discuss and illustrate how outlines work to organize the components of your speech.

preparation outline
an essentially detailed outline that uses full sentences next to symbols in an effort to help you organize the speech

Introductions need to accomplish five main goals, and outlines help ensure you do just that. First, introductions need to get the attention of the audience. They then need to state your thesis or argument, which simultaneously introduces the topic of your speech and makes it relevant your audience. Third, the introduction needs to establish your credibility on the topic. Then the introduction needs to preview the main body of the speech. Finally, you need to finish the introduction by transitioning to the body of your speech. Let's look at how an outline organizes information and helps you accomplish these goals.

> **Introduction**
> I. Attention-getter
> II. Introduce topic
> III. Thesis statement [introduces topic/relates to audience]
> IV. Credibility statement
> V. Preview statement
>   A. Preview first main point
>   B. Preview second main point
> [Transition to body]

It is important to note that if it takes more than one sentence to accomplish the attention-getter, thesis statement, or credibility statement then according to the outlining principles we discussed earlier you drop down and use capital letters to continue that segment of your speech. Doing that allows you to subordinate your ideas and more clearly demonstrate an organized and logical speech.

Also notice that the transition does not receive a symbol designation. This is because the outline must follow the principle of coordination, whereby each symbol designates items of the same level of significance. Transitions are not main points of an introduction or any part of the speech for that matter. They also are not subpoints or subordinate ideas to other elements of the section of the speech. For that reason they are "set aside" in their own place in an outline.

The body of a speech follows the same principles that the introduction does, but contains different elements. The body, for instance, does not contain attention-getters and credibility statements; rather, it includes main points and subpoints. Like introductions, however, it does make use of transitions between main points. Additionally, you may again recall from Chapter Ten that the body of a speech makes use of internal previews and internal summaries. These are similar to the preview at the end of the introduction, but tend to more condensed and work to keep the audience connected with the speech's thesis or argument. Let's look at how the body of a speech is structured within an outline.

Body
I. Main point #1
 [Internal Preview]
  A. Subpoint
  B. Subpoint
   1. Sub-subpoint
   2. Sub-subpoint
  C. Subpoint
[Transition]
 II. Main point #2
  A. Subpoint
   1. Sub-subpoint
   2. Sub-subpoint
  B. Subpoint
 [Internal Summary]
[Transition]
 III. Main point #3
  A. Subpoint
   1. Sub-subpoint
   2. Sub-subpoint
  B. Subpoint
  C. Subpoint
[Transition]

There are several things to notice in this example. First, you see where internal previews and internal summaries are typically inserted. Internal previews fit at the start of a main point as a way to orient listeners to what they should listen to in the immediate future. Internal summaries work best after at least the second main point as a means to recap what you have already covered. It is also important to note that internal previews and internal summaries are placed in brackets the same way transitions are for the same reason: they are not main points, subpoints or sub-subpoints.

One final aspect of constructing the body of a speech that outlines can help with is determining the number of main points. Most speeches that you will encounter should include 2-4 main points within the body. This is due to two factors: time and focus. The shorter the speech the fewer main points you can have because they take time to develop and explain. Also, the more main points you have the harder it is for you and your audience to focus on what is important.

Conclusions are essential when it comes to making sure your audience understands the important concepts within your speech, and outlines help here as well. Just like the main components of an introduction, the central tenets of a conclusion can be laid out properly in an outline. Conclusions contain three main elements. First, you need a signpost to indicate you are beginning to wrap up the speech. Some instructors place the signpost at the end of the body with the transition from the final main point, but we have put it in the conclusion; the important thing to remember is that it indicates the end of the speech is about to begin. Additionally, you should be aware that many instructors have a pet peeve about hearing "in conclusion," so it is best to consider avoiding using that phrase as your signpost. After signaling the end of the speech, conclusions need to restate the thesis and summarize the main points of the speech. Finally, conclusions need to contain a clincher. Let's look at how conclusions are structured within an outline:

Conclusion
I. Signpost
II. Summary [restate thesis]
    A. Restate main point
    B. Restate main point
    C. Restate main point
III. Clincher

In this example you begin with the signpost that indicates the speech has arrived at a conclusion. Then, the summary begins with a brief restatement of the thesis or argument and continues with restating the main points. This illustrates the principles of subordination and division in that restating the main points relates to the summary and thesis statement, while also showing how there was more than one main point that needed to be restated. Finally, the clincher statement finishes the conclusion.

So, outlines are formal structures that allow you to organize the content of your speech in a logical fashion. In this part of the appendix we looked at how the structure of an outline allows you to ensure that you incorporate all the elements of an effective speech in an appropriate and logical way. In the next section we will move from the form of outlines to a brief discussion of the linguistic content and why outlines are more useful than drafts.

Creating Your Speaking Outline

After practicing with your full sentence outline you will become more conversational in your delivery and will not need to look at your outline as much. Additionally, you will begin to remember the information in the full-sentence outline rather than needing to read it. So, to help you deliver your speech in a more natural and conversational style you use a *speaking outline*, or a truncated form of your full sentence preparation outline that does not include complete sentences unless you are using direct quotations from another source. Speaking outlines are easy to develop from a completed full sentence outline.

speaking outline

a truncated form of your full sentence preparation outline that does not include complete sentences unless you are using direct quotations from another source

The same format you used to create your full-sentence preparation outline applies to a speaking outline. When you create your speaking outline you still retain all the formatting elements of the full sentence preparation outline in terms of Roman numerals, capital letters and numbers, and you still follow the principles of outlining we discussed earlier. The only things that do not appear on a speaking outline but appear in a full-sentence preparation outline are in-text citations, your stated general purpose, and your stated specific purpose.

The core fundamental difference between the two outlines is that a speaking outline does not include sentences unless you use a direct quotation, in which case getting the quote correct is of paramount importance. There are many words in every sentence you write that you do not need to see so that you remember to say them. Let's look at this brief full-sentence example and see if we can identify unnecessary words:

> **Introduction**
>
> I. Attention-getter: Imagine yourself stranded, along with about 50 other people, on a desert island after a plane crash.
>
> A. Well, that is the premise of the critically acclaimed television show *Lost*.

When looking to cut, look specifically at the full sentences. Obviously, the terms *with, on, that, is, the, of,* and *a* do not need to appear on a speaking outline because you could easily insert them when speaking without a prompt. But what else could go after practicing? What about the entire subpoint? It would make sense to delete the subpoint because it should flow naturally after the attention-getter. In fact, you might be able to deliver this attention-getter from a mere handful of words, such as this:

> **Introduction**
>
>   I. Imagine/stranded/50 people/island /plane crash. *Lost*

This is what a speaking outline contains: words and phrases from the original prose in the full-sentence outline separated by backslashes.

Even though we believe we have made a case for the use of outlines in this manner, we feel it necessary to answer some questions you might have regarding format. First we will counter those who might suggest bullet-points instead of outlines. Bullet-points do not visually display the logical hierarchy behind the speech and also create the danger of going off on tangents and not making your case to the audience as clear as possible. Bullet-points are, for all intents and purposes, lists of items with no clear connection. Outlines provide that connection for the speaker and, consequently, the audience.

Others also might agree to an outline, but instead of indenting the tiers of information appropriately believe that it wastes space and the outlines would make as much sense all starting at one side of the page. This, although better than bullet-points, still does not clearly differentiate each level of information and its connection to the rest of the material in the speech for either the speaker or the audience. In short, it fails to properly employ the principle of subordination. So, the proper indentation of each level is essential for the speaker and the audience.

Outlining your speech begins early in the speaking process and continues until you deliver the presentation. It allows you to organize your thoughts and information into a coherent order. It provides you with something to practice from and thereby develop your speaking voice and rhythm, something altogether different from your written voice and rhythm. Most importantly, outlining is the manner by which a speaker arranges his speech from beginning to end.

Whether you are debating policy positions, factual accuracies, or the value of one solution over another, or are calling an audience to act, you can use a wide variety of organizational patterns in a persuasive message. Just like explanations, the arrangement of persuasive messages largely depends on the formulation of your specific purpose. Once that is identified, however, the message can quickly take shape. Knowing the main parts of a message and how you can organize your main points will help you to prepare your presentation. The most crucial step in message creation is organizing the product of your research into a cogent, coherent, and persuasive message.

SUMMARY

In this chapter we discussed the components of introductions and conclusions for advocacy messages. Most notably we identified the similarities and differences between constructing the parts of a persuasive message and those of an explanation. We also provided some suggestions for effective organizational patterns for persuasive appeals. Finally, we encourage you to look at the chapter on outlining to help provide the structure and coherence that you need to develop your persuasive message.

KEY TERMS

comparative advantage 271	preparation outline 277
coordination 276	problem-cause-solution order 270
division 277	problem-solution order 267
Monroe's Motivated Sequence 271	speaking outline 280
outline 275	subordination 276

THINK ABOUT IT

1. What are the four ways you can organize the main points in a persuasive message?
2. What are the five parts of Monroe's Motivated Sequence?

REVIEW QUESTIONS

1. Is there ever a good time to present your strongest argument first?
2. How could you determine whether your credibility increases or decreases during a persuasive message?
3. Is it ethical to induce emotions in a conclusion, or in any part of the speech? Why or why not?
4. How could you use the Motivated Sequence in everyday language?

ACTIVITIES FOR ACTION

1. Working in a group of three members, develop several different ways to get an audience's attention. Then, state several ways you could establish credibility. Finally, figure out a way that statements could both get the attention of the audience and establish credibility, thereby killing two birds with one stone.

2. In this chapter we discussed Monroe's Motivated Sequence. Divide into groups of three and assign each group a product on the market right now. Give each group 10 minutes to create a "commercial" in which Monroe's Motivated Sequence is used to sell the assigned product. Every person in each group must have a speaking role in the skit.

ENDNOTES

1. Toastmasters International, "What Is Toastmasters?" http://www.toastmasters.org/MainMenuCategories/WhatisToastmasters.aspx (accessed September 19, 2008).

2. Toastmasters International, "Community Service," http://www.toastmasters.org/MainMenuCategories/WhatisToastmasters/CommunityService.aspx (accessed September 19, 2008).

3. Quintilian, *The Institutes of Oratory,* translated by H. E. Butler, Loeb Classical Library (Cambridge, MA: Harvard University Press, 1980), IV, i, 5.

4. Raymie E. McKerrow, Bruce E. Gronbeck, Douglas Ehninger, and Alan H. Monroe, Principles and Types of Speech Communication, 15th Ed. (New York: Longman: 2003).

5. Winston Churchill, "Blood, Toil, Tears and Sweat," Speech to the British House of Commons, http://www.historyplace.com/speeches/churchill.htm (accessed June 13, 3011).

6. Ibid.

7. Ibid.

8. Raymie E. McKerrow, Bruce E. Gronbeck, Douglas Ehninger, and Alan H. Monroe, *Principles and Types of Speech Communication,* 15th Ed. (New York: Longman: 2003).

9. W. Charles Redding "An Informal History of Communication at Purdue," http://www.cla.purdue.edu/communication/graduate/informalhistory.pdf.

Interteaching Session

Dialogue

Prepare an argument either in support of or against one of the following claims, as assigned by your instructor:

1. UD should institute a policy prohibiting alcohol on campus.

2. UD should schedule Spring Break over St. Patrick's Day, so that students must be off campus during this time.

3. College athletes should be paid.

Another group will be paired with yours, and this group will create an opposing argument for the same claim. You and the other group should choose one of the four organizational patterns in this chapter, for making your respective argument. Be prepared to give your argument, to hear the opposing argument of the other group, and to engage in a brief conversation regarding these arguments between the two groups in which you respond to each other's arguments.

Performance

Choose a problem that you and your groupmates would like to solve. Develop a solution to this problem that you can propose to the class in a brief 2-3 minute presentation. Your presentation of your solution should reflect the tips described in the chapter. Conduct some research to find evidence to support any claims that you make.

Civility

11

Practically SPEAKING

In the Spring of 2010, the University of Mount Union's Regula Center for Public Service, the University of Akron's Ray C. Bliss Institute, and Cleveland State University's Levin College of Urban Affairs collaborated on an investigation of the quality of public discourse in Ohio. This Ohio Civility Project brought together a retired political reporter for the *Columbus Dispatch*, a former Lieutenant Governor, columnist for the *Cleveland Plain Dealer* and a former Minority Leader in the State Senate in a panel to discuss the state of civility in Ohio politics. This group agreed that incivility is a major problem in Ohio politics, and this position was supported by a summer 2011 poll that found almost three quarters of Ohioans felt incivility was either a "very serious problem," or "a somewhat serious problem."

The Ohio Civility Project issued a white paper on the subject that pointed to four primary causes of incivility in Ohio politics. Three of these they called "initiators," or groups that instigate uncivil discourse because of the benefits they gain from behaving badly. These three drivers were career-minded politicians, the dictate to win campaigns, and financial windfall provided to media by controversy and conflict. The public, though, did not drive incivility, but rather responded to it based on the emotional power in the message itself.

In addition to the causes of uncivil behavior, the Ohio Civility Project also identified some causes of this misbehavior. These include self-interest by politicians, disagreement over issues and policies, the advent of the Internet, and general poor manners by individual people. All of these, they argue, work together to intensify and augment the quantity and quality of uncivil behavior and communication in Ohio today.

Sadly, this trend is not restricted to Ohio. Just look at cable news programs that deliberately pit people of differing positions in a contest of who can yell the loudest on their shows; or look at people who use cell phones in movie theatres, smoke inside restaurants, fail to do the dishes in a shared dorm room, and who do not engage their neighbors in friendly conversation. In fact, the lack of civility in our culture has become so pervasive that college campus, like the University of Dayton, are expanding their training and focus for students to help instill civility in tomorrow's leaders. Others are joining the cause too, like Johns Hopkins University which now has the Civility Project, Project Civility that now runs at Rutgers University, and the consortium behind the Ohio Civility Project consists of colleges in that state[1].

In this chapter we will explore civility and how it can enhance our ability to communicate with one another and succeed in our professions. First, we will attempt to reconnect you with what exactly civility means and how it relates to ourselves. We will also identify some basic components to civil behavior. Second, we will explore how civility functions in society today. Finally, we will briefly analyze some areas of contemporary life where we could and should more effectively incorporate civility.

[1] See: The Ohio Civility Project: Report and Recommendations, http://www.uakron.edu/bliss/about-us/ohio-civility-project. dot?newsId=2328165, Last accessed April 28, 2014.

Prep Questions

Part 1: Key Concepts

1. Define civility. List and define its five components.

2. What is a face threat? Describe the three faces we seek to present to others.

3. Define self-monitoring and self-restraint. Explain how each is necessary for creating civility.

4. List and describe the three foundational behaviors for civility.

5. What are three dimensions of communication that can differ across cultures that can complicate people's efforts to engage each other in civil ways?

Part 2: Application

1. Give an example of a time when you felt that someone interacted with you in an uncivil manner. Which of the five components of civility were lacking in that interaction? Explain briefly how.

2. Reflect briefly on a time when you had to disagree with someone without being disagreeable. How successful were you at doing this? Consider the tips for how to disagree without being disagreeable in Table 11.1. Which of these did you incorporate into your communication with the other person? How did you do this?

CIVILITY AS A FOUNDATION FOR DIALOGUE

Many people today confuse the notion of civility with a form of fakery, where people hide their own feelings about something or someone to avoid conflict. Others view civility and politeness as a form of weakness that invites bullying and leads to sacrificing personal positions, goals, and feelings for no good reason. These misconceptions make the idea of civil behavior appear useless and ineffective in society. Unfortunately, by abandoning the practice of civility we create a society that is closer to Thomas Hobbes' pessimistic notion of the natural state of man, which is to say it is "nasty, brutish, and short."[3]

Instead, it is useful to conceive of civility in relation to "civilization" and "being civilized." *Civility* in these contexts does not mean fakery. Rather, it means the ability to have lasting, stable, and peaceful interactions with others. If we consider the world we live in today as civilized, it is because we practice civility, and without treating such practices as sincere we risk degrading the civilization in which we live. Civility is a foundation for communication in such a society. Without civility, communication is likely to degenerate into destructive conflict whereby one party attempts to compel others to adopt their views, estrangement whereby each party refuses to engage the other, or outright force. In the next chapter, we will explore in some depth the process of dialogue, a process whereby people strive to create mutual understanding in a manner free from any expectations of agreement among them. Without civility, dialogue is impossible.

civility
the use of tact when dealing with others; a genuine and reciprocal expression of respect for ourselves and other people through our actions and statements

In this part of the chapter we will explore some of the components that serve as the foundation of civility. Understand that each of these is a component of civility, but on their own they are not synonymous with it. We will begin with some definitional terms, and then discuss how civility functions with regard to the way we present ourselves. We will conclude this section with an overview of some civil behaviors in different contexts.

Components of Civility

"Civility" is a broad term that encompasses parts of several other concepts in its application. Any one of these behaviors on its own does not constitute civility, but rather their combination helps lead us to an understanding of what it means to actually be civil. In this section of the chapter we will discuss five different concepts that when taken together create a more substantial definition of civility.

Politeness

polite
showing consideration for others in accordance with social decorum

We mentioned a moment ago that civility is often confused with politeness. This is understandable because politeness is a component of civility; however, the two are not the same thing because civility encompasses more than simply being polite. The term *polite* refers to showing consideration for others in accordance with social decorum. At times it can mean being polished or elegant, but on a basic level politeness is the use of tact in dealings with others. Politeness, therefore, may be best understood in contrast to rudeness, which is acting in a way that violates social decency or demonstrates a lack of social skills and appreciation for others. On the one hand, people who are deemed polite have made some effort to consider other people and how they feel. On the other hand, we sometimes view politeness in others not as a nicety, but as a tool to manipulate and deceive us or as a condescending form of communication. [4]

To understand this odd approach to politeness, let's look at how the term is used. If we attend a concert or a comedy club act and the performance is not very good we still feel the need to give "polite applause" to those on stage. If we cannot, or do not, want to go to a reception or other event we issue a "polite reply" telling the host we will not attend. Then there are times where we feel that the truth may hurt someone's feelings, so we deliver a "polite lie." Each of these instances makes it appear as though we are hiding our feelings, or protecting the feelings of others at the expense of honesty. Politeness is also seen as indirect communication, but one can be direct and polite at the same time. We often conflate directness in communication with rudeness, by being short and not respecting the other person. Envision a scenario in which a person in your class whom you do not know invites you to join a study group, but you prefer studying alone. You could tell very bluntly, "I'm not interested," or you could send the same message by saying, "Thanks for the invitation but I prefer to study on my own." The latter is polite, the former rude.

As you can see, politeness can mask our own feelings, but being civil requires us

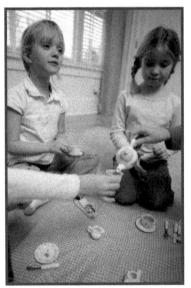

to assert our feelings in a respectful manner. A civil person is honest, but not in a way that offends the other party. Civil politeness requires that we not be polite just to help spare others the truth, but to make both them and us feel good about our deeds and actions through an honest and respectful delivery of information. For instance, there should not be a need to issue a polite lie, because it comes across as disingenuous and simply plays upon the perception most people have today when someone is "just being polite." Rather, polite civility issues the truth in a way that does not intentionally hurt anyone involved. This is, as you can imagine, a challenging task to accomplish. Politeness, though, is only one part of the civility equation.

Good Manners

The second component of civility might remind you of children because they are constantly reminded to say "please," and "thank you" as an element of good manners. *Good manners* refers to behaviors that societies deem as appropriate and positive ways of interacting with others. As you can imagine, when understood this way good manners are not restricted to children, nor are they as simple as just saying "please" and "thank you." In fact, we have even gone so far as a society to police certain types of manners to ensure they are practiced.[5]

good manners
behaviors that societies deem as appropriate and positive ways of interacting with others

There are policies in place in a variety of contexts by both companies and government entities designed to promote the practice of good manners. When we go to the movies we are asked to silence cell phones before the start of the film because holding a conversation and texting during a show distract others from enjoying the movie. Additionally, one of the reasons behind the Federal Aviation Administration's regulations regarding cell phone usage during a flight is, to be sure, safety; however, it is also meant to keep people from having phone conversations in crowded areas. After all, you do not want others to know your personal business, and they do not want to be disturbed by your conversation. These are just two examples of public efforts to maintain good manners.

Despite policies and rules regarding certain behaviors, not all good manners can and should be legislated. In fact, there are other good manners people should practice simply because they demonstrate an appreciation for other people. Here are a few behaviors that are usually considered good manners in American culture with which you may or may not be familiar:

1. Be on time for meetings and appointments.
2. Don't gloat when you win, or sulk when you lose.
3. Don't talk with your mouth full.
4. Patiently wait in line.
5. Don't ask intimate or sensitive questions—even if you ask permission first.
6. Don't make rude or sarcastic comments that devalue the work of others.

These are just a few good manners that respect the other person in an interaction. Such behaviors are a core element of civility and represent practicing politeness. Civility is, however, even more than being genuinely polite and practicing good manners.

Courteousness

A third component of civility is *courteousness*, which refers to showing consideration and attention to others. The term itself derives from "court," but not in the legal sense—rather the courts of kings where people who sought to speak with the monarch displayed an elegance and deference to those of higher stature. Today, courtesy is not as formal, nor does it involve status; rather we talk about certain behaviors as being "common courtesy." Such behaviors are often understood as polite, good manners, and civil, as well.[6]

courtesy
showing consideration and attention to others

We often refer to courtesy as *common* because it is generally expected that everyone exhibit these basic behaviors. Common courtesies include things like holding a door open for the next person to come through, standing up to greet someone when they enter your room or office, and acknowledging drivers who allow you into traffic in front of them. These are the small gestures we can do in a day that cost nothing but generate good feeling by letting others know we value and pay attention to them. At their heart, common courtesies involve an understanding of one's surroundings and respect for others, which brings us to our next component of civility.

Respect for Others

respect
....
an acknowledgement of the inherent humanity and existence of other people

Civility requires that we be polite, practice good manners, and extend courtesy to others because it is fundamentally about respecting other people. By *respect* we mean to say an acknowledgement of the inherent humanity and dignity of other people. Respect does not require deference to others, but rather an acknowledgement of them and an attempt to understand how they may feel about a statement, action, or event. One of the worst things we can do to other people is ignore them or behave as though their thoughts, feelings, and opinions do not matter. When such things are done to us we get upset and feel like we do not belong. There is no situation where behaving in such a way toward another person is acceptable.

Respect can come in different levels. It can mean we place individuals or their opinions in high esteem and value them more than others because of an existing relationship or some type of expertise they bring to the table. It can also mean an appreciation for an honor or even the position a person holds. At a minimum, however, we should respect everyone as individuals and acknowledge their feelings and thoughts. Doing so will encourage reciprocity where they return that respect in their interactions with you. This is the road to creating a culture of civility. There is, however, one more dimension of civility we must discuss.

Assertiveness

assertive
....
the ability to clearly and confidently state our positions

After detailing the first four elements of civility, it may seem as though it largely asks us to suppress our own ideas and thoughts in deference to others, but nothing could be further from the truth. In fact, civility demands honesty and the ability to clearly and confidently state our positions. This is what it means to be *assertive*, but it is essential we assert ourselves respectfully and not in an effort to dominate or devalue other people and their ideas. Assertiveness is a vital part of being happy and creating a civil society.

It may seem easier to simply try to please others by allowing them to state their positions while we keep ours to ourselves, but such actions actually do not demonstrate a respect for ourselves. One of the hardest things to assert is also the first word many children learn: the ability to say "no." As P. M. Forni, a noted Italian professor who teaches and writes about civility at Johns Hopkins University, notes, "'No' to others is nothing but a 'yes' to ourselves," and in doing so we aren't "taking something that belongs to others; we are simply keeping something that is rightfully ours."[7] Simply put, when people ask something of us, we are not required to give it, nor are we required to explain why to them though we may feel it right and necessary to do so in some situations. The ability to say "no" to others and "yes" to ourselves is a key element of civility.

We may believe that saying "no" will injure, or perhaps even destroy, our relationship with the other person, but in not protecting our own interests and time we might be doing that anyway.[8] In freely giving our time, treasure and talents to others, even when we do not want to, we may create an unbalanced relationship with the other person. By this, we mean the other person may come to expect us to always give of ourselves and may not reciprocate. It also can engender our quiet and unexpressed resentment of the other and consistent devaluing of our own ideas, time, and feelings. This is not healthy, nor is it civil. Being assertive simply means we respect ourselves just as much as we respect others. Without this final piece, civility is nothing more than sacrificing oneself to the interests of the other. To that end, we define civility as a genuine and reciprocal expression of respect for ourselves and other people through our actions and statements.

Now that we have explained the characteristics of civility, we will turn our attention to how we practice civility. In the next section we will discuss some communicative dimensions of civility as it relates to how we present ourselves. We will then follow that with covering some basic principles of civil behavior.

Civility and Self-Expression

Creating a civil society naturally involves the way we communicate with each other. This occurs in many different contexts and requires a specific set of abilities for us to effectively, respectfully, and civilly interact with each other. In this part of the chapter we will discuss this set of skills and how they relate to civility.

Facework

Everyone desires others to see them in the best possible light, and so we present our face in a manner that we believe creates that type of impression. The behaviors we employ to maintain this positive image with others are called *facework*. There are three faces we seek to present to others, and each occurs within a different context. These faces also are sometimes threatened by the actions of others or external events we cannot control.

facework
the behaviors we exhibit to maintain a positive impression of ourselves by other people

We all have a desire to be liked and appreciated. In fact, social relationships and our own psychological and physical health depend on such connections with others. The need to have others like and respect us is fulfilled through the expression of our *fellowship face*. We want others to perceive us as approachable, likeable, and friendly, so we try to create that impression through the way we interact with

fellowship face
an effort to fulfill the need to have others like and respect us

others. This type of behavior can especially be seen in our initial interactions with new people we meet.

Take, for example, the case of Lynn who has just moved into her dormitory room. During the move-in process she meets her new roommate, Olivia, who is still unloading her belongings from her car. After introducing herself to Olivia, Lynn offers to help unload Olivia's car and move her into the room. This behavior is a manifestation of civility, and also creates a positive fellowship face for Lynn with Olivia.

competence face
....
our efforts to promote our expertise on subjects to others so they respect us

The second face we seek to create is less about developing friendships and more about engendering respect from others. When we want others to listen to what we have to say on a topic, we both need and want them to see us as competent, and so the *competence face* refers to efforts to promote our expertise on subjects to others. We all are good at something, and we like it when others recognize our talents, so the competence face is how we want others to see us when it comes to those things we know or are good at doing. This is especially important when we are asked to explain material to non-experts, because we want them to respect what we have to say.

autonomy face
....
the perception that we can do things on our own and our desire to avoid others making decisions for us

The third, and final, face we seek to maintain with others is related to assertiveness. We all want to be seen as capable individuals in our own right who can make decisions and take action on our own without the assistance of others. This is the expression of our *autonomy face*, which refers to when we seek to avoid others' making decisions and doing things for us by being seen as capable in our own right. When we are assertive and respect ourselves, we demonstrate this autonomy, and when we do not we are seen by others as more dependent. As with anything, we are not entirely autonomous or dependent, but we do need to maintain the perception we can do some things on our own.

face threats
....
things that threaten to damage the image we work to present to others

Sometimes we encounter things that threaten to damage the image we work to present to others. These *face threats* can come from both internal and external causes. For instance, we may feel like we did not do enough research, practice our presentation enough, or even study enough for an exam. These internal feelings turn into threats to our competence face as the effects of those beliefs may make us appear as less of an expert to others. On the other hand, we may also be in a situation where others around us make jokes at our expense, and we feel the need to respond because these jokes damage our ability for others to like or respect us. How we manage threats to our face is just as important as the face itself. Facework is directly tied to civility, because when people are rude, lack good manners or are not courteous we perceive it as a threat to our face and thus conflict can ensue.

Image Management

We have no single image that we present to all parties. For instance, we seek to have our parents perceive us one way, our friends another, and our colleagues at work yet another way. We also try to maintain consistency with the images each group has of us. You may be familiar with the term "two-faced", which is what we sometimes call people who present two different and conflicting images of themselves in different sorts of situations. Managing multiple images with

Spotlighting Theorists: P. M. Forni

P. M. Forni

Pier Massimo Forni is an award-winning Italian literature professor at Johns Hopkins University, where he has taught for the majority of his career. Forni graduated from the University of Pavia in 1974, and received his doctorate in Italian Literature in 1981 from UCLA, where he studied the works of Italian Renaissance author Giovannie Boccaccio. Over his career his work moved toward a discussion of ethics and a commentary on civility in society, particularly the United States, his adoptive home.

In 1997 Forni cofounded the Johns Hopkins Civility Project, which brought together academics and community outreach programs in an effort to assess "the significance of civility, manners, and politeness in contemporary society." He also co-directed an international symposium in 1998 entitled "Reassessing Civility: Forms and Values at the End of the Century." He has delivered numerous workshops and written several books, including *Choosing Civility: Twenty-Five Rules of Considerate Conduct*, *The Thinking Life*, and *The Civility Solution: What to Do When People are Rude.*

Dr. Forni's work on civility has appeared in a number of press outlets, and he himself has made appearances on numerous television programs to discuss civility in contemporary society. He currently teaches at Johns Hopkins University, where he is also director of the Civility Initiative. His work has inspired similar efforts at a number of other institutions.[9]

---

various groups is both collaborative and complex, but effective management of our situations is a hallmark of being civil.

When we say that *image management* is collaborative, we mean it is a constant result of the interaction between ourselves and others. We seek to present ourselves in a specific manner, and other people either accept or do not accept that presentation. In the event they accept our image, we continue to behave in ways that reinforce that image with that particular group. If, however, our image does not seem to be accepted by others, we may adjust and adapt our own understanding of ourselves. This is a way of managing behavior and personal interactions with both ourselves and others in mind.

image management
the constant attempt to control the presentation of ourselves to others

Image management is also complex because of the multiple audiences with whom we seek to cultivate relationships. To say we present ourselves one way to our friends is even a bit too broad, because we all have different groups of friends with whom we associate and each sees us differently. For instance, a college athlete may have friends on a sports team, in the dormitory, in classes, and from high school who attend different institutions. Each of these groups knows different versions of the student, but the student seeks to maintain an image with each group. We also present different images to our family. This gets even more complex and difficult to manage when different groups are in the same situation. Just think about the first time you and a significant other had dinner with your parents. Which image did you seek to present? This is the challenge of image management, but when we adhere to the principles of civility it lessens the burden of such complicated interactions.

Self-Monitoring

To effectively manage our image and present faces the way we want we must be good communicators, and a major aspect of competent communication is *self-monitoring*. This skill refers to the ability to be aware of your own behaviors and statements and how they affect other people. To identify your ability level when it comes to self-monitoring, think about it as a line, somewhere upon which you fall. At one end of the line there are low self-monitors, and at the other end are high self-monitors.

Low self-monitors speak and act without thinking of what the effect on others will be. In short, they do not pay attention to what they are saying and doing beyond the immediate moment. This can often cause hurt feelings, emotional outbursts, and misunderstandings and it cultivates the image of a selfish individual. Being civil requires that we think before we speak and act, thus making it necessary for people who tend to act and speak impulsively to become better self-monitors.

High self-monitors, on the other hand, are aware of their behaviors and statements, as well as how they will potentially affect and influence those around them. As we have discussed, being civil requires a genuine respect for others and yourself, and so high self-monitoring is a necessary skill set for a civil society. It allows us to think through what we want to say, and then say it in a manner that respects the other party while still maintaining our own ability to assert our position. It may sound easy enough, but monitoring and thinking about our behavior and statements before we do or say something is a very challenging task.

Self-Restraint

It might seem a bit odd to include *self-restraint* as a principle of civil communication when we already said you must be able to assert yourself and your ideas, but it is important to remember to be balanced. Just because you have an idea or a thought does not mean it must be stated or asserted. In fact, learning *when* to assert yourself is an important situational skill in any profession. To borrow from country singer Kenny Rogers, you have to know when to hold them and know when to fold them.

It is not always imperative that you respond, let alone respond immediately, to comments from others. In fact, often it is best if you wait to do so, especially in emotionally charged situations. If you are upset over something, a grade for example, wait a day before contacting your professor to discuss it so that you can have a calmer and more rational conversation. If someone says something to you that you disagree with, consider what your goal is in responding. The chances of changing the other person's mind may be very small, in which case you may not even want to say something. P. M. Forni, the Italian civility scholar we mentioned a little while ago, notes that silence is not a failure to communicate, but rather an informed choice to process and reflect upon information. Shooting from the hip in response to something often creates a more combative and negative environment that invites uncivil behavior.

Self-restraint does not imply you deny your own right and ability to assert yourself; instead, it calls for us to concentrate on the best possible way to assert our opinions and positions. Timing and tone are everything. Remember that people will respond to the tone of your voice first, even before they think about what you said. The tone with which you speak can go a long way toward creating a supportive climate for conversation and preserving civility in an interaction. The same words said with a different tone can convey completely opposite things to another person, so measuring your tone of voice and paying attention to the emotions you try and convey when speaking is vital for having productive interactions with others, especially when the topics of discussion are sensitive or controversial. Keep this in mind before you choose to respond and take a minute to process what the other party said.

In today's fast paced society we often feel the need to immediately respond, since everyone seems to be available at almost any time thanks to email and cell phones. Just because you receive an email that demands a reply, it does not require that you reply as soon as you are done reading it. Also, just because someone calls in while you are speaking to someone on the other line does not mean you need to answer it. Self-restraint means we must try to control our inclination to "run after something shiny as soon as we see it" and concentrate on the moment in which we currently reside. It is, simply, thinking before acting.

Foundational Civil Behaviors

We could spend an entire book explaining and discussing specific behaviors that are civil, but that is not the aim of the book or this chapter. Instead, we wish to acquaint you with some foundational concepts that inform civil behavior so that they help you understand how to engage in an effective dialogue with other people. To that end, we have covered the root terms of civility and how it relates to the presentation of ourselves to others. The final component of explaining what civility is, however, is a discussion of three foundational behaviors that all civil communication has in common: mutual respect, listening, and disagreeing without being disagreeable.

Mutual Respect

A civil culture depends on its members valuing mutual respect. That is to say, members of society must respect all other members as well as themselves and must be willing to develop and engage in the skills we have discussed in the chapter. Each individual must value the ideas and opinions of others and begin with the precept that everyone seeks the good of the community as whole, until such time as someone demonstrates he or she is not out for that goal. In short, believe in the best that people can be, and respect their values, experiences, and expertise in the same way you wish them to do for you.

SPEAKING of CIVIC ENGAGEMENT

First Inaugural Address
by President John F. Kennedy

Delivered January 20, 1960

John F. Kennedy, a senator from Massachusetts, was elected president in November 1960 and took the oath of office on Friday January 20, 1961. The Democrat, Kennedy, defeated Republican candidate Richard Nixon and took over as the youngest president in US history for the man who was then the oldest ever to hold that office, Dwight Eisenhower. In his narrow victory, Kennedy also became the first Roman Catholic president in American history. At the time the United States was deeply ensconced in the Cold War with the communist Soviet Union, during which both countries aggressively pursued nuclear weapons and fought for influence over smaller states around the globe.

Kennedy wrote the speech along with his close advisor, Ted Sorenson, over the course of three months. At 1,364 words the speech took only 13:59 minutes to deliver, making it the fourth shortest inaugural in presidential history. In the address, which presidents use for many purposes including laying out the broad principles of how they plan to govern, Kennedy sought a more collaborative relationship with countries around the globe, including the Soviet Union. His desire for this was embedded in this call: "So, let us begin anew—remembering on both sides that civility is not a sign of weakness, and sincerity is always subject to proof. Let us never negotiate out of fear, but let us never fear to negotiate. Let both sides explore what problems unite us instead of belaboring those problems which divide us."[11] This quotation illustrates a civil approach to public discussion and debate and shows that even when two sides appear to be at such starkly different positions, there is always an opportunity for engagement.

Mutual respect is not driven by a person's achievement, position, or title, but rather by his or her inherent humanity and value as a person. All people bring something to the table that we can learn and we must respect that for them to respect what we have to offer. Without genuine mutual respect, we cannot have a civil society. This is not to say that everyone must behave this way for it to work; in fact, that is not the case even today. It is, however, an invitation to begin the effort of making society more civil by respecting those with whom we come into contact.

Even at the height of the Cold War our leaders were able to, at times, express mutual respect and a desire for civil interaction. In one of the more famous speeches in the twentieth century, then newly elected President John F. Kennedy used his inaugural address to both assert American ideals and extend an invitation for dialogue and negotiation with the Soviet Union. He actually even mentioned civility specifically in an effort to tone down tensions and begin more collaborative communication with the Soviet Union—a communist country at that time understood as a superpower and chief rival to the United States in international affairs.

Listening

Earlier in this book we discussed listening and how it related to public speaking, but its importance is much broader than simply attending to messages in formal situations. To be civil we must listen to what the other party is saying, in effect giving them our undivided attention. We may believe we can multitask and pay attention to multiple things at once, but this is a myth. In his book *Brain Rules*, John Medina explains that it is actually physically impossible for our brains to focus on two things at once,[10] making paying attention to more than one person impractical in addition to uncivil.

We owe it to others to give them our attention when we expect the same in return when we speak. The idea of listening transcends conversations and speaking situations, to include emails, text messages, and phone conversations. We all have had situations in which we tried to do something else while on the phone with a friend, but when we do that we are not truly listening. It would be much better to actually say we needed to do something else and arrange another time to talk, or to even have a shorter more focused conversation in which we actually listen to the other party. Genuine listening is the manifestation of respecting other people and being there with them.

Listening also entails the ability to come to an understanding of what the other person is saying. This may require asking clarifying questions, paraphrasing messages, or other forms of perception checking. Remember that making sure you understand the other person is a hallmark of genuine listening, and not a rude behavior. It does not mean, however, that you agree with the other person, just that you understand them. In fact, the third and final civil behavior we will discuss in this section involves the ability to assert disagreement.

Disagree without Being Disagreeable

As we mentioned earlier, civility requires us to express ourselves and assert our positions. This does not limit itself to moments of agreement. We also must be able to express ourselves when we disagree. Unfortunately, people tend to view agreement and disagreement as the only two options available, when in fact they are not absolutes. More often than not we find ourselves wanting to agree with parts of a person's argument while disagreeing with other aspects of it.

To express such complicated positions in which we both agree and disagree with another person at the same time calls for specific and delicate skills. In order to do this, it is important to first stress areas of agreement with the other party. This establishes a more comfortable climate for the interaction and enables both parties to see the exchange in a positive and constructive light. When focusing on areas of agreement, be as detailed as you would be with those things with which you disagree. Then, after expressing agreement, detail those things with which you disagree and explain why. The explanation is important because it shows you listened to the other party, but have information of your own to offer to the discussion. In more tense situations it may also be necessary to conclude with a statement reinforcing that just because you disagree with all or parts of the other person's argument it does not mean you do not like or appreciate that person. The position is not the person.

Agreement and disagreement are not "all or nothing" propositions. In fact, things are always more complicated than they appear and we must be able to articulate that complexity when we explain how we agree and disagree with someone. By detailing both agreement and disagreement we can preserve aspects of the person's argument without seeming to devalue everything he or she had to say. This respects other people's willingness to express themselves while also explaining yourself appropriately as well.

Now that we have established the basics of civility, we will explore how it has functioned in human history. The idea of respect for other people and ourselves is nothing new, and has played a role throughout human history. In the next part of this chapter we will briefly explore the practice of civility today.

Table 11.1

Tips for Disagreeing without Being Disagreeable
1. Describe instead of evaluate
2. Focus on the problem, not controlling the outcome
3. Acknowledge the feelings of others
4. Be provisional instead of certain
5. Control your own facial expressions
6. Do not interrupt someone when they are speaking
7. Do not disparage others when they are not present
8. When disagreeing, describe the points with which you disagree and agree

PRACTICING CIVILITY IN A DIVERSE WORLD

The fact of the matter is that civil behavior affects our quality of life in myriad settings, and all it takes is a small effort to take the feelings of others into consideration before acting or speaking. To be sure, every area of our lives is complicated, from the boardroom to the dining room table. But in today's technologically advanced world where we are all so closely and quickly connected, taking a moment to think before we speak and incorporating civility into our approach is more necessary than ever. Moreover, our world is becoming increasingly diverse. In our everyday lives, we are likely to be working next to someone who comes from a different cultural background than the ones that are familiar to us. As we strive to engage others in civil ways, perhaps to open a space for dialogue between us, we cannot assume that what counts as civil behavior to us will do so for others. Each element of civility—that is, politeness, good manners, courteousness, respect, and assertiveness—might be understood differently between any two cultures. In this part of the chapter, we will discuss some fundamental dimensions of social interaction that can differ across cultures and then explore how we can recognize these aspects of social interaction and engage others in a civil manner in the face of such differences.

Three Dimensions of Communication that Vary Across Cultures

In every relationship, from the business world to the classroom to the home, multiple variables influence the way we interact with each other. All of these things are also aspects we must be attuned to in order to effectively incorporate civility into our approach to others. Three dimensions of communication that can vary across cultures are the degree to which a culture is individualistic or collectivistic, the degree to which a culture is high or low power-distance, and differences across cultures in the way in which gender is constructed.

Individualism-Collectivism

Not every culture, country, or society holds the same values as do Americans. In fact, not all Americans hold the same values to the same degree. If we were to conceptualize measuring cultural values, we would recommend thinking about it as a linear continuum. On one end of the continuum are collectivistic societies, and the other individualistic. Any culture can be placed at some point along that continuum. In this section we will examine what each of those categories means and how they might affect our ability to be civil.

A *collectivistic culture* is one that values harmony in group and societal relationships. Collectivistic cultures tend to have very strong family units, strong ties within their communities and high levels of loyalty to employers. These cultures also do not value conflict and direct communication the way most Americans do. In fact, they handle conflict in a much more indirect fashion, because it helps maintain social harmony. On the other hand, in *individualistic cultures* people feel the strongest loyalties lie with themselves and not their social groups. It should come as no surprise that the United States today falls much closer to individualistic than collectivistic on this scale.

collectivistic culture
• • • • • • • •
values harmony in group and societal relationships

individualistic culture
• • • • • • • •
people feel the strongest loyalties lie with themselves and not their social groups

This has not always been the case, however. In the mid-twentieth century some of the most popular groups were the Kiwanis, Knights of Columbus, and other such social and service clubs. Additionally, communities worked together to maintain their neighborhoods and raise families, and often went bowling together. Today, in places like Las Vegas, homes are built with large stone walls blocking homes from neighbors, and, more significantly, as author Robert Putnam notes in his book *Bowling Alone*, membership in social groups has drastically dropped off from just a few decades ago. People today just do not interact with each other the way they used to, and this lack of connection contributes to both an exaggerated individualistic society and a culture where civility is less prevalent than in prior times.

With these differences in mind, one can see how what counts as civility can differ across communicators depending on the individualistic-collectivistic orientation that they have inherited from their cultures of origin. For instance, in a collectivistic culture, politeness might mean not taking credit for desirable outcomes that come from one's conduct, but rather attributing those outcomes to the strength of one's family, group, or organization. One might experience praise that focuses on him or her as an individual as misguided, inappropriate, or even discomforting, even though someone coming from an individualistic culture might understand giving such praise as a polite thing to do. Good manners might mean taking a long time to build bonds of collaboration, giving much space to establishing trust through rapport-oriented talk and inquiry about one's family or group, and seeking the input of all people before any decisions are made, so that the will of the group as a whole can be ascertained. However, in an individualistic culture, giving such time to these concerns, in the extreme, could be seen as rude and an inappropriate use of other people's or even one's own time. Assertiveness in a collectivistic culture might be appropriate in voicing the needs and views of one's group, but less so in voicing one's personal needs and viewpoint, while in an individualistic culture, the emphasis might be the converse. When communicators are aware that other participants in the communication come from different cultural backgrounds, then they need to proceed with additional flexibility and sensitivity, being even more conscious about potential face threats, more vigilant about how image management might be shaping the interaction, and exercising a higher degree of self-monitoring and possibly self-restraint.

High and Low Power-Distance

No matter how hard we may try, there is always a power dynamic in any relationship. Just think of some of the clichés bandied about in the world today, like "the customer is always right." Power exists in any relationship, and it can and does affect our ability to be civil with each other. Sometimes we speak respectfully because of someone's title or ability to reward or punish us, but this is not, by our definition, civil. Rather, it is being polite or courteous based on the other person's power or position, not because of the respect he or she should be accorded as a human being.

low power-distance cultures
members value equality and believe no one person should dominate

high power-distance cultures
where there is an uneven distribution of power and one person or a specific group of people dominate

Power, much like culture, can be thought of on a linear scale based upon how a particular group or society understands it. On the one end of this scale are *low power-distance cultures* where members value equality and believe no one person or group should dominate. These groups are indicative of democracies like the United States. On the other end of the spectrum are *high power-distance cultures* where there is an uneven distribution of power and one person or a specific group of people dominate. These cultures often are reflective of monarchies and dictatorships. Interestingly, if you think back to the origins of the term "courtesy" from earlier in the chapter, you will see it has its roots in the latter of these two types, which is yet another reason it is not synonymous with our definition of civility.

Power influences our communication with each other in many ways, and we can often "feel" its presence. Some people, like bosses, have power based on their positions; others have power thanks to their knowledge about certain things. Some jobs come with the power to reward or punish others as well. The fundamental thing to take away from all this, however, is that power is not static; rather it is fluid. One person wields power in one area of his or her life, but not others. If we think about that for a moment, we realize then that being civil in all situations and not abusing power when we do have it can increase our ability to create a culture of civility.

As in the case of differences among communicators in terms of individualism and collectivism, if communicators come from cultures with different expectations about power, then they need to proceed with additional sensitivity and flexibility. Any of the elements of civility might be understood differently between individuals who come from a high power-distance culture and those who come from a low power-distance culture. For instance, respect in a high-power distance culture means understanding the differences of rank and station that people in a situation hold and treating those with higher rank or station with greater deference than how one would interact with someone from a lower rank or station. In a low power-distance culture, treating someone in an obviously preferential manner can be seen as disrespectful to others. Communicators need to recognize as quickly as possible differences among communicators that relate to power distance and adjust their expectations in ways that ensure that they neither offend the other nor are offended, if possible. It might not be possible to avoid clashes of expectations in every case, for out of a desire for personal integrity, people might not be willing to adjust their behavior beyond a certain point. However, if such clashes can be avoided, avoiding them can help to create a stronger foundation for mutual understanding.

Differences Relating to Gender

In addition to culture and power, gender also plays a role in our interactions. It is also important to note that gender and sex are two different things. *Gender* refers to the socially constructed expectations and roles that accompany a particular sex, which vary between cultures. *Sex*, on the other hand, is a biological distinction between men and women. There is a considerable body of research in the field of communication relating to differences in how men and women communicate. Overall, the similarities between men and women in terms of how they communicate exceed the differences. However, scholars have observed key differences between men and women.

gender
the socially constructed expectations and roles that accompany a particular sex, and these vary between cultures

sex
a biological distinction between men and women

One of the key differences between how men and women communicate involves what role they attribute to communication in relationships. Women tend to view communication as the primary vehicle for expressions of intimacy and the maintenance of close bonds between partners. Men, on the other hand, tend to view communication more as a tool for accomplishing tasks and completing projects. In short, women tend to use communication to express feelings and establish connection with others; men tend to use it to accomplish tasks.

This difference can often lead to problems in relationships, for when men listen to women express feelings and discuss problems and challenges they respond by

Table 11.2

UD Commitment to Community Pledge

Civility is important to develop and uphold community. Here at the University of Dayton, we express the Catholic and Marianist values of the community in our own Commitment to Community, C2C. You might say C2C is our articulation of the values of civility and respect. C2C highlights three Catholic and Marianist principles for learning and living in community and seven key habits for living that are derived from them. C2C shapes the spirit of campus hospitality, calls us to academic rigor integrated with faith and life, and challenges each community member to take up the hard work necessary to build the intellectual, spiritual, religious, moral, physical, and social dimensions of community.

Every student at the University of Dayton takes the Commitment to Community pledge at New Student Orientation. As members of the UD community, all students are called to understand these principles and develop the habits in daily life. Doing so strengthens our educational community and prepares you to live as a mature member of society. Here is the pledge:

COMMITMENT TO
COMMUNITY
Catholic and Marianist Learning and Living

The University of Dayton's Catholic and Marianist mission calls us to develop our character and integrity as leaders committed to building community in our world. We accept this challenge and make the following pledge:

We commit ourselves to learn in and through community.

We commit ourselves to respect the dignity of every person in thought, word and action.

We commit ourselves to promote the common good.

As a contributing member of this educational community:

I will treat myself and others with respect and compassion.

I will be honest, truthful and live with integrity.

I will develop a life of faith and/or reflection, and will respect the religious traditions of others.

I will integrate what I learn with how I live.

I will take responsibility for myself and for my community.

I will practice servant leadership.

Together, we promise to strengthen our role in building communities of hope and respect, peace and reconciliation in our world.

UNIVERSITY *of*
DAYTON

commitment2community.udayton.edu

offering solutions. On the surface this can seem like a supportive gesture, but it is not always what women wish from the interaction. In these situations, men should listen carefully before jumping to the conclusion that there is a problem to be solved, so they can understand what their conversational partner wants from the interaction. This does cut both ways, though, in that women, or men who exhibit this behavior, should to appreciate the fact that when men offer solutions it's a way of expressing support. Here we see the importance of listening attentively in an effort to have a more civil interaction.

There are other differences in how men and women construct messages that are worth noting. Women tend to ask more questions in a conversation and more openly discuss emotions than men. Men in turn tend to use more self-references and judgmental adjectives when describing things to others. To be civil you must understand these gender distinctions in behaviors so that you do not get frustrated by expecting others to conform to your way of interacting.

The extent to which differences come biological factors or are the product of differences in how men and women are socialized is not known. The term "gender" focuses on the ways in which masculinity and femininity are constructed among people. What it means to be a man and what it means to be a woman can differ considerably from society to society, even between groups within a given society. In Chapter 1, we introduced the concept of discourse and suggested that people come to understand their reality in particular ways through their participation in particular discourses. There are many discourses relating to gender in any given social space. Some of these discourses might be generational in character. For instance, you might have noted particular differences between how you understand what it means to be a man or what it means to be a woman between your peers and your parents. Such differences might be even more pronounced if you consider how your grandparents talk about men and women. These discourses also might carry certain expectations about how a person who is identified as being male or female is supposed to act. You might recall the term *script* from Chapter 4: a script is a mental representation that organizes information about a topic that involves a sequence of behavior. Communicators might not have the same scripts about how men or women are supposed to act. Other differences relating to gender might be ethnic or cultural in character. People from one part of the world might understand maleness in a way that differs considerably from how people in another part of the world understand it. In addition, in recent decades, discourses that approach gender, as well as related concepts of sexual preference and sexual identity, in ways that do not reflect traditional binary constructions have gained prominence in society and shape how many people today think about sex and gender. When such differences among communicators are present, they must exercise greater sensitivity and flexibility in how they strive to create a foundation of civility among them. This might demand higher degrees of self-monitoring and even self-restraint as they engage others who hold views and behave in ways that contrast with or even contradict their own.

Now that we have covered some of the basic dimensions of interpersonal interactions and cultural influences on how people relate to one another, let's examine some contemporary environments where we can use this information to enhance civility in our own communities.

Contemporary Contexts for Civility

In this section of the chapter we will briefly discuss five settings in which we can apply civil communication to improve understanding and general wellness in our social relationships. We begin with those in your own immediate context: the classroom. We then will discuss how civility can operate and improve our interpersonal relationships with friends and significant others. Third, we will look at the professional world which you will enter in just a few short years. Next, we will examine the general lack of civility in news media, before we conclude with a discussion of civility in social media.

Civility in the Classroom and on Campus

Learning for every student in a classroom depends upon a civil atmosphere, and the responsibility for creating this falls on both instructors and students. In fact, every student at UD has seen and recited the pledge in UD's Commitment to Community (see Table 11.2). This document represents a collective promise to engage in behaviors that create a civil, responsible, and connected community at UD. That promise manifests itself in dormitories, the Student Neighborhood, and even the classroom. Additionally, both the faculty and students have responsibilities to uphold this commitment. On the one hand, instructors should allow students to express their questions, comments, and thoughts about course content without fear of reprimand or mockery. They also should listen when students have questions regarding grades or requests for accommodations. Finally, instructors should welcome student visits during office hours to discuss course material and academic progress.

Students also bear a significant portion of the burden for creating a civil classroom climate. Students should not argue with instructors for the sake of arguing, nor equate instructor experience and knowledge with opinion. Students should also begin emails and visits to the office with cordial introductions and conclude them with a genuine note of gratitude. They also should treat each other with respect and listen to peers when they offer questions and commentary and rather than judge them for their ideas, engage them to understand the thinking behind the statements their peers make. Finally, students should follow course rules and policies as outlined in the syllabus, particularly those regarding laptop and cell phone use. Being on the Internet or texting a friend during class is very rude to the instructor and your fellow classmates.

Simple behaviors like this by both instructors and students will create an environment in the classroom more conducive to learning.

Civility in Relationships

As we briefly covered earlier, you maintain multiple relationships in your life. These include those with friends, family, co-workers, and even the barista at your local Starbucks. Each of these relationships is an opportunity to connect with a larger, more robust community and a chance to learn about different people, cultures, and experiences. The trouble is that we all know how difficult these relationships are to maintain and develop over time, especially when we have disagreements with members of each group. That said, practicing civility can help enhance these relationships in every situation.

At home, you naturally behave with respect toward your parents, brothers, sisters, and significant others, but conflicts often do arise. With your friends you also practice a degree of civility, but sometimes you may say something to which they might take offense. It is ironic, but people generally are accepting of genuine apologies, but these apologies are also simultaneously the hardest thing for us to issue. We do not like admitting when we are wrong, and even when we do admit it we often qualify the apology with some explanation. If you are going to apologize, do so earnestly and without a qualification. This civil practice can go a long way toward maintaining healthy relationships with those closest to you.

Civility, however, also extends to those you encounter elsewhere but with whom you may not be close. Salespeople, hotel front desk agents, and even the person who makes your morning coffee all deserve the same type of respect and civility you accord to family and friends. Sometimes, simply having a brief conversation in which you ask about their day or just say "good morning" can go a long way toward improving their life in that moment. It is also important to recognize that people in these roles have lives you do not know, and they are people too. So, if someone in one of these roles says something or behaves in a way that frustrates or upsets you, concentrate your disapproval on the behavior or statement and not the person. If you do this, you will more likely come to a quicker and more acceptable resolution, while not unnecessarily upsetting or ruining someone else's day. This is an example of being able to disagree without being disagreeable.

Civility in Business

To conduct business effectively requires civil conduct by people in various positions. These behaviors can be as simple as respecting the time of others by not being late to scheduled meetings, or calling well in advance to reschedule them if necessary. It also includes things like knocking before entering offices, not taking calls in the middle of meetings, and learning the names of those present at a meeting. Business relationships occur between two or more people, and the emphasis should be on the fact they are people first. People are very quick to change providers or go with a different company if they feel they are treated as numbers instead of valued clients.

In an increasingly global environment, successful business relationships also require that people learn and value the cultural background of all parties. This means adhering to cultural expectations of host countries, but also understanding how other people operate. In some Asian cultures, for example, direct discussion of business only comes after a lengthy socializing process so all involved get to know each other. In fact, people often make business deals with others with whom they feel the most comfortable, not necessarily those who submit the best offer. It is important to know that up-front blunt communication may not always be the best route to go.

When negotiating for a new position, there are also certain behaviors to keep in mind. First, do not mention or discuss salary until an offer has been made or the company brings it up. Additionally, begin all interactions with greetings and conclude them with gratitude. Finally, be prepared with questions when you interview, as this reciprocity is expected. There are multiple other elements to successful interviewing, and other courses will provide you with that type of instruction, but for the purposes of our discussion here just know civility can go a long way in the interviewing process.

Civility in News Media

Unfortunately, today we need look no further than the news media and talk radio for examples of incivility and disrespectful communication. In spring 2012 talk show host Rush Limbaugh called a female Georgetown law student a "whore" for testimony she issued to Congress regarding the cost of contraception for women. In April 2007, morning talk show host Don Imus referred to the Rutgers

University women's basketball team as "nappy headed hoes." Finally, just look at all of the news programs and talk shows that pit members of opposite sides of an argument against each other. These shows devolve quickly into, at best, a recitation of talking points, or, at worst, a shouting match. In both instances nothing of substance is ever truly discussed, and emotions overshadow content.

Rutgers University women's basketball team

These are the models of civility people are exposed to every day. As we have discussed, civility demands that we assert our own ideas, and these shows definitely allow for this to take place; however, it also calls for respect and understanding, which many of these shows do not demonstrate for the public. If these programs are an example of civil society, then civility is most definitely on the wane today.

That said, there are examples of dialogue and civility in the news media. Sunday morning talk shows often bring in diverse viewpoints and rarely culminate in shouting matches. Instead, ample time is afforded to participants to express their views, explain their data, and listen to counterarguments. This type of exchange, although ineffective at changing minds of those on the show, at least disseminates information for people in a way that does not encourage emotional outbursts. Alas, these shows are often broadcast at times when people generally do not watch television.

Civility and Social Media

More and more people today use social media to stay in touch with friends and family, conduct business, and promote themselves and their products. Facebook, Twitter, and LinkedIn are just a few of the social media tools employed to accomplish these tasks. Even though these resources do not allow for face-to-face communication, they do not reduce or eliminate the need for civil communication. Civility is more than just behaving well to others when they are in front of you; it is a lifestyle where we always genuinely think about how what we say and do can affect other people.

To this end, it is instructive to think before posting status updates to Facebook, issuing a tweet about how you feel regarding an event or issue, or even uploading your résumé to LinkedIn. Remember that you need not share everything on Facebook, and that what you choose to share is now on the Internet. The Internet is like plastic—it never goes away—so you should make sure that what you post will be acceptable later as well as now. Take care when issuing comments to others as well, and even if you disagree, do so with respect and make sure it's the position and not the person with which you disagree. There are people who have lost their jobs over what they posted to Facebook, after all.

Bill Maher
(left) comedian

Tim Tebow
(right) football player

Twitter presents just as many issues for expression and it is, like Facebook, a place where self-restraint could come in handy. In late 2011, comedian Bill Maher issued a tweet mocking the religious beliefs of then-Denver Broncos quarterback, Tim Tebow. Others have issued similarly scathing tweets that have caused more problems than the expression was probably worth. In fact, in response to a negative *New York Times* review of his movie *The Avengers* in May 2012, actor Samuel L. Jackson castigated the writer in a tweet that was then met with harsh criticism across the country. Just because you may feel a certain way and can post it through social media does not necessarily mean you should. Additionally, we communicate more and more through email, but that medium is not always used in a way that promotes civil correspondence between people. Make no mistake email is an extraordinary tool for communication, but it is also rife with potential pitfalls. Table 11.3 shows some guidelines for email use that will help ensure you use it to maximum effect while also remaining civil in the tone of what you write.

Table 11.3

Some Things to Consider When Writing an Email
In General
1. Use email to request or provide succinct pieces of objective information
2. Avoid discussing sensitive issues through email
3. Use email to publicly praise, but not to blame employees
4. Use email to share insights, not to instigate confrontation
5. Judiciously use blind copy function
As Sender
1. Give email a clear and direct subject heading
2. Get to the point
3. Avoid hedgers and qualifiers as phrases
4. If asking a question, be sure to ask the question (don't issue evaluation)
5. Specify who should respond
6. Be clear about when you need a response
7. Provide relevant context
8. One message, one topic
9. Provide brief summary when sending an "FYI" or forward email
10. Don't use sarcasm
As Receiver
1. Don't make assumptions about sender's emotional state
2. Don't escalate by sending an emotionally charged response (sleep on it; perhaps don't reply by email)
3. Don't respond right away
4. Be careful quoting emails out of context in a reply

SUMMARY

Communication is a unique and powerful characteristic of being human. It allows us to connect with others and express our own ideas and feelings, but how we choose to do it matters as much as having the ability to express ourselves. Civility in our communication and actions allows for greater understanding and healthier society. In this chapter we defined what civility means and how it relates to other terms such as politeness, courtesy, respect, and good manners. We then explored how civility has been practiced during different periods of history, before concluding with a discussion of five areas in which civil communication could improve life today.

KEY TERMS

assertive 313	good manners 293
autonomy face 296	high power distance cultures 304
civility 295	image management 297
collectivistic culture 303	individualistic cultures 303
competence face 296	low power-distance cultures 304
courtesy 275	polite 292
face threats 296	respect 313
facework 313	self-monitoring 291
fellowship face 295	self-restraint 298
gender 305	sex 305

REVIEW QUESTIONS

1. What are the five defining characteristics of civility?
2. What are the four ways civility influences how we present ourselves to others?
3. What are the three fundamental components of any civil behavior?
4. What are the three foundational dimensions of interpersonal interactions?
5. What are five contemporary arenas in which civility can improve our quality of life?

THINK ABOUT IT

1. Are people naturally civil, or is this a psychological restraint put on our natural state of being?
2. Have you ever been uncivil in your dealings with an instructor or friend? How so?
3. Does today's mediated environment make it less or more difficult for us to be civil toward one another? Why?

Activities for Action

1. Watch a series of political advertisements or a listen to an airing of a political talk show. Write down what you believe the central message to be, and also the ways the person makes the case. Were they civil in their approach? Did the host or the guest try to understand the views of the other side? What behaviors encouraged or discouraged dialogue and understanding? What behaviors could have been employed to encourage understanding?

2. Write down a list of simple kind behaviors you could do in any given day. Include things like opening a door for a stranger, helping someone carry groceries, and engaging in a simple discussion with a barista or salesperson you come into contact with. Then, the next day, see how many of these behaviors you can accomplish. Also, pay attention to how many times someone else does these things with you. At the end of the day, compare the two lists.

Endnotes

1. For a complete account of "Miss Manners" visit her website at: http://www.missmanners.com/home/about-miss-manners.html (accessed June 6, 2012).

2. Ibid.

3. Thomas Hobbes, *Leviathan,* Part I, Chapter 13.

4. P.M. Forni, *Choosing Civility: The Twenty-Five Rules of Considerate Conduct*, (New York, NY: St. Martin's Press, 2002), 10.

5. Ibid. 11.

6. Ibid. 10.

7. Forni, 112.

8. Ibid.

9. For more information on Dr. Forni, visit his website at: http://krieger.jhu.edu/civility/background.html.

10. John Medina, *Brain Rules: 12 Principles for Surviving and Thriving at Work, Home and School* (Seattle, WA: Pear Press, 2008).

11. For a complete transcript of the address, see: http://www.americanrhetoric.com/speeches/jfkinaugural.htm.

12. Rod L. Troester & Cathy Sargent Mester, *Civility in Business and Professional Communication,=* (New York, NY: Peter Lang Publishers, 2007), 30.

13. Ibid. 33.

14. Ibid.

15. Jon Meacham, *American Lion: Andrew Jackson in the White House,* (New York, NY: Random House, 2008).

Interteaching Session

Dialogue

You are finishing up a course in which the textbook and classroom discussions have questioned some of your most closely held beliefs and values. In general and even though you put in the time and energy needed to learn the course material, you feel as though you did not get as much out of the class as you had hoped. It is now time to complete the anonymous Student Evaluation of Teaching (SET) for this class, and you want to make sure that someone hears about your experience.

1. Does the expectation of civility in the classroom extend to SET? If so, in what ways? If not, why not?

2. What is your obligation to the instructor in terms of UD's Commitment to Community and other core values?

3. How do you believe your comments in SET impact faculty teaching and the classroom experiences of future students?

4. How might you express your concerns within the framework of civility?

5. How do you believe department chairs (who see all SET results for faculty in their departments) respond to student comments within SET that are not civil?

Performance

At the conclusion of class, the professor returns your latest examination. You discover that you earned a grade lower than you expected on it and are quite disappointed. In fact, it puts you at risk of failing the class entirely. You disagree with the grade and want to bring it up with the professor.

1. How do you go about approaching the instructor? When, where, how, and using what language do you initiate contact?

2. Consider using email to make contact. Write the email to the instructor.

3. Consider an in-person meeting. Detail how you would go about doing this and provide a brief script of what you would say. Be prepared to role-play your skit for the class.

Dialogue

12

Practically SPEAKING

Kerry Patterson is an award-winning consultant and corporate trainer. While studying for his Ph.D., Patterson began doing research on how to develop healthy organizations. In his book *Crucial Conversations*,[1] Patterson and his coauthors tell a story about a startling discovery in a study of what made certain people successful and influential corporate leaders. In an effort to find out why some people are more effective than others, Patterson and his colleagues wanted to develop a detailed understanding of how the most effective leaders did their jobs. To do so, they widely surveyed within companies to learn which people were regarded as highly influential. They wanted to find only those people with widespread reputations for truly remarkable effectiveness.

Upon identifying an extraordinarily effective person, the researchers trailed this person at the job to see what he or she did that worked so well. One person they studied was a man named Kevin, who was one of eight vice presidents in his company. After following Kevin for nearly a week, the researchers had seen nothing out of the ordinary and began to wonder why he received such high recognition from so many people in his company. Then they sat in an important meeting in which the CEO was to make a decision about moving the company offices. Two vice presidents presented their plans, and both faced intense scrutiny. Next, the CEO presented his proposal, which the researchers observed "was both unpopular and potentially disastrous."[2] Efforts from several vice presidents to question this plan were met with defensive responses and they backed off. Then Kevin calmly spoke up, skillfully questioning the CEO and ultimately even suggesting that the CEO was going against his own principles in making this decision. Surprisingly, the CEO thoughtfully accepted Kevin's critique and admitted that he needed to rethink. In the end, a decision was reached that was better for the company.

After the meeting, one of the others said to the researchers, "Did you see how he did that? If you want to know how he gets things done, figure out what he just did."[3] How was Kevin able to question, and even critique, his superior in an environment where others had been intimidated into backing down? In their ensuing 25 years of research on effective employees, Patterson and his colleagues found time and again that the common element was that these extraordinary people were masters of dialogue. Their ability to use dialogue in crucial conversations gave them an ability to succeed where others less skilled at dialogue could not.

We share this story to show how powerful dialogue can be. But what is truly impressive is that the story only begins to illustrate the importance of dialogue. Yes, dialogue will enable you to make some amazing accomplishments at work. It is also central to the ability to maintain healthy and satisfying social relationships, such as friendship, marriage, and family. But, even more important, dialogue is an essential tool for engaging in the Marianist *Commitment to Community* (C2C) principles for living in a community, as well as for developing relationships with people who are different from you. And, it is a necessity for communicating ethically in some situations. While dialogue is a powerful tool in oral communication, its greatest importance lies not in what it can do for you, but in what it allows you to do for others.

Now look around you. Watch how people treat each other on reality TV. You won't find much dialogue there. Dialogue has been largely absent from political communication as well,[4] both among politicians and among the media (think Rush Limbaugh or Keith Olbermann). Jerry Springer, a former mayor of Cincinnati, has made millions from a show featuring people doing the exact opposite of dialogue.

Dialogue requires considerable effort, humility, ability to suspend judgment, and willingness to listen carefully to someone with qualities or views we initially dislike. These skills require strength of character many people have not developed. But those who can master dialogue discover its value in helping them achieve success at the workplace and in their personal lives. They discover how much richer it makes the quality of their lives and those around them.

PREP QUESTIONS

Part 1: Key Concepts

1. Compare and contrast monologue, debate, and dialogue.

2. Detail the four skills that you must master to engage in dialogue effectively.

3. Explain what it means to suspend judgment.

4. Define unconditional positive regard and spirit of mutual equality, two attitudes that are essential to dialogue.

5. Describe five general situations identified in the chapter in which dialogue would be helpful.

Part 2: Application

1. Construct a statement that exemplifies each of Gibb's six supportive behaviors that one might say in a dialogue with one's roommate about expectations for how you will organize your dorm room.

2. Consider the following excerpt from news sources, and imagine that it has been said to you by someone over lunch:

   "Like health care, prices are rising rapidly for higher education because of the predominant role of third-party payments—federal student loans and grants, state government support for institutions and students, private philanthropic gifts and endowment income. College seniors who borrow to finance their education now graduate with an average of $24,000 in debt, and student loan debt now tops credit card debt among Americans. When someone else is paying a lot of the bills, students are less sensitive to the price, thus allowing the colleges to care less about keeping prices under control. And the nonprofit nature of institutions reduces incentives for colleges and universities to be efficient. The key to getting costs under control is contained in three words that begin with the letter "I"—information, incentives, and innovation."

   c. Create two clarifying questions that you could ask the other person after listening to what she or he has said here.

   d. How would you paraphrase what the other person has said? Write what you would say in the space below.

A Brief History of Dialogue in Our Society

Although principles of dialogue have existed as long as people have had a spoken language, dialogue drew widespread attention both in our society and in communication research and theory in the 1960s. As Americans struggled with difficult questions about social and political issues (such as equal rights regardless of race or gender), people started to see dialogue as an important means of nonviolent response to differences. They looked at the writings of influential scholars like Carl Rogers and Martin Buber, and they began to see dialogue as a means by which we should communicate with each other in a wide variety of situations.[5] Dialogue wasn't just seen as a technique for communication; it was seen as an ethical requirement.[6]

This identification of dialogue as an ethic instead of a technique has had important implications for its history. The movements of the 1960s left a lasting impact on American culture. Martin Luther King, Jr. became a national hero, and the decade's social movements had a permanent impact on race relations, women's rights, and other social issues. However, while some enduring ideas were carried forward, certain fads were left behind. Most would agree that some of the fashion statements of the 1960s and 1970s are best left as historic relics. By the late 1970s, many people saw an excessive emphasis on dialogue as one of the fads of the 1960s, and the teaching and study of dialogue diminished greatly.

In the mid-1990s, however, an interesting change took place. Scholars started to realize that they made a mistake in abandoning dialogue, and they began once again to write and theorize about it. However, their theoretical approach changed. Instead of thinking about dialogue as part of the social movements of the 1960s, they began to think about dialogue from different theoretical perspectives. Dialogue was no longer seen as an ethical requirement for all interpersonal communication, but instead as a way to develop better understanding and build relationships in situations where those were important goals. Despite this change, the ethical elements of dialogue have never been completely forgotten. After all, the interactions in which we use dialogue require that we make moral choices. So, rather than being seen as an ethical obligation for how people must communicate, dialogue now tends to be seen as a form of communication in which ethics are one essential element. As we introduce you to dialogue, pay attention to how much of a role ethics play in our discussion of the topic. And notice how important *integrity*

integrity
a quality of discerning and acting on one's ethical principles

Air Conditioning

On a muggy Saturday in August, when the temperature reached almost 100 degrees, the air conditioning in one of the authors' homes failed. With an 8-month-old baby in the house who couldn't tolerate heat the way an adult would, he called a repair company right away. A wire attached to the compressor had broken, so the repair worker simply fixed that wire. The entire job took about 15 minutes and involved no parts. The customer was astonished to see he had been charged $225.

Unhappy at what seemed like unreasonable pricing, he called the company. He told the customer service agent that he wasn't calling to make a threat or ask for anything, but he simply wanted to let them know his reaction as a customer to his experience. He mentioned that while he knew it was their right to set pricing as they wanted, he wouldn't be using their services again because of the cost. He also mentioned that he was pleased with the work itself. The customer service agent looked into how the bill had been calculated. Although a standard service call was $75, the company had to pay employees time-and-a-half for weekend work. And they had to pay the employee's time not only for the service call itself, but also for the trip to and from the customer's house. But the major factor affecting the bill was that any job involving the compressor was classified as a major repair and a large surcharge was applied for that. The customer acknowledged these factors and noted that even though the compressor was involved, no work was done on it, and so in his opinion this didn't meet their definition of a major repair. No changes resulted from the conversation. The customer ended the call by thanking the representative for helping him better understand the process, but noted that he still disagreed with how the bill had been calculated.

About an hour later, the customer's phone rang. It was the customer service representative. "I've been thinking," she said, "Our policy guarantees satisfaction or the job is free. Since you weren't satisfied, we'd like to offer that we make this job free." The customer thought for a moment, then said, "That isn't right. I needed the work done, and your technician did a great job. Taking that work for free would be ripping you off, and my ripping you off is no better than you ripping me off." There was a surprised silence at the other end of the line for a moment, then the agent asked, "Well, what price do you think would be appropriate?" The customer thought for a minute. "I originally thought $75 would be appropriate, since it was a quick job involving no cost in parts. But, I didn't know that you had to pay driving time and overtime for weekend work. That makes me think that $125 would cover your costs and give you an appropriate profit as well. That is about what it would have been if it wasn't classified as a major repair." The customer service agent agreed, and the bill was adjusted.

The customer's goal was never to get the price changed. He merely wanted the company to understand how customers felt about what seemed like unfair pricing. In the process he learned more about why the price had been set, and learned of some shortcomings in his expectations.

It is possible that an angry threatening call might have also resulted in a price adjustment or a free repair, but that would certainly have led to resentment on the part of at least one party. Dialogue met its goal of mutual understanding, and it also led to relationship building. The mutually satisfactory pricing was merely an unanticipated side effect. And as is always the case when dialogue happens, ethics played a vital role in this exchange.

and ethical character are to those who wish to use dialogue in their daily and workplace lives. A person with no moral compass cannot fully understand and employ dialogue.

DIALOGUE: WHAT IT IS, AND WHAT IT IS NOT

Dialogue is a communicative event in which people with different perspectives seek to understand each other's views. Dialogue is, essentially, speaking so that others want to listen and listening so that others want to speak. Dialogue neither demands nor expects that people adopt each other's views or even come to agreement. If different perspectives are in conflict, dialogue often leads to an effective and satisfying resolution to the problem—typically much more satisfying than any other means of interaction can produce. However, those outcomes are a byproduct of the process, not the goal of it. To see how that can happen, take the case of one of the authors of this book, who encountered a challenging situation at home when the bill for fixing a broken air conditioner arrived and it was well above the expected cost. Many experts will tell you that engaging in dialogue changes you and leads to growth in understanding and character. One writer so strongly considers growth to be part of the nature of dialogue that he defines the concept as "a process of *inter*action through which human beings listen to each other deeply enough to be changed by what they learn."[7]

> **dialogue**
> an interaction in which people with different perspectives seek to understand each others views; speaking so that others want to listen and listening so that others want to speak

Dialogue can be contrasted with monologue.[8] *Monologue* is a communicative event in which only one voice is present. Commonly, monologue refers to one person speaking without really listening. This may happen when someone is either oblivious to the importance of listening to the other, or if a person feels that the other's voice just isn't important. For example, a supervisor who has made a decision at work might simply tell workers what they must do without inviting their input. While this form of monologue can sometimes reduce the quality of work that gets done, it might also be appropriate in cases where there is no need for the supervisor to listen or where listening could even be problematic. Certainly, the military uses monologue to great advantage in many operations. An army could not function effectively if everyone were to share an opinion with the general over how and when each operation should be conducted.

> **monologue**
> an interaction in which only one voice is present.

However, monologue can be much more aggressive when it consists of a speaker shutting down or oppressing the voice of another. This can happen when someone knows the audience may disagree with a message or the message might even be detrimental to the audience. In these cases, monologue has sometimes been used as a form of violence against another.[9] For example, when powerful people mistreat those with less power and unjustly try to keep them from telling anyone about it, then monologue is a means of oppression and it is an unethical weapon used to maintain control. Organizations and individuals who take away the opportunity for individuals or groups to speak on topics important to them exert a damaging form of monologue. Propaganda, brainwashing, and other manipulative tactics are other forms of monologue that have done great harm to humanity over the centuries.

debate
....
a form of
communication in
which participants
present opposing
arguments and attempt
to make a case
through reason and
evidence

Dialogue can also be contrasted with debate, another form of communication. *Debate*, as it is generally understood, is a form of communication in which participants present opposing arguments and attempt to make a case through reason and evidence. It is important to note that debate can be practiced in many ways; not all debates have the same character, structure, or approach. Classroom debates, for instance, are a form of communication whereby participants might present opposing arguments for the purpose of analyzing different sides of an issue. The oppositional nature of the interaction is created deliberately as a way of examining the oppositional positions one could take regarding the issue under scrutiny, such as arguments for and against a particular proposal. Such communication, although oppositional, requires civility, much as dialogue does. Indeed, in many ways, this sort of interaction might resemble closely dialogue as we have defined it in this chapter. Such interactions help participants to hone their skills for argumentation, by providing them with an opportunity to work with logic and evidence as they create and deliver persuasive arguments. Debates of this sort need not have a winner or a loser, given that their purpose is to explore the opposing sides of an issue, such as a policy under consideration. In some cases, such as in competitive debate, there is a winner or a loser. The University of Dayton has a debate team that participates in such competitions. Although the participants are trying to win the competition through the presentation of their particular argument, the overall purpose is still educational, with expectations of civility as the foundation for the interaction. The debaters in these cases are opponents, but in a sense they are also collaborators who are working together to explore opposing sides of an issue.

Interactions, however, can be approached as a game to be won at all costs, even by resorting to aggressive or otherwise uncivil behaviors. People might use terminology relevant to the interactions previously mentioned to describe this interaction: they might call it "debate" or say that they are having an "argument." However, the opposition in these cases has become more personal and less about the issues for the purpose of enhancing understanding of the opposing arguments that one could take. The participants are more concerned about "defeating" the other. Sometimes people can engage others in this sort of interaction, whether in their personal lives or in interactions in public settings, such as in a business context or through the course of one's participation in community life. Such interactions risk devolving quickly into destructive conflict, in which participants doggedly defend their positions while attacking others whom they see as their opponents. In communication of this sort, participants are not seeking creative solutions, since their goal is to win the argument. Whether they win or lose, their interaction might weaken the trust in their relationship, which likely took much time to build but can be destroyed quickly, if they are not careful.

Dialogue differs from these sorts of interaction in that it does not assume any sort of opposition between participants. There are not predetermined sides in a dialogue that participants are expected to defend. People may begin by stating contrasting or even contradictory positions, but as the conversation continues, they are free to change or even abandon these positions in favor of ones that others have expressed. At any point, there also can be a clash of opinions in dialogue, as participants express differing ideas. Sometimes the interaction can be quite intense, if people feel strongly about the ideas that they are expressing. However, what distinguishes this interaction from debate is that there is no opposition in dialogue. Though participants' ideas might clash with each other, they do not interact with each other as opponents, for they are not expected to hold any particular position at any point in the conversation, let alone one side of an issue that they are expected to defend. In some conversations, the success of the communication depends fundamentally on the participants not seeing themselves as being in opposition to each other, for there might already be a real temptation for them to do so. Talks involving people who identify with different racial, ethnic, tribal, religious, political, or other social groups who have a history of conflict might have a higher capacity of building understanding across their differences if they can be encouraged not to see each other through an oppositional lens.

Think about your interactions with others on a daily basis. How many times have you gotten into an argument with a friend, classmate, or colleague over something because you wanted to "win" the discussion rather than reach some sort of understanding, even if you don't agree in the end? How many times have you wanted to explore an issue but assumed that debating different sides was the only way to do so? Our purpose in this chapter is to encourage you to understand that dialogue is a promising way of exploring different views among communicators precisely in that it is not premised on opposition between the participants. In the next section, we will explore some attitudes and behaviors for creating dialogue, especially when differences among the participants otherwise might be a basis for tension or conflict.

ATTITUDES AND BEHAVIORS FOR DIALOGUE

Dialogue is a complex activity. Entire volumes have been written about what it is and how to do it well. This chapter can only give the briefest overview, so consider it a starting point in your understanding of dialogue, rather than a complete description. We encourage you to continue exploring dialogue throughout your time at UD through reading more about the topic, through practice and application in other classes that discuss difficult and controversial topics, and through your interactions with other members of the university community.

To explain how to engage in dialogue effectively, we address four areas that you must master: listening, developing attitudes that foster dialogue, creating a supportive climate, and appropriately shaping your messages.

Listening in Dialogue

Listening is the most prominent element of dialogic communication. Although there are vital qualities in sending messages that are essential, good dialogue begins with the way a person listens. If communicators do not listen effectively, dialogue cannot take place.

listening
the mental processing of what a person has heard

You will recall from an earlier chapter that *listening* is the cognitive processing of what is heard, and that people routinely hear without listening. Dialogue requires that participants make a commitment to listen fully and completely to the other party. In order to make this happen, people need to do a variety of actions. Although this list is not complete, a person who does all the behaviors below is likely to be a highly effective listener in a dialogue.

Give complete attention

Giving complete attention, often referred to as being "fully present" in the interaction, means that people focus all of their attention on the interaction and the people to whom they are listening. As a first step, this means eliminating elements of the environment that could be distracting. Putting away communication devices (phone, laptop, etc.) is an essential start. Turning off other devices that could be a distraction (e.g., television or radio talk show) might also be necessary in some settings. It may even be useful to move to a location where other people or activities won't disrupt the conversation. Being physically capable to participate is also necessary to be a fully present participant in any interaction, so obviously it is hard to give full attention to someone when you are intoxicated or sleep deprived.

presentness
giving full attention to someone in dialogue

A difficult part of *presentness* can be setting aside mental distractions. Notice how hard it is to pay attention in class just after you got really good or bad news, or when you are nervous about an event right after class? It's difficult not to think about those topics and to direct your full attention to the class. Being fully present in dialogue requires the ability to tune out mental distractions. If you cannot do that, then rescheduling the conversation may be the best option.

One widely shared misconception people have is thinking that they can multitask while listening. While it is possible to multitask in certain ways, such as listening while walking, the research is conclusive with regard to one aspect of multitasking: *For cognitive functions that require you to pay attention (such as listening, reading, driving, or texting), **it is impossible to multitask**.*[10] This limitation is not something you can overcome with practice or experience, such as having texted all your life. Rather, this is a physical limitation. As molecular biologist John Medina notes, "We are biologically incapable of processing attention-rich inputs simultaneously."[11] Just as your physiology makes it impossible for you to jump 50 feet in the air, the physical design of your brain makes it just as impossible for you to pay attention to two different mental inputs at once. Instead, you shift rapidly between the two objects of attention, and in so doing, you not only miss one when paying attention to the other, you also miss out on *both* as you transition between the two.

So, if you believe you are good enough at texting that you can do it while paying attention to something else, you are mistaken. There can be no argument: In order to listen effectively in dialogue, you cannot multitask with another activity that requires mental attention.

Notice that being present—like all the listening skills we discuss as part of dialogue—will have a significant impact on your success as a student. If you spend time in class texting or checking social media online, or if you come to class hung over or too tired to pay attention, your listening will be diminished, and that will hurt your ability to do your best in class. And here is the payoff: Depending on your listening habits at present, you may be able to improve your grades at

UD without any additional study time simply by applying the listening skills of dialogue in your classes.

It is also important to know that multitasking is regarded as rude in many settings. While workplace norms are still developing to accommodate today's rapidly changing communication technology, checking your messages or texting in a business meeting is likely to be viewed as offensive to others in the meeting, and may reduce others' respect for you. In class, almost all professors consider it rude when students engage in activities unrelated to class on phones or laptops. Just think: If you have to hide doing something so the other person will not notice it, then it is not an ethical approach to dialogue or civil behavior. So, realize that multitasking in this manner likely has a negative effect on your relationships with others who may be important to you and your success.

Allow the other to speak fully

One of the most common mistakes people make in conversation is failing to let the other party complete what they want to say. This can be caused by a variety of reasons, from the seemingly positive (e.g., the listener got so excited about the point that he or she couldn't wait to jump in) to the seemingly negative (e.g., the listener wanted to keep someone from making his or her points). But regardless of the reason, interruptions keep the listener from getting all the information the speaker wanted to share. And that information may include not just the content of the message, but also the other information that is inherent in communication, such as information about the speaker's emotional state or about the speaker and listener's relationship. In some cases, speakers may be happy enough with the outcome that they might not mind never having a chance to finish, but in most cases people feel frustrated when the listener doesn't even give them a chance to say what they wanted to say.

To allow the other to speak fully, you must put aside your desire to respond and instead focus on your role as a listener. It is helpful to think of yourself as a detective who is seeking all the clues. If you make an agreement with yourself that you won't speak until you have a full understanding of the other, you'll be more effective as a listener.

Ask clarifying questions

Once a person has spoken fully—or during the course of their speaking turn if appropriate—ask the speaker any questions needed for you to have complete understanding. Since asking a question is an an act of speech, it may seem unusual that we consider it as an important component of listening. However, asking clarifying questions demonstrates that you were listening closely enough to identify the areas of the message you didn't fully understand. These questions allow you to fill in information that was missing from the message. You may wish to ask about relevant facts; about a person's reasons, assumptions, feelings; or about anything else that will fill in missing pieces. But wait until they are done to respond; otherwise, you disrespect the other person by rudely interrupting him or her.

The most important point about follow-up questions is that they must be intended and worded to obtain information. Many people ask questions that are intended to criticize or attack, rather than to solicit information. Such questions are destructive to dialogue. "Why would you do something so stupid?!" is a criticism phrased as a question, rather than a true attempt to better understand. Consider the case in which an international student speaks in class about foods his family eats that most Americans would not. Other students ask the following questions:

"How do you make that food?"

"Do you eat that as an everyday staple, or just on certain occasions?"

"How desperate would you have to be to eat that stuff?"

"Now that you're used to good food here, could you ever go back to eating that?"

It is easy to see that the first two questions help the listener better understand the food and its social context, whereas the latter two questions reveal prejudice and might even be intended to demean the people and cultures under discussion.

Make sure your questions function only to solicit information, not share your own opinions. A clarifying question should result in a flow of information from the speaker to the listener, not the other way around.

Suspend your judgment

One of the more difficult skills essential for many dialogic encounters is the ability to suspend your judgment during a conversation when a person seems wrong, unlikeable, or even unethical. Listening in dialogue must happen with an open mind. This is not to say that you should not interpret, or even state, moral judgments where yours are different from a dialogic partner's. But if a listener cannot seek understanding without conveying judgmental messages against the partner, dialogue will not take place. You may wish to make judgments after a dialogue, but only do so after you have collected all relevant information.

What may surprise you is that getting to understand other people often reduces negative judgments. Once you understand their situation, their reasons, and their perceptions you often find that they are people like you, who have feelings and values you understand, external pressures they navigate every day, and commitments they seek to keep. That is not always the case, of course, and the opposite can even happen—you might like and respect a person even less when you get to know him or her better. But the only way to know what the outcome will be is to withhold judgment about other people until you have gotten to know their perspective with an open mind.

Suspending judgment requires you to be honest with yourself. It is possible to pretend to be open minded and even to fool others into believing you are open minded when in fact you are not. But if you go into a dialogue with judgments about the other person already set, you will reduce the effectiveness of the dialogue and deny yourself the opportunity to find out what you might have thought. At the outset of this chapter, we noted that dialogue requires strength of character that can be difficult for many people. The ability to suspend judgment while you listen to someone who has positions you find offensive or that you disagree with is hard to do, and may take years of practice to do well.

Plan your responses later

Another of the more common deficiencies in listening is being focused more on your response than on what the other person is saying. This happens often because it is a natural reaction to statements we disagree with. It differs from the problem of not letting speakers finish because when people do this they often let the speaker finish. But in this case, it doesn't matter what the speaker is saying because the listener isn't paying attention. The listener is preoccupied by formulating the perfect comeback.

Like suspending judgment, there isn't an easy technique that will prevent this problem. It just takes mental discipline. If you find yourself thinking of a great response to something that was said, consider jotting a keyword down so you won't forget that topic, and then put the issue out of your mind.

Practice accurate empathetic understanding

The goal of listening to another is to develop a complete understanding of that person's position, experience, attitudes, or ideas. Although it might be sufficient to list this only as a cognitive goal to understand the content of the message, you need to know the importance of the emotional side of human behavior. Nobody functions in a solely rational manner like the fictional Vulcan Mr. Spock, on *Star Trek*. Instead, all of our work and social interaction involves elements of both reason and emotion (logos and pathos). Scholars explain how our brains work using the metaphor of a rider on an elephant.[12] The rider (the rational, cognitive functions) tells the elephant (the emotional part of the brain) what to do, and the elephant provides the motivation and force to make actions happen.

Often, both reason and emotion work together seamlessly, but sometimes they conflict. When they do, it can be difficult for reason to triumph over emotion. This is the challenge with losing weight. No matter how much the rational side of the brain says "Don't have a second piece of cake," it can be difficult to exert that control. The same is true of social interaction. Often we say and do things we know we shouldn't, because our emotions get the better of us. In contrast, when our emotions are taking us in a direction that our rational side supports, we can be highly effective. And in other cases, emotions don't really seem to have any bearing on the outcome of a situation. You just have to assess it. Regardless of what, if any, role emotions play in a situation, it is essential as a listener to pay attention to a person's feelings if they seem to be showing through in a conversation, and consider how that person might feel given a particular piece of information, phrase, or vocal inflection. To that end, it is important to also listen for clues as to what triggered an emotional response from the other person. Often a person's past experiences or current circumstances may help explain their emotional state and reaction. When engaging in dialogue, heeding these clues can help you avoid getting sidetracked while also respecting the other person and where they are at emotionally and mentally in a given moment.

The importance of understanding another person's feelings does not mean that you should necessarily ask about them. Doing so might make you seem like an aspiring therapist. A person who tells her boss, "Before you made that decision yesterday, I had information I wanted to share," probably doesn't want a response of "How did my not asking about that information make you feel?" So, the message about accurate empathetic understanding isn't that you must explore the inner landscape of a person's feelings in every dialogue. Instead, you should be aware of the importance of emotions, be attentive to that information, and understand it to the degree it is relevant to the situation. In many situations it is not relevant at all. But in cases where emotional information seems to be coming through in the dialogue, pay attention to it (see Table 12.1).

Table 12.1

Listening Behaviors That Build Dialogue	
Dos	**Don'ts**
• Take notes when someone is speaking • Let the other person speak fully • Ask questions to clarify what was said • Bring appropriate materials to a meeting • Arrange appointments in advance • Use a person's preferred name or title (and if you don't know it, ask them what they prefer to be called)	• Play on your cell phone or iPad • Interrupt other speakers • Assume you know what a person means • Show up without appropriate materials • Barge into a person's office • Use abbreviated names/ nicknames without permission

Attitudes Necessary for Dialogue

Dialogue is a meeting of *people*, not just an exchange of information. The character that each person has shapes the nature of the interaction. Every conversation is different because of the personalities of the people in it. Two different sets of people talking about an event they both just experienced may have very different interactions, just as two sets of people negotiating for the same goal may have conversations that sound quite different.

You have already seen some important attitudes reflected in the guidelines for listening (such as the value of presentness). But there are several attitudes that writers identified as being essential for dialogue that need to be considered here, because they influence every facet of the interaction. Two that we will discuss are unconditional positive regard and a spirit of mutual equality.

Unconditional positive regard

The term *unconditional positive regard* was coined by psychologist Carl Rogers, as a central tenet in his person-centered therapy. Rogers believed that therapists

unconditional positive regard
accepting and respecting others as they are without judgment or evaluation

needed to create a nonjudgmental environment in which patients saw that therapists showed an acceptance of, and positive attitude toward, clients as human beings. This attitude suggested that the therapist wished them well, regardless of what they thought or said. To Rogers, unconditional positive regard was essential for therapists because it made clients comfortable speaking about whatever issues were troubling them. It is important to note that this positive regard did not mean that the therapist approved of a client's destructive behaviors, only that the therapist wanted the best for that person regardless of what the client said or did.

Unconditional positive regard is helpful for dialogue because it establishes good will even when people have goals that seem to conflict. An attitude of unconditional positive regard tells the other person, "We may or may not agree, but I value you as a person and will treat you with respect and dignity." This message can have a powerful impact on making dialogue possible, even in cases where differing positions could cause antagonism in the conversation. Consider again the story of Kevin, from the beginning of this chapter. It is reasonable to assume that Kevin showed positive regard for his boss, even though he had concerns about the soundness of his plan. It seems likely that had Kevin not shown unconditional positive regard, that conversation would not have turned out the way that it did.

This example helps show that dialogue cannot just be reduced to a set of techniques but rather, it also depends on the character of the people involved. Unconditional positive regard can seem difficult to enact at times when you encounter someone hard to like. Even when you disagree with a person's beliefs, attitudes, or actions, the ability to respect another person's humanity and desire the best for her or him is a powerful force in enabling dialogue to take place. Showing goodwill may open communication options you thought were impossible. One of the most common ways we can express unconditional positive regard is through "agreeing to disagree." When we do this you allow for the other party to hold their position, while you hold yours, and the relationship is not damaged. You accept the fact you disagree and harbor no ill will toward the person for their beliefs. The practice of unconditional positive regard involves separating the areas of disagreement and "annoying behaviors" a person exhibits from your relationship because those things do not cause you serious distress or harm.

Think about a case where your roommate has left dirty dishes in the sink. Rather than getting upset with the person for this annoying behavior, you could engage them in a a conversation about it. You might find out your roommate had a bad day or emergency to attend to that caused them to not do the dishes. Just because the dishes were not done does not make your roommate a bad or lazy person.

Spirit of mutual equality

Having a spirit of mutual equality means that participants in dialogue consider each other equal as human beings, even if they have differences in social esteem or organizational authority. Thus, parents and children or bosses and subordinates see each other not as different in authority or rank, but equal as two people. This equality does not eliminate the fact that one party has greater power than the other, but it means that their communication treats each person as equal in value as a person rather than treating one person as superior to the other. Communication scholar Richard Johannesen describes the spirit of mutual equality this way: "Although society may rank participants in dialogue as of unequal status or accomplishment, the participants themselves view each other as persons, not as objects to be manipulated or exploited. The exercise of power or superiority is to be avoided. Participants do not impose their opinion, cause, or will."[13] For a list of behaviors that do not exhibit a spirit of mutual equality, and try instead to exercise power and superiority in an interaction, see Table 12.2 below.

Table 12.2

Behaviors that Encourage and Discourage a Spirit of Mutual Equality	
Encourage	**Discourage**
• Paraphrase what was just said • Encourage others to speak • Allow others to speak • Let conversation develop • Collaborate on solutions • Treat conversation as an unfolding process	• Seek to comment on every comment • Work to achieve your own goals • Compete for attention • Try to control conversation's direction • Desire final say on decision • Treat conversation as a game to be won

Maintaining a spirit of mutual equality is important in dialogue. If it is clear to a lower-ranked participant that the higher-ranked person does not treat his or her perspective as equally worthy, there is little reason to engage in conversation. Think of someone who seems to look down on you as being of lesser intelligence or experience. How much do you disclose to that person? Probably not as much as with someone who values your perspectives. Or consider a boss who treats you as less capable than him- or herself. How willing are you to offer your thoughts about improving the workplace? On the other hand, consider a teacher you have had who truly valued and respected your ideas in class. You are likely much more willing to share your thoughts with that teacher than with the others, despite your large deficit in education and experience on the class topic, because that person treats you with a spirit of mutual equality. You may have less education or fewer credentials on the topic, but if the teacher acknowledges that you might have interesting ideas that he or she never thought about, it invites you to participate fully in the conversation.

As the preceding examples make clear, a spirit of mutual equality does not eliminate status or power differences. What it does is remove them from the effort to gain mutual understanding. Once that process has taken place, the party with authority needs to make an appropriate decision. Remember, dialogue means a free exchange of ideas with a goal toward understanding, not agreement.

Creating a Supportive Climate for Conversation

A necessary condition for dialogue to take place is the creation of a *supportive climate*. Supportiveness is the opposite of defensiveness. A *defensive climate* exists when people feel threatened or attacked, and believes that messages they send may be used against them. Johannesen notes that a person who creates a supportive climate "allows free expression, seeks understanding, and avoids value judgments that stifle. [That person] shows desire and capacity to listen without anticipating, interfering, competing, refuting, or warping meanings into preconceived interpretations."[14] People feel much more comfortable sharing ideas, brainstorming, and self-disclosing in supportive environments. That is not the case when they feel the need to defend themselves. Consider a time when you felt threatened by another person, and knew that anything you said would potentially be used against you. How likely were you to open up and share honestly with that person? Probably not at all. This is why defensive climates eliminate the possibility of dialogue. Attention to creating a supportive climate is important for everyone, but it is especially important for those who hold greater social or organizational power than the person with whom they are speaking. The *chilling effect* of defensiveness is amplified when combined with power. As an example of the chilling effect at work, let's consider a conversation with a parent about the classes you are considering taking. The student wants input and advice, and is ultimately responsible for choosing their classes, while their parents pay their tuition. The student's father makes it clear that he feels the student should take Economics, the class that is the least interesting to the child. Rather than explaining why, the father states, "It's foolish and stupid to take the history class because you can always read about it later from a book at Barnes and Noble, so you should learn economics from an expert." The student feels like further conversation will not be helpful because of the way their father conveyed his opinion and thoughts, and also worries that if they do not take Economics they will lose their parent's support for their school bills. No threat was made in this example, but the way the subject was addressed by the one party did not create a climate in which conversation about all the options could be explored. The dialogue was chilled.

How can you create a supportive climate? Communication scholar Jack Gibb wrote an article in 1961 that is still used today to guide behavior in creating supportive climates.[15] Gibb provided six contrasting behaviors that promote either supportive or defensive communication, see Tables 12.3a and b.

supportive climate
a communication situation in which a person feels he or she can speak freely without risk of harm

defensive climate
a communication situation in which a person feels threatened

chilling effect
an action that discourages others from speaking their mind

Table 12.3a

Supportive behaviors		
Description	Explaining how one's view contrasts with another without judgment or criticism	"Your view and my view differ in a number of ways…" "You seem to be assuming that X is true, while I don't share that assumption…"
Problem Orientation	Inviting others to collaborate in the search for a solution to a common problem	"Let's work together in addressing this…" "Here is the information that I have about this issue. What information can you share?"
Spontaneity	Articulating one's views in a way that makes clear one's goals, purposes, or intentions	"I want to be explicit about what I hope will come from this interaction…" "These are my priorities in the interaction. What are yours?"
Empathy	Expressing concern for the well-being of others	"I am concerned about what you need in this interaction…" "You seem to be uncomfortable with how this is going. Is everything ok?"
Equality	Communicating to others that one sees them as having the same value and capacity to contribute to the conversation	"Your viewpoint is as integral to this conversation as mine is…" "We haven't heard from you about this yet. I'd like to hear what you think."
Provisionalism	Stating one's views in a way that acknowledges that they are based on one's experience and limited knowledge	"In my experience…" "It seems to me…"

Defensive behaviors		
Evaluation	Passing judgment or criticizing others or their views	"You're clearly uninformed about this topic." "How could you say something so ridiculous?"
Control	Seeking to impose a specific solution	"We need to do it this way…" "If you don't side with me on this, then I'm not going to continue with this conversation."
Strategy	Manipulating others or the situation through a preplanned and perhaps undisclosed approach	"You and I need to stand together on this, once the conversation with the others begins…" "We need to make sure that this information does not come out in the conversation…"
Neutrality	Expressing a lack of concern for the well-being of others, apathy	"I don't care what you need…" "Whatever."
Superiority	Communicating to others that one thinks that one has more value and capacity to contribute to the conversation than others do	"What you think about this is irrelevant…" "Perhaps when you have more experience, you'll have more to contribute…"
Certainty	Stating one's views in a way that presumes that they are absolutely correct and not reflective of one's experience	"X is true, Y is false. What is there to discuss?" "Clearly, you don't see the truth here…"

Table 12.3b

Consider how these behaviors work to create supportiveness or defensiveness with the following example. A doctoral student, Reyna, was having difficulties completing her dissertation because her adviser was not reading drafts of her work and giving her feedback within a reasonable time. Reyna needed the professor's feedback and his eventual approval in order to take her dissertation to the committee that would judge whether her research passed or failed. She contacted the department's Director of Graduate Studies (DGS) to see if he could help. The DGS wanted to resolve the issue but he had no authority over the adviser, who was a faculty peer. Stop and think for a moment about how the DGS could use the strategies above to address the issue and help Reyna while minimizing the adviser's defensiveness.

In this case, the DGS stopped by the adviser's office so they could talk in person. He told the adviser that the student felt she wasn't getting feedback in a timely manner, and said that he wanted to learn more about the situation. He indicated that he hadn't formed any conclusions about what was happening because he hadn't yet listened to the adviser. As the conversation unfolded, the adviser provided some information that seemed contradictory to what the student said, but also some information consistent with the student's claims. The DGS expressed sympathy at one point for the adviser's busy schedule. The two explored some ideas together for resolving the issue, and eventually they worked out a plan that seemed like it would suit everyone's interests. The DGS relayed this information to the student, and within a month the dissertation was done.

How did the DGS create a supportive environment? First, the conversation began with a description ("Here is what the student said") rather than an evaluation ("I've heard that you're not doing your job well enough"). He showed empathy by noting the adviser's busy schedule. He treated the adviser with equality, and allowed both of them to work out a solution together. The collaboration on solutions resulted from a problem orientation, and also allowed room for discussion instead of certainty in their conversation. Together, these behaviors created a supportive climate for the conversation, rather than making the adviser defensive.

It is important to note that dialogue won't always result in a positive outcome. The adviser could have reacted negatively to any suggestion that he was negligent, he could have promised actions that he didn't follow through with, or he could have become angry at the student's allegations and become a harsher critic of her work. We don't suggest that dialogue is a magic potion that makes all problems end well. But we can say this: if the DGS had created defensiveness in this initial conversation, it's a pretty safe bet that a problem which proved to have an easy solution wouldn't have worked out so well. What this example illustrates is not that dialogue solves all problems, but that it opens possibilities that non-dialogic approaches preclude. And even if a non-dialogic solution could have helped the student complete her dissertation, it is a reasonable to assume that the DGS and adviser's relationship would have been lower in quality going forward than it was a result of the dialogic approach.

Principles of Speaking in Dialogue

We have saved principles of speaking for last in our discussion of how to promote dialogue for two reasons. First, we wish to emphasize that your attention in dialogue should foremost be on listening and maintaining the requisite attitudes. Although dialogue is a two-way interaction, it works best when both parties are more concerned with listening than with getting their message across. Second, the attitudes and guidelines for creating a supportive climate provide considerable guidance for how to frame your messages in a dialogic encounter. We could almost have left speaking out of our discussion of how to engage in dialogue without hurting your ability to do it well. But, there are a few specifics beyond what we have mentioned that are worth noting.

Don't confuse judgments and facts

When sharing your views, there are many types of information you might share—facts, your feelings, opinions, positions you take, judgments you make,

SPOTLIGHTING THEORISTS: RONALD ARNETT

Ronald Arnett

One of the most influential contemporary scholars on the subject of dialogue is Ronald Arnett, currently a professor at Duquesne University. Arnett received his graduate education in the early 1970s, and read widely from the writings on dialogue of the 1960s. He was interested in helping people better understand and practice dialogue in everyday life. Some of his early books, such as *Dwell in Peace* and *Communication and Community* offered insights into the philosophy underlying dialogue and issues people needed to be aware of to better understand and apply it. Other books considered dialogue in certain settings, such as *Dialogic Education*, which gave teachers ideas of how dialogue could lead to better educational outcomes.

As well-versed as any scholar at the philosophical foundations of dialogue from the 1960s, Arnett began to see shortcomings of some of the ideas from that era. At the same time, he also saw the value that dialogue had for society. Arnett began to think and write about some limitations of older conceptions of dialogue and to present alternative philosophical perspectives.

Arnett's books have so much depth that beginners cannot always appreciate all the ideas in them, but they have helped reshape the way contemporary scholars think about dialogue. Newer books such as *Dialogic Civility in a Cynical Age* or *Dialogic Confession: Bonhoeffer's Rhetoric of Responsibility* explored not only dialogue, but also the intersection between dialogue and larger societal issues.

If you are interested in dialogue, try reading one of Arnett's books now, then reread it ten years later. You'll find a whole new layer of wisdom that eluded you when you first read it.

preferences, and much more. When talking with someone whose perspectives are different from yours, it is important that your claims be appropriate to the type of information in question. If facts are called for, then it is important not to mix in opinions and present them as fact. If your attitudes or feelings are relevant, then talking about them as such is perfectly appropriate.

"I received the paper at 8:58" is a fact, whereas "The paper was late because she has time management problems" mixes fact with assumption. Confounding those two can create problems in dialogue if you are just trying to sort out the facts. On the other hand, sticking with the facts alone might not be helpful in a dialogue if someone really wants to understand your opinion about the situation. It is important, though, to always own your own feelings and beliefs when you present them as such. When we blame others for how we feel we actually diminish respect for ourselves and make it appear others can control our emotions and beliefs. For examples of how to change common "you" statements to respectful "I" statements see Table 12.4.

Table 12.4	Phrases for Owning Your Feelings and Opinions
	"I feel upset by this" INSTEAD of "You don't care about my feelings" "I believe I have not explained myself yet " INSTEAD OF "You never let me tell my side of the story" "I don't believe you are being honest" INSTEAD OF "You don't keep your word" "I am not enjoying myself" INSTEAD OF "You are no fun" "I do not believe that is true" INSTEAD OF "You don't know what you are talking about" "Please give me a moment, I feel a little frazzled" INSTEAD OF "You're driving me crazy"

Genuineness

Genuineness refers to being "direct, honest, and straightforward."[16] When acting in a genuine manner, you are not being strategic or manipulative, but instead speaking openly and honestly with the other person. This authenticity is important in dialogue, because it promotes trust and allows for a true flow of information. People who hide behind a façade or communicate in a tactical manner designed to create a strategic advantage eliminate the possibility of mutual understanding, which is the very purpose of dialogue. Furthermore, when people suspect that their conversational partners are not being genuine, an environment is created in which wariness and distrust dominate and lead to further degeneration of dialogue. Communication scholars Charles Brown and Paul Keller noted, "The reason truth . . . is important is that people cannot build bridges between them that crumble when tested."[17]

risk
• • • •
an action with either positive or negative outcomes

However, the importance of being genuine raises one of the great dangers of dialogue. In being genuine, you expose yourself to *risk*. Any behavior that can have either good or bad consequences is risky. If there is no element of danger, then the action is a safe bet, not a risk. When one person is genuine and the partner is not, the person being genuine can easily be taken advantage of.

This risk creates a circular dilemma. If a person is untrustworthy, then it is not likely a good idea to be genuine. Yet without genuineness, it is hard to build trust. So, what can you do? Strategy and manipulation are wrong in dialogue, so engaging with someone who is untrustworthy means you will need to be guarded. Being honest and direct, but being careful about what and how much you disclose, is probably the best approach. That allows as much genuineness as possible without exposing yourself in ways that could ultimately be harmful. In this process we encourage you to be realistic about your assessment of how trustworthy others are. People who are distrustful of *everyone* often become reclusive and withdrawn. On the other hand, people who are too trusting often get hurt.

There is a great paradox about risk. Taking risk means you will get hurt some of the time, but never taking risks doesn't assure positive outcomes; in fact, it ultimately leads to negative outcomes. In the long run, playing it safe can be the most dangerous course of action. People who fear rejection and thus never show their feelings or ask out people they are attracted to avoid the pain of rejection—but they may also never find love. So, the unwillingness to take a risk does not necessarily keep a person from ever failing; instead it often keeps a person from ever succeeding. By definition, risk requires the possibility of failing and getting hurt. But never taking risk almost assures it.

Life is not safe, so you will have to take chances some of the time. Just don't be reckless about them. In the movie *Batman Begins* a young Bruce Wayne falls down into a cavern and when his father comes to get him Bruce is upset at falling. His father asks him, "Why do we fall?" to which the child responds, "So we can learn to get back up again." Risk involves being willing to fall, because only when we stumble can we grow and learn. Experience, even setbacks, can be the greatest teacher.

Disagree with respect

In 2010, Holocaust survivor and Nobel Prize winner Elie Wiesel spoke at the Schuster Center as part of UD's speaker series. One of the subjects of his address was dialogue. In his speech, Wiesel told the university community that dialogue is vital to us because of the "need to disagree with elegance and respect." As follows from being genuine, it is essential to note that dialogue requires that people be honest with each other. Dialogue does not ask us to withhold our true feelings in an effort to be nice to others. Instead it asks us to be honest and disagree as appropriate—but to do so in a manner that shows caring and respect. Just because we disagree with an idea someone has, or a position they hold, does not make them a bad person, poor thinker or not worth our time; we can, should, and need to be able to have disagreements and live together knowing we hold different opinions. It is essential for a civilized open society to express and accept disagreement in a respectful manner.

TAKING NOTES DURING A DIALOGUE

Dialogues take place in a variety of situations, from a lunch conversation with friends, to family dinners, to meetings with colleagues and co-workers. Not all of these situations call for taking notes, but when the issue is important, the topic controversial or complex, or when a record of what was said might be useful in the future, it is important to take notes during the discussion.

When discussing something important, like the family budget, plans for an upcoming event, or a potential job opportunity, taking notes is not only useful, but necessary. It allows you to track what is said and determine what things you might misunderstand and thus ask a question about. Notes keep you from interrupting by recording the question you want to ask so you do not forget, while not having to cut someone off mid-statement.

The same holds true for dialogues about controversial or complex topics. These situations might arise in classrooms during discussions, visits with doctors or lawyers, applying for a mortgage, or during business meetings. When topics are controversial our passions might get the better of us and result in interrupting others, shouting, making impulsive assumptions about the other party, and getting argumentative. Note-taking allows us to slow down our emotional reactions, clarify what we want to know, and ask it at the appropriate time. This allows the other person to speak fully and ensures we learn what we need to properly understand the other person's position.

There are also dialogues when the notes we take serve as records of the conversation. Whenever you have a meeting with someone, be it a job interview or discussion with a faculty member about a class, taking notes can be very helpful for having an accurate record of what was said. Going in with prepared questions, taking notes about the answers provided to those questions, and jotting down other things that came up also helps you have a clear understanding of what transpired. Without notes, you rely entirely on memory which is actually not very accurate—in fact, the further you get from the conversation the less you recall accurately. Notes help fill that gap. They help you remember what tasks you were told to complete, how to improve your grade, and even what salary and compensation was offered. Notes help us keep important information straight, and are thus an essential tool for success in dialogues.

You might be wondering, "What should these notes look like?" That answer varies with each person and situation. When preparing notes before the dialogue, such as walking into a meeting with a professor about a grade or entering a job interview, they should contain the key points you want to make clear as well as the questions you feel you need to ask. When your comments express disagreement, make sure you clearly lay out the other person's original position as well as where and why you disagree in your notes. They should have proper references to resources that support your position, especially in case someone asks for that information. They also should not be so burdensome to make it seem like you are reading off your notes—in other words, not a manuscript. Generally, you just want to write key words and phrases.

It is also important in taking notes to be able to discern which information is more important and what is less important, so you can focus your note-taking on the important information. In high school, teachers often give handouts for class notes that tell the students what the most important ideas are. But in college—and in life—you rarely have someone else do the thinking for you. If your boss is explaining a project you need to do or giving you feedback on your work, she or he will not usually begin by giving you a handout telling you what to listen for. You need to develop this skill yourself. So, begin by asking yourself what makes some information in any type of communicative situation (class lecture, group meeting, conflict, etc.) more important.

When taking notes during the dialogue, everyone develops their own version of shorthand. It is not important that you write down everything that is said—if you did this you would not be listening and thinking about the other person's comments. What is important is that you record who said the piece of information you feel is important to recall, and if that statement prompted you to think of a question, write the question down so you don't forget it or who it is directed towards. These notes can also contain "notes to self" that remind you to examine something prompted by the dialogue at a later point. These notes help you keep up with the conversation and identify places where you can or need to contribute with added information or questions for clarification.

Throughout your undergraduate career every class you take at UD provides an opportunity to hone your dialogue skills, specifically those related to note taking. We too often believe that note-taking is something done during lecture, but it is a tool with much wider implications than recalling classroom content for a test. It enhances our ability understand complicated subjects, engage people on controversial topics without jumping to conclusions, and perhaps most importantly, it provides us with a clear and accurate record of important conversations. Table 12.5 provides some tips for good note-taking behaviors during a dialogue.

Table 12.5

Good Note-taking Behaviors during a Dialogue	
Dos	**Don'ts**
• Prepare questions in advance when possible	• Write down everything said
• Paraphrase position of other person with whom you disagree	• Issue judgments of others
• Identify the most important points from what is said	• Forget references
• Identify who said something that sparked a response from you	• Cut someone off
• Keep notes in a place you will remember	• Write unrelated information

DIALOGUE AND COMMUNICATION CONTEXT

Throughout the discussion of dialogue, we avoid limiting the context in which it may take place. Many dialogues happen in *dyadic* settings, such as when romantic partners discuss their relationship, when a professor and student talk about problems the student is having in class, or when coworkers discuss workplace issues. But dialogue can take place in any setting. In the workplace, dialogue is often very helpful when used in business meetings. Kevin's example from the beginning of this chapter is a good case where dialogue was used in a group setting. And dialogue is especially important at a societal level. We have noted earlier the deficit of dialogue in our political system. If all politicians worked with each other dialogically the positive impact on society would be spectacular. There are a number of organizations that exist whose mission includes fostering greater public dialogue about important social and political issues. Two of these include the Kettering Foundation, based here in Dayton, and the Center for Public Deliberation, which is housed in the Communication Studies Department at Colorado State University.

dyadic
an interaction between two people

Your classes at UD provide a rich environment where dialogue can take place, especially when you discuss controversial topics. Each student has a lot to contribute to his or her classes. The University of Dayton is especially interested in students tackling difficult issues of social and personal importance. Sharing your perspective and respectfully listening to others is an essential activity in getting the most out of class. Classes may push you to confront ideas you haven't thought about or encounter others whose viewpoints conflict strongly with your own. Use the principles you have learned in CMM 100 to engage these differences in a dialogic manner and you may be impressed with the way it expands your understanding and builds connections with other students. Dialogue will open a bigger world for you than you would otherwise have known.

When to Use Dialogue

The question of when to use dialogue is complex and cannot be answered in a paragraph. Developing judgment of when dialogue is appropriate takes years of experience to assess many elements of a situation. We offer just a couple major factors you might think about, but we encourage you to consider discussing this further in class and paying attention to it in your own life. Here are a few suggestions to get you started in your thinking. Dialogue is useful in situations in which:

- You are trying to understand a complex problem.
- People have strong interests and widely divergent views.
- Seeking new ideas and a better understanding is essential.
- You have to make a decision that has a significant impact on someone else.
- The relationship among the people is as important as the process and its outcomes.

What other criteria can you think of for judging when to use dialogue?

CRITICISMS OF DIALOGUE

When dialogue began to fall out of favor in the 1970s, critics raised a number of concerns about the merits of dialogue. Several of their points raise issues you should consider. One person who helped respond to these criticisms is Ronald C. Arnett, a professor at Duquesne University. He recognized some of the limitations of dialogue as it was practiced and discussed in the 1960s, but also saw its potential if used appropriately. This section details some of the criticisms of dialogue that manifested in the 1970s and also responses to those criticisms that were informed, at least in part, by the important work of Ronald C. Arnett.

Dialogue Is Not Always Possible

The criticism

In order for dialogue to work, all parties must follow the principles of dialogue. If one person refuses to listen, acts in a manner that creates defensiveness, or fails to be genuine, then dialogue cannot happen.

A response to the criticism

It is true that dialogue is not always possible. And not only is it impossible when some people aren't cooperative; people with abusive personalities or people with psychological disorders might not even be capable of interacting dialogically. Dietrich Bonhoeffer, a famous theologian who favored pacifism, was involved in a plot to assassinate Adolf Hitler because he felt that was the only way to effectively oppose the evil of Hitler's regime. Bonhoeffer had concluded that dialogue with the Nazi party was impossible.

So, the charges are true. This criticism, however, can sometimes be taken too far. While there are cases in which dialogue is neither possible nor ideal (see the next three criticisms for cases where it is not ideal), there is a large set of circumstances in which dialogue would be possible for people skilled enough at making it happen, and where it would be beneficial if only people made an honest attempt. Assess for yourself when dialogue is possible, but be careful not to rule it out too swiftly. It will work more often than most people think. Take a case that occurs for most students at least once during their academic career. If you have a large paper due and feel that you cannot complete it by the instructor's deadline you have several choices:

1. Miss the deadline, and appeal after the fact;
2. Hand in what you have finished;
3. Speak with the teacher in advance.

Of these, the most frightening and least employed by students is the third—but it is also the most effective. By engaging with your instructor beforehand and having a dialogue about your situation and the assignment's due date you will probably be able to generate some acceptable positive outcomes. Making the assumption that the instructor will not speak with you leaves you no viable options, so take the leap and try speaking with the instructor in advance of the deadline and see what happens.

In relationships you choose to form, you and your partner mutually create the rules of interaction. Romantic relationships are very important to many people and to society. Realize that you have total control over the way that you and a partner respond to differences. We encourage you to practice dialogue in romantic relationships. Doing so will set you up to beat the societal statistics on failure of long-term relationships. And if you find that a person you are dating is unwilling to meet differences dialogically, you might ask whether this is someone you want to commit to long term. You are going to encounter a *lot* of difficult issues to resolve over a lifetime together.

Dialogue Makes You Vulnerable

The criticism

Being genuine and open when others are being manipulative makes it easy for others to take advantage of you—and some will.

A response to the criticism

Like the first charge, this one is true as well. We have already discussed this issue when we talked about risks of being genuine. We revisit this criticism in this context as a reminder that dialogue requires some risk, but that you should be intelligent in judging risk. We also offer a suggestion on managing these encounters: Be careful how much information you share. In most situations you can establish a supportive climate, maintain your integrity, and listen dialogically without putting yourself in any jeopardy, and that alone can do quite a lot to reap the benefits of dialogue even in the presence of someone who is not to be trusted.

Dialogue Requires Too Much Effort

The criticism

Dialogue takes a lot of time and effort. In cases in which a person has the authority to make a decision, all the effort of dialogue may not be worth it. That time and energy come at the expense of something else, and for busy people (like business leaders) the time and effort spent on dialogue may require that time and effort be taken away from other areas.

A response to the criticism

Like the previous critiques, we include this because it contains an element of truth. Dialogue does take more time and effort than a command decision. The question to consider is what consequences you are seeking. If the decision is simple and no one is highly invested in any particular outcome, then the effort of dialogue might offer no gain—and it will certainly cause negative outcomes if people feel frustrated with dragging the process out. In these cases, dialogue is not the best choice.

But, in cases where the decision is important and there are significant differences, then dialogue is likely to build greater support for a decision and better relationships among the people affected by it. Furthermore, if a decision is unpopular, there may be appeals or resistance to it, and in the long run those consequences may require more time and effort than the initial dialogue would have taken. Keep in mind, though, that engaging in dialogue doesn't assure that people will be satisfied with a course of action. It only increases the odds in the immediate situation, and encourages engagement and respect in future endeavors. Human behavior is so complex that we can rarely make perfect predictions about outcomes.

This criticism raises important questions you should consider when deciding how to act in the face of difference:

- How large are people's differences, and how strongly do they feel about their positions?
- How important is it that people understand each other or support a decision?
- What consequences are likely to follow from this situation?

Use that information to decide whether dialogue is worthwhile. Don't use dialogue when it is an unnecessary waste of time and energy.

Dialogue Is Not Appropriate for Every Relationship and Situation

The criticism

Dialogue is great for building relationships, but no one needs to have a meaningful dialogue with the plumber, tax accountant, or grocery clerk. And you definitely don't want to settle in for a long dialogue about the best way to get out of a burning building.

A response to the criticism

True again, and this was one of the reasons why dialogue initially fell out of favor. In the 1960s dialogue was sometimes seen as a cure-all, and some people advocated using it too widely. You *don't* need to engage in dialogue while paying for your groceries or getting your drain unclogged. And if the building is burning, efficiency in communication definitely trumps the relationship-building capacity of dialogue.

Dialogue, in its fullest sense, is not necessary in any situation in which you interact with someone as a role rather than as an individual. In a brief service encounter, your concern is largely that the person in uniform is capable of doing a job well, not in building a meaningful and lasting personal relationship with that individual. In those situations, a simple businesslike transaction will usually suffice. That being said, there are still many elements of dialogue that can be implemented with no more effort than not doing them. For instance, treating the plumber as an equally worthy human being (showing *equality* instead of *superiority*) doesn't take any more effort than being condescending, and it's likely to have a positive effect. So, even though it's probably a bad idea to ask probing follow-up questions to the plumber about how the stubborn clog in your drain makes them feel, treating them with some respect is likely to be a good idea. You shouldn't implement every aspect of dialogue in every situation, but using a few simple and appropriate elements is a good idea even when dialogue is not necessary.

DIALOGUE AT THE UNIVERSITY OF DAYTON

Because dialogue is essential for building community, the Marianists are strong advocates of mastering and using dialogue. Dialogue is specifically mentioned in *Commitment to Community* when talking about treating others with respect: "Learn to handle conflict with respect, dialogue, understanding, and forgiveness." However, dialogue is much more widely infused through *C2C* than in just that phrase. Taking responsibility for yourself and your community means you will need to "be aware of the weakest and most vulnerable around you and seek to serve them." Developing your faith life means you'll need to "learn about and show respect for the religious traditions of others." And being honest, truthful, and living with integrity requires that you "practice behavior that is not insulting,

Virtues for Constructive Conversations:
The University of Dayton Pledge
Revised: May 16, 2018

As a member of the University of Dayton community informed by the Catholic and Marianist traditions of education, I pledge to seek the truth and to create a culture of encounter through constructive conversations where truth can be more fully known and serve the common good. Constructive conversations focus on a question and provide a space where persons can exchange their arguments and conclusions that address the question within an environment of respectful listening, honest advocacy and a mutual commitment to learning from one another. As I participate in political, social, economic, cultural and religious conversations, I pledge to practice, to the best of my ability, to practicing these virtues. I especially commit to practicing these virtues in my exchange with those whose views and values differ from my own.

Creating a Culture of Encounter: I will create opportunities for conversations on important questions that shape our society with persons, who not only share my perspectives, but also with people who hold different perspectives. In these encounters, I will respect the dignity of each person in the conversation.

Respectful Listening: I will listen carefully and thoughtfully to arguments that are different from mine. I will temporarily suspend my judgments in an effort to understand the experiences, perspectives and logic of the others arguments. I will ask questions that help me empathically understand their experiences, perspectives and logic and I will endeavor to understand their arguments before I argue against them.

Honest Advocacy: I will endeavor to grasp the issues involved in the question being considered. I will make arguments based on my experience and perspectives and formulate arguments in a logically coherent manner. I will realize that others have different experiences and perspective on the question and I will endeavor to respect and incorporate as much as possible these experiences and perspectives in my arguments. I will invite others to test my arguments and the experiences and/or the facts contained in my arguments.

Engaged in Learning: I engage in conversation with others so that we together can enrich our personal and shared experiences, perspectives, and insights into the truth and the common good.

Intellectual Humility: I will always consider the possibility that my arguments may be deficient or wrong. When I come to the realization that my arguments are deficient or wrong, I will readily acknowledge it.

Prophetic Courage: When called for, I will speak clearly and forcefully for premises and arguments that I believe to be true but may be unpopular or even reviled. I will persist in speaking for my arguments even when mine is a minority voice.

Staying at the Table: When conversations are difficult and I am tempted to exit the conversation, I will deepen my commitment to stay at the conversation table. I will reflect on the conversation and ask what constructive moves I might undertake to improve the quality of the conversation.

Practical Wisdom: I will work to develop the wisdom to know which virtues apply in which situations, and how my arguments may ultimately contribute to the common good.

demeaning, destructive, or harmful to you or others" and "respond truthfully and respectfully when your behavior is questioned by another." These actions can only be fully accomplished through dialogue.

Consider the statement, *Virtues for Constructive Conversations: The University of Dayton Pledge*, developed by Brother Raymond Fitz, in the "Speaking of Civic Engagement" box in this chapter. This statement pledges a commitment to seeking truth through the creation of constructive conversations with others. As defined by the statement, **constructive conversations** "focus on a question and provide a space where persons can exchange their arguments and conclusions that address the question within an environment of respectful listening, honest advocacy and a mutual commitment to learning from one another." The ideals in the statement reflect many of the attitudes, behaviors, and environmental conditions that we have identified in this chapter as integral to dialogue. We encourage you to take up this pledge as you engage faculty, staff members, fellow students, and other community members here at the University of Dayton, whether in the classroom or in other spaces where you encounter diverse others and their views.

constructive conversations
....
focus on a question and provide a space where persons can exchange their arguments and conclusions that address the question within an environment of respectful listening, honest advocacy and a mutual commitment to learning from one another

Dialogue is an essential means of communication in many of your classes. The Common Academic Program asks you to engage in ideas that may be different from what you learned growing up. It asks you to understand a diversity of perspectives, and to wrestle with complex issues that even great thinkers have struggled with. You will need to engage in dialogue with your professors, with students, and with other members of the university community in order to get the most out of your college education and experience. And don't hesitate to challenge your professors in a dialogic manner. The key is that you challenge yourself and others with the respectful approach to dialogue we have discussed in this chapter.

Dialogue is essential at UD outside of class as well. Using dialogue to address conflicts in your residence hall or in the ghetto can help develop better community. Off-campus service learning projects or other interactions with the broader Dayton community can benefit from dialogue as well. As UD diversifies its student body, the opportunity to understand those who are different from you can truly enhance your education. With over 1,000 international students, there is a great opportunity for all UD students to learn from cultural similarities and differences. We encourage you, regardless of your background, to step out of your comfort zone and dialogue with those of different cultural experiences. Invite each other to events or just to have dinner together and talk about your life history and how you ended up at UD. You'll be amazed what you learn and how that can enrich you and our community.

SUMMARY

We conclude by repeating a point we have made several times before: Dialogue is not a magical cure-all that makes all things good. All it does is offer an opportunity for understanding. Beyond that, the outcomes of an interaction are a result of what you choose to do. If you can master dialogue, it won't solve all problems or make your life perfect, but it will offer possibilities that are unimaginable for those who cannot use it effectively.

KEY TERMS

chilling effect 333

constructive conversations 347

debate 324

defensive climate 333

dialogue 323

dyadic 341

integrity 321

listening 325

monologue 323

presentness 326

risk 338

supportive climate 333

REVIEW QUESTIONS

1. How has our thinking about dialogue changed and stayed the same over the years?
2. What is dialogue, and how does it compare and contrast with other modes of communication?
3. What behaviors are essential for dialogic listening?
4. What attitudes and speaking behaviors are necessary for dialogue?
5. Why is character important to dialogue?
6. What are four criticisms of dialogue, and how should we respond to them?
7. How should you apply dialogue at UD?

THINK ABOUT IT

1. In what ways do people most commonly deviate from dialogue when communicating about difference?
2. If everyone mastered dialogue in high school, what impact would it have on our lives and society?
3. How have digital communication technologies affected the use of dialogue in everyday life?
4. How can you use dialogue to make UD a better community?

ACTIVITIES FOR ACTION

1. Watch some government action on C-SPAN. In what ways do the representatives engage in or violate dialogue? What aspects of dialogue could be employed to offer outcomes better for the people of the local, state, or federal government? Now, watch a reality TV show in which contestants have significant interaction. How do they model or violate dialogue? Considering that they are competing against each other, are there ways they could use elements of dialogue without hurting their chances in the game? Then compare and contrast what you observed between the contexts of government and entertainment.

2. Choose one element of dialogue you think you could use more effectively. Apply that element in class and in your personal life for a week. Do you observe any positive impact on account of using just that one element of dialogue? What do you take away from this experience?

ENDNOTES

1. Kerry Patterson, Joseph Grenny, Ron McMillan, & Al Switzler, *Crucial conversations: Tools for Talking When Stakes Are High* (New York: McGraw-Hill, 2002).

2. Ibid. 19.

3. Ibid. 19.

4. Jon A. Hess, & Joy Piazza, "Public and Relational Communication Ethics in Political Communication: Integrity, Secrecy, and Dialogue in *The Contender*," In P. Japp, M. Meister, & D. Japp (Eds.), *Communication Ethics, Media, and Popular Culture* (New York: Peter Lang Publishers, 2005), 137–160.

5. For example, see: Ronald C. Arnett, *Communication and community: Implications of Martin Buber's Dialogue,* (Carbondale, IL: Southern Illinois University Press, 1986).

6. Paul W. Keller & Charles T. Brown, "An Interpersonal Ethic for Communication," *Journal of Communication, 18*(1), 1968, 73–81; Paul W. Keller, "Interpersonal Dissent and the Ethics of Dialogue," *Communication, 6*, 1981, 287–303.

7. Harold H. Saunders, *A Public Peace Process: Sustained Dialogue to Transform Racial and Ethnic Conflicts,* (New York: St. Martin's Press, 1999).

8. David S. Young, *The Gift of Dialogue,* (Westfield, IN: The Greenleaf Center for Servant Leadership, 2012).

9. Keller & Brown, 1968.

10. John Medina, *Brain Rules: 12 Principles for Surviving and Thriving at Work, Home, and School.* (Seattle, WA: Pear Press, 2008).

11. Ibid. 85.

12. Jonathan Haidt, *The Happiness Hypothesis: Finding Modern Truth in Ancient Wisdom,* (New York: Basic Books, 2008).

13. Richard L. Johannesen, "The Emerging Concept of Communication as Dialogue," *Quarterly Journal of Speech, 57*, 1971, 376.

14. Ibid.

15. Jack R. Gibb, "Defensive Communication," *Journal of Communication, 11*(3), 1961, p. 141–148.

16. Johannesen, 376.

17. Charles T. Brown & Paul W. Keller, *Monologue to Dialogue: An Exploration of Interpersonal Communication,* (Englewood Cliffs, NJ: Prentice-Hall, 1973).

18. Stephen L. Carter, *Integrity* (New York: Harper Perennial, 1996), 7.

Interteaching Session

Dialogue

Read *Virtues for Constructive Conversations: The University of Dayton Pledge*, developed by Brother Raymond Fitz, which is featured in this chapter. Explore with your groupmates the following questions as you prepare to engage in a larger dialogue involving the whole class:

1. What are "constructive conversations" as defined in the statement?

2. What are some specific ways in which the principles for constructive conversations reflect the behaviors, attitudes, and principles of dialogue described in the chapter?

3. List some situations on campus in which constructive conversations might be beneficial in building understanding and helping people to learn.

4. Think about a specific issue that creates polarization, alienation, or even conflict on campus. Generate some questions around which a constructive conversation addressing this issue might be organized?

Performance

In Summer 2012, Dan Cathy, president of the private family-owned national fast food chain Chick-fil-A, ignited a controversy over an interview he conducted with Baptist Press, where he said that the company was "guilty as charged" for endorsing what has been described as the Biblical view of traditional marriage. He furthered the controversy a few days later when he said, "I think we are inviting God's judgment on our nation when we shake a fist at him and say 'we know better than you as to what constitutes a marriage,' and I pray God's mercy on our generation that has such a prideful, arrogant attitude to think we have the audacity to define what marriage is about." It later became known that Cathy and Chick-fil-A oversee a charitable organization called the Winshape Organization that provides financial support for organizations like Focus on the Family and Exodus International. What followed included a proposed national boycott of Chick-fil-A by supporters of same-sex marriage and a counter-movement called "Chick-fil-A Appreciation Day" by those that opposed same-sex marriage. The boycott cost Chick-fil-A revenue and also created a negative perception of the company and its employees.

Have a brief dialogue with your groupmates. First, each group member will deliver a brief statement—perhaps a couple of minutes in length—in which she or he states her or his position on the case and explains her or his reasons for taking that position, along with any support or evidence. Then, after all group members have shared their views, engage each other in a conversation that lasts about five minutes about the views that each person shared. Make sure that you are applying the key behaviors and attitudes for dialogue from the chapter and are creating a supportive not a defensive climate.

Afterwards, be prepared to continue the dialogue with the class as a whole.

Sample Outlines

SAMPLE EXPLANATORY SPEAKING NOTES

Purpose: To explain to my listener the concept of ideology in the field of organizational communication.

Thesis: Ideology is a concept that scholars in the field of organizational communication use to explain why social change does not occur in some cases, even when change might be in people's best interests.

Introduction

Greeting and expression of gratitude

Question: one social problem that you would like to be overcome?

Link to ideology. Taken any courses on it?

Degree in org comm – a central concept.

Can help you to understand why X problem has not yet been solved.

Thesis: Ideology = a concept that scholars in organizational communication | explain why social change does not occur in some cases, even when might be in people's best interests.

Body

Point 1

State the Point: One function of ideology = disposes people to see the way things are as they way that they should be or even must be.

Present Material Using the Principles and Tools from Chapter 4

- *Information*: Giddens (1979), professor at Cambridge University and director of the London School of Economics, ideology = "naturalizes the present."
- *Metaphor*: A veil. Can see through but not fully. Distorted.
- *Story:* Plato's (2009) allegory of the cave. [Video 0:56-1:51]

Make the Connection between Supporting Material and the Point: Naturalization = traps a person in a particular way of seeing.

Point 2

State the Point: Another function of ideology = disposes people to see what is in interests of few as being in everyone's interest

Present Material Using the Principles and Tools from Chapter 4

- *Information:* Giddens (1979), "sectional interests" and "universal interests"
- *Definitions:* Sectional interests = what only benefits certain people; universal interests = what benefits all people
- *Narrative:* Hunger Games? Convince that system benefits all, while only the Capitol. [Video]
- *Information:* Dennis Mumby (1987), Professor of Communication at University of North Carolina, ideology as a mechanism of control

Make the Connection between Supporting Material and the Point: Said to benefit all, but really benefits the few.

Point 3

State the Point: A third function of ideology = resist that which challenges the system

Present Material Using the Principles and Tools from Chapter 4

- *Information:* Giddens (1979) "the denial or transmutation of contradictions"

- *Definition:* "contradiction" = anything that could lead people to question the status quo, an anomaly. "deny" or "transmute" = explain it away, make it less a threat

- *Narrative:* Stick to the Status Quo [Video from *High School Musical*]

Make the Connection between Supporting Material and the Point: Teaches people how to defend the ideology so that the system can continue

Summary Question

Ask listener to review points

Conclusion

Summary of Main Ideas

- **Thesis:** Ideology = a concept that scholars in organizational communication | explain why social change does not occur in some cases, even when might be in people's best interests.
- **Main Points:** Review three functions of ideology

Thanks for time, more info = can recommend readings

References

Giddens, A. (1979). *Central problems in social theory: Action, structure and contradiction in social analysis.* Berkeley: University of California.

Mumby, D. K. (1987). The political function of narrative in organizations. *Communication Monographs, 54,* 113-127.

Plato (2009). *The republic* (B. Jowett, Trans., chap. 7). Retrieved from http://classics.mit.edu/Plato/republic.8.vii.html

SAMPLE PERSUASIVE PREPARATION OUTLINE

Thesis: Universities and colleges should eliminate honors designations for college and university graduates because they do not mean much anymore.

Introduction

I. Attention Getter: Ask yourselves this question: "When everyone is an honors student, where is the honor in your achievement?"

 A. Across the country students in colleges and universities all feel like a disappointment when they do not graduate with honors.

 B. So, they pressure faculty to give them better grades in classes so they can graduate with honors.

II. Introduce Topic: The fact is, honors designations seem to mean a lot to students, but when they are over-awarded, then the honors distinctions means very little to anyone else.

III. Thesis/Argument: In order to stop this nonsense and allow grades to mean what they indicate for a student, universities and colleges should eliminate the honors graduation designation.

IV. Establish Credibility: As a student myself who values my degree I looked into this issue over the past few weeks and discovered I am not alone in wanting to eliminate honors designations.

V. Preview: Today I want to provide you with the reasons why I believe there is no honor in the honors system.

 A. To make my case I will first show you two of the popular models colleges use to determine who will graduate with honors.

B. Next, I will explain how these approaches damage the idea of graduating with honors and do a disservice to the students.

C. Finally, I will explain how eliminating the honors designation for graduates is the solution to this problem.

[Transition: The problem with honors is a function of the way in which universities choose to bestow it, as we will now see.]

Body

I. Main Point #1: Universities and colleges in the United States typically use one of two models for determining which graduates will receive honors when graduating.

> **A. Subpoint:** Most higher education institutions award the best students the designation "summa cum laude," the next tier of students "magna cum laude," and a final group of students "cum laude" to differentiate them from the rest of the students.
>
> > **1. Sub-subpoint:** Each of those three titles comes from Latin, meaning "with the highest praise," "with much praise," and "with praise."
> >
> > **2. Sub-subpoint:** The use of these titles has been practiced in academia for centuries.
>
> **B. Subpoint:** Many institutions today set GPA standards for each honors category, and students must graduate with a cumulative GPA that meets the threshold of that category to receive the honor.
>
> > **1. Sub-subpoint:** For example, on a 4.0 scale, if a student achieves between a 3.9–4.0 as a cumulative GPA then at schools like the University of Alabama, University of New Mexico, and George Mason University the student will receive summa cum laude on their diploma (Sikula, 2006, Spring).
> >
> > **2. Sub-subpoint:** On the same scale at the same schools, if a student achieves between a 3.7–3.89 cumulative GPA then they will receive magna cum laude on their diploma (Sikula, 2006, Spring).
> >
> > **3. Sub-subpoint:** Finally, students who finish with between a 3.5–3.69 will be designated cum laude (Sikula, 2006, Spring).

[Transition: The GPA standard is not the only manner in categorizing student graduation honors used by schools today.]

II. Main Point #2: Some schools choose to award honors only to the top 10% of their students, regardless of their GPA.

> **A. Subpoint:** In this selection method, students receive honors regardless of their GPA, but instead the focus is on their standing at the completion of their career—a percentage of their class rank, in other words.

> **B. Subpoint:** This method allows for only a fixed number of students to receive honors, but the top performer, regardless of their GPA is guaranteed to receive the distinction of summa cum laude.

>> **1. Sub-subpoint:** The University of Nevada Las Vegas uses a variation of such a method whereby the top 1% of graduates receive summa cum laude, the next 4% receive magna cum laude and the final 5% of the top 10% of the class receive cum laude (Velasco, 2006, April 27).

>> **2. Sub-subpoint:** New Mexico State uses a different version of this method by giving only one person summa cum laude a year, then the top 1.5% of the class receives magna cum laude and the top 15% receive cum laude (Sikula, 2006, Spring).

[Transition: Regardless of whether this method or the GPA threshold method is used, these categories for graduates do not accurately recognize student achievement and thus do more harm than good to the students.]

III. Main Point #3: If honors truly showed the best and brightest students, they would mean something, but unfortunately, as I will now show you, they do not do that.

> **A. Subpoint:** The first criticism I will make addresses the GPA threshold method, which essentially says if you meet a certain GPA you receive that category's honors designation.

>> **1. Sub-subpoint:** The problem here is related to grade inflation and the fact too many students reach the honors threshold.

>> **2. Sub-subpoint:** For example, in 2001 half of the grades received by Harvard University students were in the A- to A range ("Grade Inflation Scrutinized," n.d.).

>> **3. Sub-subpoint:** At Princeton between 2004 and 2007, 47% of grades received by undergraduates were some form of A (Bartlett & Wasley, 2008).

>> **4. Sub-subpoint:** This problem isn't recent either; in 1997 the City University of New York awarded almost 50% A's and B's to students (Arenson, 1997, July 28).

B. Subpoint: When 50% of the students are A students, what, then, is average and how can you adequately and fairly determine who deserves to graduate with honors?

[**Transition:** Even though the GPA threshold method is problematic, the percentage of class rank method is not much better at finding out who deserves honors.]

IV. Main Point #4: Using the percentage of class rank to determine who deserves honors is not much better than using GPA thresholds because it only identifies who was best in a group, not who excelled.

> **A. Subpoint:** When you take GPA out of the mix and go with class rank it is possible that a student with a low GPA could end up receiving summa cum laude.
>
> > **1. Sub-subpoint:** Take this case for example: Students who finish #1 in their class with a 3.45 GPA would, according to the class rank system, receive summa cum laude.
> >
> > **2. Sub-subpoint:** This designation does not accurately represent the student's achievement.
>
> **B. Subpoint:** Even if you don't think that is likely, what about a situation where many students finish with a 4.0, how do you differentiate who should receive summa cum laude from who should receive magna cum laude?
>
> > **1. Sub-subpoint:** For example, at UNLV in 2005 78% of the grades   given to students in the College of Education were A's, and the average GPA of students was 3.6 (Corbin, 2007, August 6).
> >
> > **2. Sub-subpoint:** When everyone is getting A's then everyone is worthy of honors.
>
> **C. Subpoint:** The third and final point I want to make here, is that students in this system do not receive a comparable degree to someone at another institution.
>
> > **1. Sub-subpoint:** By this, I mean that students from two universities, each using a different system for marking honors, who receive the same grades would not receive the same honor upon graduation thus making one degree appear better than another's.
> >
> > **2. Sub-subpoint:** This does not allow for any type of reasonable comparison between honors at two different institutions.

[**Transition:** With such an unfair system for bestowing honors upon graduates, the best solution is to just eliminate the system altogether.]

V. Main Point #5: Eliminating honors designations for graduates at the university level will help reduce grade inflation and equalize the worth of degrees from different schools.

> **A. Subpoint:** The elimination of honors will help reduce grade inflation by reducing the pressure on students to make honor rolls.
>
> > **1. Sub-subpoint:** Students will not feel like outcasts or underachievers when they do not hit a specific grade level.
> >
> > **2. Sub-subpoint:** Additionally, when students are close to the level for a type of honors they beg for grade changes, resulting in inflation; if honors are eliminated then this practice will be minimized at least, stopped at best.
>
> **B. Subpoint:** Eliminating honors is also better than the class rank percentage model because the GPA will stand for itself.
>
> > **1. Sub-subpoint:** Whereas in the class rank method of honors selection a student with a 3.8 could possibly graduate without honors, when you eliminate honors altogether that 3.8 shows that the student did very well.
> >
> > **2. Sub-subpoint:** Students with high GPAs that miss honors are cheated out of the distinction their GPA should have, so by eliminating honors for all the GPA becomes the distinguishing feature for everyone.
>
> **C. Subpoint:** Most importantly, eliminating honors designations at all universities and colleges equalizes the playing field for all graduates.
>
> > **1. Sub-subpoint:** When all employers have to go on is GPA, instead of an honors label that was determined differently for each graduate, then all students are on a more level playing field in the application process.
> >
> > **2. Sub-subpoint:** Graduates will be evaluated by performance and not an inconsistent designation of honor.

[Transition: Put succinctly, eliminating honors designations for graduates is the fairest and most equitable way to distinguish one student's performance at one school from another student's performance at a different college.]
Conclusion

I. Signpost: In conclusion, honors designations for college graduates are a terrific idea, but terrible in execution and thus should be eliminated.

II. Summary: Honors designations based on GPA thresholds contribute to grade inflation and thus make the honors label worth less than it should be.

A. Using a system based on percentages of the rank in the graduating class also is unfair because it may leave students who achieve high marks out of the honors category altogether.

B. Most problematic, however, is that both methods are used by various institutions across the country, making the meaning of honors inconsistent for all graduates.

C. To solve the problem of inconsistent and unfair honors labels we must abolish honors designations altogether and let the GPA stand as the distinguishing criteria for determining student achievement.

IV. Restate Thesis/Argument: Only when our true performance, illustrated by our GPA, is the measure of our honor and abilities will the gamesmanship and pressure for higher grades so students can receive honors designations stop.

III. Clincher: The honor in student achievement should come from performance, not some watered-down label.

References

Arenson, K. W. (1997, July 28). At CUNY, a debate on grade inflation. *The New York Times*, p. B3.

Bartlett, T., & Wasley, P. (2008). Just say "A": Grade inflation undergoes reality check. *The Chronicle of Higher Education*, 55(2), pp. A1-A12.

Corbin, A. (2007, August 6). Standardizing honors status. *The Rebel Yell*. Retrieved from http://archive.unlvrebelyell.com/print_article.php?ID=10881

Grade inflation scrutinized at Harvard and elsewhere (n.d.). Academe Online. Retrieved from http://www.aaup.org/AAUP/pubres/academe/2002/MA/NB/Grade.htm?PF=1

Sikula, A. (2006, Spring). Faculty Senate proposal. University of Nevada, Las Vegas, NV.

Velasco, P. (2006, April 27). Grad status under debate. *The Rebel Yell*. Retrieved from http://archive.unlvrebelyell.com/print_article.php?ID=9279

Key Terms

A

abstract	words are not concrete or tangible items; they are only representations
accent	nonverbal behaviors that augment a verbal message
acceptance	the third step in the persuasive process in which the audience decides whether or not to agree with the position for which the speaker advocated
accuracy	the truthfulness or correctness of a source
active listening	listening to understand a message by processing, storing and potentially evaluating a message. It also involves reactions by the listener in some form
ad hominen fallacy	when speakers attack the person making the argument and not the argument itself
ad populum fallacy	when we attempt to persuade people by arguing our position is reasonable because so many other people are doing it or agree with it
ad verecundium fallacy	an appeal for persuasion based on higher authority or tradition
alliteration	repeating the same consonant or vowel sound at the beginning of subsequent words
ambiguous	language does not have precise, concrete meanings
ambushing	selective listening where the audience ignores the strengths of a message and hears only the weaknesses
American Psychological Association Manual	preferred reference manual for social science communication scholars
antecedent	the hypothetical condition in the major premise of a conditional syllogism
antithesis	two ideas that sharply contrast with each other and are juxtaposed in a parallell grammatical structure
anxiety disorder	abnormal mental outlook in which individuals experience high levels of apprehensiveness that keep them from living life
apologia	a forensic speech that makes a defense against an accusation
arbitrary	symbols used to represent things are not intrinsically connected to those things
argument	a claim that you are making about a given topic that you support with evidence and reasons
arguments from the past	appropriating historical events, facts, or people to justify present or future actions, or explain events in the here and now

arrangement	the second canon of rhetoric in which you determine the most effective way to organize your case for the topic and the audience
articulation	physically producing the sound needed to convey the word
artistic proof	constructed by the speaker for the occasion; concerns ethos, pathos and logos
assertive	the ability to clearly and confidently state our positions
asymmetrical balance	emphasizes imbalance thus creating an impression of stress, energy and excitement
attention getter	a devise that immediately attracts the audience's interest to the subject which the speaker plans to discuss
authorship	who wrote the information and are the credible
autonomy face	the perception that we can do things on our own and our desire to avoid others making decisions for us
axial balance	formal balance that strives for equal distribution of the elements of a visual so they do not appear tilted on one side of the image

B

backing	support for the argument
background information	material that provides context for a topic
balance	the positioning of elements within the image
begging-the-question fallacy	when a speaker presumes that certain things are facts when they have not yet been proven to be truthful
bias	presenting information in a way that unfairly influences the perception of something or someone
blending	one of the more common articulation errors, and it occurs when speakers intermingle two words together

C

categorical syllogism	a syllogism in which the argument is based on membership in a group
cause and effect arrangement	orders main points first by discussing the cause of something that occurred and then moving to an explanation of the impact of its occurrence
channel	the mode through which the message is conveyed to another party
chart	a visual device that helps you summarize or list blocks of information
Chicago Manual of Style	preferred reference manual for rhetorical studies
chilling effect	an action that discourages other from speaking their mind
chronological order	arranging points in the order in which they occur, or occurred, from start to finish
civic engagement	acting upon a sharp awareness of one's own sense of responsibility to their community
civility	the use of tact when dealing with others; a genuine and reciprocal expression of respect for ourselves and other people through our actions and statements
clarifying questions	questions that seek to understand the meaning of particular words or phrases that the speaker used in the message

clarity	the ability of a speaker to clearly articulate what they wish to say
classroom response systems	devices that allow students to answer questions posed during a lecture and provide tabulated results of the poll for everyone in the room in a timely manner
clincher	the final statement in a speech
coercion	the use of the threat of force to make someone do something against his or her will
collectivistic culture	values harmony in group and societal relationships
color pattern	collection of hues in your presentation aids
communication apprehension	the fear or anxiety associated with real or anticipated communication with another or others
Communication/Mass Media Complete	an electronic database for academic journals and popular sources related to communication and journalism
comparative advantage	an organizational pattern that uses each main point to explain why the speaker's solution to a problem is better than another proposed solution
comparison	connecting new information with something a person already knows
competence face	our efforts to promote our expertise on subjects to others so they respect us
complement	when the action demonstrates the message contained in the verbal content
comprehension	the second step in the persuasive process in which the speaker provides context for the issue in dispute so the audience understands what the speaker is talking about
conditional syllogism	a syllogism in which the major premise contains hypothetical condition and its outcome
conflicting	kinds of nonverbal cues that covey a message that contradicts the verbal statements of the speaker
conjectural stasis	when the issue in dispute is whether something occurred or not
consequent	the outcome of the hypothetical condition in the major premise of a conditional syllogism
context	the circumstances in which an event occurs that influence the meaning of the moment and the message
contrast	how objects and letters stick our from the background
constructive conversations	focus on a question and provide a space where persons can exchange their arguments and conclusions that address the question within an environment of respectful listening, honest advocacy and a mutual commitment to learning from one another
coordination	all information on the same level has the same significance
correctness	the accuracy of information presented and the honest representation of the speaker
courtesy	showing consideration and attention to others
crescendo	an organizational pattern in which the strongest point is placed at the end and is built up to by smaller main points
currency	timeliness of the information

D

debate — a competitive interaction in which people attempt to make a case through reason and evidence, while showing weakness in the other's arguments

decoding — the process of taking a message that has been sent and using one's own experiences and knowledge to give it meaning

deductive argument — an argument that reasons from known premises to an inevitable conclusion

defensive climate — a communication situation in which a person feels threatened

definitive stasis — when the issue in dispute is the meaning of a term

dehumanization — making people seem less than human in order to more easily motivate action against them

deliberative message — one of two forms of persuasive messages proposed by Aristotle; it often takes place in legislative settings and focuses on discussing policies and actions to be taken

delivery — the fourth canon of rhetoric; the manner in which you physically and vocally present your message

demagoguery — speech that attempts to win over an audience through appealing to their prejudices and emotions, particularly those of fear, anger, and frustration

demographic — groups determined by select population characteristics

depth — the graphic nature of an item; involves both level of detail and the amount of background provided to the image

derived credibility — the level of credibility during a speech that comes from what you say and how you say it

Dewey Decimal Classification System — the coding system for books, magazines, and journals used in libraries

dialects — aspects of in articulation, grammar, vocabulary, and pronunciation that differ from Standard English

dialogue — an interaction in which people with different perspectives seek to understand each other's views; speaking so that others want to listen and listening so that others want to speak

discourse — communication of thought by words; talk; conversation

disjunctive syllogism — a syllogism in which the major premise includes two or more mutually exclusive alternatives

division — in order to divide a point you need to end up with two or more items

dyadic — an interaction between two people

dynamism — a social science term for strong delivery that creates the impression with the audience that the speaker has practiced and thus cares about what he is talking about

E

either-or fallacy — an argument in which you present two options and declare that one of them must be correct while the other must be incorrect

Elaboration Likelihood Model (ELM) — a theory that proposes two primary cognitive processing paths we use to make decisions

encoding — the process of attaching symbols to ideas and feelings so that others may understand them

enkyklios paideia	rounded education spread under the reign of Alexander the Great
enthymeme	a syllogism missing one or two of its parts
episteme	universal knowledge, or understanding about the common characteristics of like materials
ethos	the credibility of the speaker
evidentiary information	information that supports main points within a speech and is directly related to the topic
exigence	a decisive point at which a response is invited or required
explanation	a process of making information clear to a person who previously did not understand it
extemporaneous speech	a speech delivered with notes but not the entire speech in front of the speaker

F

face threats	things that threaten to damage the image we work to present to others
facework	the behaviors we exhibit to maintain a positive impression of ourselves by other people
famous quotation	an actual statement closely related to the topic of the speech made by individuals that the audience will easily recognize
feedback	the responses and reactions to the messages transmitted by the sender and is itself a new message sent back to the original sender
fellowship face	an effort to fulfill the need to have others like and respect us
figurative analogy	when the two cases being compared are from completely different classifications
fixed-response questions	items on a survey that allow only for prescribed answers
forensic message	an argument in which speakers debate the facts of a case and attempt to answer questions of justice
form	how items appear in terms of their representation, size and texture
formal survey	a time consuming way of gathering data on a population which employs randomized sampling to ensure reliability and validity
frame of reference	our own singular perspective on the world around us

G

gender	the socially constructed expectations and roles that accompany a particular sex, and these vary between cultures
general purpose statement	a brief statement representing what you intend to do in the speech
gesture	a physical movement used to convey a message
ghostwriting	to write for and in the name of another person
glazing over	daydreaming instead of hearing the message
global plagiarism	taking an entire speech from a single source and pawning it off as your own
good manners	handling our relationships with others in a positive way
graph	a presentation device that indicates relationships found in numerical data

grounds	evidence in the Toulmin model

H

harmony	when all parts and aspects of the presentation aid complement one another within the aid's framework
hate speech	rude and crude speech that attacks or demeans a particular social or ethnic group many times with the intent of inciting action against that group
hearing	the physiological action of processing sounds, conducted by one's ears and brain
hierarchical	language is structured according to more or less, higher or lower
high power-distance cultures	where there is an uneven distribution of power and one person or a specific group of people dominate

I

ideograph	an ill-defined, politically powerful term or phrase that can push people to action
image management	the constant attempt to control the presentation of ourselves to others
impromptu speech	a presentation done with little or no preparation
inartistic proof	all the evidence, data, and documents that exist outside of the speaker and the audience but nevertheless can aid in persuasion
incremental plagiarism	failure to give proper credit for parts of a speech that are borrowed from others
individualistic culture	people feel the strongest loyalties lie with themselves and not their social groups
inductive argument	reasoning from individual observations or events to conclude a general principle
informal survey	polling a few people based on convenience
information literacy	the ability to figure out the type of information you need, find that information, evaluate it and properly use it
initial credibility	the level of credibility a speaker has before they begin their speech
integration	the fourth stage in the persuasive process where the audience makes the speaker's position a part of their own personal philosophy and worldview
integrity	a quality of discerning and acting on one's ethical principles
intermediate knowledge	knowing what does not reflect an excess or a defect but instead what is intuitively correct to the person
internal preview	serves as an outline of what is to come next in a speech and is often combined with transition statements
internal summary	a statement that summarizes what you already covered, precedes transitions
interviewing	a direct method of gathering information from a human source that allows for questions to adapt to responses
invention	the first canon of rhetoric in which you choose the best possible arguments for your case
issue awareness	the first step in the persuasive process whereby the speaker alerts the audience to the issue requiring its attention

J

Jargon	terminology that relates to a specific activity
JSTOR	an electronic database for political journals

K

kairos	a person's ability to adapt to any occasion and deliver a message fit for that moment
kategoria	a forensic speech that makes an accusation
kinesics	nonverbal behaviors related to movement

L

leading questions	questions that are stated in the form of a question but actually express a judgment or opinion
Lexis-Nexis	an electronic database for newspapers and magazines
linear model of communication	depiction of communication process that features a sender who encodes a message and sends it through a channel where it competes with noise on its way to a receiver who decodes the message
listening	the psychological process of making sense out of sounds
listening for appreciation	listening for enjoyment; not high in cognitive commitment
listening to comprehend	listening to understand a concept or message
listening to evaluate	listening to make a judgment about a message; involves a high level of cognitive commitment on the part of the audience
literal analogy	when the two cases being compared are classified the same way
logos	the logical dimension of the appeal
low power-distance cultures	members value equality and believe no one person should dominate
lying by commission	when a speaker willfully makes untrue statements to an audience
lying by omission	when a speaker willfully chooses not to acknowledge facts about an argument that might damage its effectiveness

M

major premise	the first part of a syllogism, consisting of a general statement about the subject of your argument
manipulation	the deliberate misrepresentation of facts and evidence to an audience
manuscript speeches	when a speaker has his or her entire speech written out word for word in front of them as they speak
memory	the fifth canon of rhetoric; refers to one's ability to recall names and important information in the middle of a speech as well as to deliver a cogent speech without notes
message	the actual content you send to an audience, both intentional and unintentional
message of self preservation	message where the speaker's topic is introducing himself or herself to the audience

metaphor	comparisons that show how two things are alike in an important way, despite being quite different in most ways
minor premise	a statement about a specific case related to the general characteristics of the major premise
models	to-scale devices that depict an actual object
Modern Language Association Manual of Style	a citation style used in disciplines within the liberal arts and humanities
monologue	an interaction in which only one voice is present
Monroe's Motivated Sequence	a five-step organizational pattern that combines psychological elements with persuasion to move an audience to action
movement	the appearance of or actual activity depicted with an image
multimedia presentation	a presentation aid that combines and integrates video, audio, pictures and notes into one medium
myth	a rhetorical construction that tries to explain natural events or cultural phenomena and is used to identify with a group and justify actions or beliefs

N

narrative coherence	the degree to which a story makes sense in the world in which we live
narrative fidelity	the degree to which a story matches our own beliefs and experiences
narrative paradigm	humans are storytelling beings by nature
necessary cause	a condition that must be present for the effect to occur
noise	anything that interferes with the encoding, transmission, and reception of a message
non sequitur fallacy	when you make an unwarranted move from one idea to the next
nonlistening	providing the appearance of listening without actually paying complete attention to the message

O

object	a tangible item used in conjunction with a speech
Occam's Razor	one should not increase, beyond what is necessary, the number of entities required to explain anything
one-to-one conversation	a talk in which participants share responsibility and ownership for the interaction in a manner that is more equal than in a speech
open-ended questions	items on a survey that allow room for the person taking the survey to answer in his or her own words

P

parallelism	similarly structuring related words, phrases, or clauses
paraphrasing	relaying back to the speaker what she or he has communicated to you
passive listening	listening without reacting
patchwork plagiarism	stealing ideas from two or three sources without referencing them

pathos	the emotional dimensions of the appeal that can influence an audience's disposition toward the topic, speaker, or occasion
pentad	a framework for analyzing the messages that speakers create to influence others
perception checking	feeding back to the speaker the emotions or intentions that you as the listener are perceiving behind the speaker's words
plagiarism	to present another person's work or ideas as your own
polite	showing consideration for others in accordance with social decorum
post hoc, ergo propter hoc fallacy	from the Latin for "after this, therefore because of this;" assumes that because one event happened after another, then the preceding event caused the event that followed
posture	the position of your body
practicality	the proper places within the speech, the where, when, and how
prejudging	entering into a presentation with a judgment already formed about the message being delivered
preparation outlines	detailed outlines that use full sentences next to symbols in an effort to help you organize the speech
presentation aids	visual devices used to assist a speaker in communicating ideas to the audience
presentness	giving full attention to someone in dialogue
probing questions	questions that are used to follow-up with what a speaker says and gain additional information
problem-cause-solution order	a means of organizing a persuasive speech in which where you discuss the problem first, then its root cause, and your preferred solution that addresses both the problem and its inherent cause
problem-solution arrangment	orders points by first discussing a problem and then how it was addressed; a subset of chronological order
problem-solution order	a means of organizing a persuasive speech in which the discussion of the problem is followed by the preferred solution
profanity	coarse and irreverent language
pronunciation	the accepted standard of how a word sounds when spoken
propriety	good behavior and faithfulness to what one considers moral and just
pseudolistening	when people attempt to hide their inattention to the speaker's message
public speaking	speaking where communication moves typically from one speaker to an audience of many

Q

quadrivium	arithmetic, geometry, music, and astronomy
qualifier	a word or statement that indicates the level of probability for the argument to bear out as given
qualitative stasis	when the issue in dispute involves the morality, ethicality, or value of an action
question of fact	when a speaker seeks to persuade people about how to interpret facts

question of policy	when a speaker takes a position on whether an action should or should not be taken
question of value	a persuasive speech about the rightness or wrongness of an idea, action, or issue

R

reasoning by analogy	when you compare two similar cases in order to argue that what is true in one case is also true in the other
reasoning by cause	arguments that claim that one event or factor produces an effect
reasoning by example	the process of inferring general conclusions and making general claims from specific cases
rebuttal	a message that involves overcoming the opponent's argument by introducing other evidence that reduces the appeal of the opponent's claims
receiver	the person or persons who receive the encoded message sent by the sender
red herring fallacy	when a speaker introduces an irrelevant issue or piece of evidence to divert attention from subject of the speech
refutation	a speech that seeks to prove the opposition''s argument is wrong, or false
regulating	using nonverbal actions to help govern the course of a speech or interaction
relevance	information that is connected to the topic
repeating	when physical actions restate verbal messages
repetition	repeating either the same phrasing pattern for main points, or a phrase you just stated in order to maximize the audience's ability to receive the information
research question	the question about your topic you seek to answer
respect	an acknowledgement of the inherent humanity and existence of other people
rhetoric	the ability to speak well and persuade audiences
rhetorical question	asking the audience a question related to the subject that does not require an answer from them
rhetorical situations	moments that call for a rhetorical response
rhetors	speakers
risk	an action with either positive or negative outcomes

S

schema	a mental representation that organizes information about a subject
script	when a schema includes a sequence of behaviors
seductive details	bits of interesting information associated with your topic, but not part of it
self-fulfilling prophecy	believing that something will happen before it actually does, and then when it does come true it reinforces the original expectation
self-monitoring	the ability to be aware of your own behaviors and statements and how they affect other people; can be either high or low
self-presentation	a message used to introduce a speaker to listeners

self-restraint	the ability to refrain from comments until the time and tone are appropriate to do so
sender	the person who desires to deliver a message to another person or group of people
sex	a biological distinction between men and women
shorthand	the process of shortening words, or eliminating word clutter in the transcription process
signpost	a connective that lets the audience know what is next; most effective form of connective for moving from the last main point to the conclusion
simile	comparisons between two objects that allow each object in the comparison to retain their unique differences
single word approach	meaning is derived from individual words used in a strategic way
slang	words derived from dialects that most people understand but yet do not use in professional writing or speaking
slippery slope fallacy	a logical fallacy that assumes once an action begins it will follow, undeterred, to an eventual and inevitable conclusion
sociophobia	the fear of social situations and/or people
socratic questioning	the process of asking questions of a speaker focused on their responses to previous questions; its ultimate goal is to uncover the truth
sophists	itinerant teachers who travelled from city-state to city-state in Classical Greece, training people in public speaking
spare brain time	the time available for your mind to wander due to your ability to process messages faster than it takes to construct them
spatial order	arranges points according to geography or logical movement through an area
speaking outline	a truncated form of your full sentence preparation outline that does not include complete sentences
specific purpose statement	a narrower version of the general purpose statement that identifies what you will talk about, what you will say about it, and what you hope the audience will come away from the speech with
speech of refutation	a speech that seeks to prove the opposition's argument is wrong, or false
spotlight syndrome	the belief encouraged by the room set up that all eyes are focused on you as the speaker
stasis	the basic issue in dispute between speaking parties
straw man fallacy	when a speaker ignores the actual position of an opponent and substitutes it with a distorted and exaggerated position
style	the third canon; involves word choice, phrasing and the level of formality in the language you use to present your case to the audience
subordination	the organization of a hierarchy of ideas where the most general appear first, followed by subsequently more specific ideas
substituting	physical actions that take the place of verbal messages
sufficient cause	a condition that automatically produces the effect in question
summary	the central part of the conclusion; it is where you reiterate the speech's thesis statement and recap the main points you addressed throughout the body

summary question	a question that prompts the listener to give a brief synopsis or list of the main points that the talk covered
supportive climate	a communication situation in which a person feels he or she can speak freely without risk of harm
syllogism	basic structure of a deductive argument that comes to an absolute conclusion

T

tangential information	evidence used to provide color and capture an audience's interest
techne	experiential knowledge; knowledge of particular events in the world around us; the least reliable form of knowledge
terminal credibility	the level of credibility attained at the end of the speaking event
thesis statement	the verbalized foundation of your entire speech in a single sentence which presents your topic, main points and goal to the audience in an explicit and understandable way
tone	the syllabic emphasis on a sound that expresses emotion or meaning
topical arrangement	the arrangement of main points by sub-points that do not naturally fit together in another way
traditional aids	aids that do not apply electronic means to communicate ideas to the audience
transactional model of communication	recognizes that we simultaneously send and receive messages; a cyclical model of the communication process
transitions	signal you are done with one point, and that you are moving on to another
translative stasis	the issue in dispute is the competency of the judge or arbiter
transparencies	transparent sheets containing information illuminated by a projector
trivium	grammar, rhetoric and logic

U

undercover interviewing	the interviewer disguises either themselves or their purpose in an effort to trick someone into sharing more information than they may have if the interviewee knew to whom they were speaking

V

verbal attribution	the act of citing sources orally when you give information that you have taken from those sources
virtues	personal qualities that manifest moral excellence and make one capable of performing noble deeds
vocalics	anything that contributes to the creation or maintenance of sound in a person's voice
vocalized pauses	utterances that are not words and have no place in a speech, but are done instead of pausing the delivery of the speech

W

warrant	explains why the grounds support the claim and makes that connection clear to the audience
word cluster approaches	meaning is conveyed through more complex structures such as stories

Index

K

Kairos 214
kategoria 181
Kennedy, John F. 185, 300
kinesics 161
King, Jr., Martin Luther 236, 321
Korzybski, Alfred 234

L

leading questions 43
Led Zeppelin 95
Lexis-Nexis 130
Library at Alexandria 116
Limbaugh, Rush 310
LinkedIn 311
listening 326
listening to evaluate 43
literal analogy 212
logos 7, 229
low power-distance cultures 304
lying by commission 188
lying by omission 188

M

Maher, Bill 311
major premise 200
Malaysia Airline Flight 370 90
manipulation 188
manuscript speech 164
McCain, John 58
McGee, Michael Calvin 238
McLuhan, Marshall 70, 71
Medina, John 68, 301, 327
memory 13
metaphor 105, 237
minor premise 200
Minow, Newton 184, 185
monologue 323
Monroe, Alan H. 273
Monroe's Motivated Sequence 271
myth 239

N

necessary cause 213
Nichols, Marie Hochmuth 39–41
non sequitur fallacy 215

O

Obama, Michelle 16–18
Ohio Civility Project 288
Olivier, Sir Laurence 32

open-ended questions 68
outline 275

P

Pacino, Al 234
parallelism 240
paraphrasing 42
patchwork plagiarism 146
pathos 7, 229
Patterson, Kerry 318
pentad 246
perception checking 42
Petty, Richard E. 94
Philip of Macedon 2
plagiarism 145
polite 292
post hoc, ergo propter hoc fallacy 216
posture 161
PowerPoint 99
preparation outline 277
presentation aids 99
presentness 326
Prezi 99
probing questions 43
problem-cause-solution order 270
problem-solution order 267
pronunciation 155
propriety 8
Ptolemy I 116
public speaking 15

Q

quadrivium 116
qualifier 137
qualitative stasis 178
question of fact 179
question of policy 180
question of value 180
Quintilian 78, 177, 179, 180, 263

R

Ranganathan, S.R. 129
reasoning by analogy 212
reasoning by cause 212
reasoning by example 210
rebuttal 137
rebuttal speech 182
red herring fallacy 216
regulate 163
relevance 133
repeat 163